BLACKBEARD

Other Works by Angus Konstam

The History of Pirates

Pirates

The Pirate Ship, 1660–1730

Pirates: Terror on the High Seas

Privateers and Pirates, 1730–1830

Elizabethan Sea Dogs

Buccaneers

Ghost Ships: Tales of Abandoned, Doomed, and Haunted Vessels

Historical Atlas of Exploration

The History of Shipwrecks

Spanish Galleon, 1530–1690

Hunt the Bismarck

Duel of the Ironclads: USS Monitor and CSS Virginia at Hampton Roads, 1862

Lepanto, 1571: The Greatest Naval Battle of the Renaissance

The Renaissance War Galley, 1470–1590

Historical Atlas of the Viking World

The Civil War: A Visual Encyclopaedia

Atlas of the Celtic World

The Spanish Armada, 1588

Atlas of Medieval Europe

BLACKBEARD

America's Most Notorious Pirate

Angus Konstam

WILEY

John Wiley & Sons, Inc.

Published by John Wiley & Sons, Inc., Hoboken, New Jersey
Published simultaneously in Canada

Photo Credits: pages vi, 10, 46, 71, 105, 109, 118, 121, 158, 168, 188, 195, 235, and 292: reprinted from Captain Johnson, *A General History of the Robberies and Murders of the most notorious Pirates* (London, 1726, reprinted by Lyon's Press, NY, 1998); pages 54 and 106: reprinted from 1725 Dutch edition of Captain Johnson, *A General History of the Robberies and Murders of the most notorious Pirates*; pages 37 and 140–141: Stratford Archive; page 82: Courtesy of John de Bry; page 213: Colonial Williamsburg Foundation; pages 20, 29, 65, 131, 149, 177, 204, 227, 248, 260, and 279: author's collection.

Design and composition by Navta Associates, Inc.

For general information about our other products and services, please contact our Customer Care Department within the United States at (800) 762-2974, outside the United States at (317) 572-3993 or fax (317) 572-4002.

Wiley also publishes its books in a variety of electronic formats. Some content that appears in print may not be available in electronic books. For more information about Wiley products, visit our web site at www.wiley.com.

Library of Congress Cataloging-in-Publication Data:

Konstam, Angus, date.
    Blackbeard : America's most notorious pirate / Angus Konstam.
      p. cm.
    Includes bibliographical references and index.
    ISBN-13 978-0-471-75885-3 (cloth)
    ISBN-10 0-471-75885-X (cloth)
    1. Teach, Edward, d. 1718. 2. Pirates—North Carolina—Atlantic Coast—Biography.
3. Pirates–Virginia—Atlantic Coast—Biography. 4. North Carolina—History—Colonial period, ca. 1600–1775. 5. Virginia History—Colonial period, ca. 1600–1775. 6. Atlantic Coast (N.C.)—History—18th century. 7. Atlantic Coast (Va.)—History—18th century. I. Title.

F257.T422K66 2006
975.5'02092—dc22
[B]

2005036438

Printed in the United States of America

10 9 8 7 6 5 4 3 2 1

Contents

Blackbeard, from an early-eighteenth-century engraving used to illustrate the 1726 version of Captain Johnson's General History.

Preface

"I remember him as if it were yesterday, as he came plodding to the inn door, his sea-chest following behind him in a handbarrow; a tall, strong, heavy, nut-brown man; his tarry pigtail falling over the shoulders of his soiled blue coat; his hands ragged and scarred, with black, broken nails; and the sabre cut across one cheek, a dirty, livid white." That was how Jim Hawkins described his first encounter with a pirate in Robert Louis Stevenson's *Treasure Island*. His description of Billy Bones could have referred to any well-traveled seaman during the Golden Age of Piracy. What made Billy Bones special was that he had once shipped with Captain Flint, the most evil, cruel, and dastardly pirate ever to sail the Seven Seas. Stevenson clearly had a role model for Flint, "the bloodthirstiest buccaneer that sailed." To show just how bad Stevenson's pirate was, the author added, "Blackbeard was a child to Flint." When the Scottish author wrote his pirate bestseller in 1883, he understood that most readers would pick up the reference and would know who Blackbeard was.

This is hardly a surprise. In 1724, when the mysterious Captain Johnson first published his catalog of pirates, Blackbeard featured prominently among them. The early-eighteenth-century book became a bestseller, and it is still in print today, supported by countless books on pirates, ranging from academic studies to children's fiction. In the last century it also inspired moviemakers, and in recent years the swashbuckling pirate films of the 1930s have taken a new lease on life. Johnson's description of Blackbeard could have been taken straight from the actors' notes for *Pirates of the Caribbean*: "In time of Action, he wore a Sling over his Shoulders, with three brace of Pistols, hanging from Holsters like Bandaliers; he wore a Fur-Cap, and stuck a lighted Match on each Side, under it, which appearing on each side of his Face, his Eyes naturally looking Fierce and Wild, made him altogether such a Figure, that Imagination cannot form an idea of a Fury, from hell, to look more frightful."

It is ironic that today, while few people remember the names of the other characters in this story, such as Alexander Spotswood, they know about Blackbeard. Charles Eden, Ellis Brand, Robert Maynard, and Tobias Knight have all but faded from the pages of history, while even Woodes Rogers is a name almost unknown outside the ranks of pirate aficionados. Blackbeard's contemporaries, such as Benjamin Hornigold, Charles Vane, Stede Bonnet, and Henry Jennings, never managed to capture the public imagination, while "Calico" Jack Rackam is only remembered through his association with the far more sensational female pirates in his crew, Anne Bonny and Mary Reade.

Other pirates were more successful than Blackbeard. Henry Every captured a ship filled with the treasures of an Indian prince, and retired to tell the tale. Bartholomew Roberts was arguably the most successful occidental pirate of them all, capturing more than five times the prizes secured by Blackbeard or any other pirate of the Golden Age. However, it was Blackbeard who caught the public imagination—and who remains our archetypal pirate of the era. The reason for this may be attributed to his appearance, which was highly distinctive, and fit the image the general public had of pirates of this time. In a large proportion of the pirate books out there on the shelves, Blackbeard features on the cover—an instantly recognizable figure who screams "ferocious pirate" to whoever picks up the book. In the public imagination, Blackbeard is the ultimate pirate captain, regardless of what he actually did during his short, brutish career.

This emphasis on Blackbeard's appearance and personality hides the fact that the man was a highly successful pirate. Although his career as an independent pirate captain lasted less than a year and a half, his actions shook the very foundations of British rule in colonial America. While he was operating in the Caribbean, Blackbeard was little more than a major irritant—one of several pirate captains who fought their own private war among the islands and shoals of the West Indies. However, his blockade of Charles Town (Charleston) was something different. His actions paralyzed the port, bringing maritime trade to a halt. While this caused a crisis in the colony of South Carolina, Blackbeard's blockade had an equally dramatic impact further up the coast.

At the time Blackbeard commanded several ships and several hundred men. With a force like that at his disposal he could repeat his success off Charleston anywhere else along North America's Atlantic seaboard. For a brief period he became America's bogeyman, and nobody knew where he would strike next. Although the crisis passed, the rulers and merchants of colonial America weren't going to forget Blackbeard in a hurry. Until his death he remained a nascent threat—the one man they knew who could bring their fragile colonial economy to its knees. This all took place in 1718—the year that represented the peak of piratical activity in the Americas. It also represented a turning point—the great upsurge of piracy following the end of the War of the Spanish Succession (1701–13) between Britain, France, and Spain reached its peak during Blackbeard's time, and afterward the threat diminished, as the few pirates who remained left American waters for fresh hunting grounds on the far side of the world.

Indeed, the so-called Golden Age of Piracy, a phrase first conjured up by Captain Johnson in 1724, was meant to encompass the period from about 1697, when the last of the buccaneers ended their attacks on the Spanish, to around 1726, when the last mass hanging of pirates took place. In fact, the peak of piratical activity was concentrated in a far shorter period: from 1713, when the War of the Spanish Succession ended, until 1722, when the crew of Bartholomew Roberts was hanged en masse on the West African coast. In the waters of colonial America the worst phase lasted from 1716 until 1720, a period that saw the development of the Bahamas as a pirate stronghold, then the establishment of British rule in the islands, and the subsequent eradication of Bahamian piracy. Blackbeard was very much one of these Bahamian pirates, even though he quit the islands in 1717 when they were at their peak as a pirate haven, and never returned. The story of Blackbeard therefore mirrors the story of this pirate crisis.

The idea behind this book is to seek out the real man behind this dramatic façade, and to try to understand why he took to piracy, how he managed to excel as a leader of cutthroats, and why his piratical career reached such a spectacular and blood-soaked finale. For someone like Blackbeard a conventional historical narrative isn't really enough. The life he led and the world he lived in were too different from our own for that. In order to understand Blackbeard the pirate, we need to become conversant with Blackbeard's profession and the role piracy played in the era he lived in. What I have done is to intersperse chapters of narrative history with others that delve a little deeper into the maritime world Blackbeard lived in, allowing readers to become conversant with such things as pirate havens, how pirates operated, how they structured their crews, and what impact they had on colonial America. I hope you find the result as much fun to read as it was to research and write.

Acknowledgments

A lot of time and effort spent researching this book would have been wasted were it not for the help of archivists, librarians, and museum curators on both sides of the Atlantic. I would particularly like to express my gratitude to the staff of the Archives of the Indies in Seville, Spain; Bristol City Record Office and Central Library in Bristol, England; the Charleston Museum in Charleston, South Carolina; Colonial Williamsburg Foundation in Williamsburg, Virginia; the Essex-Peabody Museum in Salem, Massachusetts; the Florida State Archives in Tallahassee, Florida; the Library of Virginia in Richmond, Virginia; the Mel Fisher Maritime Museum in Key West, Florida; the Mariners' Museum in Newport News, Virginia; the National Library of Scotland in Edinburgh, Scotland; the Nautica Exhibit in Norfolk, Virginia; the National Maritime Museum in Greenwich, England; the North Carolina Department of Cultural Resources in Raleigh, North Carolina; the North Carolina Maritime Museum in Beaufort, North Carolina; the North Carolina State Archives in Raleigh, North Carolina; the Public Record Office in London, England; and, finally, the Scottish National Archives Edinburgh, Scotland.

Naming individuals in these institutions is an unfair game, as there are more people worthy of a special mention than there is patience in the average reader. You know who you are, and I thank you profusely. However, I would like to single out a handful of individuals who were especially encouraging over the years, and whose work or comments or enthusiasm have inspired me to forge ahead with the project: the late David Lyon of the National Maritime Museum was the catalyst for my interest in piracy, and whose highly constructive criticism and support were always welcome; David Cordingly, maritime historian extraordinaire, whose professionalism was and still is an inspiration; Peter Martin and Rodney Broome, relatives and historians from Bristol and Seattle, respectively, whose help in navigating the pitfalls of Blackbeard's early life was priceless, and Madeleine Burnside in Key West, who encouraged me to curate a pirate exhibition several years ago, and so started the piratical ball rolling. Above all, I'd like to single out my old friend and colleague Dave Moore, now on the staff of the North Carolina Maritime Museum. He's probably forgotten more about piracy than I will ever know, and his long discussions on the subject fueled an interest in Blackbeard that never went away. I've also long since forgiven him for trashing my Fantasy Fest pirate boots by falling down the back stairs of Key West's Bull & Whistle!

A Date with History

Diary writers in Blackbeard's day must have been a little confused, as two types of calendars were being used at the same time. The older Julian calendar (supposedly named after its Caesarean inventor) began its year on March 25 and counted every fourth year as a leap year. Over the centuries this led to a discrepancy between the calendar and the seasons, losing one day every 128 years. In 1582 Pope Gregory XIII solved the problem by leaving out a leap year at the end of three out of every four centuries, which amazingly enough was all it took to bring the calendar and tropical year back into line. The New Year was now celebrated on January 1.

The Gregorian (or "New Style") calendar was rapidly adopted by most European countries, and by association it was adopted in their American colonies as well. Britain remained the exception, much as it does today when it comes to driving on the wrong side of the road and serving beer in pints. They retained the Julian (or "Old Style") calendar until 1752, when the British (and their American colonists) finally bowed to pressure. That year in Philadelphia, Boston, and London September 4 was followed the next day by September 14, as the two calendars were out of kilter by ten whole days. That means that the good people of Williamsburg celebrated New Year 1752 in March, and New Year 1753 just nine months later!

The problem for historians is that all British sources give us one date, while French or Spanish sources provide another, some ten days later. In most cases this hasn't been a problem with the Blackbeard story, but in cases such as his encounter with the French slave ship *La Concorde*,

French and British records differ. To maintain consistency I have given all dates in the Old Style, and changed French or Spanish sources to match. However, to avoid confusing the modern reader unduly I've also noted the New Year as taking place according to the New Style, on January 1. In many records this hasn't been a problem, as letters and reports written between early January and late March were usually dated using both years (e.g., 25 February 1718/19).

That means that the date of Blackbeard's encounter with Lieutenant Maynard of the Royal Navy was November 22, 1718, in the Old Style, or December 2 in the New Style. If you want to bring the calendar up to date, feel free to pencil in all the dates ten days after they happened, to keep things in line with the calendar we use today. Finally, I would like to apologize to readers in Britain and the Commonwealth. As the publisher is based in the United States, I have reluctantly adopted the quaint and peculiar American way of putting the day and the month in the wrong order. It wasn't how Governor Spotswood of the colony of Virginia would have written it, but it reflects how his counterpart would date his letters today. I hope you can forgive me.

1

The Pirate Apprentice

Everyone likes a bestseller. In 1724, booksellers in London couldn't stock enough copies of the latest rip-roaring success, a series of pirate yarns penned by the completely unknown sea captain, Charles Johnson. The publisher, Charles Rivington, was delighted, and immediately gave orders for the printing of a second edition, just to keep up with demand. The book contained a series of biographies of British-born or British colonial pirates whose deeds shocked and titillated the genteel readership and left them wanting more. Of the dozen or so pirates covered in the book, the most ferocious was a man the author called "Captain Teach." Today we know him as Blackbeard.

Even today Blackbeard remains something of an enigma. Like many pirates of his time, he only emerges from the historical mists when he crosses the line from law-abiding seaman to notorious pirate. This means that whatever follows about the pirate's early life includes a lot of supposition, a house of cards built on a shaky table. This said, we can make several fairly logical guesses about what happened to him during these lost years. The few facts we have about him can also be augmented with other, more verifiable types of evidence. Much of what we do know is based on the writings of Captain Johnson, and one suspects that his version of Blackbeard's life was colored a little to make a more sensational story. However, Blackbeard's short but dramatic life left enough of a wake that with a little detective work we can trace his piratical career, filling in the gaps left by Johnson and breathing life into the alarming figure portrayed by the first pirate biographer.

The background of Captain Charles Johnson is almost as mysterious as that of Blackbeard himself. Before we dip our toe in the pirate-infested waters of the early eighteenth century, we need to look a little more closely at the man who single-handedly made piracy glamorous and who wrote the first piratical bestseller. What we really know about Captain Charles Johnson isn't enough to fill a paragraph in an eighteenth-century Who's Who. No such figure appears to exist, which suggests the name was a *nom de plume*. While the identity of the writer still remains a mystery, several candidates have been proposed over the last three centuries.

These include the mediocre London playwright Charles Johnson (1679–1748), the publisher Charles Rivington (1688–1742), and Daniel Defoe (1660–1731), the man who wrote *Robinson Crusoe*. In his introduction to a modern edition of Johnson's *A General History . . . of the most notorious Pyrates*, maritime historian David Cordingly quite convincingly argued that as a sedentary landlubber, the playwright lacked the background needed to write a book that was so atmospherically peppered with nautical jargon. Similarly, Rivington, who published the first edition of the book in 1724, was wedded to his profession, and never appears to have strayed far from his shop near St. Paul's Cathedral. Even a day trip to the beach would have been out of character for him.

Daniel Defoe was a different type of man altogether. The London-born newspaperman and author knew how to write sensational prose, which is exactly what Johnson's *A General History* was. In *Robinson Crusoe* (1719) and *Captain Singleton* (1720), he demonstrated an extensive knowledge of the maritime world, and his style of writing was similar to that found in the pirate book. In his 1939 study *Defoe in the Pillory and Other Studies*, historian John R. Moore convincingly argued that Defoe and Johnson were one and the same, an association that remained in vogue for over half a century. Then in 1988 P. N. Furbank and W. R. Owens published *The Canonisation of William Defoe*, where they equally effectively demolished Moore's argument. This leaves us without a strong candidate for Johnson.

What isn't in doubt is that whoever Captain Charles Johnson was, he was certainly an experienced seaman. His description of how sailing ships of the time were operated and how they performed, and of what conditions on board were like, all suggest that the author was not only well versed in seafaring, but that he also spoke with some authority. He also described sea battles like a grizzled veteran. This alone precludes Daniel Defoe, who, although he was well traveled, was no professional seaman. It has even been suggested that Johnson himself was a pirate, although no suitable candidate has appeared, nor has Johnson been identified with any experienced and well-read merchant or naval captain of the time.

He certainly seemed to understand the lot of the common sailors mentioned in his book, and at times he even appeared to take the side of the pirates themselves—something a naval or merchant captain would usually be loath to do. So far it appears that the author of *A General History* has successfully maintained the façade of his nom de plume, and both the author and the publisher took his real identity to the grave with them.

What we know about the book itself is a lot more tangible. Captain Charles Johnson's *A General History of the Robberies and Murders of the most notorious Pyrates* was published in May 1724, a simple little leather-bound octavo-sized book (about half of a letter-size sheet) by an unknown author. To our ears the title sounds clumsy, but by the standards of 1724 it was as racy as it got. It certainly found a market, because the first edition sold out within a few months. A third, and then an enlarged fourth edition followed in 1725 and 1726, and by 1734 the work had been repackaged to include accounts of highwaymen, murderers, and robbers as well as pirates. It has remained in print ever since.

The original edition included an account of the lives of Bartholomew Roberts, who died in battle just three years before in 1721, as well as the sensational story of the two women pirates Anne Bonny and Mary Read and the lives of ten other pirates. One of these was entitled "The Life of Captain Teach." In the chapter, Johnson states, "Plutarch, and other grave historians, have taken notice that several great men amongst the Romans took their surnames from certain odd marks in their countenances; as Cicero, from a mark or vetch on his nose, so our hero Captain Teach, assumes the cognomen of Blackbeard from that large quantity of hair which, like a frightful meteor, covered his whole face and frightened America more than any comet that has appeared there a long time."

One of Johnson's most notorious pirates had a nickname that caught the imagination of the public, and has remained at the forefront of piratical imagery ever since. By the time the book was published Blackbeard had been dead for six years, and the so-called Golden Age of Piracy was already over. The villains whose short and brutal lives were so vividly encapsulated by Captain Johnson were fast becoming larger-than-life characters, whose exploits entertained rather than alarmed. Their recent executions or grisly deaths provided readers with the thrilling association of recent history with the escapism provided by a series of events, locations, and circumstances that the average reader could hardly imagine, and would never experience. It is little wonder that Johnson's book became such a popular work, and that his portrayal of Blackbeard and his contemporaries would remain equally vivid to later generations of readers.

The question is, how accurate was Johnson? How much were his short biographies based on fact, and how much was created to provide sensational reading? In his recent introduction to a reprint of Johnson, David Cordingly argued that in almost all cases the accuracy of Johnson's facts has been borne out by subsequent historical research. In his introduction to a reprint of Johnson published in 1925, the pirate historian Philip Gosse wrote that "Many of the incidents looked upon as imaginary are found all to be absolutely accurate in date and circumstance."

In 1998 Cordingly went even further, saying that "the majority of the facts in Johnson's *History* have been proved to be accurate." He did add the proviso that "there are a few notable exceptions. It seems likely that when he introduces conversation into his biographies he uses considerable licence." A prime example of this is Johnson's description of the exchange between Blackbeard and Lieutenant Maynard during the pirate's final battle. While it sounds good, neither Maynard nor any other survivor of the battle mentioned any such exchange. There are a few other areas where Johnson gets it wrong, but we'll come to those as the story unfolds. Suffice it to say Johnson provides a good starting point for our study, and gives us a framework on which to fix the many other scraps of historical information that make up the story of the pirate's life and times.

That brings us back to Blackbeard. As the first real biographer of the pirate, what did Johnson say about the pirate's identity, and his early life? In brief, the answer is surprisingly little. Considering that Blackbeard was one of the most notorious pirates of the Golden Age of Piracy, and one whose activities played such an important part in early colonial American history, surprisingly little seems to be known about who he really was and where he came from. However, he did leave a trail of evidence: letters from colonial governors, the legal depositions of his victims, and even newspaper articles. These can be used to check how accurate Johnson really was.

He began "The Life of Captain Teach" with the following paragraph: "Edward Teach was a Bristol man born, but had sailed some time out of Jamaica in privateers, in the late French war; Yet although he had often distinguished himself for his uncommon boldness and personal courage, he was never raised to any command, till he went a-pirating, which I think was at the latter end of the year 1716, when Captain Benjamin Hornigold put him in a sloop that he had made prize of, and with whom he continued in consortship till a little while before Hornigold surrendered."

When Blackbeard joined forces with his mentor, Benjamin Hornigold, we find surer ground, as the man was well known in pirate circles, and later became a poacher-turned-gamekeeper when he turned his back on his former career and became the chief pirate hunter for a British colonial governor. However, that leaves us with little or nothing to go on if we want to fill in Blackbeard's life before 1716. After that his deeds began to speak for themselves, as archival documents trace the path of his piratical career: the depositions of merchant captains whom he attacked, letters from colonial merchants to their governors, letters from the same governors to their superiors in London, and then the records of the officers and men of Britain's Royal Navy who were charged with hunting down the pirates who infested America's Atlantic seaboard.

Captain Johnson was clear about naming Bristol as Blackbeard's birthplace, and that he pursued a career as a privateer (a shipowner with a letter of marque from his government, which gave him the right to prey on enemy ships) before becoming a pirate. There also remains the possibility that Captain Johnson was wrong and that Blackbeard's early life followed an altogether different course. For instance, in 1900 the distinguished Virginian Thomas T. Upshur claimed that Blackbeard hailed from Accomack County, Virginia, but he never offered anything to help substantiate this rather wild statement. In the late seventeenth century this peninsula between the Atlantic and the Chesapeake, extending southward from Delaware to Cape Henry, formed part of the Virginia Colony. It is therefore unlikely that, given the publicity surrounding the trial of Blackbeard's surviving crewmen in Williamsburg in 1718, nobody commented on the pirate captain's Virginia roots. It's a pretty safe bet that Upshur got it wrong.

That leaves us with Bristol. From the descriptions of him provided by eyewitnesses, we can assume Blackbeard was a little under forty when he died, which means he would have been born around 1680. At that time the English city was a bustling port, the city's merchants growing rich on the back of transatlantic commerce, most notably the slave trade. Bristol was founded sometime during the Dark Ages, and by the time William the Conqueror reached those parts after 1066, Bristol was already a small but prosperous trading post sited on the north bank of the tidal River Avon. Slaves were big business in those days, too, a highly profitable slave trade existed between Bristol and Viking-held Dublin, a few days' voyage away across the Irish Sea.

The Normans built castles, churches, and bridges in the town, and brought stability to the land around it. Bristol prospered during the Middle Ages thanks to the wool trade, and merchant guilds ensured that the city was able to stand its own against the feudal landowners who ruled its hinterland. By the mid-fifteenth century Bristol was regarded as one of the four biggest towns in England, despite the setbacks caused by the occasional plague or famine, and her merchants began to look further afield for new commercial opportunities. That was when the port really came into its own.

In Spain, conquest might have been the driving force behind voyages of discovery, but in England the impetus was commerce. Although these Bristol explorers made less of an impact than their Spanish or Portuguese counterparts, they did manage to open up whole new markets for their West Country sponsors. In 1480 and 1481 John Jay the Younger ventured into the Atlantic in search of the "Island of Brasil," but both times he was forced to return home to Bristol without sighting any such island.

The Venetian immigrant John Cabot was more successful, and in 1496 he secured the patronage of King Henry VII of England. His charter stated, "We have given and granted to our well-beloved John Cabot, citizen of Venice, to Lewis, Sebastian, and Sanctius, sons of the said John . . . leave and power to sail to all parts, countries, and seas of the east, of the west, and of the north, under our banners and ensigns . . . to seek out, discover, and find whatsoever isles, countries, regions or provinces of the heathens and infidels whatsoever they be." King Henry had little to lose and a lot to gain. He finished, "For every their voyage, as often as they shall arrive at our port of Bristol (at which port they shall be bound and holden only to arrive), all manner of necessary costs and charges by them being deducted, to pay unto us in wares or money the fifth part of the capital gain so gotten." In effect, when John Cabot set sail in the *Matthew* of Bristol in May 1497, he became the first in a long line of Bristol mariners to cross the Atlantic in search of riches, albeit in the name of his king. It was also an early example of the old privateering rules under which the national treasury demanded a 20 percent cut of the profits. The Spanish overseas empire was built on exactly the same divide between private initiative and state profiteering.

John Cabot and his son Sebastian might well have been the first Europeans since the Vikings to set foot in North America—although a case could be made that Hugh Elliot, one of Cabot's ship captains, had actually visited the place before the explorer did! After all, Cabot thought he was in China, which doesn't say much for his sense of direction. However, the Cabots opened up a new continent to trade and settlement, paving the way for all the Bristol mariners who followed. During the sixteenth century Bristol sailors concentrated their efforts on Newfoundland, gathering lucrative catches of fish and whales, but made no great effort to settle the coastline beyond the fishing grounds. Others established trading links with Russia, and Bristol continued to develop as a port of international renown. However, not all Bristol seamen were so peaceable. The port also developed a reputation as a haven for pirates.

During the Middle Ages pirates based in Bristol became notorious for attacks on shipping in the Severn Estuary and the Irish Sea. By the sixteenth century Bristol pirates were venturing further afield. The shipowning brothers Andrew and John Barker waged their own private war against the Spanish after one of their ships was seized off the Azores in 1570, preying on Spanish shipping off the Canaries. In 1575 Andrew, too, took two ships as far as Trinidad and the Spanish Main, capturing a Spanish guard ship and looting whatever they could. Barker was killed during a mutiny, and the surviving crew were arrested and imprisoned when they returned home. Bristol captains also played their part in Sir Francis Drake's raids on the Spanish Main in the late sixteenth century, and in preventing the Spanish Armada from landing troops on English soil in 1588. This all meant that well before the first English colonists landed in North America, Bristol seafarers were crossing the Atlantic in search of plunder. Blackbeard was simply following a long and dishonorable tradition.

The seventeenth century was a time of colonization as well as discovery, and ships from Bristol participated in the founding of settlements in Newfoundland, New England, and Pennsylvania. Civil war in the three kingdoms of England, Scotland, and Ireland caused a temporary halt to these voyages of settlement, but the conflict also created opportunities for Bristolians of a more aggressive bent.

At the start of the war Bristol was held for Parliament, and with their ships in control of the seas there was little opportunity for privateering. However, in the summer of 1643 Prince Rupert captured the city for the Royalists, thereby gaining a port of strategic importance. Bristol remained in Royalist hands for two years, and Bristol ship captains made the most of their time. Royalist privateers based in Bristol scoured the waters of the Irish Sea and the English Channel for enemy merchantmen while trying to avoid the patrolling warships of the Parliamentarian Navy.

Blockade runners carried much-needed men and arms from Ireland to Bristol, while some Bristol privateersmen even joined the Royalist privateering fleet in Ireland, and helped in large-scale attacks on Parliamentarian shipping. When the Parliamentarians recaptured Bristol in September 1645, most privateers returned to more legitimate pursuits, or else escaped across the Irish Sea to the privateering den at Kinsale, in southern Ireland. Trade flourished under Cromwell's English Republic, but memories of lucrative piratical or privateering remained, and new enemies, the Dutch, French, and Spanish, all provided fresh opportunities. Blackbeard's father would have been brought up during this period, when adventurous privateersmen could make an easy fortune in plunder.

Privateering was little more than officially sanctioned piracy. In time of war, shipowners or captains could approach their government and obtain a "letter of marque," which entitled them to prey on the enemies of the state on the high seas. In effect, it was a cheap form of economic warfare, setting merchant captains and their ships in search of enemy merchantmen. It didn't cost the government anything, and in fact the government stood to make a profit. Most letters of marque stated that when a prize was brought into port it was to be sold at auction, and the government that issued the privateering license claimed a significant portion of the profit, usually a quarter of the total value of the captured ship and its cargo. Everyone was a winner, apart from the foreign shipowners and their insurers, of course. Privateering was certainly a lucrative business.

Just how big a business it was can be shown by a few statistics. During the Second Dutch War (1665–67), Dutch privateers captured 360 English merchantmen, and a similar number were taken during the Third Dutch War (1672–74). By contrast, English privateers captured approximately 160 Dutch ships in the first war, and 270 in the second. However, this was privateering on a small scale compared to the War of the Grand Alliance (1688–97), when the French embraced privateering with a vengeance. The French port of Dunkirk became a major privateering port, and French corsairs played merry havoc in the cold, congested waters of the English Channel. They even cruised as far north as Orkney and Shetland, where they preyed on the fishing fleets that were vital to the economy of both Scotland and England. The English replied in kind, but their main effort was concentrated in the Caribbean. There a stream of French merchantmen brought goods and slaves to the wealthy French-held sugar-producing islands such as Martinique and Dominique, and returned laden with sugar and rum. It was a time of rich pickings for the privateers based in Barbados and Jamaica, and by the time the war ended in October 1697 the economy of the islands had been severely damaged, with over 280 French ships captured in the Caribbean alone, roughly one every three weeks.

War broke out again in 1701, when the French king Louis XIV placed his grandson Prince Philip of Anjou on the vacant Spanish throne. This, the War of the Spanish Succession (1701–13), or Queen Anne's War, soon became a conflict fought on a worldwide scale. The maritime powers of England and Holland were reluctant to see France gain control of the Spanish Empire, so they backed a rival contender, the Archduke Charles of Austria. Philip, now King Philip V of Spain, managed to gain control of most of the Spanish army and navy, and while the English, Austrians, and Dutch fought the French in Spain, the same powers instigated a civil war in Spain itself.

The war dragged on until both sides were exhausted some thirteen years later, but while the armies fought their way around an embattled Europe, the privateers in the Caribbean were enjoying a period of almost

Henry Every (or Avery), the most successful pirate of them all. In 1694 he captured the flagship of an Indian moghul, then retired with his plunder. His success would have encouraged seamen like Blackbeard to follow in his footsteps.

unlimited prosperity. With both French and Spanish merchantmen to prey on, the English and Dutch privateers had the entire Caribbean basin to hunt in, and they made the most of their opportunity. This later privateering war was the one Blackbeard participated in, but as a youth he would have been weaned on sailors' stories of the rich pickings to be had on the far side of the Atlantic Ocean during the earlier decade-long round of fighting.

To a child growing up in Bristol during this time it would have seemed that war was normal, and that the opportunities presented by privateering would never come to an end. Blackbeard's enthusiasm would have been fueled by reports of the buccaneers in the Caribbean—men who often pursued their own private war against the Spanish, and who frequently returned to their buccaneering ports laden with plunder from the Spanish Main. It was enough to grip the imagination of any boy brought up in a seafaring town.

A local (and wholly unconfirmed) Bristol legend claims that Blackbeard's father was a privateersman during the Dutch Wars, returning to Bristol before 1680, the time when Blackbeard would have been born.

Another even more persistent version of the tale places his father on a privateer operating out of Port Royal in Jamaica during the War of the Grand Alliance, where he would have been well placed to participate in attacks on both the French and the Spanish. Of course this is mere supposition, and no sailor with the correct surname has so far been found among the scanty records that survive concerning Jamaica-based privateersmen.

That brings us neatly to the next big problem: What was Blackbeard's real name? Most of the historical records describing the career of the pirate provide us with a variety of spellings, all of which were essentially the same name. Captain Johnson calls Blackbeard Captain Edward Teach, and given his accuracy with other, more provable facts, he was probably quite correct. However, other spellings crop up in official documents during his short career, and indeed most use the surname "Thatch." Had Johnson misread his sources? Given the level of information he supplied on the life of Blackbeard and other pirates, it seems likely that he had access to official transcripts of trials, to the affidavits submitted by Blackbeard's victims, and possibly even to the correspondence between colonial or naval officials and their superiors in London.

The name "Teach" was hardly mentioned, except as one of several phonetic variations on "Thatch" such as Thach, Thatche, Tatch, and Tatche. From this it seems far more likely that Blackbeard was called "Thatch" rather than "Teach." Official letters were often dictated to a clerk during this time, and the poor writer did the best he could, often spelling unknown words or names phonetically. With no dictionaries or spell-checkers to hand, it was little wonder that the records were inconsistent.

To complicate matters even further, there is no guarantee that the pirate wasn't operating under a pseudonym. While this might explain the difference between the two main spellings of his name, it is far more likely that if he did use a pseudonym he would have chosen one that sounded completely different from his given surname. One other name crops up. One historian, Robert E. Lee, suggests that Blackbeard might actually be Edward Drummond. Drummond was a Scottish name, derived from the Gaelic words *druim* (back) and *monadh* (mountain). Could the pirate have been Scottish? This seems highly unlikely, as during the early eighteenth century, just a decade after the political union of Scotland and England into Great Britain, the Scots tongue was still markedly different from that used in England.

While old Scots as used by Robert Burns and others was based on English, many words, speech patterns, and intonations were unique to Scotland. It can be argued that as Blackbeard was a sailor, his native tongue would have been diluted by years spent amid predominantly English crews, but he would still have been left with an easily noticeable brogue. No ship captain who encountered him and described the encounter mentioned any such Scots brogue, so we can pretty safely dismiss the possibility that Blackbeard was one of the author's fellow countrymen. While it might be possible that Blackbeard's parents moved to Bristol from Scotland and departed again before their name appeared on any city records, this must be considered pretty unlikely.

We are left with the Thatch or Teach problem. Both are unusual surnames in late-seventeenth-century England, although the variant Thatche is a little more prevalent. The authorities in Bristol conducted a census in 1698, when Blackbeard would still have been a teenager, and it was hoped that this might shed some light on the problem. Unfortunately, the census never mentioned anyone called Teach, or Thatch, or even a variation of the two, although the name Thatcher did appear. Incidentally, no Drummonds were listed, either. That takes us back where we started. Given the prevalence of the name Thatch in contemporary documents relating to the pirate, it would be tempting to opt for this version of his surname.

However, the popularity of Captain Johnson's account means that the surname Teach has been closely associated with the man since May 1724. Therefore, with some reluctance we should side with convention and refer to Blackbeard as Edward Teach, at least until the day some further evidence comes to light. There's always the hope that in some dusty archive or attic some old family papers or official document might shed new light on the matter. Until then, while we should really opt for Teach, to keep things consistent we'll use the cognomen Blackbeard unless we really have to.

Building anything based on the word of Captain Johnson is something like building a home on shifting sands. He might well have been right about the Bristol connection, or the surname Teach (or even Thatch), but given the evidence of the 1698 survey, it is unlikely he was right about both. There is always the possibility that Blackbeard wasn't from Bristol at all, but only sought employment as a mariner there, in which case he could have been born just about anywhere in England. There is also the even more likely possibility that his original family name is somewhere in the census, but we simply don't know what it was. We have already raised the possibility that he used a pseudonym when he took to piracy in an attempt to cover his tracks. If so, he wasn't the first pirate to do so, but it doesn't help us discover who he really was.

There is one possible clue that may help suggest he had some link with Bristol after all. It involves Woodes Rogers (circa 1679–1732), the Bristol-born privateer who became the governor of the Bahamas in 1718. He showed a knack for privateering as a youth, during the last years of the War of the Grand Alliance, and when war broke out again in 1701 he returned to his old trade, this time as a ship's captain, working on behalf of a group of Bristol merchants. The plunder must have been pretty good, as he bought himself a house in Bristol's fashionable Queen's Square.

Even greater triumphs were to follow. In 1708 his backers gave him the command of a small squadron of two custom-built privateers, the *Duke* and the *Duchess*, and he sailed off from Bristol to the South Seas, rounding Cape Horn to enter the Pacific Ocean. The best-known incident from the voyage came in early 1709 when he put into the remote island of Juan Fernandez to pick up water. Instead he discovered the marooned Scottish mariner Alexander Selkirk. This castaway was of course the role model used by Daniel Defoe when he wrote *Robinson Crusoe*. Later that year Rogers cruised off the Peruvian coast and sacked the town of Guayaquil. The squadron returned to Britain in 1711 after completing a circumnavigation of the globe, a feat that won Rogers wide acclaim. This celebrity only increased the following year when he published a swashbuckling account of his voyage.

Woodes Rogers and Blackbeard would have been much the same age, and in a city with a population of just under twenty thousand, there is a possibility that if Blackbeard was indeed raised in Bristol, the two men would probably have known each other, at least by sight. While Rogers was raised in the old heart of the city itself, local legend has it that Blackbeard was brought up in Redcliffe, a less salubrious riverfront suburb on the opposite bank of the river. Whichever part of the city he came from (if indeed he was raised in Bristol at all), from all accounts Blackbeard was a literate, somewhat educated man rather than an illiterate seaman. Presumably he received a modicum of formal schooling. If he went to one of Bristol's half-dozen schools during the last decade of the seventeenth century, the two would surely have met at some stage.

As adventurous boys who could read, it is possible that they had access to the first racy account of privateers, buccaneers, and pirates: A. O. Esquemeling's *Bucaniers of America*, which was first published in Amsterdam in 1679, and translated into English for a bestselling book published in London in 1684. Surely copies would have circulated fairly widely in a port where privateering and maritime adventure were part of the city's heritage. Then Blackbeard would have been in his late teens in 1697 when William Dampier published the first of three *Voyages*, one of the world's first bestselling travel books, an account of his voyages in the Caribbean and the South Seas. Further volumes followed over the next decade, by which time Dampier was as well known as a Bristol-sponsored privateer as he was as an explorer and naturalist. If Blackbeard and Rogers read the works of Esquemeling and Dampier as teenagers, then it was little wonder they took to the high seas in search of adventure when they were older.

Later on both men served as privateersmen, albeit Rogers was by far the more successful of the two. It is therefore quite likely that during their careers their paths crossed, or at least that they heard of each other's exploits. In other words, Rogers would have known Blackbeard by sight, and might have recognized him if the two men met. In 1717 Rogers obtained a commission as the governor of the Bahamas, which was then a den of pirates. As part of his drive to stamp out piracy in the area he offered a pardon to any pirate who was willing to change his ways, a policy adopted by several other colonial governors soon afterward. Blackbeard was well aware of this, as his mentor, Benjamin Hornigold, and many of his fellow shipmates took Rogers up on the offer. Blackbeard decided not to, and went pirating instead. However, after his attack on Charleston he seemed to change his mind, and sought a pardon.

It is interesting that Blackbeard opted to sail to North Carolina rather than the Bahamas to take up the offer. Was he trying to avoid Governor Rogers? If Blackbeard was indeed operating under a pseudonym, the meeting could well have led to Rogers (who would of course know his true identity) recognizing the pirate. While it is unlikely that Blackbeard cared about maintaining the family name, as has been suggested by some, he was probably keen to avoid revealing his true identity. Doing so would reduce his chances of slipping inconspicuously back into Britain and British society, as the pirate Henry Every had done. Most pirates dreamed of retiring to live off their loot, and Blackbeard may well have been planning for such a future. While there were other reasons why North Carolina proved attractive, New Providence in the Bahamas had been his base, it was where his former shipmates were, and it was a place where an enterprising former pirate could earn the favor of the governor and establish a new career as a pirate hunter. Blackbeard chose to turn his back on all this, and the Woods Rogers connection may well have been the reason why.

Although no official records appear to survive from Blackbeard's youth in Bristol, long-standing local legends provide at least a suggestion of what might have been. That these stories are so detailed bears testimony to the way Bristolians have embraced their notorious townsman as their own, and most probably fleshed out his background to strengthen the connection between pirate and place. It would be nice to discover that they had some grain of truth in them, but unless some new piece of evidence is uncovered, they remain little more than unsubstantiated tales about Bristol's most notorious son. They also help explain how Blackbeard took to the sea in the first place.

It is claimed that Blackbeard was indeed born Edward Teach, and hailed from the seafaring community of Redcliffe. It was said that his father died in 1693, when Blackbeard would have been in his early teens, and that shortly afterward his mother remarried. The story goes that this newcomer took a cordial dislike to his stepson and beat him regularly. After a few years of this, the youth couldn't take any more and turned on his stepfather, beating him half to death. The sixteen-year-old had no alternative but to flee his home, and so he went to the waterfront and signed on as a cabin boy on the next ship to sail from the city. This vessel was a merchantman bound for Port Royal in Jamaica, and so in about 1697 the young Edward Teach arrived in the Caribbean. He proved to be a highly capable seaman, and within two years he had become a fully fledged sailor, serving on Caribbean-based merchant ships. From there he went on to become a privateer.

While this tale would be highly revealing if it were true, there is absolutely no evidence to support the legend. Searches of city records reveal no such attack being reported by anyone called Teach, Thatch, or Drummond, and no charges were brought against anyone of the same name. Indeed between 1690 and 1700 there was no report of any serious domestic violence that might fit the story. Therefore how Blackbeard left Bristol and ended up in the Caribbean will probably remain a mystery, despite the attractiveness of the local legend. This lack of information on Blackbeard's past is hardly surprising. The lives of most seamen in the eighteenth century went completely unrecorded, and even the most sophisticated governments of the age kept very little in the way of information on their citizens. In those days illiterate sailors signed on to a ship by marking the ship's papers with a cross or mark, or, more often, no written records were kept, and the contract between seaman and captain was sealed not by a piece of paper but by a handshake.

Even though Blackbeard was literate, it is hardly surprising that tracing the career of one young seaman is almost impossible, at least until he crossed the line between law-abiding sailor and maritime outlaw. The pirate historian Robert E. Lee summed this up when he wrote that "Historians . . . can pinpoint documented records of the capture of ships, with details of longitude and latitude, inventories of looted cargo, and minute particulars relating to atrocious conduct; but they can discover little or nothing about the pirates' personal lives before they committed acts of piracy."

What we do know of seamen of the time often comes from court testimony, the statements of men who crossed the legal line from seaman to pirate and were caught. These accounts provide us with a glimpse into the life of the ordinary seaman during the early eighteenth century, and show why so many turned their backs on authority and became pirates. Much if not all of this would have applied to Blackbeard.

In his history of English merchant seamen during this period, Peter Earl posed the question "What sort of life did they lead?" He continued:

> One might imagine it was a life of poverty, brutality and great hardship, toiling in leaking sailing ships across the oceans, subject not just to the storms and threat of shipwreck with which the modern sailor is familiar, but also to the threat of capture by the numerous predators who plied the seas and to the arbitrary discipline of captains and boatswains ready with lash and cane to drum their crews into obedience. These men had few mechanical aids, no electronic wizardry to tell them where they were, no wireless to call for aid, no cans to preserve their food. They ate salt food, slept when they could in crowded leaking forecastles, lived in damp, smelly clothes and relied on muscle, common sense and knowledge of the sea to carry their ships across the globe. They were cheated and short-changed by officers

and ship-owners; duped ashore by victuallers and prostitutes, abused and reviled by those who made their living on land.

It was certainly no easy life, and the hardships, injustices, and dangers facing a seaman of this period is a theme we will return to a little later. Still, it was a career that men were increasingly drawn to as the number of merchant ships increased during the late seventeenth and early eighteenth centuries, and the number of seafaring jobs rose accordingly. Where a century before transatlantic voyages were a rarity, by 1700 merchantmen were plying a regular trade between the Caribbean and the American colonies and Europe. In addition, slavery was becoming big business, and the number of vessels engaged in the "triangular trade" between Europe, West Africa, and the Americas increased dramatically during Blackbeard's life. There was plenty of work to be had, and it is estimated that by 1700 over thirty thousand English sailors were employed on the high seas, in addition to those from the colonies, from Scotland, and from other European maritime nations, most notably France and Holland.

These opportunities increased even further in 1698 when the Royal Africa Company withdrew its monopoly of trade with African ports, opening up the market to independent slavers who had hitherto only engaged in the slave trade as interlopers. The most profitable trading route of the eighteenth century was the triangular trade route from Britain to West Africa, then on to the Caribbean or the American colonies, then back to Britain. Trade goods were taken from Britain and exchanged for slaves on the African coast.

The slavers would then make the notorious transatlantic Middle Passage to the Caribbean or the Southern colonies, where the slaves would be sold or exchanged for a local cargo, sugar in the Caribbean and tobacco or rice in America. The ship would then make the return leg to Britain. Another version of the triangular trade involved New England merchants who transported flour, meat, and other provisions to the West Indies, where the food would be exchanged for sugar or rum. The New Englanders would transport this to Britain, where it would be exchanged for manufactured goods to be brought back to the colonies.

Not every English or French merchantman engaged in transatlantic commerce was engaged in the slave trade. The lucrative business of supplying the American colonies or the Caribbean islands with European manufactured goods was also important, although the profits it generated were usually nowhere near as spectacular as those created by the slave trade. By contrast, slave ship owners could recoup the cost of building a vessel in one or two voyages. By 1730, Bristol had surpassed London as the slaving capital of the world. While few slaves ever set foot in either port, the profits from this inhumane traffic poured into the home ports of the slaving ships. Of course, the sailors themselves saw little of this profit, and their lot remained unremittingly harsh, with the added risk of contracting a fatal tropical disease while they laid off the African coast.

As the number of slaves shipped to the plantations of the West Indies and the Southern colonies of British America increased, so, too, did the production of raw materials and manufactured goods to export. Sugar was king in the Caribbean, followed by its refined spirit derivative, rum, and demand for both increased markedly during the period from 1680 to 1720. Meanwhile, the export of rice from the Carolinas, tobacco from Virginia, and lumber and furs from the northern colonies all became increasingly big business.

The cargoes of transatlantic trading vessels reflected this commerce. For example, an outgoing ship of 400 tons, the *Mercy*, sailing from the Virginia Capes to London in 1721, carried "360 tons of tobacco, laden, 24 barrels of herbes of divers sorts, 14 hogges of spirit, 120 bales of flax and 32 barres of pigge [iron]." The diversity of her cargo almost certainly reflects small amounts of private cargo carried by passengers and crew in order to turn a small personal profit from the voyage. Accounts of cargoes looted by pirates in America during the same period also reflect the nature of transatlantic trade at the time, and show what cargo was carried on smaller ships from port to port along the Atlantic seaboard, and from the American colonies to the Caribbean.

The pirate captain John Martel was, "in the month of September 1716, cruising off Jamaica and Cuba, about which time he took the Berkley galley, Captain Saunders, and plundered him of 1,000 pounds in money, and afterwards met with the sloop called the King Solomon, from whom he took some money and provisions, besides goods, to a good value." In December he encountered the *Greyhound* of London, and "as soon as they could get out of her all her gold dust, elephants teeth and 40 slaves, they sent her upon her voyage."

Even the accounts of Blackbeard's piratical attacks reveal something of the nature of maritime trade. In 1718 he encountered two French ships off the Carolina coast, "one of them loaded with sugar and cocoa and the other light. Both bound to Martinique." A few months later he claimed he found another abandoned French ship, so presumably its crew had seen the pirates coming. He took the ship and cargo to Bath Town, North Carolina, where "a court was called and the ship condemned: the governor had 60 hogsheads of sugar for his dividend . . . his secretary and collector for the Province 20, and the rest was shared amongst the other pirates."

We have no evidence to support how or when the future Blackbeard first reached the Caribbean, but as he sailed from Bristol it can be assumed that the ship he first served on was engaged either in the transport of man-ufactured goods to a port such as Jamaica, or else the transportation of African slaves. Of the two the latter is by far the most likely. As for when, we can surmise that he made his first Caribbean landfall during the last years of the seventeenth century. While we know nothing of the ship he joined, we do know a little about slave ships of this period.

A prime example is the English slave ship *Henrietta Marie*, which sailed on its first triangular trade voyage in 1697. She was typical of the numerous small merchant ships that transported slaves to the Americas during this period. She was about 60 to 70 feet long, and displaced around 120 tons. She began her working life as a small French merchantman, but she was captured during the closing stages of the War of the Grand Alliance, when English and French privateers scoured the English Chan-nel and its approaches for prizes. She was three-masted, with a rounded bow, a square stern, and a relatively commodious cargo hold. On slave ships this was converted to hold tiers, allowing more slaves to be crammed into the limited space available.

In September 1699 she sailed from London laden with trade goods, bound for West Africa. Captain John Taylor planned to exchange these beads, iron bars, and pewter for slaves when he reached the trading station of New Calabar on the African coast. She arrived there in the middle of December, and remained there throughout the winter. She embarked on the leg of the triangular trade route known as the Middle Passage in the spring of 1700, her 'tween-decks crowded with her human cargo of two hundred African men, women, and children. It was said that you could smell a slaver from a mile downwind, so bad was the stench of unwashed, maltreated humanity on board.

A twelve-gun British sloop in naval service, pictured at anchor off Boston in 1722. Although this vessel was in naval service, she was typical of the well-armed sloops used by Blackbeard and his compatriots during this period.

Accounts of the horrors of the Middle Passage are legion—the terror of the captives, the suicides of those who preferred to jump overboard rather than endure any more, and the lack of air, space, and privacy on the overcrowded slave decks. Given the small size of the *Henrietta Marie*, archaeologists and historians have worked out that the slaves barely had enough room to lie flat, while there was insufficient room to do more than sit upright. Conditions on the *Henrietta Marie* must have been better than most, as only sixteen slaves died during the voyage. On other less fortunate or well-managed ships the death toll could reach as high as 50 percent, although one death in five was considered average.

On the morning of May 18, 1700, the *Henrietta Marie* put in to Port Royal, Jamaica, whereupon her crew washed and cleaned the surviving slaves ready for the auction block. Then came the sale. The slaves were usually auctioned off in groups of up to a half-dozen at a time, with prices ranging from £12 to £18 each, depending on sex, age, and health. Captain Taylor made £827 on the transaction, a profit he immediately reinvested in local goods that he planned to export back to London. Eighty-one barrels of muscovado sugar, fourteen bales of cotton, eleven barrels of indigo dye, and twenty-one tons of logwood (used for the dying of cloth) were loaded aboard the ship in Port Royal, all goods that would fetch an extremely good price in London. Captain Taylor must have looked forward to the completion of a highly profitable voyage. She set sail from Jamaica bound for England around the middle of August 1700, sailing westward along the southern coast of Jamaica.

The officials who watched her sail were the last people to see any of the crew again. Off Negril Point she set course for the Yucatan Channel. Sailing ships were governed by wind and current, so the best route home for the *Henrietta Marie* was to round the Peninsula de Guanahacabibes, the most westerly tip of Spanish-held Cuba, then head northeast into the Florida Straits. It was there that fate took a turn, and the *Henrietta Marie* was caught up in a hurricane, which came howling up over the mountains of Cuba, lashing Havana and then picking up force as it headed out into the Straits. The slave ship never stood a chance. She was dashed against New Ground Reef, an outlying spur of the Florida Keys, and the ship sank with all hands.

The only reason we know so much about the *Henrietta Marie* today is that in 1972 treasure hunters found her while they were looking for the remains of the fabled Spanish galleon *Nuestra Señora de Atocha*, which sank in the same area almost eight years before the slaver. When the divers began recovering shackles and English cannon rather than Spanish gold and silver, they left the wreck alone and resumed their search. Mel Fisher and his divers were finally rewarded for their long search in 1985 when they found the remains of the Spanish galleon, complete with her precious cargo. While the treasure hunters may well have been disappointed with their earlier find, archaeologists working for the salvors were not.

No shipwreck of a slave ship of this period had ever been found. It would be another two decades before anything was done with the finds, but in 1995 these artifacts formed the basis for a successful traveling exhibit called "A Slave Ship Speaks: The Wreck of the Henrietta Marie." During the preparation of the exhibition researchers traced the story of the small slave ship, and curators were able to use the objects themselves to tell the story of the transatlantic slave trade far more eloquently than any book. The exhibition is still touring cities in the United States.

What has all this to do with Blackbeard? Well, quite simply, if he decided to go to sea on a Bristol-based ship during the late 1690s, then the chances are that he would have signed on as a crewman on a slave ship. It would have followed a nearly identical course to the one followed by the *Henrietta Marie* two or three years later, and the young pirate in waiting would have made his first foreign landfall at a port on the West African coast such as New Calabar. As Captain Johnson suggests that Blackbeard subsequently became a privateer based in Jamaica, then it is likely the ship he served on would have completed her transatlantic passage at Port Royal in Jamaica, just like the *Henrietta Marie*. That later ship carried a crew of eighteen men, and her crew size was fairly typical of the bulk of the slaving vessels that operated the triangular trade.

A ship of her size could have been sailed with far less, probably as few as eight to ten competent men, but additional crew were carried to watch the slaves, and to help ensure there was no slave insurrection. We know from shipping returns that crewmen often elected to leave their ship in Port Royal, either because they fell out with their shipmates, because they proved troublesome to the captain, or simply because they saw new opportunities in the Caribbean. A few others had originally signed on as a means of paying their passage to Jamaica, Barbados, or the other slaving ports, and planned to make a new life for themselves when they arrived in the New World.

Although we don't know which of these categories Blackbeard belonged to, later accounts suggest he was a popular captain, a successful seaman, and a man of some considerable charm. It therefore seems likely that if he chose to leave his ship in Port Royal, he did so of his own free will. Then again, by 1697 France and Spain were at peace with England, and so there would be no opportunity to work as a privateer. It is more probable that Blackbeard remained as a sailor on merchant ships during the next few years, learning his trade and gathering the skills he would later put to good use as a pirate. However, if Captain Johnson is right, then Port Royal would soon become Blackbeard's home port.

In the late 1690s Port Royal was a mere shadow of its former self. In its heyday it had been the premier port of the Caribbean, with some 250 ships entering its harbor every year from England, West Africa, and the North American colonies. It was also the buccaneering, freebooting capital of the world, a frontier town on the edge of the mighty Spanish Empire. Like a bank that never closed, the treasure ports of the Spanish Main were visited by these buccaneers with almost monotonous regularity during the later seventeenth century, and much of the plunder was brought back to Port Royal, where it was usually squandered on drink and whores. It is little wonder that Port Royal earned itself the title of "the Sodom of the New World."

A settlement was established there soon after Cromwell's Jamaican expedition captured the island from the Spanish in 1655. The English found that the south side of the island site contained an easily defended natural harbor, and so on a spit that contained nothing but sand and land crabs they rebuilt the Spanish earthwork fortification there, then created a small port. With little help from England, Jamaica's governors were forced to look to the buccaneers for help in protecting their newly won island. The term "buccaneer" comes from the Arawak word "*buccan*," a fire used to smoke meat. In the 1620s and 1630s the name was appropriately used to describe the European outlaws who roamed the Spanish-owned island of Hispaniola, hunting wild cattle and selling their produce to passing ships. These rough, lawless men clashed with the Spanish, but were relatively safe from Spanish patrols in the mountainous hinterland and jungle-fringed coast of the island.

A buccaneer haven was established on the nearby island of Tortuga, and by the 1640s the majority of these men had turned their backs on their cattle and had taken to piracy. While this was good for Spanish landowners in Hispaniola, it was disastrous news for the Spanish government. They began with small-scale attacks on ships passing through the Windward Passage, but by the time the English had secured Jamaica they were ready to move on to greater things. By offering the buccaneers a refuge from the Spanish, the English authorities of Jamaica began an association between Port Royal and the buccaneers that would last until the end of the century.

Known as "the Brethren of the Coast," these buccaneers were mostly English and French, although their ranks included outlaws of all nations, creeds, and colors. By the late 1650s they had begun to attack Spanish coastal settlements, and under the leadership of buccaneering captains such as Christopher Myngs and Jean l'Olonnais they waged their own private war against the Spaniards. This was a war fought regardless of minor diplomatic inconveniences such as England, France, and Spain being at peace with one another. The old Elizabethan seadog's expression of "no peace beyond the line" applied to these buccaneers as much as it did to men like Sir Francis Drake.

The most successful of all these buccaneers was Sir Henry Morgan, a Welsh-born seaman who terrorized the Spanish Main for the best part of a decade. With the connivance of the Jamaican governor he used Port Royal as his base for devastating raids on Puerto Principe and Porto Bello in 1668, then Maracaibo and Gibraltar the following year. His most spectacular achievement was his capture and sack of Panama on the Pacific coast in 1671, a feat achieved by capturing the Spanish fort at the mouth of the Chagres River, then leading his buccaneers across the steaming jungle-clad Isthmus of Panama to fall on the city. This jewel in the Spanish colonial crown was captured after a brief but bloody battle. Although recalled to England to answer for his actions, he returned to Jamaica, where he was able to retire to the estates he bought with his plunder. He got out of the business just in time, as new laws came into force in 1681 outlawing unsanctioned attacks on the Spanish.

Henceforth anyone conducting buccaneering raids on their own initiative were labeled as pirates—which of course they were in the first place. By the time of his death in 1682 the heyday of the Jamaican buccaneer was all but over, and the port resorted to more legitimate forms of income. As Europeans developed a sweet tooth and demand for sugar soared, Port Royal developed into a major trading port, where slaves, sugar, and rum became the cornerstones of the island economy. Its population grew to over sixty-five hundred people, making it one of the busiest ports in the Americas, and as big as Boston.

Even without hordes of buccaneers spending their loot on rum, women, and cards, Port Royal was a notoriously rough place. One somewhat biased visitor claimed that "its population consists of pirates, cutthroats, whores, and some of the vilest persons in the whole of the world." It was said that the port boasted more bars and brothels than any other port in the Americas, and the critics may well have been right. Then, shortly before noon on June 7, 1692, the whole lawless freebooting boomtown phase of Port Royal's existence came to an abrupt end.

The first tremors of a massive earthquake rocked the town, and scores of buildings collapsed. Other even more severe shocks followed, and a tsunami-like tidal wave thrown up by the earthquake swept over the port like an avenging angel. Within minutes it was all over, but in those few seconds almost every building in the port had been destroyed, and the two-thirds of it facing north toward the anchorage had been inundated by the sea. It has been estimated that some two thousand people died in the disaster, followed by roughly the same number over the next few months as disease took its toll on the survivors. Port Royal never recovered. One wag claimed that the earthquake was the wrath of God, meted out on "that wicked and rebellious place."

The young Blackbeard must have arrived there only a few years after the disaster, and would have heard tales of the port in its buccaneering heyday. By that stage new buildings were springing up in Kingston, across the bay to the north, but the remains of Port Royal still served as the island's main port until well into the eighteenth century. He and his shipmates probably first arrived as slavers, and would have been immersed in the mechanics of the sale of their human cargo. To them Port Royal would still have appeared a fascinating place, with its lush tropical backdrop, its clear blue waters, and its bustling humanity. While the days of the buccaneers were over, the port did enjoy something of a revival during times of war. If Bristol legend is to be believed, Blackbeard's father was based here while he served as a privateersman during the War of the Grand Alliance (1688–97). If we are to accept Captain Johnson, his son performed the same role there during the War of the Spanish Succession (1701–13).

During that long war a growing number of privateersmen gathered in Port Royal, preying on French and Spanish ships from Newfoundland to the coast of Brazil. French and Spanish privateersmen did exactly the same, although the bulk of the French privateering fleet was based in St.-Malo and Dunkirk, on the French coast. They still managed to sail as far as the Caribbean and the Indian Ocean, and over a thousand British or Dutch merchantmen were captured during the war. The political union of England and Scotland in 1707 opened up Jamaica to Scottish seamen, and the few records that survive show that a sizable number of these men took advantage of this opportunity.

Eager to gain the edge in commercial mayhem, in 1708 the British government decreed that they would no longer demand a 20 percent share of the profits from the sale of captured vessels and cargo. A new wave of privateering ships put to sea, and soon it was the French who were on the defensive in both European and American waters. As an example, no less than 125 privateering expeditions sailed from Bristol alone during the latter years of the war, and the story was repeated in most other British ports that boasted a merchant fleet that could be converted into privately owned warships. Port Royal was even busier, with thirty-nine privateering vessels based there in 1711 alone, crewed by up to four thousand plunder-hungry privateersmen.

A typical purpose-built privateer of the time was the *Cinque Ports*, a newly built vessel that accompanied William Dampier's *St. George* on a privateering expedition that left British waters in September 1703. She was described as a galley, but she was quite unlike the oared warships of antiquity. The 90-ton vessel had a full set of masts and sails, just like a regular square-ended three-masted sailing ship. However, a series of oar ports lined her side, and sweeps or oars were provided so she could be rowed into action against target ships when there was no wind.

Among her sixty-eight-man crew was Alexander Selkirk, the man who became the model for Daniel Defoe's Robinson Crusoe when Captain Stradling of the *Cinque Ports* marooned Selkirk on the Pacific island of Juan Fernandez, some five hundred miles off the coast of Chile. She carried sixteen guns, and so was more than a match for any Spanish merchantman she encountered during her voyage. She was also provisioned with enough supplies to last six months, allowing her to reach the unprotected Spanish shipping lanes in the Great South Sea (the contemporary name for the Pacific Ocean). However, most of the privateers operating out of Jamaica seem to have been smaller vessels than the *Cinque Ports*, mostly sloops or brigs with an armament of twelve to sixteen guns, and a crew of about forty to sixty men.

The war ended with both sides exhausted and nearly bankrupt. A temporary secession of hostilities was announced, and then in April 1713 the embattled French signed the Treaty of Utrecht with Great Britain and Holland. In the treaty the French ceded their possessions in Newfoundland and parts of what is now Canada to the British, and in return Queen Anne's government recognized Philip V as king of Spain, but any political union between France and Spain was officially dissolved. The following year the Austrian Empire signed its own peace agreement, and in 1715 the Treaty of Madrid brought an end to the war between the last contenders, Spain and British-backed Portugal.

While the end of the war might have been good news for the majority of Europe's population, it was decidedly a disaster for the seamen who had made a good living out of wartime plunder. It has been estimated that the end of the war, and consequently the canceling of all privateering contracts, put upwards of forty thousand British and Dutch seamen out of a job. Many of these would have been cast ashore in home ports such as Amsterdam, Bristol, London, Plymouth, or Leith, but several thousand of them found themselves stranded in the Caribbean and the North American seaboard.

The figure of six thousand British seamen in this predicament has been suggested, and the streets of Port Royal, Boston, New York, Charleston, and Bridgetown would have been littered with discharged privateersmen, all looking for work. While peace brought an increase in trade and an expansion in the number of merchant ships, this didn't help many of these former privateersmen. For a start, their ships were purpose-built for their role — lean, fast, heavily armed, and well manned. They lacked the cargo capacity of regular tubby merchant ships, and were expensive to operate. While many privateersmen turned their back on a period of plenty and signed on as seamen on board merchant ships, others looked for more lucrative and less legal means of employment.

Captain Johnson claims that Blackbeard "sailed some time out of Jamaica in privateers, in the late French war; yet though he had often distinguished himself for his uncommon boldness and personal courage he was never raised to any command, till he went a-pirating." Although we have no firm idea when Blackbeard began his privateering career, Johnson does suggest he was good at his job. If we assume that he began his seagoing career as a merchant seaman, it is likely that he became a privateer several years before the end of the war. A possible date is around 1708, when the British government's decision to waive its right to 20 percent of profits led to an upsurge in privateering numbers. If he first went to sea during the late 1690s, then he would have been a highly experienced seaman in his late twenties by that stage, and a prime candidate for recruitment into a privateering crew.

Although the war ended when the Treaty of Utrecht was signed in April 1713, the Spanish were still at war with Britain's Portuguese allies, so even after word that peace had been declared reached Jamaica in the summer of 1713, privateersmen might have been able to take advantage of this for a few more months, until clarification of the political situation reached the Jamaican governor in September. During this last summer of legitimate plundering hundreds of British and Dutch privateers would have been at sea, and would only have learned of the unfortunate advent of peace when they returned to port with their now-worthless prizes. However, by the late summer of 1713 almost every privateer in the Caribbean would have realized that the party was over.

By that time Blackbeard would have been looking around for fresh opportunities, legitimate or otherwise. There was little gainful employment to be had. One possible avenue of hard but honest work was already being closed to men like Blackbeard. For over half a century communities of logwood cutters had been scattered along the Caribbean shoreline of Central America. The majority worked on the shores of the Bay of Campeche, so they were also sometimes called "bay men." These primitive settlements were places that many privateersmen knew as friendly havens on a hostile coast. In fact, many of these settlers were former buccaneers and privateersmen, and the hardships endured by most logwood cutters meant that many were willing recruits when a privateer anchored offshore and asked for volunteers.

Logwood was the boom crop of its day, producing a vivid red dye that transformed the clothing industry in Europe. It was the Spanish who first discovered the strange leguminous tree growing along the coastal fringe of the Yucatan Peninsula. It had a deep red heartwood that was similar to the brazilwood found in South America, and the value of this red timber as a dye soon became apparent. The logwood tree (*haematoxylum campechianum*) was duly harvested for this heartwood, and the Spanish maintained a monopoly on its harvesting until English interlopers arrived in the area. The buccaneers discovered that the first captured Spanish cargoes of logwood sold in Europe for over £100 a ton, making it a highly valuable commodity.

This was almost all profit, as in 1676 William Dampier claims that the logwooders sold their cut heartwood for £5 a ton. By the time Blackbeard was looking for work, a single merchant ship leaving Jamaica with 50 tons of logwood in her hold could sell her cargo in London for upwards of £2,500. Although the price had now stabilized at around £50 a ton, the timber was one of the most valuable exports the Caribbean could produce, although the problems of gathering the heartwood meant that quantities available for sale were substantially lower than those of rum, sugar, rice, or tobacco. Between 1713 and 1716, some 4,965 tons of logwood were

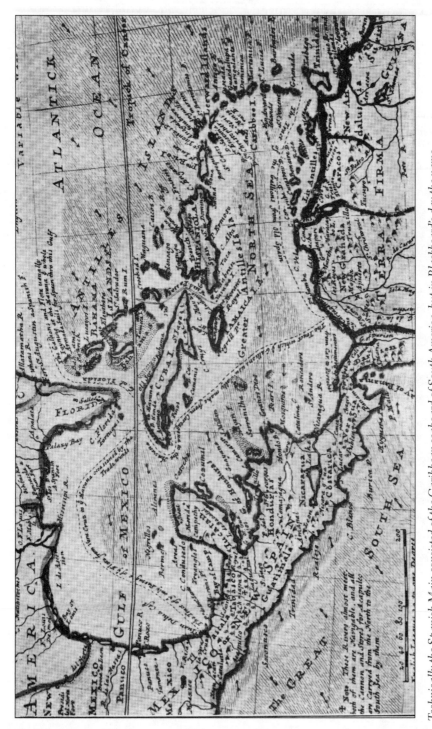

Technically the Spanish Main consisted of the Caribbean seaboard of South America, but in Blackbeard's day the name encompassed all Spanish dominions in the Caribbean. This map of 1720 shows the routes taken by the Spanish treasure flotas, while arrows show the direction of the prevailing wind.

shipped from the Caribbean to Britain, an export valued at more than £60,000 per annum. At the same time the colonies of Virginia and Maryland were exporting five times that value of tobacco leaves every year. Still, logwood remained a small-scale but highly profitable business.

While there was money to be made, conditions in these logwood camps were extremely primitive, and the camps perched on the edges of mangrove-fringed bays plagued by mosquitoes, alligators, and snakes. William Dampier provided a valuable firsthand account of this life in his book *Voyages and Descriptions*. In fact, he argued that these men were less of a threat to the Spanish as logwood cutters than they were as pirates or privateers. When a ship arrived, the logwooders would celebrate with bacchanalian excess, and often exchanged logwood for rum, regardless of the commercial value of the timber. Dampier also claimed that many logwooders used their spare time to raid neighboring Native American villages, or even passing Spanish merchant ships.

In a way the logwooders of Blackbeard's time resembled the early buccaneers who made a living on the coast of Hispaniola during the early seventeenth century. By 1713 the number of logwood cutters had dropped to less than a thousand, as the Spanish stepped up their systematic harassment of the logwooding communities. Spanish ships would arrive in the bay, and although the loggers would hide in the jungle, sailors and marines would burn their settlement and seize any tools, weapons, and timber they found. The end of the war meant that the Spanish could devote fresh resources to driving off these interlopers, and by 1715 most British logwooders had packed up and left.

Historian David Cordingly claims that "Driven out of the Bay of Campeche, many of the logwood cutters headed for the Bahamas. The harbor of Nassau on the island of New Providence became the headquarters for another community of pirates, and acted as a meeting point for pirate ships operating throughout the Caribbean and the Atlantic Ocean." This is where Blackbeard ended up, and it is in Nassau (or New Providence) that we can replace the supposition that surrounds his early life with a substantial body of verifiable facts. It was in the Bahamas that he would meet his mentor, Benjamin Hornigold, and where he turned his back on the law.

Given the lack of hard evidence, the suggested course of Blackbeard's early life outlined above remains little more than educated guesswork, a foundation laid on shaky ground. However, as soon as a pirate began attacking merchant ships and their captains and crews lived to tell the tale, people started writing about his exploits. Until he arrived in New Providence he was little more than one of the thousands of shadowy, nameless figures who contributed to world events without leaving a mark. From that point on, he would become an infamous and much-reported figure in his own right, leaving a growing trail of evidence behind him to mark his passage through history. As Captain Johnson put it, Blackbeard was about to burst on the scene "like a frightful meteor," and his coming "frightened America more than any comet."

2

A Pirate's Life

The crowd had been gathering all morning, crowding around the gallows like expectant vultures. In the harbor sailors climbed into the rigging for a clear view of the hanging, while the wealthy of Charles Town lined the verandas overlooking the open ground on the city's southern edge. The noise grew as the prisoner's cart approached, flanked by two files of colonial militia. The date was December 10, 1718, and the condemned man was Captain Stede Bonnet, onetime gentleman farmer from Barbados, and more recently the piratical partner of the infamous Blackbeard, the man who a few months before had held the city to ransom. Bonnet could expect little mercy as he was led to the scaffold. After he gave a short speech of repentance the cart was pulled away, and, clutching a posy of flowers, the unlikely pirate captain was left jerking his way to oblivion.

The message executions like this sent was that piracy didn't pay. Colonial America was fighting a bitter war for its very survival, her fragile and nascent economy solely reliant on unrestricted maritime trade with the mother country, Europe, Africa, and the Caribbean. A wave of piratical attacks from Newfoundland to Florida threatened to cut this trading lifeline, and so when authorities captured pirates like Bonnet they used them to send a dreadful warning to other sailors not to follow the pirates' lead and turn to a life of crime. The only end a pirate could expect was a bloody one, or else death at the hands of a hangman.

If this message was so powerful, then it does beg the question, why did Blackbeard turn to piracy? He obviously knew the risks—he knew what fate almost certainly had in store for him. Were his experiences typical of others, or if not, what made him stand out from the crowd? Did he sail to the Bahamas specifically to turn his back on the law, or was it a career option he chose when he met the cutthroats who settled there? To find answers we need to look at what he found when he arrived in New Providence, the place where it all started. We also need to see how he and other pirates began their careers as highwaymen of the seas.

Piracy was clearly not an occupation to enter into lightly. When Blackbeard took up piracy in 1716, recent history was littered with examples of the fate awaiting pirates once they were caught. In May 1701 Captain Kidd swung from the riverside gallows at Execution Dock in London, a crowd of thousands watching as he kicked and breathed his last. Ten days later the crew of the French pirate ship *La Paix* followed him to the same gallows, a mass execution of Captain Louis Guittar and two dozen pirates unlucky enough to be cornered by an English warship in the mouth of Virginia's James River.

As recently as December 1715 the Scottish-born pirate Captain Alexander Dolzell (Dalziel) repented his sins on the same scaffold before being executed as a crowd watched him embark on his final voyage. Public hangings always drew a big crowd, and pirate executions were even more entertaining than most. For a start, the gallows were always erected on the shore or riverside between the high and low tide marks. On the day of the execution a large crowd would gather, while yet more spectators watched the event unfold from boats moored just offshore. In London the condemned pirate was forced to ride in a cart as part of a solemn procession that wound its way from the Marshalsea prison on the south bank of the river across London Bridge, past the gloomy walls of the Tower of London, then on to Wapping and Execution Dock. At the head of the procession was the imposing figure of the Admiralty Marshal or his deputy, flanked by an official carrying the silver oar that represented the authority of his office and of the Admiralty. A chaplain rode with the prisoner, no doubt berating him for his sins and demanding he repent them before he met his maker.

The actual business of hanging was always something of a pageant, with the condemned man given a last chance to speak before the sentence was carried out. If he failed to come up with anything suitably apologetic or moving then, there were plenty of journalists ready to put words in his mouth. Within hours of the execution copies of the pirate's last testament were being distributed throughout London, the words eagerly awaited by a public that reveled in the tale. After the pirate had been hanged, it was customary to cut him down and retie him to a post on the foreshore, where three tides were allowed to pass over the body before it was cut down again. After that the pirate was buried in an unmarked grave or, worse, was carted off to the Surgeon's Hall for dissection.

In the case of Captain Kidd, the body was used to make a point. It was customary to display the corpses of the more notorious pirates at prominent locations at the entrance to a harbor or waterway, so that passing seamen were reminded that piracy didn't pay. Captain Kidd's corpse was daubed with tar to delay the decomposition of the body, then was placed in a man-shaped iron cage. This was then suspended from a gallows on desolate and windswept Tilbury Point, several miles downriver from London. This meant that all ships entering or leaving the great port would have to pass by the macabre spectacle. His decaying body remained swinging there for several years, an attention-grabbing warning to any would-be cutthroats. All sailors knew that they could expect no mercy once they embarked on a piratical career. Like the other former privateers congregating in the Bahamas, Blackbeard was well aware of all this, but it didn't deter him.

We don't know when Blackbeard first arrived in the Bahamas, as the first historical mention of him comes in the summer of 1717. Johnson remained vague about when exactly Blackbeard began his new career, writing, "which I think was at the latter end of the year 1716, when Captain Benjamin Hornigold put him into a sloop that he had made prize of, and with whom he continued in consortship till a little while before Hornigold surrendered." This seems an unlikely start, as however skilled and charismatic Blackbeard was, Hornigold would never have raised him into a position of command without having watched him in action for some time.

It is far more likely that he was already part of a pirate crew, run by Hornigold or even someone else, and that he was given command of the sloop as a reward for his excellence as a pirate, and as a natural leader of cutthroats. If we assume that Blackbeard arrived in the Bahamas at least a year before Captain Johnson's date, then that places him in New Providence during 1715, just over a year and a half since the last legitimate privateering contracts or "letters of marque" were canceled. Then, like thousands of other seamen, Blackbeard found himself out of a job. We know that many of these former privateersmen congregated in the Bahamas during 1715, along with hundreds of logwoodsmen who sought fresh employment as seamen. It is highly likely that Blackbeard was one of these incomers.

By the time he arrived in the Bahamas, the islands had become a bustling place, filled with the human detritus of the Caribbean and the Americas. For a few brief years New Providence would also become the pirate capital of the New World. The islands sat on the edge of the relatively narrow Bahamas Channel and the Florida Straits, each less than a hundred miles wide. Given a radius of visibility of twenty miles on a clear day, two or three pirate ships working in concert just within sight of each other could cover most of the channel, ensuring that they stood a good chance of encountering any ships that fell into their net. Both passages were the preferred route for ships heading home to Europe, and for the growing number of smaller vessels that plied the route between the Caribbean and the British colonies of North America.

While the Spanish and occasionally the British maintained naval patrols in the region, their ships were generally too slow to cause the pirates much concern. If threatened, the smaller and faster pirate ships could seek refuge in the shallow waters of the Bahamas, where there were numerous islands and cays to hide behind and jagged reefs to snag the unwary. In other words, the waters between the Bahamas and Florida, and between the Florida Keys and Cuba, were a perfect hunting ground for any pirates based in New Providence. That wasn't the only place where rich pickings could be had.

The Bahamas also lay just to the north and northwest of two important passages that lead from the Atlantic Ocean into the Caribbean Sea. The first of these is the Windward Passage, a fifty-mile-wide gap that runs between the eastern tip of Cuba and the northwestern corner of Hispaniola (now Haiti and the Dominican Republic). The former buccaneering base of Tortuga lays a little to the east, off the northern coast of Hispaniola. While it no longer offered an unrestricted welcome to pirates and privateers due to its proximity to the lawful French harbor of Port-de-Paix, the island still remained a popular watering place, and somewhere pirate ships could shelter while they waited for prey.

Most merchantmen bound from Europe or West Africa to Jamaica passed through the Windward Passage, making it one of the busiest waterways in the Americas. On the far side of Hispaniola the Mona Passage runs

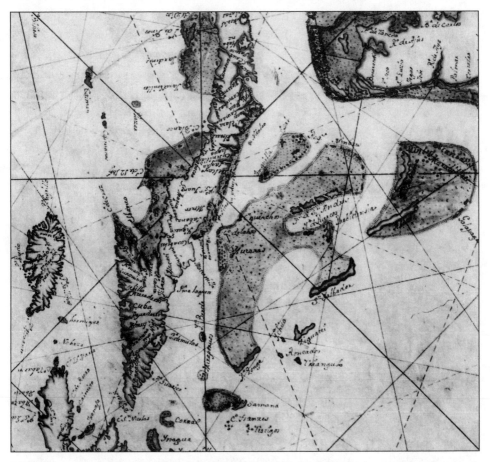

The Bahamas, from a detail of a Spanish chart dated 1747. In the original, west was at the top of the map, with Cuba running down the center. New Providence (marked "Providensia" on this chart) is shown in the center of the Bahamas archipelago.

between Hispaniola and Puerto Rico, and this equally narrow waterway was also a popular means of entering the Caribbean. The Bahamas were an ideal location for pirates during this period, and it is little wonder that the largely uninhabited cluster of islands became such a den of cutthroats during the second decade of the eighteenth century.

The other good thing about New Providence, or all of the Bahamas for that matter, was that nobody really owned it. Technically the islands belonged to the Spanish, as Columbus first dropped anchor in the New World off San Salvador, on the Bahamas' outer edge. The Spanish called the island group "Baja Mar," meaning inland sea, which is how the first explorers saw the network of channels and sounds fringed by balmy islands and reefs. Nobody bothered to ask the native Arawaks what they called the place, so the name stuck. However, the Spanish never settled the Baja Mar, so it was left to the English. Charles I of England and Scotland grandly claimed the islands as his own when he did the same with the Carolinas, but nobody actually sailed there and planted a flag on a beach. Colonists from Bermuda in search of religious freedom of expression established a colony on Eleuthera in 1648, founding a settlement that struggled but survived. In the process they corrupted the Spanish name for the place to the Bahamas.

Never slow to miss an opportunity for imperial advancement, the English government formally declared the Bahamas to be their territory in 1670, although it would be almost half a century before a government official ever set foot in the place. Administratively the islands came under the control of the Lords Proprietor, a group of six absentee landlords who with two others also managed the British colonies of North and South Carolina. These men, Carolina rice barons, English noblemen, and leading plantation owners, never once visited the islands. After all, there was hardly anyone there, just a few colonists in a few sand-blown islands of no real economic value.

New Providence was first settled in 1666, and in 1695 the tiny harbor of Charles Town was renamed Nassau, to avoid confusing it with the properly established Charles Town in Carolina. The poor settlement had been attacked and plundered by the Spanish in 1703, 1706, and 1709, and what the colonists were left with was probably not worth having. By 1713 Nassau was still just a minor settlement with a handful of palm-roofed huts, struggling for survival, with no government worth mentioning and no defenses. That left the way free for the pirates to move in. Therefore, when

Blackbeard and his cronies arrived in New Providence, the islands were to all intents and purposes lawless, empty, and ungoverned.

Today, the island of New Providence is dominated by the bustling city of Nassau, the capital of the islands. Luxury hotels, casinos, and shops line the beaches and waterfront, while the warm tropical breeze rattles the rigging on hundreds of sleek white-hulled yachts and cabin cruisers in the marina. Ugly boxlike liners disgorge thousands of cruise ship passengers who roam the streets in search of local color. The only similarity between Nassau now and the port when Blackbeard first arrived there is that there was certainly plenty of color to be had along the waterfront. In 1715 the port was a small but bustling settlement of wooden shacks and tents, where prostitutes, bartenders, and merchants all vied for the attention of passing seamen. Actually, the island hasn't changed that much, as all three groups still do their best to make the visit a memorable one.

The pirate historian George Woodbury captured the scene quite vividly: "It was no city of homes; it was a place of temporary sojourn and refreshment for a literally floating population. The only permanent residents were the piratical camp followers, the traders and hangers on; all the others were transient. The shanty town of impoverished tents and palm-leaf shelters would have been squalid were it not for the almost incredible beauty of the island." Historian Robert E. Lee went even further: "In Blackbeard's time, it was nothing more than a mariner's resort, a place where the ordinary sailor or pirate could go for a few days to whoop it up and let off steam. For nearly every dozen pirates there was a bar with entertainment. And if a sailor wanted a woman—and few men of the sea did not—there was an ample supply of all ages, shapes, and tints. The half-breed prostitute was in greatest demand."

What is interesting here is the infrastructure. When Port Royal was a privateering base and New Providence an island of empty white beaches, the prostitutes, traders, and bar owners plied their wares in Jamaica. When privateering came to an end, so did the influx of money, and so like the sailors themselves, many of these people drifted away. It seems that a large proportion of them congregated on the shore facing what is now Paradise Island. Any pirate base needed two types of traders: those who supplied the pirates with what they wanted, and those who bought plundered goods from the pirates, then shipped them off to be sold elsewhere. The former needed regular supplies of rum, food, and tobacco, which in turn generated a profitable minor smuggling industry, while the real merchants would have obtained the promise of safe passage for their sloops as they loaded up the less consumable goods brought into the island and sailed off to sell them in other more legitimate markets.

Of all the groups on the island, it was the pirates who were the top dogs, probably because they had the firepower. What law and order existed was based upon the collective wish of the pirate captains who happened to be in the harbor at the time. The best the piratical hangers-on could hope for was to buy the protection of some of the most powerful pirate captains, and hope that their crew paid attention to their elected leader. Blackbeard would have realized that the pirates were the elite of the island, and with his background and abilities it is unlikely that he wasted much time signing on as a member of a pirate crew.

We can therefore assume that Blackbeard turned to piracy because it was the most attractive option open to him. He knew the risks, but somehow in that carefree, sun-kissed place amid his fellow seamen the threat of Royal authority must have seemed so distant as to be almost inconsequential. The same must have been true for other former privateersmen who landed up on New Providence. As the numbers of successful pirates grew, and their attacks became bolder, then more captured vessels would come available, all needing a crew. This introduction to piracy is somewhat unusual. For reasons only Blackbeard knew, he took passage to New Providence, and no doubt he was fully aware of what was going on there. In effect, he strolled down the beach and offered his services.

Whether he first shipped with Benjamin Hornigold or another pirate captain remains unclear, but he certainly signed on with somebody. Hornigold was the most likely candidate. Possibly some of Blackbeard's fellow privateersmen vouched for him, mentioning the courage he displayed in battle that Captain Johnson refers to at the start of his biography. We shall return to the opening phase of his piratical career in the next chapter, but first we need to take a broader look at pirates and piracy. From the historical accounts it seems pretty clear that Blackbeard was a gifted leader, with the charisma to win men over to his side, and the common sense to understand what motivated them. To understand Blackbeard, we need to understand his crew. We also need to take a broader look at why these men turned to piracy, and what sort of life—and death—they could expect.

We can be reasonably sure that the majority of the pirates who made up

Blackbeard's crew in 1717 were highly professional seamen in the prime of their working life, which for a sailor was in his late twenties. By this stage Blackbeard was a decade older, an age gap that would have given him an air of authority over his shipmates. Most of these pirates were former merchant seamen or privateersmen, although the odd logwood cutter, fisherman, or even landsman made his way into the crew. The bulk of these seamen became pirates when the merchant vessel they served in was captured. These men were rarely threatened with death, as executions were usually reserved for merchant captains, although even then these cases were fairly rare.

Many pirate volunteers seized the opportunity, begging the pirates to let them sign up. Occasionally the others had no option. While landsmen or nonvolunteers might be marooned (put ashore) or simply left on board a vessel stripped of everything apart from the hull and sails, the volunteers sailed off to start new and usually brief lives as pirates. This trend of sea-men volunteering to become cutthroats certainly worried the authorities. Several governors and colonial officials wrote to London expressing their concern. For instance, in 1718 Colonel Benjamin Bennett of Bermuda wrote, "I fear they [the pirates] will soon multiply for so many are willing to joyn with them when taken." If captured soon afterward they usually claimed they were pressed into service by the pirates, but both seamen and the authorities knew that pirate crews rarely recruited sailors against their will. The majority of men who tried this defense were strung up with the rest of their shipmates.

Several seamen who would later become successful pirate captains were recruited in this way; "Edward England went mate of a sloop that sailed out of Jamaica, and was taken by Captain Winter, a pirate." Speak-ing of the Welsh pirate Howel Davis, Johnson records, "The last voyage he made from England, was in the *Cadogan*, snow of Bristol, Captain Skinner commander, bound for the coast of Guinea, of which Davis was chief mate: They ere no sooner arrived at Sierra Leone on the aforesaid coast, but they were taken by the pirate Edward England, who plundered them." Davis joined England and was rewarded with the command of the *Cadogan*, turning her into a pirate ship.

The next man in the chain turned into one of the greatest pirates of his day: "Bartholomew Roberts sailed in an honest employ, from London aboard of the *Princess*, Captain Plumb commander, of which ship he was second mate: He left England, November 1719, and arrived in Guinea about February following, and being at Anamboe, taking in slaves for the West Indies, was taken in the said ship by Captain Howel Davis." The list could go on, but it is already clear that not only did merchant seamen volunteer of their own accord, but some took to piracy as if born to the profession.

Unlike their mercantile counterparts, former privateersmen were well versed in the martial skills needed to be a successful pirate, and indeed there was little difference between piracy and privateering apart from a piece of paper giving the privateering captain an excuse to attack the enemies of his government. Privateersmen enjoyed higher levels of pay than most merchant seamen, their living conditions were often better, and above all they had the prospect of a share in plunder. However, privateersmen were still answerable to authority, both through the captain and his officers on board the ship, and the lawmakers and enforcers in the ports they used as their bases. Some privateers were run on such strict lines that the discipline on board resembled that of the Royal Navy, and this sometimes caused resentment. Many privateersmen would have deserted an unhappy or overstrict ship, while another privateering crew based in Jamaica "sett their Captain ashore and turned pirate" as soon as they learned that the Treaty of Utrecht had ended their chance of legitimate piracy.

Certainly the end of the war had been a testing time for these men. The profits of war that encouraged men to become privateers ended when peace returned, and not unnaturally some refused to stop. One such man was Blackbeard's mentor, Captain Benjamin Hornigold, who, like the buccaneers of old, continued his own privateering war against Queen Anne's former enemies. Hornigold even claimed as much to the captain of a French ship he captured: "They meddle not with English or Dutch, but that they never consented to the Articles of Peace with the French and Spaniards." The arrogance of this is incredible, as if Louis XIV, Queen Anne, and the States General of Holland should have consulted the Jamaican privateering captains before they ended a war that had brought Europe to its knees!

Others such as Philip Cockram and Henry Jennings followed Hornigold's example, choosing their victims as if they were still following the rules of wartime privateering. Whether this was mere delusion on their part or just an attempt to build a case for their defense if they were captured is unclear. Certainly the new generation of pirates such as Blackbeard would have little time for such niceties. They just attacked whomever they wanted.

Word soon spread that the Bahamas were becoming a haven for pirates, and this news alone would have been sufficient temptation for many to sign up under the pirate flag. The other options left to these seamen were to return to the poorly paid drudgery of regular mercantile work if a job could be found, or else face starvation in some harbor somewhere, becoming a beggar or a thief in order to survive. This is what probably drew Blackbeard to the profession, as there is no indication that he was ever part of Hornigold's crew while the older captain was a privateer. It seems unlikely that Blackbeard formed part of a privateering crew that voted en masse to turn from privateering to privacy, although we have already seen that some were all too ready to cross the legal divide into lawlessness.

The most celebrated and controversial example of this slide from privateer to pirate involved Captain Kidd, the man hanged in Wapping's Execution Dock in May 1701. The Scottish-born captain sailed from England in a purpose-built privateer, the *Adventure Galley*, charged with rooting out pirates and the French enemies of the Crown. Instead he turned pirate himself, attacking English East Indiamen or their allies on the high seas without much success. By the time he returned to New York with his plunder he was a marked man, and he was shipped off on the next ship bound for London, where he stood trial and was executed for his crimes.

After former privateersmen and merchant seamen, another, smaller group of pirate recruits reached New Providence from the fishing grounds of Newfoundland. Captain Johnson claimed that British-based deep-sea fishing vessels and whalers "transport over a considerable Number of poor Fellows every Summer, whom they engage at Low Wages, and are by their Terms to pay for Passage back to England." Like the logwood cutters of the Bay of Campeche, or even the men working the turtle-hunting boats of the Caribbean, these men grasped the opportunity to quit. They all found their living conditions to be so hard and the profits to be gained so meager that the opportunity of turning to piracy must have seemed really attractive.

The same applied to landsmen, mainly those who arrived in the Americas as indentured servants, forced to work off the cost of their transatlantic passage by a number of years working as little more than slaves. Many entered indentured servitude out of their own free will, while others were less fortunate, being shipped from Britain to the Americas as servants as a means of paying for crimes or misdemeanors they committed back home. For example, following the Jacobite rebellions in Ireland in 1689–90 and Scotland in 1689 and 1715, many sympathizers of the exiled King James II were sent to the colonies as servants, a convenient way of ridding Britain of those men the authorities deemed to be politically suspect.

While the average term of indenture lasted for two or three years, the terms of these criminals or political prisoners could last for fourteen years. Given the climate of the Caribbean, this amounted to a death sentence. It is easy to see why many indentured servants tried to escape, and the only place to run on a Caribbean island was out to sea, taking passage on a vessel whose captain and crew wouldn't ask too many questions. Of course it would have helped if the runaway was actually a sailor, but well-built landsmen could also be useful when it came to simple tasks of seamanship, or to fighting. To a lesser extent the same applied to slaves, and often a sizable proportion of a pirate crew could be made up of former African slaves. While many of these runaways were used as menial help on board pirate ships, others could become fully integrated members of the crew. A prime example of the latter was Black Caesar, the man who tried to blow up Blackbeard's sloop during his captain's final battle.

In 1718 the Jamaican governor, Nicholas Lawes, wrote to his superiors in London to complain about the problem of former criminals running away to sea:

> Those people have been so farr, from altering their evil courses and way of living and becoming an advantage to us, that the greatest part of them are gone and have induced others to go with them a pyrating, and have inveigled and encouraged severall negroes to desart from their masters and go to the Spaniards in Cuba, the few that remains proves a wicked lazy and indolent people, so that I could heartily wish that this country might be troubled with no more [of] them.

Finally, there were the mutineers. Occasionally a crew would feel that they had no option but to rise up against a particularly repressive captain and seize the ship. The unfortunate Scottish pirate John Gow turned to piracy this way, as did several others.

The details of his mutiny were particularly brutal, but the scene might well have been repeated on other ships.

> On the 3rd of November [1724] the George Gally . . . weighed from Santa Cruz in order to sail to the straits, but at ten that night was the time they [the mutineers] fixed for their bloody execution, when all the persons to be scrificed were asleep, except Captain Fernau who then had the watch on deck; accordingly Winter went down to Thomas Guy, the surgeon; Peterson to the chief mate, Bonadventure Jelphs; and Daniel MacCawley to the poor scriven, and presently cut their throats; in the meanwhile Melvin and Rawlisson seized the captain to throw him overboard, but in struggling he got away from them, though meeting Wintr with the bloody knife in his hand, got a gash in his throat from him, but it missing the windpipe the two former laid hold of him again, and endeaavoured to throw him into the sea, but still struggling with his murderers, Gow came up with a pistol and shot him through the body . . . While this scene was acting they secured Belvin the boatswain, Murphy the carpenter, with Phinnis and Booth who were upon the watch, in the great cabin; and threatened the rest with death if they stirred from their hammocks, so that there was not the least opposition offered. When all was over, all hands were called upon deck, and Gow being declared Captain, said to them, "If hereafter, I see any of you whispering together, you shall be served in the same manner, as those that are gone before."

This happy band then sailed off into the sunset, the Jolly Roger flapping in the breeze. Once the deed was done, mutineers had only two options. They could abandon their ship and slip ashore, hoping to mingle back into maritime society without being linked to the mutiny. If this wasn't an option, then they had no choice but to turn to piracy, as returning to any law-abiding port would have invited arrest, trial, and a date with the gallows. The historian Marcus Rediker estimated that "at least thirty-one mutinies erupted on merchant ships during the 1710's and 1720's, many of them on vessels involved in the African slave trade. Roughly half these crews moved into piracy."

George Lowther was a mate on the *Gambia Castle*, a Royal African Company ship that arrived off the West African coast in May 1721. He fell out with Captain Russel, so after soliciting the help of an army officer named Captain Massey he laid plans to seize the ship. When Russel rowed ashore to confer with the governor, Captain Massey and some of his men looted the governor's residence, took his son as a hostage, and rowed out to join Lowther. Lowther and his men took control of the *Gambia Castle*, and despite running her aground in the Gambia River, he succeeded in slipping away to sea. The governor's son was cast loose once they were clear of danger. Then the mutineers "knocked down the cabins, made the ship flush for and aft, prepared black colours, new named her, the *Delivery*, having about fifty hands and 16 guns." In other words, they became pirates.

Pirates careering a ship in a secluded bay near the Gulf of Honduras. The figure in the foreground is meant to be the pirate captain George Lowther, who operated in American waters during 1721–1722.

Whatever the reason a sailor had for becoming a pirate, he was well aware that once the die was cast there would be little chance of returning to his old life, and even if he took advantage of a pardon, he would be marked as a troublemaker by any future employer. Most would have a short, brutish career for a few months or years before succumbing to death by battle, disease, or the noose.

We have already said that the majority of pirates were in their late twenties. Several historians have analyzed the records of known pirates, mainly by looking at the information gathered about them during their trials. While these statistics could be skewed, it seems pretty clear that some 60 percent of named pirates were men in their twenties, with a few younger and the rest older seamen in their thirties and early forties. In the unlikely event that an early-eighteenth-century seaman reached his late forties, he was considered too old to perform the tough physical tasks expected of him.

This was as true in merchant ships and warships as it was in pirate ships, and the range of ages is therefore pretty typical of the crew of most sailing vessels of the time. The one exception was that pirate ships contained fewer boys than was normal on other vessels, mainly because they were considered unsuitable for a piratical life. This means that the majority of pirates might have lost a few teeth or the odd finger, or had a toe shot off, but the majority of them were prime, fit, experienced seamen. These men had already served their apprenticeship at sea, and they turned to piracy of their own free will. They knew the risks and the odds stacked against them.

As for nationality, the same records list where these pirates came from, although the town or port they listed and their actual birthplace were probably not always the same. For instance, several Welsh-born seamen would have worked out of Bristol, which was their nearest major port, and so Bristol is the place that is listed in the records. Given these limitations, the statistics allow us to build up a reasonably accurate picture of where these men came from. While a handful of seamen from various European maritime countries, such as France, Holland, Spain, Portugal, Sweden, and Denmark, are listed, the majority were British, a group which also included the American-born descendants of British colonists settled in North America or the Caribbean. Of these roughly half were English, a quarter were from the American colonies, and the rest were divided fairly equally between Irish on the one hand and Scottish or Welsh on the other.

Pretty obviously the majority of these men came from the great port cities or from coastal communities. The English sailors tended to come from the riverside boroughs of London, from ports such as Bristol or Plymouth, and from counties with strong seafaring traditions in the West Country or the Channel coast. The Irish ports of Dublin and Cork, the Welsh port of Swansea, and the Scottish ones of Leith (by Edinburgh) and Aberdeen are all mentioned, while a handful came from other smaller seafaring communities.

Although all spoke English of a sort, these crews would have encountered strong linguistic differences between the different nations and even regions that made up Great Britain. It would take a fairly long voyage for an Orcadian and a Cornishman to begin understanding each other. Meanwhile the Irish and Welsh seamen always had the option to retreat into their native language, which would have been completely unintelligible to the rest of the crew. As for the sailors from the American colonies, the majority of these men were from Barbados or Jamaica, with a smaller group hailing from the colonies of Massachusetts, New York, or the Carolinas, among others. In this respect pirates would have been typical of most bluewater crews of the period, with sailors coming from all corners of the Atlantic maritime world.

While French, Spanish, and Dutch pirates existed, the statistics are skewed toward those pirate crews who operated in the Caribbean, North American waters, West Africa, and the Indian Ocean, where a majority of the ships at sea were from some corner of Britain's nascent empire. However, when asked where they came from, many pirates would claim that they had no country, and were loyal only to their floating community and their black flag. Nationality and place of origin were transcended by the unity created by a common purpose. A government official writing in 1697 claimed that pirates "acknowledge no countrymen, that they had sold their country and were sure to be hanged if taken, and that they would take no quarter, but do all the mischief they could."

These figures miss out one vital group. At one stage in late 1718, Blackbeard commanded a sloop where almost half of his crew were of African descent. Granted, this proportion was highly unusual, but the evidence remains that while the rest of the seafaring community saw Africans as chattels, pirates often viewed them as a source of recruits. Pirates were certainly no multiracial pioneers, and often when a slave ship was captured the slaves themselves were viewed as nothing more than cargo, to be sold for a profit as quickly as possible. However, many African slaves joined pirate crews, either by running away from their plantations or volunteering when the ship transporting them was captured. Several Caribbean islands had mulatto communities, where groups of runaway slaves lived in the hills, a little like the Hispaniola buccaneers of old. These and other free Africans also found their way on board pirate ships.

Like many landsmen, they would have been given menial tasks to perform—cooking, cleaning, fetching water, and so on—but in time these men would learn the art of seamanship, and would play a more integral part in the running of the pirate ship. The only reason these men often fail to appear in official records is that when they were captured they were usually treated not as pirates, but as runaway slaves. They would be stripped, beaten, and then returned to the auction block. These men would have watched their shipmates swing from the gallows, and thought the dead were the lucky ones.

African slaves joined pirate crews to escape captivity, which was completely understandable. It was their one chance of freedom. Less easy to understand is what drove whole crews to rise in mutiny against their captain, giving themselves no option but to become pirates. What made others step forward and volunteer when their merchant ship was taken, thereby turning their backs on everything they had known? They must have realized that they could never see their families again, and that they would eventually be called to account for their actions. What made men like Blackbeard seek out pirate communities and sign on as a member of a pirate crew? Clearly something must have driven eighteenth-century seamen to take such drastic measures.

Usually the answer seems to be authority. When a sailing ship put to sea in the early eighteenth century, the captain had complete power over his crew. Some literally got away with murder. Even if the captain was a just man, sailors often had to contend with sadistic officers and boatswains, or corrupt owners who denied them the food they needed to remain healthy, or the wages they deserved at the end of the voyage. The injustice of all this was reflected in the final speech of the pirate William Fly, who was hanged on Boston waterfront in July 1726, just eight years after Blackbeard's crew met the same fate in Williamsburg. Condemned men were usually allowed the opportunity to say a few last words as they stood beneath the gallows, and in most cases they begged God and society to forgive them their sins.

Captain Fry was cut from a different cloth. He used the opportunity to rail against the injustices that drove him to piracy in the first place, demanding "all Masters of Vessels might take Warning by the Fate of the Captain that he had murder'd, and to pay Sailors their Wages when due, and to treat them better; saying, that their Barbarity to them made so many turn Pyrates." He summed up his demand with the phrase "Bad Usage"— shorthand for the maltreatment of sailors by their captains, and the appalling conditions sailors often had to endure for little reward. His dying words were for justice. It is little wonder that some sailors saw pirates as heroic, fighting for the rights of all sailors against a tyrannical and uncaring system.

Captains and shipowners naturally saw matters in a different light. After spending some time as a prisoner of Howel Davis and his pirates off the West African coast, Captain William Snelgrave wrote of his captors that "they pretend one reason for their villainies is to do justice for sailors." He remained unconvinced of the argument, and like most he considered the main motives for men turning to piracy to be greed and sloth.

Still, the pirates had a point. Merchant and naval seamen found that shipping with a tyrannical captain could turn a routine voyage into a living hell. For instance, Captain Haskins of the *Laventon Galley* took such a dislike to one of his crew, a John Phillips, that he went belowdecks one night and punched the sleeping crewman in the face, then battered the poor sailor around the head with a marlin spike. Evidently Phillips was late going on watch, as Captain Haskins duly sent the bleeding man aloft to set the topgallant. Dressed only in his blood-soaked shirt and breeches, Phillips braved the freezing rain and swaying mast to perform his task as blood poured over his eyes. He began to convulse due to the shock caused by loss of blood, but when his fellow sailors worked their way aloft to help him Captain Haskins roared out that he would shoot the first man to help the sailor. While this account is shocking in its brutality, it is far from unique.

Accounts of sailors being whipped almost to death for the slightest fault, forced to spend whole days aloft in terrible weather, or tortured at the whim of the captain are not uncommon. Several other statements made by condemned pirates under the shadow of the gallows tell the same story—

that many were driven to desertion, piracy, or mutiny by the callous actions of those placed in positions of authority.

In theory the state should have paid attention to these last words of condemned men. The Admiralty Courts were designed to hear cases of gross abuse of this kind, but although seamen frequently cited cases of extreme brutality, the authorities invariably sided with the ship captains, and the complaints never came to trial. The law even argued that the authority of a merchant captain over his crew was "analogous to that of a parent over his child, or a master over his apprentice or scholar." The same applied to the payment of wages, or the supply of sufficiently edible food for the crew. Wage regulations for seamen only came into effect in 1726, and although it was never said, piracy might have played its part in this legislation. By limiting the worst excesses of shipowners, the authorities were acknowledging the legitimacy of one of the pirates' most common grievances.

A picture is emerging of the typical pirate crew of the time—most were British-born seamen in their late twenties, with several years of experience beneath the mast. They were often disillusioned with their lot, particularly their maltreatment by those in power. While most took to piracy when the opportunity presented itself, seeking greater rewards for their efforts and a less demanding physical life, some took matters into their own hands. These people rebelled against authority, becoming outcasts and fugitives. Their actions left them no refuge except the brotherhood of pirates.

What happened next? Clearly these sailors-turned-pirates had no wish to replace one draconian system with another, so they had to come up with a workable scheme for operating a ship and choosing where it went and who it hunted. They needed some form of structure, an authority they could all follow. They also needed to have a say in what or who this authority was and what it did, but there was still a need for some form of structure, a set of rules that governed how they lived. The result was a unique system of command, a piratical contract that bound the crew into something other than an anarchic mob. This meant they replaced a draconian authority with one that was accountable, and they were governed by simple rules that protected their own communal interests rather than those of the hated shipowners.

These pirates already had a model for this. Most seamen who had been based in Jamaica would have come across former buccaneers, and would have heard of "Jamaica Discipline." This buccaneering code was not as egalitarian as later pirate codes, but at least it offered buccaneers a say in what happened to them. It is possible that elements of this reasonably fair system were used on board many of the Port Royal privateers during the wars of the Grand Alliance and the Spanish Succession. In this case former privateersmen would have brought these surprisingly democratic notions with them when they left Jamaica for New Providence.

The real arbiter of power on a pirate ship of this period was the crew itself, not the captain or his officers. Pirate ships were run along democratic lines, where every man had a say in almost every decision. Meetings were held to decide the division of food and drink, the election of officers, whether to attack a particular target, and what to do with prisoners once they were captured. While the captain might have undisputed authority on board once the shot started flying, the rest of the time he was simply another voice in the crowd. The notion of electing officers would have been anathema to the merchant and naval fleets of the world, but for the pirates this played a vital part in maintaining their freedom. A captain would be answerable to his men, and woe betide any commander who went against the wishes of his crew.

Electing a captain was a fairly straightforward business. The pirate Walter Kennedy recounted how this was done on board his pirate ship:

> They chose a captain from amongst themselves, who in effect held little more than that title, excepting in an engagement, when he commanded absolutely, and without control. Most of them having suffered formerly from the ill-treatment of their officers, provided carefully against any such evil, now they had the choice in themselves. By their orders they provided especially against quarrels which might happen among themselves, and appointed certain punishments for anything that tended that way; for the due execution thereof they constituted other officers besides their captain, so very industrious were they to avoid putting too much power into the hands of one man.

Pirates were free to build their own social order, unrestricted by the constraints of convention. In fact, as we have seen, they took great efforts to ensure that they remained free from the tyrannies they had suffered while working as law-abiding seamen. They created a utopia for the common sailor, and that might well have frightened the authorities even more than their piratical actions. After all, the early eighteenth century was hardly a time of world revolution, and any suggestion of overturning what the authorities saw as the natural order of things was viewed as a dangerously radical sentiment. It was important that such notions be quashed before they had a chance to spread. This political fear may have explained why the British authorities went to such great pains to stamp out the decade-long wave of piracy that began after 1713.

Pirate captains had no special privileges. They shared the same fare as their shipmates, they dined in the company of their fellows, and they even had no guarantee of privacy, as the rest of the crew had as much right to sleep in the captain's cabin as they did. The one great strength of the pirate captain was that he had been elected into the job by a majority of his peers. If he could keep most of the crew on his side, and bring them success and plunder, he was fairly certain of keeping his job. Examples of pirate captains being removed from power include Charles Vane, whose crew marooned him on a deserted island. Then there was none other than Benjamin Hornigold, whose crew refused to go along with his notion of "limited piracy," when he limited his attacks to the ships of the wartime enemies, France and Spain. Of course, some captains were harder to remove from office than others. It would take a brave crewman to cross the likes of Blackbeard or Bartholomew Roberts in mid-ocean. That said, we will see that even Blackbeard was afraid of being ousted by his crew, and of sharing the fate of Charles Vane.

The captain wasn't even the most influential figure on board. That role was reserved for his supposed deputy, the quartermaster. While the captain guided the crew by his example and plotted the stratagem that would bring them plunder, the quartermaster controlled the ship. He was responsible for keeping the peace on board, and mediating the inevitable drunken dispute. He selected the men who would lead the attack on a prize, or would form the boarding party if it surrendered without a fight. The first men on board a captured vessel would inevitably have the pick of what they found. Once the cargo and any money were brought back on board the pirate ship, it was the quartermaster who divided the loot, or was responsible for storing the plunder until it could be divided up or sold.

Above all, he was elected as a check on the captain, preventing him from assuming too much power and privilege. Like the captain, the quartermaster was elected into office by his shipmates, and could be removed from power just as easily. He could also be promoted. If the decision was made to convert a prize ship into a new pirate vessel, then the quartermaster was a prime candidate for election to the new command.

One skill that pirates demanded of their two leading officers was that they could tell where they were. They had to be able to navigate, to read a chart, work an astrolabe, and steer a steady course. This required a degree of education and training, and many pirate crews had to make do with officers who had little more than a rudimentary knowledge of navigation. It is hardly surprising that any seaman who displayed any knowledge in this "black art" was considered a suitable candidate for command. Conversely, the pirate crew would have to think twice before demoting a captain or a quartermaster if nobody else on board could steer a ship by the stars.

Once a pirate crew elected their officers, they then established their set of rules that governed life on board. Much has been made of pirate codes, and some historians have elevated them to the status of a holy writ. It seems more likely that they were guidelines, the basic tenets by which the pirates

Bartholomew Roberts, from a Dutch edition of Captain Johnson's History *published in 1725. He was something of a dandy, and Roberts's appearance was in stark contrast to Blackbeard's, who favored undecorated clothes to help enhance his ferocious image.*

could ensure that their shipmates lived together without too much rancor. These rules almost always governed the way plunder was divided, and set a rate of compensation for injuries suffered in battle. Most laid out punishments for those who fragrantly broke the rules, and some attempted to include a code for living together that was designed to avoid divisions within the crew. As we have already seen, the buccaneers had drawn up similar documents in their time, and these might well have served as a model for the pirates.

The rules they laid down covering the division of plunder followed the democratic lines by which they made decisions, and as the former ship's cook Barnaby Slush noted, captains had to work hard for their extra portion of the loot: "Pyrates and Buccaneers, are Princes to [sailors], for there, as none are exempt from General Toil and Danger; so if the Chief have a Supream Share beyond his Comrades, 'tis because he's always the Leading Man in e'ry daring Enterprize; and yet as bold as he is in all other attempts, he dares not offer to infringe the common laws of Equity; but every Associate has his due Quota."

What is interesting is the use of the words "Enterprize" and "Associate," as if they were a business rather than a ship filled with cutthroats. It shows just how seriously they took the notion of equality, and how important their pirate articles were to them, a businesslike bill of rights and profit that ensured everyone would benefit. The most detailed set of pirate articles that has survived was drawn up by the mutinous crew of the merchantman *Rover* (later the *Royal Fortune*), who turned pirate in 1721 and elected Bartholomew Roberts as their captain. Captain Johnson quotes the document in "The Life of Captain Roberts":

I. Every man has a Vote in Affairs of Monument, has equal Title to the fresh Provisions, or strong Liquors, at any Time seized, & use them at pleasure, unless a Scarcity make it necessary, for the good of all, to Vote a Retrenchment.

II. Every man to be called fairly in turn, by List, on Board of Prizes, because they there on these Occasions allow'd a Shift of Cloaths: But if they defrauded the Company to the Value of a Dollar, in Plate, Jewels, or Money, MAROONING was their punishment.

III. No Person to game at Cards or Dice for Money.

IV. The Lights & Candles to be put out at eight o'Clock at Night. If any of the Crew, after that Hour, still remained inclined for Drinking, they were to do it on the open Deck.

V. To Keep their Piece, Pistols, & Cutlash clean, & fit for Service.

VI. No Boy or Woman to be allow'd amongst them. If any Man were found seducing anny of the latter Sex, and carried her to Sea, disguised, he was to suffer Death.

VII. To Desert the Ship, or their Quarters in Battle, was punished with Death, or Marooning.

VIII. No striking one another on Board, but every Man's Quarrels to be ended on shore, at Sword & Pistol Thus: The Quarter-Master of the Ship, when the Parties will not come to any Reconciliation, accompanies them on Shore with what Assistance he thinks proper, & turns the Disputants Back to Back, at so many Paces, Distance. At the Word of Command, they turn and fire immediately, (or else the Piece is knocked out of their Hands). If both miss, they come to their Cutlasses, and then he is declared Victor who draws the first Blood.

IX. No Man to talk of breaking up their Way of Living, till each has shared £1000. If in order to this, any Man shall lose a Limb, or become a Cripple in their Service, he was to have 800 Dollars, out of publick Stock, and for lesser Hurts, proportionably.

X. The Captain and Quarter-Master to receive two Share of a Prize; the Master, Boatswain, & gunner, one Share and a half and other Officers, one and a Quarter.

XI. The Musicians to have Rest on the Sabbath Day, but the other six Days and Nights, none without special Favour.

While not all articles were as detailed, the basic tenets were the same. What they left out is almost as revealing as what they decided to include. These articles don't mention the right to elect or demote officers, as that was taken for granted, these situations being "Affairs of Moment." They say nothing about the day-to-day running of the ship, as that was second nature to these men. Compared to a merchant ship, a pirate vessel was extremely heavily manned, which meant that the seamanship tasks that required half the crew would now need less than a quarter. Therefore there was no detailed watch system, or list of duties, apart from the article dealing with desertion in battle.

The articles designed to reduce the chances of rancor among the crew—sex, gambling, drinking, and disturbing shipmates' sleep—were laid out in some detail. It is even more revealing that the most expansive article covers the settling of arguments, making the procedure so involved and open to chance that many would have settled their differences before the pirate ship could find a suitable spot to fight the duel.

The final article covering musicians stands out from much of the rest. It serves no real purpose, apart from ensuring that the musicians on board have one day of rest per week. Music has long been a feature of shipboard life, with dancing, singing, and fiddling being mentioned in numerous accounts from the earliest days of sail until the nineteenth century. Traditionally sea chanties were sung accompanied by a fiddle as sailors worked the capstan or hauled in sheets. It seems the pirates did the same, but the articles suggest that this musical accompaniment might not always have been voluntary. David Cordingly claims that when Bartholomew Roberts's crew stood trial, Nicholas Brattler was one of two musicians on board, and his defense centered on his nonparticipation in pirate attacks. He had been forced to join the pirate crew when his ship was captured, and forced to play his fiddle for their entertainment. He was acquitted, as was James White, "whose business as music was upon the poop in time of action."

By contrast, the first article is not only the most important, but also says a lot about the piratical interpretation of freedom. As merchant seamen or naval ratings they would have been used to poor, meager rations, and even starvation. They also would have had a limited and highly regulated access to liquor. Now the right to have equal title to fresh provisions and strong liquor was enshrined in their own articles, as close to a guarantee as they could have that they would no longer have to go hungry, or even sober. This provision meant that when a prize containing a cargo of rum, wine, or brandy was captured, the result was inevitable.

Pirates such as Bartholomew Roberts and "Calico" Jack Rackam were overtaken by warships when their crews were still recovering from a bacchanalian night of excess, drinking the spoils until most of the crew were too incapacitated to fight. Even more unfortunate were the crew of Sam Bellamy's *Whydah*, who became so drunk after capturing a prize that they were unable to claw their ships off the rocks near Cape Cod when a storm took them by surprise. Most of the crew were drowned.

Pirates became known for their ability to have a good time, indulging in hedonistic excess to an extent that must have seemed impossible in the days before they turned to piracy. A common invitation to fellow cutthroat crews was to come aboard and drink a bowl of punch, which inevitably contained a mixture of sugar and whatever alcohol came to hand. Drink also went hand in hand with pirate democracy. An account of Howel Davis's piratical career reported that "a counsel of war was called over a large bowl of punch, at which it was proposed to choose a commander; the election was soon over, for it fell upon Davis by a great majority of legal pollers, there was no scrutiny demanded, for all acquiesced in the choice: as soon as he was possessed of his command, he drew up articles, which were signed and sworn to by himself and the rest, then he made a short speech, the fun of which, was, a declaration of war against the whole world."

The moral was that if you wanted to become a pirate captain, you laid on a party. Just how the men signed the articles was never mentioned, but as most were illiterate, the document must have contained a good number of shakily scrawled crosses. Captain Snelgrave, who spent time as a prisoner of Davis, added a little more detail as he watched them pillage his ship. The pirates "made such Waste and Destruction that a more numerous set of such Villains would in a short time, have ruined a great City." Finding half-barrels of wine and brandy, they "knock'd their Heads out, and dipp'd Canns and Bowls into them to drink out of." Inevitably the transfer of the cargo led to scenes of wild excess. When they reached Snelgrave's own stock of liquor the pirates "would not give themselves the trouble of drawing the cork out, but nick'd the Bottles, as they called it, that is struck their necks off with a Cutlace; by which means one in three was generally broke. . . . In a few days they had not one Bottle left." It is little wonder that it took them three days to plunder Captain Snelgrave's ship.

Then there was the unfortunate captain of the Dutch vessel *Flushing*, who was forced to watch as his pirate captors raided his shipboard chicken coop and plundered his larder before inviting him to dine with them. "It was a melancholy request to the man, but it must be complied with, and he was obliged, as they grew drunk, to sit quietly, and hear them sing French and Spanish songs out of his Dutch prayer books, with other prophanes that he (though Dutch man) stood amazed at." Other merchant captains tell similar tales of excess, so the pirates' propensity to "make merry" is not the invention of pirate fiction.

When Blackbeard first joined Benjamin Hornigold, this was exactly the kind of volatile, boisterous crown he had as his shipmates. His crews were men open to excesses of violence and debauchery, but who still operated under their own strictly followed set of rules. These pirates would have made great play of their individual and collective rights, and made sure that no man, even Blackbeard or Hornigold, was allowed to assume a position of complete power over them.

Blackbeard would have learned quickly that to be successful as a pirate captain you had to promise your crew a steady stream of prizes and a never-ending supply of food and drink. He would have to make a play of deferring to his crew, while bribing them with plunder in order to keep them loyal. It was a delicate balancing act. Hornigold failed as a captain, despite being a father figure to many of his crew. By comparison, Blackbeard had the charm and charisma to ensure the loyalty of his shipmates, while he also had the Machiavellian intelligence to outsmart them.

3

The Scourge of the Caribbean

William Howard must have cursed the day he set foot in Williamsburg. It seemed like the perfect place to sell his two slaves and so treble his money. After all, he had £50 on him, the equivalent of $10,000 today—which was roughly what he could expect for a healthy, well-built field hand. While his African American slaves would have drawn little attention—they made up a quarter of Virginia's population in the summer of 1718—Howard himself would have stood out amid the town's two thousand inhabitants. He walked, talked, and dressed like a seaman, and in those days a seaman with money and slaves was a rare sight indeed.

Then someone recognized the seaman who spent his time drinking and playing dice in the taverns, and whispered his name to the authorities. Howard was immediately arrested, his slaves led away, and his money confiscated. The informant was correct. It turned out that William Howard was none other than a pirate quartermaster, a man who had once shipped with Blackbeard himself. By that time Blackbeard had become a serious threat to the colony, so the capture of his former quartermaster was something of a triumph in Governor Spotswood's war against the pirates.

If Blackbeard was considered a threat to a bustling colony like Virginia, then he was clearly a man whose piratical reputation was at its height. He had come a long way since he stood on the beach in New Providence, about to sign on as a pirate. Blackbeard the onetime privateer had become Blackbeard the notorious pirate, and the transformation was largely due to the patronage of the leading pirate captain of the time. While Benjamin Hornigold might not have been his first pirate captain, he was certainly the first one to be publicly associated with our hero. Clearly the pirate captain recognized the potential of his new recruit as Blackbeard flourished under his tutelage. In time Hornigold assumed the role of Blackbeard's mentor, and then, once his pupil had learned all he could, he sent Blackbeard off a-pirating on his own account. Hornigold was an important figure in Blackbeard's early career, and one who deserves investigating.

Benjamin Hornigold was an Englishman who, like Blackbeard, served as a privateer before becoming a pirate. His roots, like those of most pirates, are obscure, but the name Hornigold was and still is a popular surname in Norfolk, a county with a strong seafaring tradition. Located in the middle of England's North Sea coast, Norfolk boasted two main ports, and it is likely that Hornigold started his maritime career in one of them. The ports of King's Lynn and Great Yarmouth were important centers for fishing and coastal trade and short-haul mercantile voyages between Britain and the rest of Europe while Hornigold was growing up in the late seventeenth century. However, they faced the wrong way, looking toward Europe rather than the Atlantic, and this limited their value as long-range trading ports. Instead Norfolk supplied a pool of seamen for London ships, and it is pretty likely that as a young Norfolk sailor Hornigold began his bluewater career in England's capital and principal port.

We know nothing else definite about him until he appeared in New Providence, by which time he was already a pirate. Rumor had it that he was a veteran privateer who refused to end the fight against the French and Spanish when the war ended in 1713. He was already well established in Nassau by the time Blackbeard joined him, so we can assume that Hornigold was one of the first privateersmen to move to the Bahamas. He probably arrived there without a ship, as an account of the first pirates to operate from the Bahamas mentions them using small boats with crews of no more than twenty-five men. By late 1715 he had a sloop under his command, and circumstantial evidence suggests that by 1717 he commanded a thirty-gun vessel, possibly called the *Ranger*. Even if some of these guns were just light rail-mounted swivel guns, Hornigold's ship would still have dwarfed all others as she rode at anchor in the blue waters off Nassau.

Hornigold's new career as a cutthroat probably began around late 1714 or early 1715, as by the time Blackbeard and Hornigold are mentioned together in the summer of 1716 Hornigold was already a successful pirate. In the rootless society of New Providence he would have been the top dog, playing a leading part in the running of Nassau—a pirate king in a community of equals. The respect he commanded in New Providence survived his later demotion as captain, as the authority he still wielded in the summer of 1718 was demonstrated when he rallied the pirates behind the new British governor, Woodes Rogers.

Hornigold almost single-handedly talked his fellow pirates into accepting the king's pardon and submitting to British rule, which would have been no mean feat in such a lawless community. He even managed to form up these ragged pirates into something resembling a military honor guard to greet Governor Rogers as he stepped ashore on the Nassau waterfront. We shall touch on the whole saga of Benjamin Hornigold and Woodes Rogers in the next chapter, but for the moment we need to launch Blackbeard on his new career. It is sufficient to say that the younger pirate couldn't have picked a better teacher.

Blackbeard was already a leading member of Benjamin Hornigold's crew "at the latter end of the year 1716," when the pirate mentor reportedly captured a sloop and gave command of her to his protégé. Presumably Hornigold and his pirates spent the winter in New Providence, carousing in the makeshift taverns and brothels, and spending their share of the year's plunder. Although we know nothing about this captured sloop, it was probably the same one that Blackbeard commanded the following year. One account suggests it was the sloop *Revenge*, owned by the "gentleman pirate" Major Stede Bonnet, but the newspaper account that places the *Revenge* in New Providence in early 1717 might well be an inaccurate account of the secondhand story passed on to the journalist.

What is clear is that by the spring of 1717 Captain Hornigold was ready to begin a fresh cruise north from the Bahamas Channel into the waters of the Carolinas. By this stage Blackbeard is clearly named as Hornigold's deputy, his sloop acting in concert with Hornigold's own vessel: "In the spring of the year 1717, Teach and Hornigold sailed from [New] Providence, for the Main of America, and took in their way a billop from the Havana, with 120 barrels of flour, as also a sloop from Bermuda, Thurbar, master, from whom they took only some gallons of wine, and then let him go; and a ship from Madeira to South Carolina, out of which they got plunder to a considerable value."

It isn't hard to imagine the scene, as the two pirate sloops lay on either side of larger ship, the cowed Portuguese crew looking on in amazement as some 150 pirates set about drinking the entire cargo of Madeira's excellent white wine. Pirates didn't worry about vintages, linking the right wine with the right food, or corking the bottle. For them, quantity had a quality all of its own. The first mention of Blackbeard himself comes during this cruise, penned by the experienced captain of an armed South Carolina vessel. Earlier that spring she had been on an antipiracy patrol on behalf of the Lords Proprietor.

Unfortunately, Captain Mathew Munthe ran his sloop aground on Cat Cay, part of the Bimini group on the western fringe of the Bahamas. At least the accident gave him the chance to gather information, presumably from passing traders and local fishermen. In the report he sent to South Carolina deputy governor Robert Daniel in March 1717, the pirate hunter described the piratical vessels operating out of New Providence that spring. Conveniently for us, he also named their commanders: "Five pirates made ye harbour of Providence their place of rendevous vizt. Horngold, a sloop with 10 guns and about 80 men; Jennings, a sloop with 10 guns and 100 men; Burgiss, a sloop with 8 guns and about 80 men; White, in a small vessel with 30 men and small arms; Thatch, a sloop 6 gunns and about 70 men."

This meant that by March 1717 Blackbeard (or "Thatch") was a pirate captain in his own right, commanding a substantial crew. The report reached Charles Town in early July, by which time Hornigold and Blackbeard had not only started their cruise, but were just over the horizon from Daniell's windows, cruising the busy waters of the Carolinas and Virginia in search of prey. We have to take Captain Johnson's word for what mentor and protégé got up to in the Bahamas Channel when they started their cruise, but we do know that at some stage Hornigold and Blackbeard parted company. Captain Johnson suggests they continued to work together until November, but the historical records muddy the waters.

The privately owned sloop Fancy *in a detail of an engraving of New York Harbor in 1717 by William Burgis. This vessel, the private yacht of Colonel Lewis Morris, was typical of the smaller sloops found in American waters in Blackbeard's day.*

In the summer of 1718 the governor of Virginia, Alexander Spotswood, drew up a series of charges against a pirate called William Howard "for Pyracy and Robbery committed by him on the High Seas." Howard was none other than Blackbeard's quartermaster, and the indictment against him included a pretty detailed description of Blackbeard's activities off the Virginia coast the previous summer. According to the document, Howard "did some time in the Year of our Lord 1717 Join and Associate him self with one Edward Tach and other Wicked and desolute Persons & with them did combine to fit out in Hostile manner a Certain Sloop or Vessel Call'd the Revenge to commit Pyracys and depridations upon the High Seas."

There was no mention of Hornigold, only Blackbeard (or "Tach") and his leading crewmen. Of course, by the summer of 1718 Hornigold was a changed man, a pirate turned pirate hunter, and no longer on the list of

America's most wanted brigands. There is another good reason why the pupil and not the teacher was named. At some stage during the fall of 1717 Benjamin Hornigold was deposed as captain, a victim of the changing face of piracy. As we have seen, he was a privateer, and so when the War of the Spanish Succession came to an end in 1713 he decided to keep on attacking his country's enemies. This private war with France and Spain was something of a fiction, designed to salve Hornigold's conscience.

In May 1716 the *Boston News Letter* published an article quoting a French merchant captain whose ship was captured by Hornigold that summer. According to the Frenchman, the pirates claimed that "they never consented to the Articles of Peace with the French and Spaniards," and therefore would continue to attack them. The Frenchman added that Hornigold assured him that "they meddle not with the English or Dutch." It was pretty obvious why Hornigold was trying to maintain the façade of being a law-abiding privateer—a maritime version of those Japanese soldiers who didn't know the war was over. After all, Henry Morgan had kept attacking the Spaniards after England signed a peace treaty with her old enemy, and he still went on to be knighted and become the deputy governor of Jamaica.

Hornigold knew the British government operated a carrot-and-stick policy, switching from chasing pirates across the oceans to offering them pardons in an attempt to reduce their numbers. This happened in the few short years of peace between 1697 and 1701, and there was no reason to suppose it wouldn't happen again. Hornigold was clearly on to something, as although the British authorities had little time for pirates whatever their professed national loyalties, less than two years later Woodes Rogers arrived offering pardons for all. Benjamin Hornigold was one of the few pirates who got out of the business at the right time, and no doubt his fiction of selective attacks helped him gain the trust of Rogers when the time came.

Some British officials saw through the fiction. In 1716 Virginia's Governor Spotswood wrote to his superiors in London, expressing his doubts over Hornigold's claim. He told them that Hornigold claimed his men "will only content themselves with making Prize of all French and Spanish they meet with," then added the barb, "yet there is so little trust to be given to such a People, that it is not to be doubted they will use all Nations alike whenever they have an advantage." Benjamin Hornigold wasn't alone in maintaining this delusion, as his fellow Bahamian pirates

Philip Cockram and Henry Jennings made similar claims. However, they appear to have changed their tune relatively quickly, probably because their crews saw through the charade.

Hornigold enjoyed greater loyalty from his men, and tried to remain true to his word—pushing the loyalty of his pirate crew to the limit as they saw a stream of plump British merchantmen sail past them without Hornigold lifting a finger. The inevitable result was that at some stage during the late summer his crew declared they had enough. Their captain had let one too many merchantman sail away over the horizon, so his crew called a council and voted to attack any target they chose. Hornigold must have protested the decision, because in the process he was deposed as captain, spending the rest of the cruise as a seething bystander as his men turned their guns on British ships. We don't know if Blackbeard was involved in this decision, but if he was, then despite his torn loyalties he would have sided with the majority. His subsequent actions show that it was a move he would have approved of.

Unlike Hornigold, men like Blackbeard harbored no illusions. The entire maritime community was united against them, and so maintaining a quasi-legal façade was pointless. The report of the stranded Captain Munthe clearly shows that Blackbeard and Hornigold operated in two different sloops, although until the "mutiny" Hornigold would have remained in nominal command of the expedition, with Blackbeard's sloop treated as an auxiliary. In fact, a later account suggests that the two vessels were cruising independently, so the first that Blackbeard might have heard of the revolt was when the two pirate ships met at a prearranged rendezvous some weeks or months later. The demotion of Hornigold might well have occurred fairly early on in the cruise, since if the plan was to limit attacks to French or Spanish shipping, then there was no need to cruise the waters off Virginia and Delaware.

A much better hunting ground would have been the Florida Straits and the Bahamas Channel. If the incident took place anywhere, it was somewhere off the Florida coast, and a betting man might put his money on a date in early September. Hornigold probably saw the revolt as a setback rather than a disaster, as he was still held in high regard in the Bahamas. He returned there to lick his wounds, probably when Blackbeard headed south into the Caribbean that November. Hornigold was still in New Providence when Governor Woodes Rogers arrived there the following year. Released from any restraint placed upon him, Blackbeard was free to steer his own course.

Meanwhile, the course Blackbeard steered during the late summer and fall can be traced by following the documentary trail—all mentioning encounters during this voyage of destruction, which brought shipping in the mid-Atlantic port of Philadelphia to a standstill. It was clear that by late September the pattern of pirate attacks had changed, as had the pirates' area of operations. This time it would be British and colonial American merchants who bore the brunt of the pirate assault.

If we turn to Governor Spotswood's case against Blackbeard's quartermaster William Howard, we learn where and when Blackbeard struck. They claimed:

> That in pursuance of the Said Felonious and Pyratical Combination [Blackbeard and Howard] the said Willm Howard did together with his Associates and Confederates on or about the 29th day of Septr in the Year Afforsaid [1717] in an Hostile manner with force and Arms on the high seas near Cape Charles in this Colony [Virginia] within the Jurisdiction of the Admiralty of this Court attack & force a Sloop Calld the Betty of Virginia belonging to the Subjects of our said Lord the King, and the said Sloop did then and there Rob and plunder of Certain Pipes of Medera Wine and other Goods and Merchandizes and thereafter the said Wm Howard did Sink and destroy the said Sloop with the remaining Part of the Cargo.

From this it seems that Blackbeard had already parted with Hornigold by late September and was cruising independently, or else the senior pirate was a hostage on his own flagship. The document only mentions one sloop, called *Revenge*, so we don't know what happened to the second pirate vessel. The phrase "with his Associates and Confederates" might suggest that two pirate sloops were working together, with Hornigold in nominal charge of one and Blackbeard the other. As Blackbeard wasn't mentioned in this charge, it is possible that he was cruising somewhere on his own. However, a later charge against Howard describes an incident where Blackbeard was most definitely present.

That means that it is just as likely Blackbeard was in charge of the *Revenge* when she met the *Betty*, and Howard was still acting as the pirate's quartermaster. Hornigold isn't mentioned at all in the document. It also seems as if Blackbeard and Howard had problems controlling their crews, as all they took from the *Betty* was wine, and they then sank their prize with her nonpotable cargo still aboard her. By now the pirates would have developed quite a taste for Madeira. The next report comes just two weeks later. The early November edition of the *Boston News Letter* carried a report from Philadelphia, which had been filed on October 24, 1717. It said, "Arrived Captain Codd from Liverpool and Dublin with 150 Passengers, many whereof are Searvants. He was taken 12 days since off our Cape by a Pirate Sloop called Revenge, of 12 Guns, 150 Men, Commanded by one Teach, who Formerly Sail'd Mate out of this Port."

Their common cause with the underdog would also have played a part in ensuring that the ship commanded by Captain Codd was allowed to complete her voyage into Philadelphia. The same article included a report that "Two Snows, outward bound, Spofford loaden with staves for Ireland and Budger of Bristol in the Sea Nymph loaden with Wheat for Oporto" were captured by pirates as they left the Delaware River. It adds, "They also took a sloop Inward Bound from Madera [Madeira], Peter Peters Master . . . an other Sloop one Grigg Master, bound hither from London . . . another sloop from Madera, bound to Virginia . . . also said they took a Sloop from Antigua, belonging to New-York." It was claimed that the pirates kept the *Sea Nymph*, and converted her into a pirate ship, doubling the size of Blackbeard's force. Presumably the pirate they mentioned was Blackbeard, so clearly Delaware Bay was providing a happy hunting ground for him.

Captain Codd was in no doubt that Blackbeard was responsible for the attack on his ship, as "Teach" is clearly named. As the ship was carrying indentured servants, it is unlikely that the pirates found much to plunder. These attacks place Blackbeard off the Delaware Bay around October 4–12. The cape referred to in the newspaper article was probably Cape May, which marked the southern tip of the New Jersey colony. The pirates were certainly keeping the *Boston News Letter* correspondent in Philadelphia busy. The November copies of the paper carried three more reports of piratical attacks, and from reading closely it appears that most of them took place during the same short period in October.

You could almost feel sorry for Captain Farmer, who had already been stopped by pirates on his voyage from Jamaica. When Blackbeard found that his vessel had already been looted, he let him continue on his way—after stripping him of his spare masts, anchors, and cables. A Captain Sipkins had his "great sloop" captured, and this time the pirates kept the vessel, converting her into a twelve-gun pirate sloop. Then, "on 30th past arrived Capt. Goelet, who was lately taken by Teach the Pirate, coming hither in a Sloop from Curacao, half loaden with Cocoa, which the Pirates threw overboard." Blackbeard and his men kept the sloop and sent their prisoners off in the slower *Sea Nymph*. By now Blackbeard had a small flotilla of three sloops under his command.

As Captain Goelet sailed off to safety in the *Sea Nymph*, he watched the pirates capture three more vessels—a ship, a brigantine, and a snow (which was a form of brig). The next news report is a little more confusing. It mentioned Captain "Prichard from St. Lucia, who on 18th October in Lat. 36 and 45 was taken by Capt. Teach, in Compa[ny] with Capt. Hornygold." "In compa with" doesn't sound like "under the command of." Hornigold's name appears one more time after this, and again it suggests that it was Blackbeard and not Hornigold who was leading the expedition.

Finally, the article claims that Blackbeard then captured a ship sailing from London to Virginia, but after rifling through its holds the pirates only took part of her cargo, then let her go. She might well have been the ship from London described in the newspaper as arriving in a Maryland port— presumably Baltimore—after being "taken off the Capes of Virginia by Teach and Hornigold." All the pirates took from her was a new suite of sails and rigging. Although the date given for the attack is two weeks before the paper was printed, this is almost certainly an error. By that time Blackbeard was far away in sunnier climes. These newspaper reports listed one more fascinating gem of information. The article describing the attack on Captain Codd's vessel concluded with a piece of news that showed that at some stage over the preceding month, Blackbeard had joined forces with another pirate.

> On board the Pirate Sloop is Major Bennet, but has no Command, he walks about in his Morning Gown, and then to his Books, of which he has a good Library on Board, he was not well of his wounds that he received by attacking a Spanish Man of War, which kill'd and wounded thirty to forty men. After which putting into Providence, the place of Rendevouze for the Pirates, they put the afore said Capt. Teach on board for this Cruise.

This throws everything on its head. There is little doubt that Major Bennet was actually the same Major Stede Bonnet whom Captain Johnson

*Stede Bonnet, the gentleman pirate, whose encounter with Blackbeard
in 1717 led to an enforced sojourn on board the* Queen Anne's
Revenge *as Blackbeard's guest. After being double-crossed by the
pirate, he carved his own piratical path, only to be cornered and
captured in the Cape Fear River.*

described as "a gentleman of good reputation in the island of Barbados,
was master of a plentiful fortune, and had the advantage of a liberal education." Captain Johnson devoted a whole chapter of his book to Major
Bonnet, but claimed that he and Blackbeard first crossed paths the following year, somewhere between St. Vincent and the Central American coast.

It now seems likely that the two met a lot earlier than that, and the
newspaper article even suggests that Blackbeard took Bonnet into his care
before he and Hornigold left the Bahamas on their summer cruise. This
would have been around the time the unfortunate Captain Munthe of

South Carolina reported that Blackbeard was still in New Providence. We will return to the question of Bonnet in a minute, but first we need to complete the story of Blackbeard's cruise off the Delaware Capes.

Governor Spotswood's second charge against Quartermaster William Howard allows us to pick up the tale:

> That the said Wm Howard and his Associates and Confederates did on or about the 22d of Octo^r in the year aforesaid in the Bay of Delaware in America wthin the Jurisdiction of the Admiralty of Great Britain & of this Court Pyratically take and Rob the Sloop Robert of Philadelphia and the Ship Good Intent of Dublin both bound for Philadelphia aforesaid and divers goods and Merchandizes then on board the s^d Ship & Sloop belonging to the Subjects of our Lord the king did felonously and piratically take seize and carry away.

This places Blackbeard and Howard in the same spot as the earlier spate of attacks some ten days later. Presumably Blackbeard had decided that Delaware Bay was a prime spot to intercept ships bound for Philadelphia. However, both were inbound ships, so we have to assume that by that stage word of the pirate threat had spread through Philadelphia like wildfire. While the authorities don't describe the cargo carried by the *Robert* and the *Good Intent*, we are left with the impression that the pirates took the cargo and left the vessels to continue their voyage into Philadelphia. While the *Robert* was just a small coastal sloop, the Irish prize was described as a ship, meaning she was a square-rigged three-masted vessel, with enough cargo space to make a long transatlantic voyage a profitable concern.

She wasn't necessarily particularly large. We have already mentioned the English slave ship *Henrietta Marie*, which displaced 120 tons and was just 60 to 70 feet long. The *Good Intent* was probably similar, most likely carrying a cargo of manufactured and luxury goods, spirits, and other luxuries. Her cargo would have fetched a good price in Philadelphia if Blackbeard hadn't intercepted her soon after she made landfall off the Delaware coast. The limited cargo space in the *Revenge* and the other two sloops must have been filled to capacity, and Blackbeard clearly needed a larger ship to hold his plunder. The Irish vessel was considered unsuitable, probably because she was too slow. Blackbeard was therefore on the lookout for a fast, well-founded ship, and that is exactly what he found.

To say that by the end of October the weather off the New Jersey coast is autumnal is something of an understatement. We know from British naval records that heavy cold winds were sweeping inshore from the Atlantic. For example, while Blackbeard was off Cape May, the British twenty-gun brig HMS *Phoenix* was 130 miles to the north, lying at anchor in New York Harbor. On October 31 her Officer of the Day noted in the ship's log that a strong, fresh wind was blowing in from the east-southeast, and that it was raining. A similar report was filed on board HMS *Lyme*, anchored in Virginia's James River. She had just returned from New York herself, where she had been escorting a convoy up the coast from the mouth of the Chesapeake Bay to Sandy Hook, at the head of the Hudson River.

The *Lyme* must have passed Blackbeard's sloop as she headed north, but her lookouts never spotted the *Revenge*. Quite possibly the pirate sloop was not even at sea, as Captain Johnson claimed that at some stage during the cruise Blackbeard careened his ship in some deserted cove on the Virginia coast. This involved beaching the sloop, then scraping off any barnacles and marine growth that would have reduced her speed. He certainly would have done this monotonous chore before the onset of the equinoctial storms of late September—meaning she was safely tucked away when the *Lyme* sailed past.

Unlike merchant sailors or naval ratings, pirates had no need to endure the worst that a North American winter could expose them to. From early June until the end of October the Caribbean was a potentially dangerous place for a small sailing ship, as those five months covered the hurricane season. At any time during this period a ship could be overhauled by a cataclysmic vortex of 150-mile-an-hour winds and surging waves. As recently as 1715 an entire Spanish treasure *flota* of a dozen galleons were caught by a deadly hurricane in the shallow waters of the Bahamas Channel. One by one these proud ships were dashed onto the reefs and sandbars of the Florida coast, scattering the bodies of more than seven hundred sailors and some fourteen million pieces of eight along 30 miles of storm-ravaged coast. Incidentally, this disaster played a significant part in the establishment of New Providence as a pirate base, but more of that in the next chapter.

For Blackbeard and his men, the end of October meant the end of the hurricane season, as the equinoctial gales gave way to winter storms off

New Jersey. The pirates decided to head south toward warmer weather and into less violent seas. By the last day of October the *Revenge* was heading south-southeast, steering a course that would take her east of the Bahamas and into the sun-kissed waters of the West Indies. However, before we take up the story of Blackbeard's next great venture, we need to return to the problem of Major Stede Bonnet.

Although Captain Johnson fails to give us any dates, he suggests that the two men crossed paths after Blackbeard encountered a "large French Guineaman" off Martinique, and then supposedly fought off the British warship HMS *Scarborough* somewhere off the West Indian island of St. Vincent. As Captain Johnson described it, Blackbeard in his newfound flagship had already decided to quit the Windward Islands, and had set a course for the Spanish Main.

> On his way he met with a pirate sloop of 10 guns, commanded by one Major Bonnet, lately a gentleman of good reputation and estate in the island of Barbados, whom he joined. But a few days later, Teach, finding that Bonnet knew nothing of a maritime life, and with the consent of his own men, put in another captain, one Richards, to command Bonnet's sloop, and took the major on board his own ship, telling him that as he had not been used to the fatigues and care of such a post, it would be better for him to decline it and live easy and at his pleasure in such a ship as his, where he should not be obliged to perform duty, and follow his own inclinations.

While Captain Johnson might have described the encounter with some accuracy, he was wrong about the time and the place. Many historians follow Johnson and place the encounter sometime after December 1717. In fact, the pirate historian Robert E. Lee claimed the two men met while Blackbeard was sailing from the Carolinas to the Gulf of Honduras "sometime in early March 1717/1718." The discovery of that article in the early November edition of the *Boston News Letter* changes everything. Remember that the paper's Philadelphia correspondent reported that a twelve-gun pirate sloop called the *Revenge* commanded by "one Teach" with 150 men on board was operating in Delaware Bay. As the report was filed on October 24 and the first pirate attack happened "12 days since," then we can assume Teach made his first capture in the area around October 12. The mysterious "Major Bennet" who "has no Command" was clearly mentioned as being on the same sloop when the pirates seized Captain Codd's ship. Change "Bennet" to "Bonnet" and the picture is clear—the two pirates first met each other during Blackbeard and Hornigold's summer cruise off the Virginia and Delaware coast in the fall of 1717.

That's a full six months before Lee's date, and in a whole different part of the ocean. However, unraveling the historical trail is rarely that simple. The same article finishes by saying that "Major Bennet" was injured during an earlier attack on a Spanish warship. He took his battered vessel into New Providence for repairs, where "they" (presumably Hornigold and his peers) put Blackbeard in command of the damaged pirate ship. The newspaper correspondent would have talked to Captain Codd, and possibly his passengers and crew. Evidently some of them saw "Major Bennet," and someone heard the story either from him or from a member of Blackbeard's crew. To unravel the mystery, we need to take a look at what Captain Johnson has to say about Stede Bonnet.

In "The Life of Major Bonnet" Captain Johnson claims that the soldier turned pirate came from Barbados, but was unable to explain why he decided to throw everything away and become a pirate:

> He had the least temptation of any man to follow such a course of life, from the condition of his circumstances. It was very surprising to every one, to hear of the major's enterprise, in the island where he lived; and as he was generally esteemed and honoured, before he broke out into open acts of piracy, so he was afterwards rather pitied than condemned, by those that were acquainted with him, believing that this humour of going a-pirating, proceeded from a disorder of his mind, which had been too visible to him, some time before this wicked undertaking; and which is said to have been occasioned by some discomforts he found in a married state; be that as it will, the major was ill qualified for the business, as not understanding maritime affairs.

It wasn't clear whether his "disorder of the mind" was caused by his unhappy marriage, but from what followed, his behavior defied any rational explanation. It seems harsh to blame his poor abandoned wife for what happened next. The historical records help flesh out what we know about the man. He was born in 1688, the son of a well-respected sugar planter from St. Michael's Parish. He inherited the family estates, married a neighbor's daughter, and even became a major in the island militia. He was twenty-nine when he gave all this up and escaped to sea, so he didn't even have the excuse of a midlife crisis to explain his uncharacteristic behavior.

He then broke all the rules of piracy and bought his own sloop—a real pirate would have stolen her. He spent good money fitting her out with ten guns and enough provisions for a season's cruise, and capped this shocking display of nonpiratical decency by hiring a seventy-man crew, paying them wages out of his own pocket. Captain Kidd would have turned in his unmarked grave. History didn't record what he told his respectable neighbors or his wife. Presumably he claimed that the sloop would be used for interisland trading. He left Barbados, never to return, setting a northerly course toward the tip of the Leeward Islands and fresh exciting horizons. As soon as the island faded into the distance, he ordered the Union flag hauled down and raised the black flag of piracy in its place. He called his sloop *Revenge*, although just what he planned to avenge was never made clear.

Although he lacked any knowledge of seamanship, he must have hired the right men in the taverns of Bridgetown, as he managed to follow the outer rim of the Bahamas to make landfall off the Virginia Capes. He set to his new trade with enthusiasm: "He took several ships, and plundered them of their provisions, clothes, money, ammunition, etc. in particular the Anne, Capt. Montgomery, from Glasgow; the Turbet from Barbados, which for country sake, after they had taken out the principal part of the lading, the pirate crew set her on fire; the Endeavour, Captain Scot, from Bristol, and the Young from Leith."

That was a successful start for any pirate—two Scottish, one English, and one Barbadian prize in his first few weeks on the job. The captain of the ship from Barbados must have recognized Bonnet, and would have been amazed at the planter turned pirate. Captain Johnson continued the saga of Stede Bonnet's first cruise, claiming that he left the Virginia coast and sailed north to a new hunting ground off New York. He captured another sloop outward bound from Boston to the West Indies off the eastern tip of Long Island, and then put in for supplies to Gardiner's Island, where Captain Kidd had hidden his plunder before returning to New York some two decades before. True to form, Captain Bonnet paid the locals for the provisions he took. According to Captain Johnson, this took place sometime in August 1717—roughly the same time that Blackbeard and Hornigold were in the Bahamas Channel.

This is where the story becomes a little confusing. He headed south again, and Captain Johnson wrote that his next attack took place "off the bar of South Carolina," meaning Charles Town Harbor. His first prize was a Barbadian sloop under the command of Master Joseph Palmer, bound for the Carolina port. The lucrative haul included rum, sugar, and slaves, but before they could settle down to drink themselves into insensibility, a second vessel appeared. This, a brigantine bound for Charles Town from New England under the command of Master Thomas Porter, was plundered but then left to continue her voyage. Bonnet decided to keep the Barbadian sloop, and the two vessels headed north a little to find a deserted spot where he could careen his own sloop. Captain Johnson is a little unclear at this point, claiming that they found a suitably deserted inlet on the North Carolina coast, then "careened her, then set her on fire." Whether this was an accident or whether Bonnet decided he didn't need the second sloop is unclear.

It is highly probable that not all was well with the crew, who must have realized that their nonelected captain didn't know what he was doing.

> After the sloop was cleaned they put to sea, but came to no resolution what course to take; the crew were divided in their opinions, some being for one thing, and some another, so that nothing but confusion seemed to attend their schemes. The major was no sailor as we have said before, and therefore had been obliged to yield to many things that were imposed on him, during their undertaking, for want of a competent knowledge in maritime affairs.

The careening probably took place in the mouth of the Cape Fear River, a spot Bonnet would return to the following year. That placed Stede Bonnet and the *Revenge* square in the path of another group of marauders. By now it would have been mid-September—the same time Blackbeard and Hornigold were heading north toward the Virginia Capes on their summer cruise. They would have passed within sight of Cape Fear, and if Blackbeard and Bonnet did meet on the high seas, this was the time and place for it.

From the case against Blackbeard's quartermaster, William Howard, we know that Blackbeard and possibly Hornigold were "on the high seas near Cape Charles" in Virginia around September 29. Less than two weeks later the *Boston News Letter* places Blackbeard 120 miles to the north, off

Cape May in New Jersey, at the mouth of Delaware Bay. By that time his formerly unnamed vessel had become the *Revenge*, and the report read that "on board the Pirate Sloop is Major Bennet." From naval records we know the weather was fair off the mid-Atlantic seaboard at this time, and that the predominant wind was fresh, from the southeast. That would have put him off Cape Fear around September 15.

We would be fairly sure that this was when the paths of Bonnet and Blackbeard crossed if it weren't for that description of Stede Bonnet's cruise that didn't fit Captain Johnson's outline. It claimed he was wounded "attacking a Spanish Man of War," and put into New Providence for repairs. While most accounts of Blackbeard and Bonnet follow Captain Johnson's claim that the two met on the high seas, Professor Joel Baer based his account around the article in the *Boston News Letter*. He supports the theory that after he left the Carolinas Bonnet headed south toward the Bahamas, but fell foul of the Spanish warship, presumably in the Bahamas Channel. He continues: "In September 1717 the badly damaged sloop limped into New Providence, where, in return for provisions, repairs and reinforcements, Bonnet agreed to let Thatch command the Revenge on a cruise along the northern colonies."

While this makes perfect sense if Bonnet did indeed encounter a Spanish warship that killed and wounded half his crew, the timing is wrong. It would have taken a sloop the best part of three weeks or more to sail from the Bahamas to Delaware Bay, meaning that Blackbeard and Bonnet would have had to slip their anchorage off Nassau by mid-September at the latest. Similarly, if we take Captain Johnson's statement that Bonnet was off Long Island in August, then the whole story begins to look even shakier. He would have been hard put to fly south under full sail to Charleston, capture two ships, careen two sloops, fight a battle, limp into New Providence, and repair his ship in the time available—six weeks at most. To make it even harder, Blackbeard was off the Virginia Capes in late September, a near-impossible voyage from Nassau even in the fastest, sweetest sloop in the Americas.

Regrettably, we have to assume that the Philadelphia correspondent for the *Boston News Letter* muddled his story, one he presumably heard third-hand from a prisoner on board the *Revenge* who landed in Philadelphia two weeks later. While it is not impossible, we have to assume that Stede Bonnet fabricated the story about the encounter with the Spanish man-of-war, which after all sounded far more heroic than saying he meekly threw up his hands when Blackbeard overhauled his sloop. We've already seen something of the relationship between the two men. A hardened seaman like Blackbeard must have seen that Bonnet was completely out of his depth and that his crew was losing any respect for him. Bonnet must have known that, too, and faced with someone as intimidating as Blackbeard, it is little wonder that he allowed himself to become a passenger on his own vessel.

From the account of Captain Codd that mentioned that Bonnet "walks about in his Morning gown, and then to his Books," we can see that by October 12 at the latest, Stede Bonnet had resigned his command to Blackbeard, who was in full control of the *Revenge*. Captain Johnson claimed that "to him [Blackbeard] Bonnet's crew joined in consortship, and Bonnet himself was laid aside, notwithstanding the sloop was his own; he went aboard Blackbeard's ship, not concerning himself with any of their affairs." In other words, while Blackbeard maintained the charade that Bonnet was his guest and a passenger, the Barbadian major was little more than a prisoner, rejected by his own crew and completely dominated by the charismatic figure of Blackbeard.

If we assume that the *Revenge* fell into Blackbeard's clutches in mid-September, and that Blackbeard moved from his own six-gun sloop into the more powerful twelve-gun *Revenge*, then by late September his force contained three vessels, and the *Revenge* acted as the flagship of the pirate flotilla. The rest of the force consisted of Blackbeard's old sloop and what Captain Codd described as "a Consort Ship of 30 guns"—presumably Hornigold's *Ranger*. While this might have been a different vessel from the ten-gun sloop the stranded Captain Musson claims was under Hornigold's command earlier that year in New Providence, there is no indication that the force had gained an extra ship. Then came the two weeks in October when Blackbeard kept, then released the snow *Sea Nymph*, and added Captain Goelet's sloop to his force. By the time Blackbeard, Hornigold, and Bonnet headed south, the force consisted of four ships.

The next time we hear of Blackbeard in mid-November, he only had two ships under his command, and Hornigold and his former protégé appear to have parted company. We have to assume that Hornigold returned to New Providence as Blackbeard sailed past the Bahamas in early November, and took one of the two sloops with him. As Blackbeard is next mentioned having an eight-gun and the twelve-gun sloop under his command, one might well have been his original small 40-ton Bermudan sloop, with her armament augmented by two looted guns. The other was the *Revenge*, with poor Major Bonnet still reading his way through his library in the stern cabin. Hornigold must have returned to port with his own thirty-gun vessel and the sloop taken from Captain Goelet. The parting of the two pairs of ships must have been a time of mixed emotions for Hornigold and Blackbeard. The mentor was never to see his protégé again.

After the two pirate groups parted company, Blackbeard sailed his remaining sloops southeast, a fast run with a cool but brisk northeasterly wind blowing in from the north Atlantic. The pirates would have made landfall off Anguilla or Barbuda at the northern end of the Leeward Island chain early in the second week in November, but Blackbeard elected to steer a course to windward (east) of the islands, sailing south-southeast under easy sail. The idea was to lie in wait of well-laden ships trying to make landfall in the sugar islands of the Lesser Antilles, and the plan worked to perfection.

By November 17 he lay some 60 miles west of the French colony of Martinique, gently rolling in what was described in Barbados that morning as a gentle onshore wind. The lookouts spotted a sail to the east-southeast, and Blackbeard gave the order to intercept. Captain Johnson gave a surprisingly terse account of the encounter: "They returned to the West Indies, and in the latitude of 24, made prize of a large French Guineaman, bound to Martinique . . . Aboard of this Guineaman Teach mounted 40 guns, and named her the Queen Anne's Revenge." Fortunately others were more verbose, particularly the French captain, who reported the capture of his ship to the French authorities in Martinique. The intendant (the manager of public affairs) in Martinique, Charles Mesnier, sent a detailed report of the incident to his superiors in Paris.

The French vessel was a slaving ship called *La Concorde*, whose home port was given as Nantes, a major port on the River Loire that opened out into the stormy Bay of Biscay. He listed the owner of the slaver as Monsieur René Montaudouin of Nantes, and her master as Captain Pierre Dosset. Given the constraints of eighteenth-century bureaucratic reports, the tale Charles Mesnier told was a dramatic one.

Last 28 November [French dating], being within 60 miles from here [Martinique] at 14 degree 27 minutes north latitude, having been attacked by two boats of English pirates, one of 12 and the other of 8 guns armed with 250 men controlled by Edouard Titche, English, was removed by these pirates with 455 negros who remained with him . . . the afore-mentioned Dosset with his crew to the Grenadines onto the island of Becoya [Bequia], near Grenade [Granada].

Captain Dosset and his deputy, Lieutenant François Ernaud, survived their ordeal. We also know that at the time of her capture the forty-strong crew of the French slaver had suffered from scurvy and dysentery during their transatlantic voyage, and only twenty-three men were in any kind of fit state when the pirates appeared over the horizon. When the two pirate sloops overhauled La Concorde, she had little option but to surrender without a fight.

After boarding her, "Edouard Titche" and his men escorted their prize to the south. They finally dropped anchor in the sheltered anchorage of Bequia, an island small enough to lack a British or French garrison, and a long-established watering place for buccaneers, privateers, and pirates. There Blackbeard and his men set to work, building a slave holding pen, landing La Concorde's human cargo and crew, then converting La Concorde for their own use. Blackbeard had already decided that with a little work she would make the perfect pirate flagship.

We know a little about the French slave ship. Like many slavers she was built for speed, as a fast Middle Passage meant fewer deaths in the slave holds and therefore a larger profit for the shipowners. However, she was never designed as a slaving vessel, but rather began life as a privateer. After all, the requirements were similar—a clean, fast hull, ample cargo capacity, and three masts, providing a maximum press of sail for a vessel of her size. In other words, she was built for speed.

According to the report of Captain Dosset, his ship displaced 200 tons and carried fourteen guns. His deputy Lieutenant Ernaud placed her arma-ment at sixteen guns, but the difference can probably be explained by the way that slavers operated. One of the greatest fears of European crewmen during the Middle Passage was that the slaves might break free of their shackles and rise in revolt. There are several instances of this, and woe betide the slaver crew who were caught unawares. It was therefore common to build a barrier between the waist of the ship and the quarterdeck, so that the stern of the vessel could be turned into a miniature fortress if need be.

This sleek French merchantman shown in an engraving dated 1714 is very similar to the description of La Concorde, *the Nantes slave ship Blackbeard took as his flagship. He renamed her* Queen Anne's Revenge, *and turned her into a floating fortress of upwards of forty guns.*

For extra security, when the slaves were brought up from the hold to be exercised or washed by hand-pumped hoses, they were penned into the waist, and crewmen armed with small arms standing on the quarterdeck guarded the wretched sea of humanity below them. It was also common to mount swivel guns or even small guns loaded with grapeshot on the quarterdeck, their arc of fire designed to sweep the waist of the ship in case of a rising. While this might have been seen as a last resort, as it played havoc with the shipowner's profits, the guns might be all that lay between the crew and a grisly death at the hands of their captives.

The most dangerous times for the crew were when the ship left the West African coast and when they arrived in the Caribbean—when the slaves saw land they thought they might have a chance to escape. Therefore a prudent captain would make sure any guns covering the waist were loaded and ready for action when the slave ship was about to make landfall. When *La Concorde* was captured she was within sixty miles of her destination in the Martinique harbor of Fort de France, so Captain Dosset would have already given the order to prepare these small guns. That explains the discrepancy—either the two missing pieces were just small rail-mounted swivel guns, or they didn't form part of the ship's main broadside armament, but instead were placed so the crew could fire them into the waist of their own ship.

La Concorde was built in Nantes on the River Loire during 1709–10, designed along the lines of a naval frigate, only on a smaller scale, which would have made her a superb purpose-built privateer. Her first privateering job came in August 1710. This was a strange assignment as a hired vessel working for the French government, when she helped escort a convoy of fourteen sail from the Roads of Mindin off the mouth of the Loire to the bustling naval port of Brest. As soon as she was free of her convoy she headed south, bound for the West African coast.

In late September she captured a Portuguese merchantman off Sestre or Setera [now Sesstown] on the Grain Coast near Cape Palmas, then continued east to cruise off the Rio de Lahou, on the Portuguese-held Ivory Coast. She wintered there, and by early February 1711 La Concorde had quit the African coast and was heading out into the Atlantic. She made landfall near Martinique, and after cruising off Tobago she headed north. By April the French privateer was cruising off the colony of Santo Domingo in Hispaniola (now the Dominican Republic), where she captured a small British merchantman. She touched in Havana for supplies before heading home, and in September 1711 she captured a small colonial vessel from Boston off Barbados, which she ransomed and released. The privateer arrived back in Nantes two months later. All told, her maiden voyage was a success. However, like all privateers her value was directly linked to warfare, and as rumors of imminent peace spread through France her owners dropped her like a hot potato.

La Concorde was bought by René Montaudouin, a prosperous shipowner and slave trader from Nantes, and he refitted his new acquisition as a slaver. She began her first voyage in the spring of 1713, and after collecting more than five hundred slaves on the coast of Benin she made a fast Middle Passage, arriving in Martinique in time for Christmas. Four hundred and sixty-five slaves were sold on the auction block in Fort de France, and she arrived back in Nantes the following July, completing a hugely profitable voyage.

The following year he sent La Concorde out again. This time she collected her slaves from the mouth of the Congo River, and in November

1715 she sold them in Leogane, a bustling little French port on the western coast of Saint Dominique (now Haiti). She returned to Nantes early in 1716, and once again Monsieur Montaudouin was delighted. Her third slaving voyage was to prove her last. On March 24, 1717, she slipped down the River Loire toward the open sea, bound once more for the sweltering and unhealthy Gold Coast. By July she lay at anchor off Whydah (now the port of Lomé on the coast of Benin), and by September 1717 she was ready to make her Middle Passage, as a full cargo of 516 terrified men, women, and children were crammed into her slave decks.

Given the time of year, she made a good passage, that is, until November 28, when she met Blackbeard. The pirate had served as a privateer during the War of the Spanish Succession, and he recognized a dream ship when he saw her. *La Concorde* was everything a budding pirate leader could want, and Blackbeard immediately decided to make her his new flagship.

Although we don't know exactly how Blackbeard set about converting the privateer turned slaver into a pirate ship, we do have plenty of accounts of other prizes that went through the same process. For a start, Captain Johnson describes a handful of prizes that were converted by pirates, and of course, we now have the wreck of Blackbeard's flagship to provide further clues. In Captain Johnson's "The Life of Captain England" he included a passing mention to just such a conversion, when in early 1719 "Captain England took a ship called the Pearl, Catain Tyzard commander, for which he exchanged his own sloop, fitted her up for the piratical account." England renamed his prize the *Royal James*. Unfortunately, Johnson never explained what fitting the ship up for the piratical account entailed.

He provided a little more information in "The Life of Captain Lowther", which said that when George Lowther incited the crew of the *Gambia Castle* to mutiny in 1721, he and his men set about converting the slaver into a pirate ship. "They one and all came to the measures, knocked down the cabins, made the ship flush for[e] and aft, prepared black colours, new named her the Delivery, having about fifty hands and 16 guns." Then, in "The Life of Captain Roberts", we have the description of what Bartholomew Roberts and his men did to the large frigate-built slave ship *Onslow*, owned by the Royal Africa Company.

The pirates kept the Onslow for their own use, and gave Captain Gee the French ship, and then fell to making such alterations as might fit her for a sea rover, pulling down her bulkheads, and making her flush, so that she became, in all respects, as complete a ship for their purpose as any they could have found; they continued to give her the name Royal Fortune and mounted her with 40 guns.

We can see that converting a merchantman into a pirate ship was a big job, something akin to converting a merchant ship into an auxiliary cruiser in the First and Second World Wars. First the pirates removed many of the temporary bulkheads set up in the hold, which were used to prevent the cargo from shifting. This meant that whatever was captured was on view to all, and nobody could accuse the captain or quartermaster of hiding plunder away. Even communally held money chests were left unlocked, for the same reason. After all, it went against the articles for anyone to plunder from his own shipmates. If this lower deck space contained an extra level above the waterline, then it could be used to hold additional ordnance, after holes were cut in the sides of the ship to create crude but effective gunports. Most merchant ships, including *La Concorde*, carried no more than sixteen guns, and these were always mounted on the open upper deck or beneath the quarterdeck. Of course, on a slave ship like *La Concorde* the hold space was already divided up into tiers to accommodate the maximum number of slaves.

In essence, what the pirates did was to convert their prize from a merchant vessel into a makeshift warship, using additional pieces of ordnance taken from earlier prize ships. Most vessels used stone for ballast, a counterweight to keep the vessel floating upright. In pirate ships, captured guns often replaced the ballast stones. These extra guns could either be used as additional armament if needed, or else sold off when the pirate crew found a suitable market. In the case of *La Concorde*, Blackbeard would have stripped any suitable pieces from the smaller of his two sloops, then winched up any extra guns from the hold of the *Revenge*. Additional swivel guns would be placed around the upper rails of the ship, particularly on the forecastle and quarterdeck. *La Concorde* was now well on her way to becoming a maritime fortress.

Next, in line with the egalitarian nature of the way the pirates ran everything, most internal cabin bulkheads were knocked down, creating an open space behind the quarterdeck, in the forecastle, and on any lower deck. Not only did this reduce the risk of flying splinters when the pirate ship went into action, but it also prevented the captain or the quartermaster from setting themselves up above the rest. It seems that Blackbeard's crew made an exception for the "gentleman pirate" Stede Bonnet, who was transferred from the *Revenge* to Blackbeard's new flagship, together with his library and his morning coat.

The pirates then went one stage further. Most merchant ships of the time had large quarterdeck, poop deck, and forecastle structures, the former two housing cabin space and a small gun deck, and the latter being a space for the crew to sleep and for the housing of stores. With the opening up of the lower decks this became unnecessary. Both Roberts and Lowther made the main deck of their ships flush fore and aft, tearing down the forecastle and lowering any superstructure "abaft" (behind) the mainmast. This created a smooth, open, flush-decked vessel without any break from bow to stern, apart from the break between waist and quarterdeck. In most cases the pirates knocked down any roundhouse located under the poop deck abaft of the mizzenmast, but in a few cases this also involved tearing down the whole quarterdeck structure as well. We don't know to what extent Blackbeard's crew did this to *La Concorde*, but with luck, future archaeological work on her suspected wreck site might shed more light on the conversion job.

The spaces once occupied by the roundhouse and the forecastle were now used to house more guns, both large pieces and swivel guns. More ad hoc gunports were cut in the side of the hull, and possibly extra bow chaser and stern chaser ports were cut as well. This turned the ship into a superb fighting platform. For the same reason, the pirates tended to remove any impractical decorated rails and decorations that might get in the way during a fight. Remember that pirate crews greatly outnumbered merchant ones, so not only did the ship have to house more men than it was designed for, these pirates needed to be able to flood another ship with boarders. This open, unimpeded upper deck space gave them the ability to do just that—and it also helped the crew squeeze as much ordnance on board as the ship could carry.

All this work would almost certainly have altered the sailing qualities of the ship itself, which meant rerigging the vessel. If the pirates disliked the existing sail rig they would change it, as while a merchant captain might be reluctant to carry so much sail that his ship could damage sails or rigging, the pirates cared little for this. After all, any damage could be replaced from the next prize. Captain Johnson underlined this when he described how Bartholomew Roberts plundered the *Samuel* of London: "They carried with them sails, guns, powder and cordage, and 8,000 or 9,000 pounds of the choicest goods." For pirates the emphasis was on speed, and so the sail rig would often be redesigned to squeeze the last drop of power out of the wind. This conversion work might involve replacing lateen yards with square-rigged ones on the mizzenmast, or even stepping the mainmast back a few feet to improve the sailing qualities of the newly converted ship.

By the time they were finished, poor Captain Dosset would have been hard-pressed to recognize his old ship. The new pirate flagship now carried up to forty guns, and her upper decks were stripped and her rig altered to suit Blackbeard's needs. She also acquired a new name. From now on Blackbeard's flagship was going to be called *Queen Anne's Revenge*. She was named after the Queen Anne who reigned over England and Scotland from 1702 until her death in 1714 and who oversaw the union of the two kingdoms in 1707.

She was the last of the Stuart dynasty, and on her death without an heir she was succeeded by George I, a Hanoverian whose succession owed more to his Protestantism than to his lineage. Anne was the daughter of the King James who was overthrown and exiled in the Glorious Revolution of 1688. Many pirates expressed their support for the exiled James, so creating the "Jacobite" cause that remained a nascent threat to the Hanoverians for another three decades. By including the term "revenge" after "Queen Anne," Blackbeard might have been suggesting he supported the last of the Stuarts and saw his actions as a form of revenge against the usurping Germans on behalf of the Jacobite cause. He would not be the only pirate of the era to claim some form of legitimacy by linking himself with the deposed British monarch.

The whole business of unloading the slaves and stores, refitting the ship, and rearming her would have taken at least one or two weeks, which meant it was probably late November before Blackbeard was ready to put to sea again. The pirates gave the smaller of their two sloops to the prisoners, probably after removing all her guns and most of her stores and rigging. According to Lieutenant Ernaud the small sloop was of "Bermuda fabrication, of 40 tons or thereabouts." The French aptly renamed her the *Mauvaise Rencontre*, which translates as "Bad Meeting."

Captain Dosset and his crew must have set sail for Martinique soon after the pirates arrived in Bequia, as the report sent by Charles Mesnier from

Martinique was dated December 10, 1717. The French were still using the Julian calendar, which is ten days behind the Gregorian version used by the British. This means that the French crew must have completed the 130-mile voyage to Martinique by the end of November, meaning Blackbeard would have released them within a few days of capturing the ship. We can guess that Blackbeard recruited some of the more promising Africans as reinforcements for his pirate crew, but the rest were left behind when the pirates sailed away. The abandoned slaves enjoyed only a brief taste of freedom, as the *Mauvaise Rencontre* returned for her human cargo, and these remaining slaves were then transported to Martinique in two trips.

We do know that Blackbeard was back at sea again before the end of November. Again it is the *Boston News Letter* that chronicled his next move. It reported that in late November "a great Ship from Boston was taken at or near St. Lucia or St. Vincent by Captain Teach the Pirate in a French Ship of 32 Guns, a Briganteen of 10 guns and a Sloop of 12 guns." The article continued on to name the vessel as the *Great Allen*, and said that Captain Taylor of Boston was kept in irons for twenty-four hours and was whipped to see if he had hidden any money on board. "The pirates plundered her of what they thought fit, [then] put all their men ashore upon the island above mentioned [St. Vincent], and then set fire to the ship." A little more information is supplied by a deposition filed by Governor William Hamilton of the Leeward Islands in January 1718. He claimed that the pirates "had a great deal of plate on board, and one fine cup they told despondent they had taken out of Capt. Taylor, bound from Barbados to Jamaica, whom they very much abused and burnt his ship."

Evidently Blackbeard was working his way up and down the chain of islands, looking for rich pickings among the British sugar islands of the Grenadines. In the first report the thirty-two-gun French ship is clearly the *Queen Anne's Revenge* and the sloop is the twelve-gun *Revenge*, but what is a little more confusing is the mention of a ten-gun brigantine. Evidently the pirates captured another small prize before their encounter with the *Great Allen* of Boston off St. Vincent, but how Blackbeard found the men to crew her is something of a mystery. By all accounts he had at least 150 men with him at that stage, and this force now had to be split among three vessels.

The *Great Allen* certainly wasn't his only victim in the waters off St. Vincent and St. Lucia. On November 30 Richard Joy, the master of the Antiguan sloop *New Division*, was overtaken by "two pirate ships and a sloop." Blackbeard asked what Joy knew of shipping in the area, then left him to continue on his way—after taking on board a sailor who wished to join the pirate crew.

On the same day Captain Benjamin Hobhouse of the *Monserrat Merchant* saw a small convoy of two ships and a sloop approaching. He thought two were Guinea slavers and the third one was a Bristol ship, so he foolishly heaved to, then lowered his boat to ask for news and letters. "They desired us to come on board, but seeing Death Head [Skull and Crossbones] in the stern we refused it etc. . . . They report the pirates name is Kentish and Captain Edwards belonging to the sloop, and they report the ship had 150 men on board and 22 guns mounted, the sloop about 50 white men, and eight guns." We know that Stede Bonnet later used the alias "Captain Edwards," but this deposition gives us the first clear sign that Blackbeard used aliases himself. He must have thought "Captain Kentish" had a nice ring to it. The other part of this is the suggestion that not all of Blackbeard's men were Caucasian. It might be that he selected some of the fitter and more suitable slaves from those carried on board *La Concorde* and pressed them into service as extra crew. From the numbers involved, he might have recruited as many as seventy or even more, although he might well have also augmented his crew with volunteers from *La Concorde* and the *Great Allen*.

Another seaman to join the band was Thomas Knight, who was reputedly taken prisoner when Blackbeard encountered the *Monserrat Merchant*. He later reported to Governor Hamilton that the pirates headed north, back up the chain of islands until they reached Nevis. They looked into the island's main harbor of Charles Town, but "among the rest they took on[e] for the Mon of Warr." Nevis was a British island, so the warship they spotted was most probably HMS *Scarborough*, a thirty-gun fifth-rate ship of the line commanded by the highly experienced Captain Francis Hume. Interestingly, Knight reported that "they said they would cut her out, but the Captain being ill prevented it."

This near encounter may help explain one of the great Blackbeard mysteries. According to Captain Johnson, soon after the pirates destroyed the *Great Allen* they ran into Captain Hume. "A few days later, Teach fell in with the Scarborough man-of-war, of 30 guns, who engaged him for some hours; but she finding the pirate well manned and having tried her strength, gave over the engagement and returned to Barbados, the place of her station, and Teach sailed towards the Spanish America."

This makes for a great story. Unfortunately, it seems that the closest HMS *Scarborough* and the *Queen Anne's Revenge* ever got to trading blows with each other was when the pirate ship sailed past Nevis on her way north. The log of HMS *Scarborough* is still available, as are the reports and letters of Captain Hume. None of them mentions any such battle. While conspiracy theorists might claim that the reports were doctored to spare the blushes of the good captain, this just wasn't practical. After all, a standup fight would have caused a lot of damage to both ships and emptied the shot locker of the *Scarborough*. However, there are no reports of her putting in to the naval yard in Barbados for extensive repairs, and she had no need to replenish her stocks of powder and shot. To cap it all, Governor Hamilton made no mention of such an encounter, although he had plenty to say about Blackbeard's cruise through the Leeward Islands.

As he quit the West Indies, never to return, Blackbeard made two last captures. Henry Bostock, the master of the sloop *Margaret* of St. Christopher, filed a deposition with Governor Hamilton in Antigua on December 19, 1717. He claimed that on December 5 he was off Crab Island near Anguilla when "he met a large ship and a sloop. He was ordered on board and Capt. Tach took his cargo of cattle and hogs, his arms books and instrument." Governor Hamilton's report added that "they did not abuse him or his men, but forced 2 to stay and one Robert Bibby voluntarily took on with them . . . They said they had burnt several vessels, among them two or three belonging to these Islands, particularly the day before a sloop belonging to Antego [Antigua], one McGill owner."

The pirates held him for eight hours, then let him go, along with the rest of his crew and their sloop. He told Hamilton that Blackbeard's flagship carried thirty-six guns and was very full of men. In fact he estimated that Blackbeard now had a crew of three hundred, and they had no shortage of provisions. Bostock added two more snippets. One was that he heard the pirates say they planned to sail to Samana Cay in Hispaniola (now in the Dominican Republic), where they would careen their ships, then lie in wait for a Spanish flotilla that they heard was due to sail past with a substantial payroll on board.

Bostock also claimed that "they had much gold dust aboard." Pirate gold was the stuff to fuel the imagination of any red-blooded treasure hunter, but from later accounts it seemed as if someone was teasing the captive with tall stories. Certainly *La Concorde* might well have been transporting a small amount of gold dust when she was captured—it was a common enough thing for slavers to pick up on the West African coast. Unfortunately, there is little to suggest that this formed a substantial part of the cargo, as Captain Dosset never mentioned it. It is more likely that if any gold dust was carried, it was a small amount that individual French sailors or officers had been shipping for their own benefit—until the pirates robbed them of it. Like the *Scarborough* encounter, while it makes for a good swashbuckling story, it probably wasn't true.

Finally, Bostock provided a little information on the pirate captain himself, describing "Capt. Tach" as "a tall spare man with a very black beard which he wore very long." This is the first description of Blackbeard we have, and it was this account that first gave the pirate his nickname. The pirate was no longer a man hanging on the coattails of Benjamin Hornigold, or a small-time cutthroat who was more an irritation than a threat to the maritime establishment. He now commanded one of the largest warships in the Americas, he had cut a swathe of destruction through the West Indies, and he was clearly a pirate leader of uncommon ability. The man was also developing a fearsome reputation, which of course was good for business. He now had a nickname that would strike fear into the hearts of ship captains from Newfoundland to the Spanish Main. In other words, Blackbeard had come of age.

4

Mixing with the Wrong Crowd

N ew Providence was more than a pirate haven. For five years it was a place where the flotsam and jetsam of the Caribbean washed up, an island that attracted some of the most unsavory people in the Americas. It also served as a finishing school for pirates, where seamen like Blackbeard could learn their trade, then set themselves up on their own account. Plunder and slaves could be bought and sold there, captured ships could be refitted and recrewed, and successful voyages could be celebrated in an orgy of riotous indulgence. Above all, it was a place where pirate captains could meet, exchange, swap intelligence, and plan even darker deeds for the future.

Blackbeard wasn't the first pirate to call New Providence home, but he was one of the last. The list of cutthroats who spent part of these years drinking rum on the beach at Nassau reads like a list of the most notorious cutthroats of the Golden Age of Piracy. Most of them knew one another, and in later years when the pirate scourge spread to the West African coast and the Indian Ocean beyond, it was hard to imagine that all this mayhem began on that palm-fringed subtropical beach in the Bahamas. The Golden Age may well have ended on Africa's Gold Coast, at the gallows beneath Cape Coast Castle, or in a festering native village in the Madagascar jungle. However, it began much earlier, when an English pirate with a great sense of timing combed the Bahamas for somewhere to stash his loot.

The phrase "the Golden Age of Piracy" was something dreamed up by historians, a convenient shorthand for a few years, a decade at the most, when piracy appeared to be rampant. To colonial American and British merchants it must have seemed that law and order had broken down and that nobody was safe once their home port slipped over the horizon. As we shall see, it should really have been called the silver age of piracy. It was Spanish silver that first drew would-be pirates to the Bahamas, and it was this plunder that attracted the dregs of the Caribbean to the Nassau waterfront.

On July 24, 1715, a Spanish treasure fleet (or *flota*) threaded its way past the Morro Castle, which stood sentinel over the great port of Havana, and then, raising sail, set a course to the northeast. Few knew it at the time, but this *flota* was one of the last of its kind, a pale shadow of the great treasure fleets of the past that since 1526 had carried the wealth of the Americas from the New World to the old. For two centuries the Spanish ran a highly organized transatlantic convoy system, with two annual sailings between Seville and the Spanish Americas. The New Spain fleet left Spain in April, bound for what is now Mexico, while the Tierra Firme fleet followed in August and sailed to the Spanish Main—the Caribbean coast of South America. After collecting a cargo of Mexican silver, oriental spices, porcelain, and other luxury goods, the fleet wintered in Vera Cruz, then sailed to Havana the following summer.

Meanwhile, the Tierra Firme fleet wintered in Cartagena after collecting a huge cargo of silver from Porto Bello. This represented a fifth of Peru's annual silver production, hacked out of the mines of Potosi and Cuzco by slaves, then transported by ship and mule to Panama and then across the isthmus to Porto Bello. This cargo belonged to the Spanish crown, their quinta, or fifth, a tax that the government claimed as its own. This flow of silver made Spain a superpower in the sixteenth century, and the king came to rely on the safe arrival of his annual Peruvian income.

While the bulk of this cargo consisted of seventy-pound silver ingots, the rest was shipped as coins—the "pieces of eight" so beloved of pirate fiction. These were minted in Peru and to a lesser extent in Mexico, the majority being shipped in the form of eight-*real* coins—hence the pirate nickname. Each of these contained an ounce of the purest silver and was stamped with the emblems of the Spanish king. Before the Tierra Firme fleet sailed north to join their colleagues in Havana, they filled any remaining cargo space with emeralds from Colombia, small quantities of gold from Venezuela, and pearls from Equador. Gold coins were produced, too, although in significantly fewer numbers than their silver counterparts. One *escudo* was equal to sixteen *reals*, and like the silver coins, most were shipped as eight-*escudo* coins. These were known as *doblons*, giving rise to another much-loved pirate coin. This meant that each gold "doubloon" was worth sixteen silver "pieces of eight."

In addition to carrying the king's share of New World production, the fleet reserved space for private cargoes—the worldly wealth of people who had made their fortune in the New World and now planned to return home to Spain while they still had the health to enjoy their riches. In such a highly regulated business, every royal ingot of silver, every private gold "finger" bar, and each shoebox-sized coin chest was weighed, labeled, and recorded in duplicate—one set of ledgers traveling with the fleet and the other remaining behind on dry land for safekeeping. This is what the ships commanded by General Don Antonio de Echeverz y Zubiza carried in their holds as they slipped out of Havana that late July morning.

Six of the ships were from the Tierra Firme fleet, four were from the New Spain fleet, and two more were prizes, Portuguese ships unlucky enough to run into the Tierra Firme fleet off the Spanish Main. Unlike the cumbersome *galleones* of the previous century, most of these vessels were either well-built frigates or else smaller support and supply vessels. They must have made a brave and impressive display as they headed up the Florida Straits and into the Bahamas Channel, where they picked up the easterly wind that should have helped them on their way. Instead the storm clouds gathered on the starboard beam, and the sky became dark with ominous purple streaks over the cays of the Bahamas.

Don Antonio ordered his ships to make sail, cramming on all the canvas they could to clear the narrow channel before the gathering storm broke upon them. It was too late. By noon on July 30 the fleet was struck by a howling easterly wind, which soon rose to storm force and beyond.

The fleet had been caught in the path of a hurricane. The winds and seas rose to a crescendo, and by midnight all hope had gone. One by one the ships were driven against the reefs fringing Florida's eastern shore, and as the hulls broke apart cargo and crew fell into the raging sea.

Dawn revealed the true scale of the disaster. All but one of the dozen ships that had left Havana a week before had been dashed to pieces. The survivor, a forty-gun French fifth-rate called *Grifón*, limped back to Havana with the news. The Spanish wasted little time sending out rescue parties, and amazingly they found that almost fifteen hundred sailors had somehow survived the hurricane. While some had set up camp on the beach, others had managed to reach the safety of the Spanish town of St. Augustine, 120 miles to the north.

In Havana, Governor Corioles then set about recovering the treasure. A salvage expedition was organized, complete with a team of native divers, professional Spanish divers with a diving bell and a handful of survivors to tell them where to look. The man in charge of the operation, Don Juan de Hoyo Solórzano, wisely insisted that a company of soldiers were added to the list, charged with guarding whatever was recovered. It took weeks of backbreaking work to recover the silver, and by the end of the year the salvors had gathered a substantial pile of treasure. Unfortunately news of the disaster and the salvage effort had leaked out, and others were preparing to play their part in the saga.

In November 1715 Lord Archibald Hamilton, governor of Jamaica, sent the former privateering ships *Bathsheba* and *Eagle* out on an antipiracy patrol. Captain Henry Jennings was placed in charge of the expedition, a man who clearly had his own plans for the voyage. He recruited three more former privateering sloops, then set off for the Spanish salvage camp on the Florida coast.

Sometime in the last week of November a force of three hundred men stormed the camp, drove off the sixty soldiers guarding it, and made away with all the treasure they could carry, some 60,000 pieces of eight. On the way back to Port Royal, Jennings stopped and plundered a Spanish merchantman, recovering enough treasure to double his haul. We don't know how much the governor knew of Jennings's plan, but he certainly seemed to turn a blind eye to the celebrations when the men returned with their loot. Jennings raided the camp again on January 26, 1716, netting another 120,000 pieces of eight. When the authorities in

Havana lodged an official complaint with Governor Hamilton, the British official promised to send an expedition to suppress the freebooters, but the Spanish suspected he was actually the sponsor of Jennings and his men.

They sent more troops to guard the salvors, and by April Don Juan de Hoyo was able to report that his men had recovered four-fifths of all the treasure that could be found. That summer two large Spanish men-of-war carried the recovered treasure to Spain, augmented by enough from a reserve fund in Havana to make up for the fifth still lying in the sand and rocks of the Florida coast. By all accounts that still left some 250,000 pieces of eight waiting to be recovered. When news of Jennings's successes spread, everyone wanted their share of the treasure. As soon as the Spaniards packed up their diving bells and went home, a swarm of British treasure hunters descended on the coast, eager for a share of the plunder.

Treasure fever swept the Caribbean. As Captain Belchin of HMS *Diamond* recalled in a letter written from Jamaica, "There have been at least twenty sloops fitted for the wrecks, and if I had stayed a week longer I do not believe I should have kept enough men to bring the ship home. I lost ten in two days before I sailed, being all mad to go a-wrecking as they put it." Henry Jennings was sent back to Florida to keep an eye on this free-for-all on behalf of the Jamaican governor, but by then he had already crossed the line. In a document dated April 22, 1716, it was claimed by a Nassau resident that "Captain Jennings arrived at Providence and brought in a prize of a French ship mounting 32 guns which he had taken in the Bay of Hounds, carrying a very rich cargo of European goods for the Spanish trade. He then went in said ship to the wrecks where he served as governor and guard ship." The governor's man had turned pirate. It also seems clear that by the spring of 1716 Jennings had already established a base in the Bahamas.

The Spanish didn't just complain about Jennings to the governor of Jamaica; the Spanish ambassador raised the matter in London. By April, Governor Hamilton received orders to stop the plundering of Spanish property.

As it was in full peace, and contrary to all justice and right, that this fact was committed, they [Jennings and his men] were soon made sensible that the government at Jamaica would not suffer them to go unpunished, much less protect them, therefore they saw a necessity of shifting for themselves; so to make bad worse, they went to sea again, though not without disposing of their cargo to good advantage, and furnishing themselves with ammunition, provisions, etc. and thus made desperate, they turned pirates, robbing not the Spaniards only, but their own countrymen, and any nation they could lay their hands on.

In short, Jennings and his fellow privateersmen turned salvors could no longer expect the tacit support of Governor Hamilton in Jamaica. Privateering was no longer a legal option, and now treasure hunting was being ruled out as an alternative. The former privateers voted with their feet, and after clearing Port Royal of whatever goods they might find useful, they quit the port before the authorities could stop them. These men and their fellows already hard at work trawling the reefs off the Florida coast needed to find a new base: "The rovers being now pretty strong, they consulted together about getting some place of retreat, where they might lodge their wealth, clean and repair their ships, and make themselves a kind of abode. They were not long in resolving, but fixed upon the island of Providence, the most considerable of the Bahama islands, lying in a latitude of about 24° North, and to the eastward of the Spanish Florida."

We have already seen how the island attracted a small number of pirates and fugitives during the years following the end of the war in 1713. These included the baymen of Campeche driven from their logwooding camps by the Spanish, most of whom sought refuge in New Providence. The governors of Barbados and Jamaica were aware of a growing problem in the Bahamas as early as April 1714, but nothing was done about it. As the maritime historian Peter Earle said, "Among these masterless men there were 'three setts of pirates' led by one Benjamin Hornigold, soon to be well known but as yet no great threat since these pirates only operated from small open boats with crews of twenty-five in each." These "three setts of pirates" would soon be joined by a fresh wave of treasure salvors, and their numbers would grow until the island became the greatest pirate haven in the Americas.

Another document, this time a statement filed by one of the original New Providence settlers, sheds some light on these first tentative steps toward a pirate colony in the Bahamas. It also illustrates the relationship between Jennings and Hornigold.

In November last [1715], Benjamin Hornigold arrived in Providence in the sloop *Mary* of Jamaica belonging to Augustine Golding which Hornigold took upon the Spanish coast. Soon after taking it he took a Spanish ship loaded with dry goods and sugar, which cargo he disposed of at Providence. But the Spanish sloop was taken from him by Captain Jennings of the sloop Bathsheba of Jamaica. In January, Hornigold left Providence in said sloop *Mary*, having on board 140 men, six guns and eight pattereros [swivel guns], and soon after returning with another Spanish sloop from the Florida coast. After he fitted out said sloop at Providence he sent Golding's sloop back to Jamaica to be returned to the owners and in March last sailed to Providence in the Spanish sloop, having aboard 200 men, but bound on a secret mission.

This means that by the start of 1716, Benjamin Hornigold was no longer a small-time privateersman turned cutthroat. He was now a full-fledged pirate, with enough crewmen at his disposal to start a full-scale war. The capture of the *Mary* also runs contrary to his later claims that he attacked only Spanish or French targets. Given the ways pirate ships were run, it was probably his crew that forced him to capture the Jamaican sloop against his better judgment. His return of the vessel less than three months later suggests that he was already trying to impress upon Governor Hamilton that he was no pirate, only a privateer who hadn't stopped fighting. The account also shows that Jennings had become the de facto pirate chief in New Providence. Even though Hornigold was gradually rising to the top, power still lay with Jennings and his salvors. After all, they were the ones with the plunder.

We know very little about Hornigold's activities in 1716, apart from Captain Johnson's assertion that Blackbeard had become a member of his crew by the middle of the summer. If, however, we assume Blackbeard signed on with Hornigold at least six months before, then he could well have participated in the attacks mentioned above. Certainly he was present in the Bahamas during the summer of 1716, when the islands became a bustling treasure-hunting center, with sloops of salvors descending on the Spanish shipwrecks from Jamaica, Barbados, and the Antilles. Inevitably, when these men tired of trawling for sunken treasure, they then turned to piracy.

On June 3 Governor Spotswood of Virginia complained to the Council of Trade in London that pirates were taking over the Bahamas. He imprisoned Captain Forbes, who as one of the original salvors had helped drive the Spaniards from their camp, before he was involved in the illegal capture of a French merchantman. While he was prepared to take a firm stance against what he saw as unsanctioned looting, he wasn't completely immune to the treasure-hunting bug himself. On June 15, 1716, he ordered Captain Harry Beverly of the sloop *Virgin* of Virginia to visit the sites of the shipwrecks and recover what he could of the Spanish silver. While this could be dressed up as a way of protecting Spanish property, it could also be interpreted as plain looting.

Governor Hamilton of Jamaica sponsored similar expeditions— attempts to seize some of the treasure before the illegal salvors picked the wrecks clean. As one report put it, "The English plunder under the pretext of clearing the coasts of pirates . . . [but] against all equity have been diving for the silver which was lost on the Flota at Palmar [now Fort Pierce]."

By 1717 most of the readily recoverable sunken treasure had been plundered, and the bulk of the salvors had signed on as pirates. However, a few remained and continued to work on the wreck sites, and when the Spanish returned in early 1718 they found that the British salvors had set up a fortified camp in the dunes. A Spanish attack was repulsed, but they returned with reinforcements that summer, and the salvage camp was overrun. In September 1718, when Blackbeard was in North Carolina, the Spanish returned to Havana in triumph with five captured sloops, eighty-six British prisoners, and ninety-eight slaves. The Spanish built their own heavily armed fortified camp, ending any further thoughts of salvage.

With the end of the salvage operation, Henry Jennings seems to have lost his power base. The royal proclamation issued by the British on September 5, 1717, came as something of a godsend for him, as it gave all former pirates the offer of a full pardon if they surrendered within a calendar year. Consequently, when Woodes Rogers arrived to take up the post of governor of the Bahamas, Jennings was one of the first to welcome him and to sign up for the pardon. The privateer turned treasure hunter and cutthroat was one of the few pirates who quit while they were ahead. He retired to Bermuda with his remaining plunder, where he ended his days as something of a local celebrity—his retirement fund unwillingly provided by the Spanish crown.

Although few could have imagined it in early 1717, the days of New Providence as a pirate den were numbered. Blackbeard left the islands in the late spring of 1717, never to return. While Benjamin Hornigold returned to the islands the following November, his pirating days were over. There were others, however, who still used the islands as a base, and who would continue the island's association with piracy until the bitter end. Some of these characters would cross Blackbeard's path in the next year or so. Others would have their future careers shaped by his activities and by the way the authorities reacted to the threat Blackbeard posed. Most of them would have known him, and some would even have shipped with him as either privateers or pirates before he set up "on his own account." In fact, one of the most fascinating things about the pirates of the Golden Age is how they interrelated. Some served with a captain for a year or so, then split off to form their own team. Prime examples are Blackbeard and Sam Bellamy, who were once both shipmates of Benjamin Hornigold, and "Calico" Jack Rackam, who once served under Charles Vane.

A common way this happened was accidental, when a pirate would capture a prize, and members of its crew would volunteer to join the pirates. One of these volunteers would rise above the rest and would eventually set up as a pirate on his own account. The process would then be repeated when another prize was captured. An example of this kind of chain begins with Captain Charles Winter, a die-hard Bahamian pirate who captured a Jamaican sloop in early 1718 off the Bahamas. The sloop's first mate, Edward England, volunteered to join Winter, and when Woodes Rogers arrived in the Bahamas, England set up on his own. In 1718 he captured a ship off the West African coast that yielded Howel Davis as a pirate volunteer, although Davis immediately broke off on his own, but was later captured and imprisoned in Barbados.

On his release Davis went a-pirating with a new crew, which included Thomas Anstis and Walter Kennedy. In early 1720 Davis captured a slaver off Guinea, and Bartholomew Roberts volunteered to join Davis's crew, creating a new link in the chain. Kennedy later served with Roberts, while Anstis broke away to become a pirate captain in his own right. John Phillips was captured by Anstis off Newfoundland, and his death in a prisoner revolt meant that he cheated the gallows in what was to become one of the last pirate executions of the Golden Age. A Hollywood scriptwriter would be hard-pressed to invent a sequence like this—a string of pirate captains recruiting fresh blood who then repeated the process when they became captain. This also means that a link can be traced from men like

Hornigold to the last pirates to hang for their crimes eight years after Davis folded away his black flag.

Others teamed up to hunt in consort with each other—Blackbeard and Bonnet (although the "gentleman captain" had little say in the matter), or Edward England and Bartholomew Roberts, Edmund Williams and Sam Bellamy, the French pirate Olivier "La Bouse" ("The Buzzard") and Howel Davis all operated in this way during their careers. All of these men apart from Roberts spent part of their piratical careers in New Providence. You could almost call them the "Bahamas set." Historian Marcus Rediker has identified some twenty pirates who began their careers in the Bahamas, and has followed often quite complex links among these men and their crews.

The result is a pirate web, with Hornigold and to a lesser extent Jennings at its center. At the outer edges can be traced the pirates who operated well into the late 1720s, or who moved to other pirate hunting grounds thousands of miles from New Providence. In almost every case some connection can be traced back to those early days in the Bahamas, demonstrating just what an important part the islands played in the outbreak of global piracy known as the Golden Age.

It is difficult to work out the scale of the pirate crisis. Exactly how many pirates were based in the Bahamas before Governor Rogers appeared to clear up the pirate den in the summer of 1718? During those five years between 1714 and 1718, did pirate numbers grow steadily, or did the men already there try to limit the competition? As we have seen, Hornigold was not necessarily the first pirate to work out of New Providence, but he was the first to be mentioned by name. By the late summer of 1715 other names began to appear: Captain Barrow, Thomas Cocklyn, and Captain West are all known to have joined Hornigold in New Providence soon after the hurricane of 1715 swept over the Bahamas. All three men were former privateers, and as they were just the captains at the top of the piratical pile, then hundreds of others must have arrived to form their crews.

In the spring of 1714 the British official line was that only an insignificant handful of pirates used the Bahamas as a base. Clearly that view needed some revision, as did the notion that these pirates only had small *jollyboats* (longboats) and *piraguas* (native canoes) at their disposal. Then came the new wave of treasure salvors, men like Jennings who slipped easily from salvage to piracy. As the number of prizes increased, so, too, did the number of pirate ships, as captured sloops were converted into pirate vessels, crewed from the growing pool of ready manpower, then sent out to sea again. Piracy must have seemed like a rapidly expanding business in those days, and as the number of attacks increased, the British and Spanish slowly began to realize the seriousness of the problem.

Both nations increased the strength of their naval patrols. The Spanish maintained a small flotilla of guard ships, mainly sloops little bigger than the pirate ships they were sent out to hunt down. They also had a handful of larger warships of the *Armada de la Guardia* at their disposal, based in Havana. These were primarily charged with providing an escort for the Spanish treasure *flotas*. However, this force could also be used for expeditions against pirates or other interlopers who were seen as a threat to the Spanish overseas empire. This *armada* had the strength to crush the pirates in the Bahamas if the Spanish could organize themselves sufficiently to launch a full-scale attack.

Unfortunately for Spain, the islands were officially the dominions of the British crown, and any such attack could have been construed as an act of war. Instead the *Armada de la Guardia* occupied itself by driving the logwooders from the Bay of Campeche, leaving Spanish shipping at the mercy of the Bahamian pirates. As we have seen, all their actions did was to increase the problem, as most of the logwood cutters escaped to the Bahamas, where they immediately turned to piracy. The weakness of Spanish power in the Americas was highlighted by their inability to protect the wrecks of the 1715 fleet and the Spanish divers sent to salvage them.

The British were in a far stronger military position, as they already maintained strong garrisons in all the major British-held islands in the Caribbean, and colonial militias backed by the occasional regiment of regular troops helped protect the British ports of colonial America. The Royal Navy was undergoing a round of postwar cutbacks at the time, but it still maintained a relatively powerful presence in American waters. A document issued by the Admiralty Office dated May 1, 1715, listed no fewer than nineteen warships in the region, although these were scattered from Newfoundland to the Spanish Main.

The fifty-gun fourth-rate HMS *Southampton* was based in Newfoundland, but was in the process of returning to Britain. Her relief, HMS *Dragon*, was still in British waters, as were the replacements for the forty-two-gun fifth-rate and two twenty-four-gun frigates that formed half of the fleet based on "the Jamaica Station." The forty-two-gun fifth-rates HMS *Roebuck* and HMS *Diamond* and the sloops HMS *Jamaica* and HMS *Tryal*, which were left behind in Jamaica, were hard-pressed to keep their crews during the treasure-hunting stampede later that summer.

Eight other small frigates and brigs were scattered throughout British possessions in the Americas, the majority having a limited brief of defending the port they were stationed in, or providing an escort for local coastal shipping. Boston, New York, Williamsburg, and Baltimore all had small guard ships of this type, while Barbados boasted a slightly larger force of three ships, including a forty-two-gun fifth-rate, as this small force had the additional responsibility of protecting British possessions throughout the Lesser Antilles. Only the Royal Navy force on the Jamaica Station had the strength to attack New Providence, but no such orders ever came—at least until the summer of 1718.

By 1716, the time Blackbeard appeared on the scene, Jennings and his salvors had already established themselves in New Providence, and fresh names had begun to appear, including Captain Paul Williams and the French captain La Bouse. The report of Captain Musson written in March 1717 added the names of Thomas Burgiss and Captain White to the list, who together with Hornigold and Blackbeard commanded a total of five ships and 360 men. This suggests an average of 70 men per pirate ship, most of which were sloops carrying between six and ten guns apiece.

Within a year the names of Charles Vane, John Martel, James Fife, Charles Bellamy, Edward England, Nicholas Brown, and others could be added, as could Blackbeard's former shipmate on Hornigold's sloop, Captain Porter. Another was Blackbeard's own crewman Richard Richards, who was given command of a prize during the 1717 cruise off Delaware and was returned to command by Blackbeard the following year, remaining with him until the pirate moved to North Carolina in the fall of 1718. Others such as "Calico" Jack Rackam spent time on the islands during this period but were raised to command only after Woodes Rogers established control over the Bahamas and the remaining pirates fled from the islands.

As for the total number of pirates in the Bahamas, several figures have been suggested, but most historians agree that no more than one thousand to two thousand were active at any one time between 1715 and 1725. In 1717 the Philadelphia merchant James Logan estimated that fifteen hun-

"Calico" Jack Rackam, the man who assumed control of Charles Vane's ship and crew. Rackam accepted a second offer of a pardon, then returned to piracy, only to be captured off Jamaica, where he was hanged for his crimes.

dred were active in American waters, of whom eight hundred were based in the Bahamas. Other contemporaries claim that at the time of Blackbeard and a little after, some two thousand were operating across the globe. Of course by that stage the diaspora from the Bahamas had already started, and many of these men were operating off West Africa or in the Indian Ocean.

As Marcus Rediker put it, "These figures seem broadly accurate. From records that describe the activities of pirate ships and from reports or projections of crew sizes, it appears that 1,500 to 2,000 pirates sailed the seas between 1716 and 1718, 1,800 to 2,400 between 1719 and 1722, and 1,000 in 1723, declining rapidly to 500 in 1724, to fewer than 200 by 1725 and 1726. In all some 4,000 went, as they called it, upon the account." Therefore, if we take James Logan's figures as broadly accurate, then some eight hundred pirates were based in New Providence in 1717, when Blackbeard launched his career.

While most pirate ships would have been sloops, a handful of slightly larger vessels such as brigs or "great sloops" might have been available,

Blackbeard, from a Dutch-language version of Captain Johnson's History *published in 1725. This depiction is closer to the original one given by Johnson in 1724, who describes Blackbeard as wearing a fur cap. In later versions this was changed to "hat."*

with an average crew of around seventy to one hundred men apiece. It therefore becomes apparent that the whole pirate crisis of the Golden Age of Piracy was caused by probably no more than a dozen small pirate ships, commanded by the pirate captains mentioned above. Seldom have so few seamen had such a disproportionate influence on American colonial history, or left such a lasting impact through the subsequent retelling of their exploits. By 1717 it was clear to the British authorities that the Bahamas lay at the center of this piratical activity, and that if the islands could be denied to these cutthroats then the waters of colonial America would be considerably safer. That was when the Bristol-born former privateer Woodes Rogers was called in to deal with the problem. The subsequent loss of New Providence as a pirate base would play a major part in the shaping of Blackbeard's activities during the latter part of 1718.

King William III had already revised the English laws that dealt with piracy—Scotland had and still has its own separate legal system, and its laws had already been updated. Before, all pirate trials were the responsibility of the Admiralty, and captured pirates had to be shipped to London to stand trial. William's new antipiracy laws of 1700 gave individual governors, major landowners, and officers of the Crown much greater powers, enabling them to hold trials within their own area. Legal loopholes were removed, and it became far easier to condemn pirates on evidence that today would be considered insufficient or inadmissible.

This decentralization gave men like Woodes Rogers and Alexander Spotswood all the legal muscle they needed to hunt down, convict, and execute pirates on their own authority. That was the legal stick used in all the pirate trials of the period, and the highly publicized trials and mass executions that followed gradually whittled down the number of pirate crews that remained at large. Without these laws, the pirate threat could never have been eradicated. However, an even more effective method was the carrot, the promise of full pardons to any pirates who surrendered to the British authorities.

On September 5, 1717, the British king George I signed a "Proclamation for Supressing Pyrates." It is a very interesting document, as it began by claiming that the Bahamian pirates "committed divers Pyracies and Robberies on the High-Seas, in the West-Indies, or adjoining to our Plantations" from June 24, 1715. That was the same day the Spanish *flota* of 1715 left Havana—a curious date to choose. Evidently the British authorities saw the attacks by Henry Jennings and his companions as the ones that marked the start of the pirate scourge.

The proclamation then came up with a novel way of dealing with the cutthroats.

> We have thought fit . . . to Issue this our Royal Proclamation; and we do hereby promise, and declare, that in Case any of the said Pyrates, shall on or before the 5th of September, in the Year of our Lord 1718, surrender him or themselves, to one of our Principal Secretaries of State in Great Britain or Ireland, or to any Governor or Deputy Governor of any of our Plantations beyond the Seas; every such Pyrate and Pyrates so surrendering him, or themselves, as aforesaid, shall have our gracious Pardon, of and for such, his or their Pyracy, or Pyracies, by him or them committed before the fifth of January next ensuing.

This was a pretty sizable carrot. Quite ingeniously, it included the time-sensitive proviso that the immunity only covered pirates who stopped their attacks within four months. As copies of the proclamation only reached Jamaica in early December 1717 and the Bahamas a week or two later, the pirates didn't have much time to make up their minds. In case they thought they might be able to continue as they had before, an extra-large stick followed the carrot: "We do hereby strictly command and charge all our Admirals, Captains and other Officers at Sea, and all our Governors and Commanders . . . to seize and take such of the Pyrates, who shall refuse or neglect to surrender themselves accordingly . . . We do hereby further declare, that in Case any Person or Persons, on, or after the 6th Day of September 1718, shall discover or seize, any one or more of the said Pyrates . . . shall have and receive a Reward."

This blood money was set at £100 for a captain, £40 for a quartermaster, master, or gunner, and £20 each for the rest of the pirate crew. That was just for "causing or procuring such discovery or seizure " of the pirates. If one or more of the crew turned their captain in themselves, the reward soared to £200. This was something of a masterstroke, as not only did it encourage maritime bounty hunters, but it also made pirate captains worry about the loyalty of their crew. This combination of stick and carrot was matched by a policy of encouraging colonial governors and naval captains to take a tougher stance. After the deadline passed, the authorities would be actively encouraged to hunt down and capture any pirates who remained at large.

When copies of the proclamation reached New Providence, pirate leaders like Benjamin Hornigold and Henry Jennings were placed in a quandary. They realized that this offer was unlikely to be repeated, and that being seen to support the drive against piracy might have its advantages. Having just returned to the island after being deposed by his crew, Hornigold saw the offer of a pardon as a means to help him recover from this indignity and regain his position as one of the leading figures in New Providence. While Jennings probably had no plans other than retirement with his plunder intact, he understood that his position would be helped if he could encourage most of his fellow pirates to follow his example and turn themselves in.

> They sent for those who were out a cruising, and called a general council, but there was so much noise and clamour, that nothing could be agreed on; some were for fortifying the island, to stand upon their own terms, and treating with the government on the foot of a commonwealth; others were

also for strengthening the island for their own security, but were not strenuous for these punctilios, so that they might have a general pardon, without being obliged to make any restitution, and to retire with all their effects, to the neighbouring British plantations.

This idea of sticking together as a pirate "commonwealth" and bargaining with the British authorities from a position of strength was completely impractical, as that would only invite the British to launch a full-scale expedition that would destroy New Providence and everyone in it. The key point for many was restitution—if they could surrender and then walk away with their plunder intact, then they would happily turn their back on piracy. Inevitably, this undermined the will of the die-hards, as the fortified pirate commonwealth idea would only work if the majority agreed to stand together at the barricades. Henry Jennings spoke in favor of accepting the pardon, and he managed to convince approximately 150 others to follow his lead.

Captain Charles Vane, the leader of the Bahamian die-hards, whose men joined Blackbeard on Ocracoke Island during September 1718. He was subsequently marooned, captured, and then hanged.

He was just in time, as in March HMS *Phoenix* sailed into New Providence's harbor, and her commander, Captain Vincent Pearce, was rowed ashore, hoping to convince the pirates to accept the offer. Surprisingly, the naval officer received a cordial welcome, and Jennings and Hornigold were among the first to sign. By the time the *Phoenix* pulled up her anchor and headed back to New York on April 6, 1718, Captain Pearce had some 209 signatures of surrender and had issued provisional pardons to all those who signed. Before he left he told the assembled rogues that he would soon be followed by a governor, a man capable of establishing British rule in the islands and of wreaking vengeance on those who refused to surrender.

Still, a significant group of die-hard pirates refused to acquiesce. The situation must have been a strange one in the months following Captain Pearce's departure. The traditional leaders of the Bahamian pirates had already submitted to British authority, which nullified any authority they might have with the hard-liners. Inevitably a new champion arose, whose antiauthoritarian stance and rhetoric threatened to rally many of the undecided pirates to the die-hards. This champion was Charles Vane, who swore that "while he was in the Harbour, he would suffer no other Governor than himself."

Vane served as a piratical salvor under Jennings during 1716, and most probably participated in the raids on the Spanish salvage camp on the Florida coast that year. By early 1718 Vane had command of his own sloop, called the *Ranger*, and made his first independent cruise in April, capturing the Bermudan sloops *Diamond* and *William & Martha* off Rum Cay in the Bahamas. He pillaged and burned the *Diamond*, but after plundering the *William & Martha* later that day, he let her go. In a deposition to Governor Bennett in Bermuda, her commander, Edward North, claimed that Vane's men had beaten him and his crew, and tortured a sailor by tying him to the bowsprit, then sticking burning matches in his eyes and a cocked pistol in his mouth. The crew of the *Diamond* who accompanied North back to Bermuda told a similar story, claiming that Vane had partially hanged one of the sailors, then slashed him with a cutlass until pulled away by his pirate shipmates. Charles Vane was developing a reputation.

He then took a small French merchantman and brought her back to New Providence as a prize, having missed the visit by Captain Pearce of the *Phoenix*. Vane categorically refused to countenance surrender, and laid plans to signal his defiance to the world. While the hard-liners joined his crew, most of the remainder were talked into accepting the British offer. Vane and his minority of supporters continued to fly the flag of rebellion. The argument rumbled on until late July, when the new British governor was sighted approaching New Providence, accompanied by a powerful squadron of Royal Navy warships. That was when Vane made his play, a dramatic gesture that was the stuff of swashbuckling fiction.

As a former privateer captain himself, the new governor, Woodes Rogers, understood the pirates who were watching him enter their lair. He deliberately laid on a show of strength. His flagship was the former East Indiaman *Delicia*, accompanied by two sloops, *Shark* and *Buck*, transporting a company of British soldiers between them. Naval muscle was provided by two warships, the thirty-gun fifth-rate HMS *Milford* and the twenty-gun sixth-rate frigate HMS *Rose*. The force arrived off New Providence shortly before nightfall on July 26, so Rogers decided to delay his landing until the following morning. Nassau Harbor had two entrances, on either side of the cay that is now called Paradise Island. In case of trouble, Rogers split his force in two, deploying his ships so that they blocked both entrances.

With little sign of impending trouble, he expected a peaceful night. Unfortunately, Charles Vane had other ideas. While the majority of the island's eight hundred or so reformed cutthroats enjoyed their last night of piratical freedom in the customary manner, Vane and some ninety supporters quietly rowed out to his sloop the *Ranger*. His crew then prepared for action, double-shotting their dozen guns and readying the sails for a swift departure. He also sent a small group to the French prize he had captured two months before.

Vane had already implemented part of his plan, having converted the prize into a fireship. Powder stocks had been lain aboard, the guns were already loaded, and flammable materials had been stowed in the hold. All his pirates had left to do was open the gunpowder barrels and lay powder trails across the deck, then douse the sails and combustible material piled on deck with rum or some other highly inflammable accelerant. When they signaled everything was ready, Vane made his move.

Both ships cut their anchor cables and made sail, aiming for the western entrance of the harbor, which ensured that the prevailing wind was blowing toward Rogers's ships HMS *Rose*, the sloop *Shark*, and possibly the former Indiaman *Delicia*. Vane gave the order for his men on the fireship to set the French-built prize alight, then rescued her skeleton crew before tucking the *Ranger* in behind the burning vessel. As the flames rose above the masthead on the fireship, her double-shotted guns began to fire off to either side, adding to the confusion.

The revels on the shore must have come to an abrupt halt as Hornigold and Jennings watched aghast as Vane demonstrated just how audacious he could be. The British ships had no option but to cut their own cables and try to get out of the way. This was exactly what Vane hoped would happen, and as the British ships raced to man their guns, Vane's sloop shot past them, firing off broadsides to port and starboard. As the fireship foundered amid a sea covered in burning debris, Vane veered away to the northwest and disappeared into the darkness. It was just about as spectacular a departure from New Providence as any pirate could wish for.

Woodes Rogers and his men spent the rest of the night sorting out the mess and keeping a wary eye out for any repeat performance. They need not have bothered, as the remaining pirates would prove as troublesome as newborn lambs. Early the following morning Rogers ordered boats to be lowered, and he was rowed ashore under the cover of the navy's guns. Hornigold and Jennings fell over themselves to welcome Rogers, lining their pirate crews up to form some semblance of an honor guard.

"The pirate captains . . . drew up their crews in two lines, reaching from the waterside to the fort, the Governor and other officers marching between them; in the meantime, they being under arms, made a running fire over his head." Captain Pomeroy of the sloop *Shark* wrote, "Governor Rogers made his entry, and was received with a great deal of seeming joy by those that stile themselves marooners." In all, about seven hundred pirates would have been on hand to welcome Woodes Rogers, but for all the efforts of Hornigold and Jennings, this colorful pageant had already been overshadowed by Vane's dramatic escape. We shall return to Woodes Rogers and the pirates later, but for the moment we need to follow Vane on his desperate voyage.

Captain Johnson puts the clash between Rogers and Vane at some time before May 1718, and he even dated Rogers's arrival as being in May or June 1718, some two months before the dates given in the historical record. Rogers only set sail from Britain on April 11, and the voyage to Jamaica routinely took three months in those days. This means that his account of Vane's last cruise used elements from his first sortie in the spring of 1718. The sequence of events in his "Life of Captain Vane" is therefore suspect. However, we can build a timeline from other sources.

For instance, we know Vane fled from New Providence on the night of July 26/27, 1718. He was reportedly off Charles Town (Charleston), South Carolina, in late August, and he was supposedly still in Carolina waters a month later. By then the South Carolinians had antipirate patrols at sea, trying to hunt Vane down. While Vane eluded capture, another pirate captain wasn't so lucky, and was trapped by these colonial warships in the Cape Fear River. We shall return to that tale later, but suffice it to say it appears that Vane had probably quit Carolina waters by the time the authorities began looking for him. Most sources claim that the confrontation between Vane and his crew took place about six weeks later, in mid-November, and the hurricane he encountered off Jamaica has been dated to mid-February 1719. We also know when he was taken to Jamaica, and his last days are well enough documented. This framework allows us to tie in Vane's activities with those of Blackbeard, Hornigold, and Rogers.

As Vane made good his escape, Woodes Rogers sent some of his force off in pursuit. Adopting the policy of "set a thief to catch a thief," he even commissioned Benjamin Hornigold as an official pirate hunter, and let him join the chase. Hornigold and Captain Pomeroy of the sloop *Shark* never caught up with the *Ranger*, but they did cross the path of other pirates. Somewhere in the Bahamas or the Bahamas Channel Vane captured a sloop and placed his quartermaster Yeats in charge of her along with fifteen men. The two sloops then headed north to the Carolinas, where they captured a string of ships in quick succession. They "took a ship belonging to Ipswith, one Coggershall commander, laden with logwood," which was released after the pirates destroyed the cargo.

Next came a Barbadian sloop commanded by a Captain Dill, a small ship from Antigua, another from Curacao, and "a large brigantine, Captain Thompson, from guinea [West Africa], with ninety-odd negroes aboard." Vane let all these ships go after plundering them, but kept the slaves, transferring them to Yeats's sloop. It is also likely that Vane kept the slave ship or one of his other prizes, as it is implied that he exchanged his sloop *Ranger* for a larger brigantine at some stage during the late summer. For some reason Yeats took offense at his sloop being used as little more than a tender, and so a few nights later he and his men slipped away to go a-pirating on their own. Captain Johnson claimed that Vane pursued Yeats over the bar into Charles Town Harbor, but unfortunately the city's records make no mention of this. The fate of Yeats is still something of a mystery.

Vane was certainly off Charles Town in late August as he captured two outbound merchant ships. This came close on the heels of a similar performance by Blackbeard, and the South Carolina authorities took a dim view of Vane's activities in their own backyard. However, Vane was wise enough not to linger too long, and instead it seems he worked his way up the coast of the Carolinas toward Virginia, reaching Ocracoke sometime in mid- to late September. It was there that he met up with Blackbeard, and the two pirate captains decided to celebrate the occasion with a weeklong drunken party on the beach of Ocracoke Island.

After about a week Vane and his men upped anchor and headed north again, although it has been claimed they dipped south, plundered two more Carolinian ships, and let them go, telling the crews they planned to head south. Vane then doubled back in the opposite direction to confuse any pursuers. Captain Johnson places them off New York in late October, claiming that "on the 23rd of October, off Long Island, he [Vane] took a small brigantine, bound from Jamaica to Salem . . . and sent her away." It then appears that like most pirates they headed south for the winter, keeping well away from the coast to avoid detection. Captain Johnson added that they went "without seeing or speaking with any other vessel, till the latter end of November." Again, he has them cruising off Newfoundland, when we know they were heading for the Caribbean.

It seems that by this stage Vane's crew were beginning to have their doubts about their captain, as a month would have seemed a long time to go without the chance of plunder, fresh food, or liquor. It seemed that the drought had finally come to an end when on November 23 they came upon a large fat French merchantman, seemingly ripe for plunder.

> Then they fell upon a ship, which 'twas expected would have struck as soon as their black colours were hoisted; but instead of that, she discharged a broadside on the pirate, and hoisted colours, which showed her to be a French man-of-war. Vane desired to have nothing further to say, but trimmed his sails, and stood away from the Frenchman; but Monsieur having a mind to be better informed who he was, set all his sails, and crowded after him. During this chase, the pirates were divided in their resolutions what to do; Vane, the captain, was for making off as fast as he could, alleging the man-of-war was too strong to cope with; but one John Rackam,

who was an officer that had a kind of check upon the captain, rose up in defence of a contrary position, saying that though she had more guns, and a greater weight of metal, they might board her, and then the best boys would carry the day.

As the captain, Vane had the ultimate say when it came to fighting, and Rackam, as the quartermaster, eventually had to back down. The result was that the pirates steered away from the pursuing Frenchman and eventually escaped to safety. While Vane had probably made the right decision, his plunder-starved crew were not willing to let matters rest. Captain Vane had backed down from a fight, and it was inevitable that some of his crew would brand him a coward. Vane was supported by the mate Robert Deal and about fifteen of the crew, but his leading critic, "Calico" Jack Rackam, managed to gain the support of everyone else. As Captain Johnson hinted, Rackam was the quartermaster, a position designed to keep the captain in check.

Rackam turned check into checkmate. He called a vote, and "a resolution was passed against his [Vane's] honour and dignity, branding him with the name of coward, deposing him from the command, and turning him out of the company, with marks of infamy; and with him, all those who did not vote for boarding the French man-of-war." With Vane out of the way, Jack Rackam had little trouble securing the vote and becoming the new captain. The pirate ship was accompanied by a sloop, possibly the Ranger but more likely a prize, and so Rackam decided to allow Vane and his sixteen supporters to take over the smaller vessel. The two pirate groups parted company, and as "Calico" Jack headed toward Jamaica, Vane and his men were left wallowing in their wake, putting the sloop to rights and preparing her for their own piratical cruise. We shall follow Rackam's adventures in a moment, but first we need to remain with Charles Vane.

The encounter with the French man-of-war probably took place off St. Domingue (now Haiti), most likely in the Windward Passage. Vane decided to try his luck in the Gulf of Honduras, some eight hundred miles to the southwest, but instead of heading there directly he followed the Cayman Trench, between Jamaica and Cuba, before turning south. He lingered off Pedro Point on the northwestern tip of Jamaica for two or three days, snapping up a Jamaican sloop and two piraguas (native canoes).

Robert Deal's loyalty was rewarded when Vane gave him command of the sloop, but the two canoes were allowed to continue on their way.

On December 16, 1718, Vane and Deal made landfall in the Gulf of Honduras, somewhere along the coast of what is now Belize. There they came across the Jamaican sloop *Pearl*, commanded by her master, Charles Rowling. The *Pearl* raised sail as soon as the strangers appeared over the horizon, and even fired her guns to warn off the oncoming sloops. The pirates ran up the Jolly Roger and fired at the *Pearl*, at which point Rowling realized that escape was impossible. He hauled down his colors, and the pirates escorted their prize to a nearby island, where they plundered her cargo. Johnson names the island as "Barnacko," which could have been one of several dozen small islands and cays lying off the Belize coast. The pirates captured another Jamaican sloop "going down to the Bay" while they were there, which again suggests that the mystery island was somewhere along the northern coast of the Gulf of Honduras.

In February 1719 Vane and Deal left their island base, but within a few days they were overtaken by what Captain Johnson described as a "violent tornado," but which was more likely to have been a severe tropical storm. The two sloops became separated, and Vane's craft must have lost her mast, as "after two days distress" the storm threw the sloop onto a reef off an uninhabited island. She broke apart, and although Vane made it to the shore, most of his men were drowned in the surf. Again, this mystery island was probably off the coast of what is now Belize, possibly around Lighthouse or Glover Reef, or even the Turneffe Islands. "Vane himself was saved but reduced to great straits, for want of necessaries, having no opportunity to get anything from the wreck. He lived for some weeks and was subsidized by fishermen, who frequented the island with small craft from the main to catch turtles, etc."

The piratical Robinson Crusoe must have been delighted when he saw a Jamaican ship put in to the island for water, and he met the crew on the beach as they came ashore. Unfortunately the vessel was commanded by a former privateer, Captain Holford, who recognized Vane as a wanted pirate. He refused to let Vane step on board, supposedly exclaiming, "Charles, I shan't trust you aboard my ship, unless I carry you a prisoner; for I shall have you caballing my men, knock me on the head, and run away with my ship a-pirating." Vane was left where he was. However, nobody on the next ship to call knew Vane by sight, so he managed to be taken on board. His run of luck ended pretty quickly. This vessel sailed down toward the Gulf of Honduras, and on the way she met Captain Holford's ship heading back north. The two ships heaved to and Holford was invited aboard for dinner. As he was working his way aft he spotted Vane and immediately told the captain who the castaway really was.

Vane was taken prisoner, transferred to Holford's ship, and clapped in irons. By November 1719, a year after he had been deposed by his own crew, Vane was safely locked away in a Jamaican jail. He was duly tried for piracy by a Vice-Admiralty Court held at Spanish Town just outside Kingston on March 22, 1720. Given his dramatic refusal to accept Governor Rogers's pardon twenty months earlier, the outcome was never in any doubt. He was found guilty and hanged at Gallows Point, within sight of Port Royal. His body was then cut down, tarred, and placed in a cage that hung from Gun Cay, as a dire warning to others not to follow in his footsteps.

The message must have been heeded. Captain Vernon, commanding the ships on the Jamaica Station, wrote, "He has been tried, condemned and executed, and is now hanging in chains . . . These punishments have made a wonderful reformation here." A similar fate befell his ally Robert Deal, who Captain Johnson claims ran into a British warship in the Gulf of Honduras soon after he parted company with Vane. He and his handful of men were also taken to Jamaica, where they, too, were tried, convicted, and hanged a few months before Vane arrived. Unfortunately, no records of his trial or execution have yet been found, so Johnson's version of events cannot be confirmed.

Charles Vane wasn't the last of the Bahamian pirates, but he represented the die-hards who refused to give in. Therefore his capture and execution was of considerable importance to the British authorities, as it demonstrated that rebellion didn't pay. However, Vane was just the figurehead of these unrepentant cutthroats who had long since gone their own way, leaving Vane to rebuild his career from scratch. It was "Calico" Jack Rackam who became the new leader of the New Providence hard-liners, so to finish the story we need to return to the point where he and Vane parted company back in late November 1718.

He headed into "the Caribee islands" (the Lesser Antilles) and reportedly captured several small prizes amid the Leeward Islands. By December he was ready to head west, and so he sailed west along the southern coast of Puerto Rico and Hispaniola to reach the promising cruising ground of the

Anne Bonny, one-time consort of Jack Rackam. In August 1720 she helped her partner steal the sloop William *in Nassau Harbor, and she served with him as a full-fledged member of his pirate crew.*

Jamaica Channel. It lay between Morant Point on the eastern tip of Jamaica and Cape Dame Marie in what is now Haiti. He came upon a merchant ship on her way from Madeira to Jamaica, "which they detained two or three days till they had made their market out of her." In other words, they drank their way through her cargo of wine. Rackam then returned the ship to her master, who continued on to Jamaica accompanied by Hosea Tisdell, a Jamaican bar owner whom the pirates had captured a few weeks before. Their paths would cross again.

Next the pirates put in to an island off the north of Hispaniola to careen their sloop. We don't know where they went, but in the buccaneering days of half a century before, the Turks and Caicos Islands were a popular careening spot. Christmas was allegedly celebrated by a drunken party, but by early January 1719 they were back at sea again, spending a fruitless two months cruising the waters off the Windward Passage. All they had to show for their trouble was a ship carrying convicts bound for the plantations of Jamaica. Although Rackam freed the prisoners and handed the ship over to them, it was captured a few days later by a British warship.

By then Rackam was heading north into the Atlantic, bound for Bermuda. Somewhere off the Bahamas he captured a British ship bound for the Carolinas, as well as a New England vessel. In May 1719 he reputedly sheltered in the Bahamas while he plundered the two vessels at his leisure. It seems the pirates hadn't reckoned on the vigilance of Woodes Rogers, and so when a heavily armed Bahamian sloop appeared, Rackam was forced to abandon his prizes and escape.

Captain Johnson claimed that Rackam fled back through the Windward Passage and hid out somewhere on the southern coast of Cuba, not venturing out to sea for several months. He even describes in some detail a spirited battle between Rackam's brig and a Spanish patrol vessel. However, there is far stronger evidence that Rackam went to the Bahamas not to plunder, but rather to turn himself in, and that the Cuban sojourn never happened. In May 1719 he was mentioned as a supplicant in New Providence, requesting and receiving a pardon from Woodes Rogers, which meant that the remainder of the die-hard pirates had also decided to turn themselves in by that stage.

Britain was fighting with Spain again, having declared war in December 1718, so beginning a conflict known as the War of the Quadruple Alliance. Although the fighting only lasted until February 1720, the British government decided it needed its old privateersmen to turn against Spanish shipping in the Caribbean. As a means to an end Governor Rogers reissued his offer of a pardon, and so Rackam and the hard-liners decided that spurning the offer twice would have been tempting fate. A handful of Bahamian privateers were outfitted, but the war ended before Rackam and his crew could play any part in the new legitimate adventure. It was almost inevitable that they would soon consider returning to piracy.

It was during this period in New Providence that Rackam met the first of two women who would not only become closely associated with him, but whose lives would completely overshadow his. He met an Irishwoman called Anne Bonny, a lady from a respectable family who had defied her father by eloping with a seaman. Rackam and Bonny began an affair, and she soon left her husband for the pirate. On August 22, 1720, Rackam rowed out to the twelve-gun Bahamian sloop *William*, riding at anchor off Nassau.

He was accompanied by Anne Bonny disguised as a sailor, and with the aid of another dozen supporters he seized the sloop and escaped in her. Amazingly the other pirates included a second woman, Mary Read, whose disguise as a man may have fooled Rackam, but not Bonny. So began a largely uneventful pirate cruise that later became the stuff of pirate legend largely because of the presence of Bonny and Read. Captain Johnson claims that Anne Bonny was pregnant when they sailed, which may explain why Captain Johnson reckoned Rackam spent so long in Cuba.

Governor Rogers immediately issued a proclamation, declaring that "John Rackum and his said Company are hereby proclaimed Pirates and Enemies of the Crown of Great Britain, and are to be so treated and Deem'd by all His Majesty's subjects." The document listed the crew, and included "two women, by name, Anne Fulford alias Bonny, and Mary Read." By the start of September Rogers had sent two sloops out in search of Rackam, so after plundering a small fleet of fishing boats off Great Harbor Cay he fled south toward his Cuban bolt-hole.

The depositions of merchant captains remain to chart Rackam's progress; on October 1 he captured two sloops off the northwest corner of Hispaniola, and two weeks later he captured and plundered another small vessel off Port Maria, on the Jamaican coast directly north of Kingston. He worked his way along the northern shore of Jamaica past Montego Bay until he reached Negril Point, on the extreme western tip of the island. That was where he met his nemesis, a privateer commander named Captain Jonathan Barnet.

Commissioned as a pirate hunter, Barnet was under orders to scout the western end of the island for any sign of the pirate after word reached Spanish Town and Kingston of Rackam's attacks. On the early evening of November 15 his twelve-gun sloop was level with Negril Point when he heard the sound of musketry coming from further inshore. He altered course to investigate. That afternoon Rackam had sighted a small piragua and ordered her to heave to. The canoe was crewed by nine British-born turtle hunters, and they offered their catch in exchange for drink. The pirates dropped their anchor and a drinking session began, during which some of the crew must have fired off their pistols or muskets in a celebration.

When Barnet appeared out of the setting sun Rackam roused himself and weighed anchor. He tried to escape, but by 10 P.M. Captain Barnet managed to overhaul the pirate sloop. He hailed them, asking the smaller sloop captain to identify himself. "John Rackam from Cuba," came the reply. That was enough, and Barnet opened his gunports and called on Rackam to surrender. Rackam or one of his crew replied by firing a swivel gun at the Jamaican ship, prompting Barnet to retaliate with a broadside and musketry. One round-shot severed the *William*'s boom, and the pirate ship turned into the wind. Barnet laid his sloop alongside the pirate ship and ordered away his boarders. With two exceptions the pirates threw up

The second female pirate in Rackam's crew, Mary Read, disguised herself as a man in order to escape to sea, and in Rackam's final battle she and Bonny were the most ferocious members of the pirate crew.

their hands and surrendered. Only Anne Bonny and Mary Read offered any resistance, cursing their drunken male companions and fighting the Jamaican seamen with cutlasses until they were overpowered.

The following day Captain Barnet landed his prisoners, turning them over to the local militia, who escorted them to the jail in Spanish Town. On November 16, the Vice-Admiralty Court tried and convicted the ten surviving male pirates, including Rackam. The case for the prosecution was helped when the barman Hosea Tisdell stepped forward and identified Rackam as the man who had attacked him two years before. Justice was swift and vengeful. Early the next morning, November 17, 1720, Captain Rackam and four of his men were marched to Gallows Point and hanged, followed by the rest the day after, this time at a gallows set up outside Kingston.

The bodies of Rackam and two of his companions were then hung in chains around Kingston Harbor as a warning to other sailors. Surprisingly, the court then went on to convict and execute the turtle hunters, whose only real crime was being in the wrong place when Captain Barnet appeared. On November 28 the court tried the two women pirates, and they too were sentenced to be hanged. However, as soon as the sentence was passed they claimed that they were both pregnant, and so the execution was delayed until the two women could be examined.

They were both telling the truth, and in a fit of clemency the two were reprieved. Mary Read died in prison five months later, still carrying her unborn child. As for Anne Bonny, "She was continued in prison, to the time of her laying in, and afterwards reprieved from time to time; but what became of her since, we cannot tell; only this we know, that she was not executed." Like many others, she probably ended her days in the gutters of Port Royal or Kingston, and her unmarked passing brought an end to a chapter in pirate history, the last link in a chain that began several years before during a hurricane off the Florida coast.

5
The Devil Off
Charles Town

Threw the week before Christmas 1717, Blackbeard was in the Leeward Islands, somewhere off Anguilla. Although the *Queen Anne's Revenge* was more than a match for most smaller Royal Navy and *Armada de la Guardia* warships, his near encounter with a larger British warship, possibly the fifth-rate HMS *Scarborough*, must have been an unsettling experience. After all, while he might have been able to match a thirty-gun man-of-war in firepower, he was well aware that when it came to training and crew quality there wasn't any comparison. The *Scarborough's* 125-man crew could probably fire three rounds to Blackbeard's two, and as long as the warship avoided being boarded, victory in a standup fight was almost a certainty for the British. Unlike that of Charles Vane, Blackbeard's crew also knew when to walk away from a fight. The pirates quietly slipped away from the Leeward Islands, never to return.

What followed is something of a mystery. According to Captain Johnson, the pirates headed toward "Spanish America," or more accurately the Gulf of Honduras. According to this timetable of events, he met Stede Bonnet along the way. We know this is nonsense, as we have documentary proof that Bonnet was already accompanying Blackbeard as early as October 12. That was some three months before Captain Johnson claimed the encounter took place. It seems that Blackbeard's first biographer confused the timing of events around this period, largely because the pirates seem to have disappeared into thin air. From the deposition of Henry Bostock of St. Christopher we know the *Queen Anne's Revenge* was off Anguilla's Crab Island in December 1717. By the following April Captain Johnson places Blackbeard in the Turneffe Islands, off the coast of what is now Belize. The next link in the chain of official reports also appears that spring, in May, by which time the pirates were back in North American waters.

The Henry Bostock deposition described an attack that took place on December 5, and we might assume that they headed northwest soon afterward. However, two other reports suggest that Blackbeard and his men didn't travel too far. In a letter he sent to London sometime before mid-December, Governor Hamilton of the Leeward Islands reported that pirates were operating off the Dutch-held island of St. Eustatius, just north of St. Kitts and just a few miles from where Henry Bostock was captured. The governor reported that two trading sloops had been captured, and a Barbadian merchantman sighted a ship and a sloop in the distance as she approached the island's harbor. The locals told him the vessels belonged to pirates. The same pirates had also reportedly captured a French ship from Guadaloupe carrying sugar, which they scuttled off the north end of St. Eustatius.

There was little doubt about who was responsible. "The [pirate] ship is commanded by Captain Teatch, the sloop by one Major Bonnett an inhabitant of Barbadoes: some say Bonnett commands both ship and sloop . . . they have committed a great many barbarities. The ship some say has 22 others say she has 26 guns mounted, but all agree that she can carry 40 and is full of men, the sloop hath ten guns and doth not want men." Henry Bostock clearly overheard the pirates say they planned to head toward Samana Bay in Hispaniola (the deposition actually said Samana Cay), where they planned to careen their ships and wait for a Spanish flotilla to sail past their hideout. It seems Governor Hamilton never sent any ships to investigate the story, probably because Hispaniola was Spanish territory, and for once the two countries were at peace with each other.

While Samana Bay was pretty remote and it was unlikely that a British force would encounter any Spanish warships, Hamilton clearly erred on the side of caution. An admittedly cursory search of the Spanish *Archivas des Indies* in Seville had failed to uncover any mention of pirates operating in the waters around Hispaniola that winter, nor were any warships of the *Armada de la Guardia* ordered to patrol the area. The colony of Santo Domingo operated a few sloops that would have patrolled the coast that winter, and they might even have searched part of the 120 miles of coastline that made up Samana Bay. Nothing was found, or at least nothing was reported to the governor back in Santo Domingo.

Hispaniola was one of the least developed islands in the Caribbean. When the Spanish first settled there in the wake of Columbus, they all but exterminated the Indians, and stripped the island of its mineral wealth. By the mid-sixteenth century the once-thriving settlement of Santo Domingo was virtually a ghost town, and in the 150 years that followed, raids by Elizabethan sea dogs and French buccaneers did little to help population growth. Those who remained raised cattle and pigs to help feed the rest of the Spanish overseas empire, a trade that kept Santo Domingo in business as a useful but minor port on the sea route between Puerto Rico and Cuba. Other people made a living from these wild cattle, too, and by the early seventeenth century the Spanish had virtually abandoned the mountainous center and the far west of the island to the buccaneers.

Eventually the French took over the western end of the island, and in 1697 this region, which now forms the modern country of Haiti, was formally ceded from Spain to France and dubbed St. Domingue. Unlike the Spanish, their French neighbors knew how to develop a productive colony using slave labor, and soon the colony became a major sugar producer. Meanwhile the Spanish part of Hispaniola (now officially called the colony of Santo Domingo) continued its decline. By Blackbeard's time, the eastern half of Hispaniola beyond the city of Santo Domingo was a deserted wilderness, apart from a handful of small impoverished towns, Catholic missions, and the odd native village or hunter's camp. It therefore made an ideal place to hide out, and Samana Bay would have offered a sheltered, hidden anchorage, a place to careen ships, an abundance of water and wild game, and a dearth of prying human eyes.

For a few months it seems as if Blackbeard went to ground, but then we find a strange report filed by Captain Hume of HMS *Scarborough* that suggests the pirates mightn't have traveled too far. On February 6, 1718, the naval officer reported that "in December I had information of a Pyrate Ship of 36 Guns and 250 men, and a Sloop of 10 Guns and 100 men were Said to be Cruizing amongst the Leeward Islands. I accordingly Salied hence the 18th of Said month for Antegoa [Antigua] to join the Seaford, there were informed the Said Pyrate Ship and Sloop were gone to Leeward, the 23 December we proceeded for Nevis, and St. Christophers, from which islands I had an Officer and 20 Soldiers put on board me for the Cruize." Clearly Governor Hamilton had little faith that the small twenty-gun frigate HMS *Seaford* could stand up to the *Queen Anne's Revenge* in a fight, so he ordered the thirty-gun HMS *Scarborough* to support her.

Of course we don't know that the pirate ships he mentioned were indeed Blackbeard's flagship and the sloop *Revenge*, but it remains a pretty good guess. The fact that Captain Hume reinforced his 125-man crew with a detachment of musket-armed soldiers shows that he expected trouble. He continued that at St. Christopher he "was here informed that Said Pyrates had been off the Islands about three weeks before and there Sunk a French Ship loaded with Sugars, we proceeded to Spanish Town, Santa Cruiz, St. Thomas's and Crabb Island, found by all account that they went Westward." With the British searching every harbor and anchorage in the Virgin Islands, Blackbeard had evidently made the right decision by fleeing the scene of his crimes. Captain Hume remained in the area for several more weeks, making sure the pirates didn't return. However, he added an interesting rumor at the end of his report: "I was further informed that they had been at Mona, and were gone down the North side of Hispaniola, this was the last account."

The Mona Passage between the islands of Puerto Rico and Hispaniola would have been a promising cruising ground for Blackbeard, and the rumor that the pirates headed north from there does reinforce the rumor that they spent some time in Samana Bay before heading further west. This sojourn in Spanish territory might also explain the dearth of hard information on the pirates' movements during the first few months of 1718. Strangely enough, Captain Johnson was also unable to shed any light on what the pirates did during those lost months. We can assume that the *Queen Anne's Revenge* was careened somewhere around Hispaniola, a process that would have taken several days or even weeks.

They might even have remained in their Hispaniolan hideout for almost three months, the time between their last sighting off the Leeward Islands and their next appearance some seventeen hundred miles away, in the Gulf of Honduras. The voyage would have taken about two weeks, providing the pirates didn't loiter along the way, looking for prizes in maritime bottlenecks such as the Mona Passage, the Windward Passage, or the Jamaica Channel. The run to the west-southwest would also have taken the pirates dangerously close to the British naval base in Port Royal, but there are no accounts of anyone spotting the *Queen Anne's Revenge* and the *Revenge* as they sailed past. Almost certainly Blackbeard would have kept Jamaica beyond the horizon as he sailed past, either by skirting the Pedro Bank to the south of the island or by keeping in the middle of the channel between Jamaica and Cuba.

By the end of March Blackbeard was cruising off what is now Belize. Captain Johnson describes the capture of Blackbeard's first prize in Central American waters:

> At Turniff [Turneffe Islands], ten leagues short of the Bay of Honduras, the pirates took in fresh water. While they were at anchor there they saw a sloop coming in, whereupon Richards in the sloop Revenge, slipped his cable, and ran out to meet her, who upon seeing the black flag hoisted, struck sail, and came to under the stern of Teach the commodore. She was called the Adventure, from Jamaica, with David Harriot master.

We shall hear a lot more about this little sloop later on. She was a well-built vessel of 80 tons and strong enough to carry up to twelve guns, although there is no record of her armament before Blackbeard claimed her as a prize. Harriot (or Herriot) had sailed from Kingston Harbor about ten days before, intending to sail up the coast looking for logwood camps. Like Blackbeard, he planned to take on water in the Turneffe Islands, and it was his singular misfortune that he chose the same haven as Blackbeard. The pirate decided to keep the *Adventure* for himself, as it made a useful addition to his force. It seems that the pirates spent about a week in the Turneffe Islands before heading south into the Gulf of Honduras itself on April 9.

By the second week in April, Blackbeard and Bonnet seem to have separated in an attempt to search a larger area for prizes. Captain Johnson is adamant that Stede Bonnet remained little more than the titular captain of the *Revenge* during this period, and a mate in Blackbeard's crew named

Richards was the real authority on the sloop. However, most accounts suggest that by this time Bonnet was already a "guest" on board the pirate flagship. As for the *Adventure*, Captain Johnson claimed that Blackbeard sent over a crew to run the second sloop, suggesting that her new captain was Israel Hands, the former master of the *Queen Anne's Revenge*. We can imagine the three vessels spreading out across the Gulf of Honduras, searching for victims. The sweep was highly successful, adding a three-masted ship and four sloops to Blackbeard's tally of prizes.

Three of the sloops belonged to Captain Jonathan Bernard of Jamaica, and the fourth was owned by a Captain James whose port of origin went unrecorded. Presumably the four sloops were in the area to collect log-wood, and all seem to have been anchored close to the shore when Richards appeared in the *Revenge* and captured the lot of them. The pirates plundered the four sloops of whatever trading goods they carried, and then Captain Johnson claims Richards set fire to the sloop belonging to Captain James "out of spite to the owner."

Richards was making an example out of Captain James, presumably because the merchant captain had the audacity to protest at the rough treatment he received. Richards and his cutthroats would have cared lit-tle for James's outburst, but they were well aware that their future success depended on showing a tough face. Given other examples of this kind of encounter, Captain James should have considered himself lucky to escape with his life. The three remaining sloops were allowed to continue on their way.

The three-masted ship was the *Protestant Caesar* from Boston, com-manded by a Captain Wyar (or Weir). Apparently she was first encountered by one of the pirate sloops, presumably the *Revenge*, but she managed to fight off the smaller vessel and escape. This was an accomplishment the pirates didn't want to encourage. Consequently Blackbeard led his flagship in pursuit of the Boston vessel, eventually cornering her further up the bay. In Captain Johnson's account, the Massachusetts crew abandoned their sloop and rowed ashore when the *Queen Anne's Revenge* appeared. As the crew hid in the jungle they would have had a grandstand view of Black-beard and his men plundering their vessel, then burning her to the water-line. That way Captain Wyar and his men "might not brag when he went to New England that he had beat a Pirate." The whole sweep must have taken about a week, and by the time the pirates had cleared the bay Black-beard was ready to head back up north.

After all, this was the pirate routine established by Hornigold and his compatriots, cruising the Atlantic seaboard of British North America in the summer and the Caribbean in the winter. Blackbeard and his snowbirds "sailed to Turkill, and then to the Grand Caymans, a small island about thirty leagues to the westward of Jamaica, where they took a small turtler." Turkill is hard to identify, although Captain Johnson could have misheard or misread the place name. The Gulf of Honduras is something of a wind trap, with strong onshore breezes predominating from the northeast. This meant that the voyage north would have been a slow one, with the wind on the starboard beam as the pirate fleet headed north up the Yucatan coast.

By sailing some 250 miles east toward the Islas de la Bahia, then, Black-beard would have had an easier run north, with greater leeway in case a storm drove him further inshore off the Yucatan Peninsula. Not only did this make sound maritime sense, but Roatán, the largest of the islands, had long been a buccaneering rendezvous where fresh water was readily available. The closest mainland settlement to the Islas de la Bahia was Trujillo, the small Spanish port that served as a trading center for logwood and local spices. This means that "Turkill" was probably a misspelling for "Turkillo" or Trujillo.

As for Grand Cayman, it wasn't the tax-free banking center it is today when Blackbeard arrived, but it was a well-known source of fresh food and water for ships plying the Spanish Main, particularly during the days of the buccaneers. The islands had been under English control since 1655, when Cromwell's troops first seized Jamaica, and Spain included the island in a peace agreement some fifteen years later, when according to the terms of the Treaty of Madrid the Spanish crown recognized "all lands, islands, colonies and places situated in the West Indies." It remained an administrative adjunct to Jamaica, and in 1718 it was still sparsely settled. Grand Cayman's main claim to fame was the island's abundance of wild fowl and sea turtles, and local turtle-gathering boats were a common sight there. Presumably the pirates decided to plunder one of these boats rather than pay for the catch.

From there the pirates headed northwest into the Yucatan Channel, which brought them out into the Gulf of Mexico. According to Captain

Johnson they skirted the Cuban coast, "and so on to Havana, and from thence to the Bahama wrecks, and from the Bahama wrecks, they sailed to Carolina, taking a brigantine and two sloops in their way." It is unlikely that Blackbeard even passed within sight of Havana, although he did appear to capture a small Spanish vessel that was outward bound from the Cuban port. This vessel was evidently kept by the pirates, as later documents refer to "the Spanish sloop."

As for the Bahama wrecks, Captain Johnson was clearly referring to the Spanish shipwrecks of the 1715 fleet, wrecked along the western coast of Florida from Cape Canaveral to the modern city of Fort Pierce. Although both the Spanish salvors and Henry Jennings and his pirates had recovered what they could from the shipwrecks, there was clearly more down there. After all, in 1964 the American treasure hunter Mel Fisher recovered hundreds of silver pieces of eight and gold doubloons from the wrecks, and his successors are still bringing up sunken Spanish treasure. It seems that Blackbeard and his companions were unable to resist visiting the wreck sites and seeing if they could recover anything for themselves. It would have been late April when Blackbeard looted his cargo of turtles in the Caymans and early to mid-May by the time he reached the treasure wrecks in the Bahamas Channel.

It was here that he would have landed the Spanish crew of the sloop he captured, where they would have sought out the fort built by Spanish troops on the coast as a deterrent to further large-scale looting. Evidently Blackbeard decided not to linger too long, as by the end of the third week in May he was three hundred miles further north, approaching the port of Charles Town, South Carolina. Captain Johnson suggests that he captured three vessels (a brig and two sloops) along the way, presumably off the Florida or Georgia coast. Again, little time was spent plundering these vessels before letting them go, as Blackbeard had a much bigger target in mind. He was about to embark on the most breathtakingly audacious piratical adventure of his short career.

During the afternoon of May 22, 1718, a small cluster of four vessels was seen approaching Cummins Point from the south, sailing on a broad reach and making good progress given the strong onshore breeze from the southeast. One was a square-rigged ship of French construction, and the other three were sloops of various sizes. Behind the marshy point Charles Town's ample harbor stretched back for three miles until it reached the

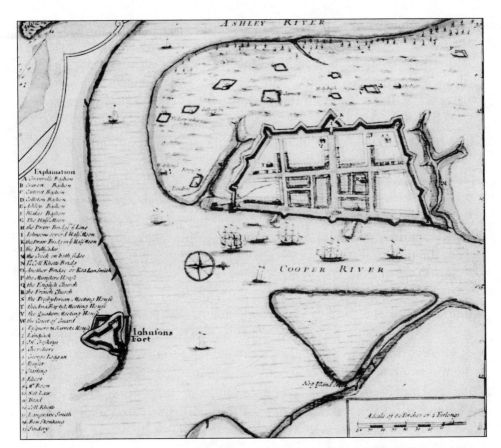

The port and inner harbor of Charles Town, from an early-eighteenth-century map. The Charles Town Bar was several miles away to the south, well away from the city's impressive but neglected defenses.

headland where the Ashley and Cooper rivers converged. There, where the deep bay offered some protection from hurricanes and the marauding French or Spanish, lay the small port of Charles Town in the colony of South Carolina, a bustling little city of some five thousand people.

The port was two years short of being half a century old that summer, and Charles Town's merchants had every reason to feel complacent. In 1700 and again in 1713 the city was hit by hurricanes, while in 1706 a joint French and Spanish expedition attacked the city, only to be repulsed by the gunfire of the local militia, manning makeshift batteries facing out over the harbor. The town had been laid out in 1680, when the Lords Proprietor decided to move the site of their main settlement across the Ashley River to the easily defensible peninsula between the rivers. Because the colony was so close to Spanish-held Florida, the defenses of the new port became a priority, and within six years a rectangular series of city walls ran roughly north to south along the banks of the Cooper River, then halfway across the peninsula where a landward wall completed the circuit of fortifications.

Most of these defenses were just earthen banks, with a ditch running around the outside. At least it followed the latest military notions, incorporating a series of nine triangular bastions that protruded from the wall on the landward side. A ninth large bastion complete with a drawbridge protected the city's main gateway in the middle of the landward side opposite the harbor. The idea of a bastion was that any attacker trying to assault the walls would come under flanking fire from the protruding triangular-shaped bulwark, allowing the defenders to sweep the space in front of the walls with musket fire and grapeshot.

However, even if they were ever fully built they couldn't have been as intimidating as the city fathers had hoped. A statute of 1704 was referred to as "an Act to prevent the breaking down and defacing of the fortifications of Charles Town." Evidently the locals thought the fortifications got in the way of urban growth, or access to the hinterland, or both. Two other statutes outlawed the free range of cattle in the city because they "damnif[ied]" the city's fortifications. After all, where cattle could cross, so too could any attacker. While these lines were not really good enough to keep out a determined assault by regular troops, they were thought good enough to deter surprise attacks by marauding Native Americans, pirates, or Spanish militiamen. Following the defeat of the Yamasee tribe in 1717, Governor Nicholson gave his approval for the city's expansion beyond the bounds set by these landward walls. Many of the bastions and sections of the old earthen ramparts were torn down and the ditches filled, creating a level site for the builders.

After all, the city was built on a peninsula, and faced with the threat of attack, the militia could always dig themselves a makeshift defensive line three miles to the north, across the peninsula's narrowest point at Charles Town Neck. The city planners realized that the most likely avenue of attack was from the sea, so that was where they concentrated their limited resources. On the side facing the Cooper River the walls were built of brick, six bricks thick at the bottom and three at the top. A string of five more brick-built bastions and a semicircular "half-moon" battery completed the seaward façade of the city, and near-contemporary prints show just how imposing Charles Town's defenses must have looked from the harbor.

The Powder Magazine on Cumberland Street was part of this defensive arrangement, and it is regarded as the city's oldest surviving building. It was completed five years before Blackbeard appeared off Charles Town Bar. It all must have seemed impressive enough to the colonists. However, the handful of guns on the half-moon battery hardly had the range to reach the far side of the Cooper River, let alone the entrance to the harbor some four miles away. In 1704 a small battery was established on James Island, but these guns in what was grandly called Fort Johnson did little more than cover the main anchorage of the inner harbor. The expensive seaward fortifications of Charles Town were fine against a direct assault on the harbor, but were useless in the face of a slow, strangling blockade.

Charles Town was certainly a city worth plundering. In 1717, the year before the pirates arrived, the decision to tear down the landward walls reflected the city's growth. The city was up-and-coming, with genteel townhouses such as the Rhett Mansion (1712) being built by the city's new merchant elite. The old earthen city walls made way for the elegant new streets and houses demanded by an increasingly sophisticated population, whose merchants and planters were growing fat on the back of trade. Ships from Britain and the Caribbean rode at anchor in the Cooper River, alongside vessels from South Carolina and its neighboring colonies. Ten ships of various sizes and types were reportedly clustered around the wharves and mooring buoys in the Cooper River the day the pirates came to town. In their holds these vessels would have carried a representative sample of the exports that were powering the economic development of the colony.

Rice first arrived in the Carolinas around 1685 when a brig bound from Madagascar put into Charles Town for repairs. Her captain presented Dr. Henry Woodward of the city with a sack of rice to help test Woodward's theory that the crop would thrive in the Carolina tidewater. Another version of the story claims that in 1695–96 seed rice was sent to the Carolinas by the treasurer of the English East India Company. However it arrived, rice-growing conditions in the tidewater area of South Carolina were ideal, and within two decades rice grew into the region's major cash crop. In 1695 Charles Town exported 438 pounds of rice, just enough to fill one and a half 3-hundredweight barrels. Thirteen years later, in 1708, the figure had grown only slightly to 675 pounds, or two barrels. However, by

1718 South Carolina was exporting a staggering 1,320 tons of rice per year, or eighty-five hundred barrels. This total would quadruple within five years. Charles Town was evidently experiencing a rice bonanza.

While rice exports would never match those of sugar or tobacco during the colonial era, it remained a near-miraculous cash crop, and the rice barons of the colony grew ludicrously rich on the profits it brought them. Most of these rice exports went to Britain, transported on medium-sized merchant ships of 100 to 150 tons. However, an increasing quantity was shipped to the Caribbean, where it was used to help feed the region's growing population of slaves. The next biggest export was indigo, the blue-dye–producing plant that grew well in the colony. It was said that indigo from the Carolinas was the equal of any imported from Asia, and its cost of transportation to Britain's textile mills was significantly lower.

Finally, there was lumber. Unlike the colonies in New England, South Carolina didn't export timber as a raw material, but as a finished product. The native longleaf pine (*Pinus palustris*) that covered the Carolina backwoods was used to produce good-quality masts and spars for sailing ships, while its by-products of tar, resin, and turpentine were bought from the backwoodsmen by Charles Town merchants, then shipped to Britain, where they fetched a healthy profit. The warehouses on the city's waterfront would have been stacked with rice and indigo, maritime stores and resin casks, while others contained the imported British luxuries that the returning ships brought to the colony: quality silverware, wines and liquor, cloth, silk, household furnishings, examples of the latest fashions, precision firearms, books—the list was long and varied.

The growing profits from rice cultivation meant that the city's mercantile elite had money to flaunt, and so as personal wealth increased, so too did the demand for luxury imports. One other cargo had become commonplace in South Carolina by 1718. Rice cultivation was a labor-intensive business, and as demand grew, so did the need for slaves. All those rice plantations used slave labor, and so slavery was becoming a growth industry in the Carolinas. While most slave ships still sailed from West Africa to the Caribbean, a few sailed straight to Charles Town. Other groups of slaves were transported north from Jamaica, Martinique, or Barbados in small trading sloops or brigantines, purchased in exchange for a cargo of rice.

There wasn't much romance in a barrel of rice, or a cask of turpentine, or a group of shivering slaves chained together in a cargo hold. For the pirates of the Golden Age there was no Spanish galleon crammed with silver waiting for them over the horizon—at least, unless it was shipwrecked in a hurricane. The ships in Charles Town harbor were typical of those that pirates like Blackbeard managed to capture, and their often mundane cargoes were what fell into pirate hands rather than anything more exotic.

In most cases these cargoes were of little use unless the pirates were based in a friendly port where the plunder could be sold without too many questions being asked. For the most part the goods were simply left on board. They could be deliberately damaged, or burned along with the ship carrying it, but more often than not the cargo remained rifled but undamaged, and the ship was eventually allowed to continue on its way. What pirate crews wanted was ready money and liquor, fresh clothes and shiny keepsakes.

Sometimes they took other items such as navigational instruments or charts, sails and rigging, or weapons. However, as we have already seen, if the cargo included rum or imported wine or brandy, then the pirates set to with a vengeance, drinking their way through the entire consignment. When Blackbeard and his men arrived off Charles Town Bar in the middle of May 1718, they knew the South Carolina port was a bustling one, and they were also well aware of what the ships they encountered might be carrying. Blackbeard wasn't there to make a fortune in plunder. He was there to make a point.

Charles Town Harbor resembled a large rectangular box some 5 miles long and 1½ miles across. Charles Town itself sat at one end, while the other faced the open Atlantic. The main anchorage was at the far end where the two rivers converged, and between this safe haven and the open sea lay a series of deepwater channels separated by shoals and sandbanks. Any sailor making the approach to the city through Charles Town Harbor needed to know what he was doing. To make matters worse, these sandbars moved around from time to time, when hurricanes or winter storms swept in from the Atlantic. Just over a century later, in 1829, the U.S. Army Corps of Engineers began building Fort Sumter on one of these sandbars, right in the middle of the entrance to the harbor.

This entrance was also blocked by Charles Town Bar, a long, submerged shoal of sand running roughly from Sullivan's Island on the north side of the bay to Cummins Point (now Morris Island) on the south side, itself marking the eastern extremity of James Island. While small sloops with captains who knew what they were doing could work their way over the bar and through the shoals of Charles Town Harbor, other, larger vessels needed help. That was why when Blackbeard's small flotilla appeared off the bar, the Charles Town pilot headed out to meet the cluster of ships riding gently off Sullivan's Island. The bar wasn't a solid wall of sand but was pierced by several channels in the same way that the waters of the harbor itself were divided beyond it.

The depth of these channels varied from a few feet to as much as 10 fathoms (60 feet), so it was always advisable for ships to wait until high tide before trying to cross the bar. The North Channel was the deepest of these, running close to the shore of Sullivan's Island, then past the submerged shoal where Fort Sumter would be built. The shallower South Channel ran close to Cummins Point before turning into the harbor itself, where it split into smaller and even shallower channels. Like all larger square-rigged ships, Blackbeard's flagship would have heaved to opposite the deeper of the two channels.

The men in the pilot boat must have thought the ship and three sloops rolling gently in the swell were harmless enough as the vessel came alongside the *Queen Anne's Revenge* and the pilot hauled himself on board. He would have been greeted by the terrifying sight of Blackbeard surrounded by his heavily armed and equally fearsome shipmates. By that time flight was out of the question, and the pilot boat crew found themselves prisoners. Before the end of the day more Carolinian sailors would join them in the dark confines of the pirate flagship's hold. The next prize was a square-rigged three-masted ship bound for London called the *Crowley*, her cabins filled with passengers and their baggage, and presumably her hold stacked with barrels of rice.

A large ship like this would have needed help crossing the bar, so it is not unreasonable to assume that her commander, Captain Clark, had followed the pilot boat out of the harbor, and was captured within minutes of his guide. The belongings of the passengers would have brought some decent plunder, but otherwise all the prisoners seem to have remained unharmed. By now it must have been getting dark, as no fishermen or watchers on the shore noticed the goings-on off Charles Town Bar. The good people of Charles Town slept secure in their beds, completely unaware that their city was blockaded by one of the largest pirate bands in the Americas. This meant that when dawn broke the following morning, the flock of ships were still riding the swell of the North Channel, and presumably Captain Clark's ship was tucked in behind the *Queen Anne's Revenge*, so nobody could identify her until it was too late. The pirates would probably have left the pilot boat where it was, as it had a perfectly good reason to be out there.

The following day the haul was even better. First came another, smaller outward-bound local ship bound for London, her commander, Captain Craigh, no doubt wondering what had happened to the pilot, and why the ships at the bar were still waiting to cross. He would soon find out, as one or more of the pirate sloops would have raised the black flag when it was too late for her to escape, and it would then have fired a warning shot. She was soon added to Blackbeard's growing tally of prizes. A letter sent from Charles Town a week later claimed that another ship, the outward-bound British merchantman *William* from Weymouth commanded by a Captain Hewes, was also captured as she crossed the bar.

By this time the identity of the mystery ships would have become clear as fishermen or others in small boats would have witnessed the encounter and would have raced back to Charles Town with the news. Certainly none of the remaining eight ships in Charles Town Harbor would put to sea while the pirate blockade remained in place. For the merchants and rice barons of South Carolina, this blockade was a disaster in the making. Visions of rotting cargoes of rice or even pirates marauding and pillaging their way through the port would have caused panic among the colony's power brokers.

Captain Johnson managed to catch something of the crisis when he wrote that the pirate attacks

being done in the face of the town, struck a great terror to the whole Province of Carolina, having just before being visited by Vane, another notorious pirate, that they abandoned themselves to despair, being in no condition to resist their force. They were eight sail in the harbour ready, for the sea, but none dared to venture out, it being almost impossible to escape their hands. The inward bound vessels were under the same unhappy dilemma, so that the trade of this place, was totally interrupted; what made these misfortunes heavier to them was a long expensive war the colony had had with the natives, which was but just ended when these robbers infested them.

Meanwhile, Blackbeard continued to capture prizes off Charles Town. Later on that second day two "pinks"—small vessels with narrow overhanging sterns—would fall into the hands of the pirates as they tried to enter Charles Town Harbor. Unfortunately, the South Carolina authorities did not bother to say what these vessels were, or where they came from. Given that the average pink was not much bigger than a sloop or a brigantine, it seems likely they were coastal trading craft, the kind of craft that would carry tobacco from Virginia to the South Carolina port, or produce from plantations further up the coast.

Fortunately, Captain Johnson provided a little more information about the next prize, which he described as "a brigantine with fourteen Negroes aboard." Another account refers to "a brigantine from Angola with 86 negroes which was mett by the pirates—they took from her 14 of their best Negroes, she comes from Bristol." It sounds as if Blackbeard asked for volunteers from among the terrified slaves, and chose the fittest of them to reinforce his pirate band. No doubt he did the same after capturing the 455 slaves on board *La Concorde* back in November, and given the same percentage of recruits, the French slaver could have furnished as many as 70 African volunteers for Blackbeard's crew. It is little wonder that when these men saw friendly black faces among the crew that liberated them, they became willing recruits. One has to wonder if any of the Bristol seamen recognized Blackbeard as one of their own. It seems unlikely, for if they did, we would have heard about it.

The same report contained a reference to another prize immediately after mentioning the captured Bristol slave ship: "a ship from Boston is also come in which was likewise plunder'd by them, etc." This might well have been one of the pinks, as that type of vessel was reputedly fairly common in New England waters. That made a total of eight prizes in just two days—unless the reports were confused and the "pinks" referred to one or more of the outward-bound ships or the ship from Boston. Eight or ten, it made little difference to the merchants of the beleaguered colony. No ship could come in or out of Charles Town while the *Queen Anne's Revenge* covered the North Channel with her guns. South Carolina was effectively sealed off from the outside world.

Inevitably the Carolina merchants turned to the governor for help. After Blackbeard and his men raised the blockade after ten days and headed north, Governor Robert Johnson wrote to the Council of Trade and Plantations in London. His letter reflected the way the Carolinians felt. "The unspeakable calamity this poor Province suffers from pyrats obliges me to inform your Lordships of it in order that his Majestie may know it and be induced to afford us the assistance of a frigate or two to cruse hereabouts upon them for we are continually alarmed and our ships taken to the utter ruin of our trade." This was fair enough. After all, New York had its own guard ship, while no less than two Royal Naval warships rode at anchor in the James River protecting Virginia's capital at Williamsburg.

However, the governor also knew that in 1718 the Royal Navy was thinly stretched. After the end of the war with France in 1713, the size of the fleet had been scaled down, and many warships were placed "in ordinary"—eighteenth-century naval jargon for "in mothballs." Worse, Europe was facing another crisis, this time involving attempts to curb the power of Spain. With a new war looming, and the nascent threat of a Jacobite invasion of Scotland or Ireland to deal with, the Lords of the Admiralty had few ships to spare. It was clear that if the governor of South Carolina wanted to protect his colony from pirates, he would have to do it himself. After Blackbeard left this is exactly what happened, as the colony raised the money to hire two sloops and then fit them out as pirate hunters. Some of the pirates off Charles Town Bar would run into these sloops before the summer was out, and the Carolinians would have their chance for revenge.

In the meantime the governor would have sent messengers racing north to spread the word and to try to stop any more local traders from sailing to Charles Town. He would also have sent word to the captains of the two Royal Navy ships in Virginian waters. However, it would take at least five days for a rider to cover the 350 miles to the James River if the ships were there and not on patrol, and at least another week for them to race south to Charles Town. It seems that the governor and his colonists might have been caught napping a second time in the space of less than a year—there is the hint that this wasn't the first time pirates had appeared off Charles Town Bar. In his report to London, Governor Johnson wrote

The port of Charles Town as it would have looked in Blackbeard's day. Shipping tended to crowd into the inner harbor in the Cooper River, where in theory it was protected by the guns of

that "twice since my coming here in 9 moneths time they [pirates] lain off of our barr takeing and plundering all ships that come into this port."

This is a little confusing, as the letter was written in late May 1718 and delivered in London on August 18. Therefore, it was written shortly after the blockade of the port by Blackbeard. Robert Johnson became governor on April 30, 1717—over a year before Blackbeard arrived—so the ambiguous passage about "nine months" must refer to the time between one pirate blockade and the next rather than his period in office. That would mean the first blockade took place in or around September 1717. This doesn't tally with Captain Johnson's claim that it was Vane who first blockaded Charles Town. According to him, Charles Vane fled from the Bahamas in May 1718, and was off Charles Town a week or so later. This was impossible, as we know the pirate was still in New Providence when Governor Rogers arrived there in late July. He therefore cruised the waters of the Carolinas during the summer rather than the spring of 1718.

It seems the only logical solution is that Captain Johnson got it wrong. Vane was certainly operating in Carolina waters in August 1718, and while he could have arrived off Charles Town Bar during his earlier spring

Fort Johnson. Although Blackbeard threatened to force his way past the weakly armed fort, his fleet remained at the outer entrance of the harbor during his weeklong blockade.

cruise, this doesn't fit in with the timing supplied by Governor Johnson. Things become a little clearer when we look at another letter, written in late May or early June 1718, after Blackbeard raised the blockade. It described the second day of the blockade, and included a useful description of the pirate force. The merchant ship *Crowley* was captured "by two pirates, one a large French ship mounted with 40 guns and the other a sloop mounted with 12 guns with two sloopes for their tenders, having in all about 300 men all English—the ship is commanded by one Teach and the sloop by one Richards, who have been upon this account [i.e., pirates] in those and other vessels about two years, and is the same sloop and company that was off our barr the last summer and took two vessels inward bound."

In other words, Blackbeard had been there before. The timing given by the governor suddenly makes sense, as that was exactly the time Blackbeard was cruising off the Carolinas. Blackbeard must have loitered off the bar the previous summer, and that was when he formed the bold idea to return with a stronger force and blockade Charles Town Harbor properly when the chance presented itself. No doubt Blackbeard had already worked out his plans soon after he seized *La Concorde*. With a pirate force that was collectively a match for any naval warship in American waters, he must have thought he could do what he liked.

This said, the South Carolina governor could have been accused of exaggeration. In the late summer of 1717 Blackbeard never imposed a tight blockade of the port, as he only loitered offshore for a few days, snapping up merchant vessels sailing in or out of Charles Town Harbor. Did the governor blow up this earlier incident of Blackbeard's first dalliance off Charles Town to strengthen his case for naval assistance? This remains one of the many little mysteries of the period. If the governor did indeed cry wolf after Blackbeard's attack, then one can have little sympathy with his plight when Charles Vane appeared off Charles Town Bar in August—three months after the governor wrote his letter.

What all the sources do agree on is what Blackbeard did next.

> Teach detained all the ships and prisoners, and, being in want of medicines, resolved to demand a chest from the government of the province; accordingly Richards, the Captain of the revenge, sloop, with two or three more pirates, were sent up along with Mr. Marks, one of their prisoners, whom they had taken in Clark's ship, and very insolently made their demands, threatening that if they did not send immediately the chest of medicines and let the pirate ambassadors return without offering any violence to their persons, they would murder all their prisoners, send up their heads to the governor, and set the ships they had taken on fire.

In his report, Governor Johnson stated that "About 14 days ago 4 sail of them appeared in sight of the Town tooke our pilot boat and afterwards 8 or 9 sail wth. Several of the best inhabitants of this place on board and then sent me word that if I did not immediately send them a chest of medicines they would put every prisoner to death which for there sakes being [I] complied with." He then continued: "After plundering them [of] all they had [the prisoners] were sent ashore almost naked."

This brief summary of Blackbeard's actions off Charles Town misses much of the subtleties involved as Blackbeard opened negotiations with the city authorities. One of the prisoners he captured on the *Crowley* was Samuel Wragg, a member of the colony's ruling council and an influential and wealthy Charles Town merchant. With hostages of this social standing Blackbeard had the perfect tool to pry concessions out of the authorities.

Like the buccaneers of old, he could extort money from the city. In the case of the buccaneers, this was demanded in return for the buccaneers sparing the city itself. In Blackbeard's case, the city itself was perfectly safe. It was the lives of the hostages and the financial value of the captured ships and cargo that were on the line.

Blackbeard's only demand was for medicine. When the pirates captured *La Concorde* they may well have seized the French ship's surgeon, although this cannot be confirmed. He would be the man drawing up the list of drugs and medical supplies, and Samuel Wragg was proposed as the man who would carry the list to the Charles Town council. He was the ideal choice, as not only was he well respected in the city, but when the pirates captured him he was accompanied by his infant son William, who would act as surety for his father's return. Blackbeard seems to have then changed his mind, as he thought that a man of Wragg's standing might not be allowed to return, regardless of his son's welfare.

Instead he selected a less prominent Charles Town resident named Master Marks to accompany Captain Richards and another pirate, allegedly a "master of one of their tenders," which probably meant the commander of the smallest sloop. Blackbeard threatened to wreak havoc if Richard and Marks failed to return, threatening to "come over the barr for to burn the ships that lay before the Towne, and to beat it about our ears."

The resident who wrote this after the event then added the telling lines, "The Towne is at present in a very indifferent condition of making much resistance if them or any other enemye should attempt it and that we were very desirous to get them off our coast by fair means, which we could not doe otherwise for want of such helps as other Governments are supply'd with from the Crown." Charles Town's militia might have had a stout seaward wall and a small fort to hide behind, but it seems they didn't rate their chances against a pirate host who would give no quarter and who would take no prisoners. Blackbeard's carefully developed and largely undeserved reputation had clearly preceded him. Blackbeard then waited for the expedition's return.

As for the men onshore, Captain Johnson provided us with a colorful account of their reception: "Whilst Mr. Marks was making application to the council, Richards and the rest of the pirates walked the streets publicly in the sight of all people, who were fired with the utmost indignation, looking upon them as robbers and murderers and particularly the authors of their wrongs and oppressions; but durst not so much as think of executing their revenge, for fear of bringing more calamities upon themselves, and so they were forced to let the villains pass with impunity." There was little anyone could do about it. Given the earlier reference to the port's defenses, Governor Johnson and his advisors would have realized they had no option but to agree to Blackbeard's reasonable terms.

After all, he wasn't asking for hard currency like the buccaneers of yore, only a chest of medical supplies, which could be gathered without much difficulty, and the cost covered by the town's medical community until such time as the governor felt flush enough to repay them. The Carolinians must have wondered just what medical emergency warranted such a preoccupation with medicines. Several theories have been proposed. For instance, before the pirates arrived off Charles Town Bar they had spent several months in the West Indies and off the coast of Central America. Both were areas known for disease, primarily yellow fever. In fact, the coastline just around the corner from the Gulf of Honduras was known as "the Mosquito Coast," and while the link between the insect and disease had not been made in Blackbeard's day, the results of prolonged exposure to the climate there were well known to all sailors of the period.

Another suggestion was that the pirates needed medicine to help cure venereal disease, which in this case would probably have meant mercury preparations—an injection of mercury being the primary treatment for syphilis in those days. Maritime archaeologists investigating the shipwreck site that they think is the *Queen Anne's Revenge* made an interesting discovery that may be relevant. Among the detritus of the shipwreck they found a metal urethral syringe, complete with its intimidating curved funnel-shaped tip. It was designed specifically to administer mercury for the treatment of venereal diseases, and tellingly enough, an analysis of residue recovered from the inside of the syringe showed a high concentration of mercury. The nasty-looking device had been used shortly before the ship went down. Its seems as if the pirates' sojourn in either Hispaniola or the Gulf of Honduras wasn't as pastoral as we might have otherwise thought.

Alternatively, some of Blackbeard's crew might have already contracted syphilis in New Providence the previous year, and the disease was only now reaching its unbearably painful second stage. Either the venereal disease or the yellow fever theory would explain why medical supplies had become such a big priority by the end of May 1718. It was just as well the pirates hadn't demanded money, as the colony's coffers were almost empty, drained by a long-running war against the Native Americans in the back-country. They could stall for time, but that would only increase the risk of retribution against the hostages or the city itself. The best course was to buy off the pirates and hope they would go away and leave the colony in peace. That way they would become somebody else's problem.

A few days passed without any news reaching the waiting ships, and no doubt the pirates became increasingly anxious. The longer they remained there, the greater the risk was of a Royal Naval warship appearing, and no doubt they were concerned about their shipmates who had accompanied Marks into Charles Town. Eventually Marks returned with the news that the pirate demands were being met. "The [Carolina] government were not long in deliberating upon the message, though 'twas the greatest affront that could have been put upon them; yet for saving so many men's lives (among them Mr. Samuel Wragg, one of the council), they complied with the necessity and sent aboard a chest valued at between £300 and £400, and the pirates went back safe to their ships." Of course, this medicine chest wasn't the only reward Blackbeard and his men collected for their efforts.

Before they released their eighty or so hostages, the pirates stripped them of any valuable and good-quality clothing, which is why they "were sent ashore almost naked." The value of the haul in gold and silver alone was estimated by Captain Johnson at around £1,500, a reasonable fortune in 1718, equivalent to approximately $400,000 in today's money. However, it wasn't much if you had to split it three hundred ways. Most of the money would have come from the passengers on the *Crowley* who, like Wragg, had traveled with enough funds to last them during their stay in Britain.

In another letter written from Charles Town soon afterward, it was reported that the pirates made away with less plunder than Captain Johnson suggests. After describing the delivery of the medicine chest, the letter continued: "Soon after the [pirates] dismissed our people and their ships having first taken from the two vessells that were homeward bound [back to Britain] what little money they had on board and all their provisions and from the two others the same, and distroy'd most of their cargoes etc. all fore pure mischief sake and to keep their hands in." Wanton destruction was the pirates' trademark, a means of retaliating against the profiteering ship-owners who oppressed the seamen working for them in poor conditions and for little pay. With some relief the writer continued: "They made no farther stay (thanks to God) but are gone to the Northward etc."

Blackbeard and his men had lingered off the Charles Town Bar for less than a week, during which time the port lay at the pirates' mercy. We have already seen that the defenses were barely up to the task of keeping the pirates at bay, and when Captain Richards returned he would have told Blackbeard as much. A determined assault would have carried the defenses, and the pirates could have plundered the city. Why didn't they? Well, Blackbeard must have realized that time wasn't on his side. If he delayed, the Royal Navy would eventually arrive on the scene, and the blockader would become the blockaded. Meanwhile Governor Johnson would have called in the militia from across the colony and would have asked for reinforcements from the neighboring colonies of North Carolina and Georgia.

Even a token defense of the port would have inflicted casualties on the pirates, and this might have deterred some of their number from supporting an assault. Blackbeard certainly threatened to destroy the ships in the inner harbor, and even to "lay before the Town and to beat it about our ears," as a resident put it, but he never once mentioned a full-scale assault. Evidently he didn't think he could pull it off. The days of the buccaneering assaults on Spanish ports were a barely remembered thing of the past, and the pirates were sailors, not trained soldiers. Blackbeard and his men would have realized that while an attack might well work, they also ran the risk of the governor's rhetoric or the arrival of fresh reinforcements galvanizing the city's inhabitants and their militia. In that case they would be met by a determined defense.

Even the option of bombarding the town and attacking the ships at anchor involved some risk if the defenders stood to their guns. A shore battery always had the edge over a moving wooden sailing ship—a point that was ably demonstrated in the same harbor in June 1776. The pirates had achieved their aim, and Blackbeard had made his point. He and his pirate band were powerful enough to dictate events, rather than to have to keep one step ahead of the authorities. They were no longer just a pirate crew, but had become a military force in miniature. Rather like the slave army of Spartacus, which terrified the landowners of Italy out of all proportion to the real threat they posed, Blackbeard and his pirates had the whole of the American seaboard wondering fearfully what the cutthroats would do next.

The ironic thing is that by that stage Blackbeard had decided that his pirate band had become too large for its own good—or, to be more specific, for the good of its leader. The attack on Charles Town had been an amazing demonstration of his piratical abilities, but it also brought problems. It certainly enhanced Blackbeard's reputation, and given the bloodthirsty threats he made there, his reputation as a hard-bitten terror would have been reinforced. This fear was important, as it made merchant captains far less likely to try and resist when they saw him approaching.

The problem was that this also drew more attention to him, and after Charles Town he became colonial America's public enemy number one. Every Royal Navy vessel on the American station would be on the lookout for him, and with a ship as big and powerful as the *Queen Anne's Revenge*, it was difficult to hide. However, hiding was what he had to do. He would have realized that he couldn't maintain this level of operation without inviting a standup fight with the Royal Navy—a fight he was bound to lose. He needed to hide out for a while, letting the outcry die down a little and any warships sent after him to return to their base. The trouble was, he was running out of hiding places.

During his sojourn off Charles Town Bar or even during his visit to the "Bahamas wrecks," he would have heard the latest gossip. Therefore, by the end of May 1718 he would almost certainly have heard about the offer of a royal pardon, and he probably knew that his old mentor Benjamin Hornigold planned to surrender as soon as he had the chance. In that case he would also have learned of the visit of HMS *Phoenix* to the Bahamas that March, and would have heard that the frigate captain left after awarding provisional pardons to more than two hundred Bahamian pirates.

Blackbeard would have realized that New Providence wasn't the place it once was. During that visit Captain Pearce of the *Phoenix* made it clear that he was just the vanguard and that before the summer was out the island's newly appointed governor would arrive with a powerful naval force and would formally demand the mass surrender of the pirates. It was clear that the Bahamas were no longer suitable for use as a pirate base, or even as a secure haven to hide in. He needed to find somewhere else to hide, and find it fast.

Blackbeard had already sailed the waters of the Carolinas and Virginia the year before, and he pretty much knew the area. He would have known that in North Carolina the governor was said to be less enthusiastic in his suppression of pirates than his neighbors, and that trade in the colony was also less developed than elsewhere on the coast, so there would be a less effective mercantile lobby to oppose him. It was in the interests of South Carolina and Virginia merchants to quash piracy, as the pirates damaged the transatlantic trade that was their livelihood. In contrast, North Carolina lacked a suitable deepwater port, and her trade was less developed than in neighboring colonies.

In many ways the colony was still in its formative stages. Her small-scale merchants shipped raw materials, not finished products, and because the North Carolina colony lacked a decent port, these were shipped to other colonies for sale to other colonial merchants. There was no transatlantic trade to speak of. This meant the merchant lobby didn't dominate the business of the colony, and the place was still economically backward enough to need supplies of basic imports in order to survive. It therefore had all the makings of an excellent pirate haven. Pirates could exchange their plunder at cut-rate prices in the colony's few towns, and as long as the governor didn't raise too much of an objection, the pirates and the settlers could coexist well enough.

Then there was the opportunity presented by the royal pardon to consider. A temporary surrender would certainly take the pressure off Blackbeard and his floating band of cutthroats. There might be some short-term gain to be had in appearing to do what the authorities wanted. In the longer term, the situation looked increasingly bleak. With the pardon in effect for any pirates willing to make a career change, others would mend their ways and take advantage of the offer. When the deadline for the offer passed, the authorities would be able to direct their efforts against a smaller number of pirate crews. Blackbeard was certainly not stupid, and he knew the odds were gradually shifting in favor of the authorities. The only question was which colonial governor to approach. Governor Robert Johnson of South Carolina was certainly out of the question after the pirates' recent visit to Charles Town, while Governor Robert Hunter of New York and Governor Robert Spotswood of Virginia were notoriously opposed to pirates and were guaranteed to make the process of surrender as difficult as possible for pirate supplicants.

That left Governor Woodes Rogers, who was due to arrive in the Bahamas, and Governor Charles Eden in North Carolina. As Rogers came from Bristol and was roughly the same age as Blackbeard, and Teach was

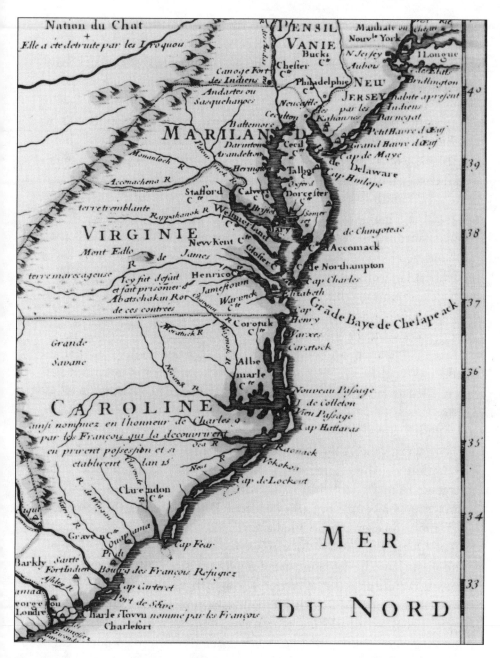

The Atlantic seaboard of Britain's North American colonies, shown in a detail from a French map produced in 1718. Blackbeard's hunting ground stretched from Delaware Bay in the north to Charles Town in the south.

almost certainly an assumed name, it has been argued that Blackbeard avoided seeking out a pardon from his fellow Bristolian for all the reasons we've discussed in the first chapter. It was equally likely that Blackbeard and his crew had too many unsettled scores in New Providence, and with Hornigold and his men supporting the governor, or even acting as his deputies, the pirates could expect little leeway. No doubt they would be watched closely for any sign that they might revert to their old ways. Therefore Blackbeard opted for Charles Eden in North Carolina, a man he would clearly have to charm and convince. That meant that when Blackbeard sailed north from Charles Town, he didn't just need a new base, he needed a protector as well.

Blackbeard would have discussed all this with his crew as they sailed north, or even before the pirate fleet left Charles Town Bar. However, what he didn't share were his plans for the *Queen Anne's Revenge*. It must have been clear to him that his pirate flagship was something of a liability. She drew too much water to slip easily through the Outer Banks into the inshore coastal waters of North Carolina's Pamlico Sound.

Like the Bahamas, the Outer Banks provided a perfect network of small islands and shoals where the pirates could evade pursuit and hide out when they needed to. However, the Bahamas also contained two deepwater channels for vessels the size of the *Queen Anne's Revenge* to navigate through, and both led directly to New Providence. In addition, the archipelago was pierced by two other channels, called the Tongue of the Ocean and the Exuma Sound, where large ships could find somewhere to hide in an emergency. Although the line of the Outer Banks was pierced by at least six channels, only a couple of these were remotely suitable for the passage of larger ships, and even these could be navigated only with extreme difficulty.

The *Queen Anne's Revenge* was just too big to operate out of his newfound pirate base. In the language of modern business, Blackbeard had to downsize. While the rest of his crew might have supported him if he explained this to them, Blackbeard had his own plans for downsizing that were best kept to himself. His plan was so draconian and Machiavellian that it exceeded anything that the most rapacious modern corporate executive could dream up.

The place he selected for this dastardly deed was Topsail Inlet, just in front of the modern town of Beaufort, North Carolina. In 1718 Beaufort was just a tiny hamlet, a ragged collection of unpainted shacks surrounded by bleached bones and the stench of rotten fish. Although a series of settlements were established along the Carolina coast during the seventeenth century, this area remained the preserve of the Coree Indians, whose land stretched from the Outer Banks down to Cape Lookout and on to the Cape Fear River.

In 1681 the Lords Proprietors who governed the Carolinas saw the Outer Banks as an area where commercial whaling might be successful, and so they encouraged the establishment of small whaling communities. Beaufort was just one of these, a permanent settlement built during the first years of the eighteenth century to replace the more makeshift whaling camps near Cape Lookout that grew up during the 1690s. From all accounts the settlement wasn't that successful, as its inhabitants lacked the boats needed to do anything more than cut up the whales that occasionally washed up on the beaches of Bogue Sound.

At the time the Coree Indians weren't considered much of a threat, as they were embroiled in a crippling war against both the Tuscaroras and the Machapungos. Those who survived were in no shape to stand up to the incursion of well-armed white settlers. Still, in 1713 acting governor Thomas Pollock of North Carolina saw the native threat as sufficiently serious to station a small garrison of North Carolina militia in the Core Sound area "to guard the people there from some few of the Cores that lurk thereabout." Five years later the same troops would be ordered to round up the pirates who arrived on their doorstep, the victims of Blackbeard's downsizing. No doubt they were all still roundly cursing their former captain when the soldiers appeared. As for the whalers, when they saw what Blackbeard had done, they must have thought their Christmas and birthday had come at once.

6

A Cutthroat Business

Henry Bostock wasn't having the best of mornings. His sloop the *Margaret* wallowed in the swell, while a cable length (200 yards) away a large, menacing pirate ship lay waiting for him, her gunports open. Wisps of smoke told him the gunners were ready, lengths of burning slow match held in their fists. Jeering cutthroats lined the rail of the larger vessel, and the taunting continued as he clambered down into his sloop's tender and gave orders to be rowed toward his tormentors. By way of diversion he would have cast his experienced eye over the pirate ship as she loomed over him. She was clearly French-built, with fast lines and a sleek appearance, a little like a naval frigate. She had already been pierced for two dozen guns, but her hull showed evidence of more recent alterations: extra gunports were cut into her gunwale and beneath her forecastle and quarterdeck, both of which had been cut down slightly, creating a flush deck fore and aft. Grinning faces looked down on him as he clambered up the frigate's side, and rough hands hauled him up the last few feet onto the pirate deck. It was then that he saw him.

Standing before him was one of the most frightening men he had ever clapped eyes on, a devilish-looking figure with wild eyes surrounded by even wilder black hair. The pirate's beard was long and unkempt, plaited and hanging down over his chest. The same unkempt hair seemed to surround his face, and more plaits stuck out on either side of his face. Surprisingly, the ends of these rat-tailed black plaits were tied with twists of ribbon, which only seemed to make his appearance all the more disconcerting. The man was dressed in a long sea captain's coat, crossed by two belts—a sword belt and a bandolier—while three brace of pistols hung from improvised holsters over his chest, making him look like a walking armory. Despite the winter sun of the Caribbean, the man wore a small brown fur cap, of the kind commonly worn by seamen in cold weather, and beneath it, as if to complete the whole devilish image, two small lengths of slow match poked out and hung down behind each ear, the tips of the impregnated rope glowing red and smoldering, with wisps of smoke framing the pirate's head. As if all this wasn't alarming enough, there were the eyes—the manic, staring eyes that glared at him from behind the hair. Henry Bostock had just met Blackbeard.

Somehow Henry Bostock lived to tell the tale. The encounter took place on December 5, 1717, when for eight long hours he and his men remained Blackbeard's prisoners, never knowing from one minute to the next whether they would live or die. The attack took place off Crab Island near Anguilla, and for the rest of the day the *Queen Anne's Revenge*, accompanied by the sloop *Revenge*, cruised the waters of the Leeward Islands in search of more victims. During that time Bostock had plenty of time to watch Blackbeard in action, and when he wrote his statement for the governor of Barbados two weeks later he was able to describe his nemesis in some detail. In fact, the master of the sloop *Margaret* was the first to provide a description of the pirate who captured him, and it was he who first came up with the cognomen "Blackbeard."

In his deposition written on December 19 Bostock described his tormentor: "The Captain by the [name] of Capt. Tach . . . was a tall Spare Man with a very black beard which he wore very long." It was hardly a full description, but it tallies with the far more vivid version provided by Captain Johnson: "So our Heroe, Captain Thatch, assumed the Cognomen of Black-beard, from that large Quantity of Hair, which covered his whole Face, and frightn'd America, more than any Comet that has appear'd there a long Time." He continued to describe the beard in even more lurid detail: "This Beard was Black, which he had suffered to grow of an extravagant Length; as to Breadth, it came up to his Eyes; he was accustomed to twist it with Ribbons, in small Tails, after the Manner of our Remellies [Ramillies] Wigs, and turn them about his Ears."

The description of Bostock's encounter with Blackbeard is drawn from Captain Johnson's dramatic visual sketch of Blackbeard, quoted in full in this book's preface. Johnson described the little flourishes that tipped Blackbeard's appearance over the edge from frightening to downright demonic. Whether his description was genuine or simply sensationalism is not really clear. It almost seems as if Johnson took Bostock's description of the pirate and exaggerated it for dramatic effect. What is clear is that Blackbeard, the consummate actor, knew how to dress for the part. It was all a calculated façade, an image designed to intimidate his opponents and to terrify his own crew to the extent that they dared not cross him. In other words, Blackbeard understood the most basic rules of piracy—appearance was everything, and fear was the key to success.

In some ways, Henry Bostock was to discover it was largely a matter of bluster. The pirates ransacked his sloop, the *Margaret*, and winched his cargo of cattle and pigs on board their own vessel. He had no plunder worth having nor rum to drink, and only a few weapons to loot, so Blackbeard contented himself with liberating Captain Bostock of his books and navigational instruments, along with the master's small collection of books—almost certainly navigational guides. This was hardly the piratical attacks portrayed in fiction—no chests filled with Spanish treasure or sacks of gold coins were to be had, only wholly unromantic livestock. Even more surprisingly, after being forced to spend a day in the company of the pirates, Henry Bostock and his men were returned to their sloop and allowed to sail off unharmed. This leniency hardly fitted with the image of the devil incarnate that Blackbeard cultivated so successfully. It just showed how good Blackbeard was at projecting an image.

There was a lot more to piracy than simply stopping ships and stealing plunder. In some ways the business of piracy resembled any other form of semiorganized crime. Suitable victims had to be identified, then cornered. It was important to avoid any unnecessary casualties, as this lowered the morale of the pirate crew. This meant that in order to discourage resistance, pirates had to cither show a display of overwhelming force, or else develop such a fearsome reputation that victims imagined that any resistance would be met by brutal retaliation. In other words, it was all a matter of fear, intimidation, and firepower, which made Blackbeard little different from the Dalton Gang or Al Capone. The only real difference was that the pirates operated in the open sea, which brought with it its own set of problems and opportunities. What set Blackbeard apart from many other pirates of his day was that he seemed to excel at the business—he was an intelligent enough man to know where to strike next, he was a good enough seaman to overhaul his victims, and he was superb at the business of forcing his prey to strike their colors and meekly wait for the pirates to board them.

Naturally enough, his appearance played a major part in this, as did his larger-than-life persona. For a start, it set him apart from his men. We have already said how pirate ships were run on egalitarian lines, with all shipmates having a say in the running of their ship, and voting on all important decisions. Of course, some were more equal than others. Blackbeard's intimidating appearance was as important a prop with his own crew as it was with the merchant captains he encountered. Henry Bostock would no more raise a weapon against Blackbeard than he would at the devil, and many of Blackbeard's shipmates clearly felt the same way. The pirate used his appearance and manners to create a fearsome image, then worked hard at maintaining it in front of his crew. He needed to show he was braver, wilder, and more violent than his shipmates. Once this persona was established, there was far less chance of Blackbeard being ousted from power, as happened to Benjamin Hornigold and Charles Vane.

Captain Johnson tells the tale of an incident that demonstrates just how good a showman Blackbeard was. As he put it:

In the commonwealth of pirates, he who goes the greatest length or wickedness is looked upon with a kind of envy amongst them, and is thereby entitled to be distinguished by some post, and if such a one has but courage, he must certainly be a great man. The hero of whom we are writing [Blackbeard] was thoroughly accomplished this way, and some of his frolics of wickedness were so extravagant, as if he aimed at making his men believe he was a devil incarnate; for being one day at sea, and a little flushed with drink, Come, says he, let us make a hell of our own, and try how long we can bear it. Accordingly he, with two or three others, went down into the hold and, closing up all the hatches, filled several pots full of brimstone and other combustible matter, and set on fire, and so continued until they were almost suffocated, when some of the men cried out for air; at length he opened the hatches, not a little pleased that he held out the longest.

Whether there was any truth in the story is largely immaterial. Johnson included it because it was believed at the time, which meant it reflected the image Johnson and his contemporaries had of Blackbeard.

The image seemed to work with Blackbeard's own crew, who certainly seemed to view their leader as an intimidating, devilish figure. Captain Johnson reinforced the image they had of Blackbeard by telling another tale. Even he had to describe it as "a story which may appear a little incredible," but added, "however it will not be fair to omit it since we had it from their own mouths," meaning Blackbeard's own crew. By this he probably meant Blackbeard's mate Israel Hands, who survived his piratical career and by the time Captain Johnson was writing his *General History* was back in London, begging on the streets. We can be fairly certain that the writer met the pirate during this period and that the latter was the source of many of the accounts of Blackbeard's career. Captain Johnson continued: "Once upon a cruise, they found that they had a man on board more than their crew, such a one was seen several days amongst them, sometimes below, and sometimes upon deck, yet no man in the ship could give an account of who he was, or from whence he came from, but that he disappeared a little before they were cast away in their great ship; but it seems, they verily believed it was the Devil." This surely referred to the *Queen Anne's Revenge*, in the weeks before she ran aground on Topsail Inlet. If Israel Hands and the rest of the crew believed the devil was a ship-mate of theirs while they were off Charles Town Bar, then Blackbeard excelled at projecting his devilish image.

What is surprising in all this is that Blackbeard's reputation was based on fear and the perception of evil, rather than on violence. In all his encounters before his final battle, it is almost certain that Blackbeard never actually killed anyone. It was almost as if his reputation was enough, and he didn't feel the need to prove himself by acts of excessive violence.

Unlike other pirate captains, there is no evidence that he subjected his victims to torture in order to find out if they were hiding anything from him, and in fact he seems to have been a relatively benign pirate. Take, for example, his dealings with Henry Bostock, where he returned the man's ship to him after a day and allowed him to sail off unharmed. Although nobody could take being captured by Blackbeard lightly, the chances were higher than with most pirates that his victims would live to tell the tale.

This compares favorably with men like Charles Vane, who seemed to take a psychopathic delight in torture and violence. In one instance Vane's crew had to intervene when their captain tied a poor sailor to the bowsprit, then tortured him by jabbing burning matches into his eyes while holding a loaded, cocked pistol in the sailor's mouth. The crew's actions saved the lives of the man and his fellow prisoners. Ironically, this tendency for violence seemed to have left little impression with Vane's crew, who unceremoniously removed him from office when they felt he was no longer doing his job properly. It is almost inconceivable that

Blackbeard, from the original version of Captain Johnson's General History, *complete with burning slow match stuffed under his tricorne hat.*

Blackbeard's crew would ever join forces to oust their leader in this man
ner. After all, seamen were a superstitious lot, and if they genuinely
believed that Blackbeard was in league with the devil, then he was definitely not a man to be crossed.

The one act of violence associated with Blackbeard was also recounted
by Captain Johnson, from a tale told by Israel Hands. The pirate mate was
captured in Bath Town by Captain Brand of the Royal Navy in November
1718, and according to Captain Johnson he was wounded following a fra-
cas with Blackbeard, who had been "in one of his savage humours." As the
story went, "One night, drinking in his cabin, with Hands, the pilot, and
another man, Blackbeard without any provocation privately draws out a
small pair of pistols, and cocks them under the table, which, being perceived by the man, he withdrew and went on deck, leaving Hands, the
pilot and the captain together." Clearly the visitor didn't risk crossing
Blackbeard by asking him what he was planning! "When the pistols were
ready, he [Blackbeard] blew out the candle, and crossing his hands, discharged them at his company." The effect of two pistol shots being fired at
point-blank range in the cramped stern cabin of a small sloop can only be
imagined. "Hands, the master, was shot through the knee and lamed for
life; the other pistol did no execution." Given the primitive medical facili-
ties onboard, a pistol shot in the kneecap could well have been fatal. Israel
Hands was lucky to survive the drunken incident.

What is revealing is what happened when the injured Hands
demanded to know why he had been shot. Blackbeard simply replied by
cursing them, then adding, "that if he did not now and then kill one of
them, they would forget who he was." If the story has any truth whatsoever,
then it shows how hard Blackbeard worked at maintaining his image. If the
incident took place during those long months spent at anchor off Ocracoke, then he would have been worried about the morale of his crew, and
their motivation to follow him. He might have felt that he needed a wild,
dramatic gesture to prove he was no soft touch. If so, it was an indication
that morale on board was not what it once was before he deliberately
wrecked his flagship at Topsail Inlet. It seems that even the devil incarnate
had to worry about crew motivation now and then.

Another part of Captain Johnson's account of Blackbeard's life tells of
a journal he kept, which was supposed to have been captured by Lieutenant Maynard of the Royal Navy. Johnson claims that "in Blackbeard's

journal, which was taken, there were several memorandums of the follow-ing nature; found writ with his own hand; 'Such a Day, Rum all out:—Our Company somewhat sober:—a Damned Confusion amongst us!—Rogues a plotting;—great Talk of separation. So I looked sharp for a Prize;—such a Day took one, with a great deal of Liquor on Board, so kept the Company hot, damned hot, then all things went well again.'" Unfortunately, no such journal was ever recorded among the pirate's possessions and correspon-dence. This is almost certainly an embellishment on Johnson's part, adding some extra spice to his account of Blackbeard. Then again, he might have used the story of a journal as a literary vehicle—a way of reflecting the situation on board Blackbeard's sloop during the latter half of 1718. He would have learned of conditions aboard from Israel Hands, not from any journal.

If there was any truth in the story of the journal and the sentiments behind the entries, then it shows that Blackbeard might have been facing a crisis. It also explains why he might have had to resort to extremes like shooting Israel Hands to keep his men motivated and willing to follow orders. Other pirate captains faced murmurings of rebellion when the basics of pirate living ran out—especially the rum. It almost suggests that Blackbeard resumed his piratical career because he needed to pacify his men, and if so this betrays a weakness that runs against the general impres-sion of a man who was willing to abandon the majority of his crew at Topsail Inlet. Given that during the last months of 1718 he had less than thirty men at his disposal, it seems unlikely that a man of Blackbeard's for-midable nature would let morale slide so much that he was faced with rebellion. His crew was small enough to dominate, and their repeated visits to Bath Town would have helped maintain morale as the Carolina winter set in.

Clearly the whole business of being a pirate captain was a balancing act, one that required a steady stream of prizes to supply the crew with the basic food, drink, and supplies they needed, and a reasonable amount of specie to spend if and when the pirates reached a port like Bath Town. During 1717 and 1718 Blackbeard did an exemplary job, attacking just the right targets to provide his shipmates with what they needed. What changed the whole pace of his operation was Topsail Inlet. After all, aban-doning 90 percent of your crew and making off with the plunder might have made the select few feel somewhat special, but they would also have wondered just how far they could trust their two-timing captain. The lack of activity during the pirates' sojourn in Bath Town might also have taken its toll on the morale of the remaining members of the crew. So, too, did concerns over their status—Blackbeard still hid behind the pretense of having reformed, even though he and his men were clearly attacking ships again. The result was that while morale might not have been as bad as Captain Johnson suggests during that winter, it was certainly not as good as it had been before Topsail Inlet.

Blackbeard was a gifted pirate captain in more ways than just understanding his crew. He was also intelligent enough to be fully conversant with the job and had fully mastered the skills needed to be a success. These were wide-ranging, from knowing the basics of navigation and seamanship to intelligence-gathering and knowing how to pursue an enemy and what to do with him when he was cornered. A gifted captain also needed to know when to cut his losses and abandon the chase or turn away from a powerful opponent—and had to be able to convince his crew he made the right decision. Some pirates such as "Calico" Jack Rackam and Stede Bonnet seemed to struggle with these skills, while others lacked the education or understanding to master them as they went along. What set Blackbeard apart was the apparent ease with which he functioned as a pirate captain. To understand how he operated, we need to take a closer look at the whole business of piracy.

Pirates didn't just randomly sail around looking for victims. Instead, they tended to operate in shipping bottlenecks or along major shipping routes, where they could virtually guarantee meeting merchant ships. We have already seen how Blackbeard operated in the relatively busy waters of the Leeward Islands, the Gulf of Honduras, the Florida Straits, off the port of Charles Town, and off the mouth of the Delaware River. Others favored the Mona Passage and the Windward Passage, both important bottlenecks and entry points into the Caribbean, while the waters surrounding the Windward Islands, the Dutch Antilles, and the Yucatan Channel were all considered good hunting grounds. Further to the north the approaches to New York and Boston, the area off the Virginia Capes (Chesapeake Bay), and the fishing grounds of Newfoundland were also considered prime locations for pirates. While the extensive waters of the Spanish Main might have been considered a prime hunting ground during the days of the buccaneers in the seventeenth century, by Blackbeard's time there was little shipping worth plundering down there. Although there was a lot of ocean out there, a good pirate captain knew exactly where to look.

The shipping booms that followed the end of the War of the Grand Alliance and the War of the Spanish Succession meant that in the periods from 1697 to 1701 and after 1713 the number of ships operating in Caribbean and North American waters increased significantly. Even more importantly, these ships tended to sail along set routes, which made the task of hunting down certain types of ships fairly straightforward. For example, British slave ships tended to make their American landfall off Barbados or the Leeward Islands, while French slavers opted for Martinique. One reason for this was the need for a speedy passage—Barbados and Martinique were both major slave markets, while the rich sugar-producing colonies in the Leeward Islands all needed a ready supply of slave labor. From St. Kitts and Monserrat the slavers also had a straight run west to Jamaica, the largest slave market in the Caribbean. Similarly, French slavers cut across the curve of the Lesser Antilles and headed straight for their sugar-producing colony of St. Domingue. Alternatively, French slavers reached Port-au-Prince after making a fast transatlantic voyage that made landfall on the northern coast of Hispaniola.

The homeward leg of the triangular trade route meant that these same slave ships returned to Europe laden with sugar or rum, making them prime targets for marauding pirates. Because of the prevailing winds, a direct voyage from Jamaica out into the Atlantic wasn't really practical, so instead these vessels sailed around Cuba, passing through the Yucatan Channel, the Florida Straits, and the Bahamas Channel before curving out into the Atlantic toward Bermuda, which was a popular watering and provisioning port of call before the final transatlantic leg of the voyage began in earnest. Similarly, shipping from the Lesser Antilles headed roughly northwest and then northeast toward Bermuda, leaving the shallow waters of the Leeward chain around Anguilla or the Virgin Islands. The dogleg was to take advantage of the Antilles Current, which swept up the eastern side of the Bahamas to join the Florida Current as it merged with the Gulf Stream.

Spanish transatlantic shipping tended to follow the age-old routes laid down by the Spanish treasure galleons, making landfall near Trinidad if the ships were bound for the Spanish Main, and Puerto Rico or Santo Domingo if they were heading toward Cuba or Mexico. The majority of

Spanish shipping tended to head home through the Florida Straits, which made the waters off Havana a rich source of Spanish merchantmen. In the waters of the Spanish Main, wind and current were often at odds, with the Caribbean Current moving from Trinidad toward the Yucatan Channel, and the North East trades crossing it at right angles, blowing from the Leeward Islands toward Panama. For the most part Spanish shipping tended to take advantage of the old but still workable *flota* system, which meant that the ships with the best cargoes tended to sail in convoys. This was bad news for pirates, who were therefore forced to prey on smaller coastal craft or non-Spanish vessels, which were pretty much left to fend for themselves.

As for shipping bound directly for the British or French colonies in North America, a minority made landfall somewhere off Newfoundland, Nova Scotia, or even New England, although this involved a relatively slow crossing, given that the ships had to go against the flow of wind and current. After making landfall, they then followed the line of the coast south to their destination. In this respect their following of the rhumb lines of Earth mirrored the routes taken by commercial airliners today. Further south, shipping hit the Gulf Stream and the North Atlantic Drift, a great conveyor belt of current that sailing ships used to speed their passage from America toward Europe. For much of the year this current was assisted by the Westerlies, the predominant wind direction that blows from New England toward Britain. Rather than fight the prevailing currents, the majority of sailing ships bound for the Americas tended to keep far to the south of this current.

The easiest way to view the prevailing wind and current patterns in the Atlantic is to imagine a big irregular circle moving in a clockwise direction through the Windward Islands and around the Caribbean to Mexico, then out again up the North American coast before heading out again past Bermuda. The reason Bermuda was such an important landmark was that to the southeast of it lies the Sargasso Sea, a patch of slack water where there is very little in the way of wind or current to help a sailing ship on its way. The North Equatorial Current picks up again between the Azores and the Leeward Islands, and although the accompanying column of easterly wind is not as pronounced as the Westerlies of the North Atlantic or the North East Trades a little to the south, they were more than sufficient to speed the bulk of transatlantic sailing ships on their way between Europe and the North American colonies. The North East Trades were the slavers' winds, blowing directly from West Africa toward the Caribbean, which usually guaranteed a speedy Middle Passage between slaving grounds and slave markets.

Experienced mariners like Blackbeard fully understood the vagaries of wind, tide, and current. They realized that by concentrating their efforts on likely bottlenecks they were assured of merchant ships to prey on. Even more importantly, rather than trying to intercept a ship in midvoyage, they tended to concentrate their efforts close to destinations, which again increased the chances of encountering a victim. That was why Blackbeard operated off Charles Town Bar—it was a major destination port for vessels from the Caribbean and for coastal shipping heading down from the northern colonies. The same was true of Delaware Bay, the mouth of the Delaware River, where all the shipping bound in and out of Philadelphia would sail into the pirate trap. It was for exactly this reason that Charles Vane loitered off Charles Town himself, and also operated immediately to the southwest of Bermuda. Shipping wasn't so hard to find if you lay between the merchantmen and their destination—that way the prey came to you. All you had to do then was corner the unfortunate vessel and force its crew to surrender.

Of course, both Charles Town and Delaware Bay had another advantage to the pirates. Both Philadelphia and Charles Town lacked a dedicated guard ship—a Royal Navy vessel whose duty it was to protect local shipping, and even to escort vessels through dangerous waters. Naval officers were just as able to figure out the pirate danger spots as the pirates themselves, which is why pirates rarely loitered long in the waters off New York, Chesapeake Bay, Barbados, Jamaica, and Nova Scotia. As the pirate crisis developed, the British deployed more warships in American waters, which gave commanders the chance to conduct antipiracy patrols rather than just remain on the defensive. In time of war the risks became even greater, as even more warships would gather in naval bases such as Barbados and Jamaica, ready for offensive operations against the French or Spanish. For their part these other maritime powers maintained their own local patrols, although neither power seemed to devote many resources to countering the threat of piracy. Fairly correctly, they saw it as a largely British problem—the majority of victims were from Britain or the British colonies in North America.

In order to take advantage of this vast pirate hunting ground, pirate captains needed to be able to navigate. In an age when literacy was the exception rather than the rule, this requirement severely limited the candidates for a pirate captaincy. The basics of navigation in the early eighteenth century meant that the captain or master needed to be able to determine his latitude with some degree of certainty using astrolabes, quadrants, or similar devices. The ability to determine longitude correctly had to wait until the invention of the marine chronometer in the mideighteenth century. In Blackbeard's day mariners had to rely on dead reckoning, guessing the speed and direction their vessel had sailed since the last measurement of latitude using the most basic of tools—a log streamed over the side to determine speed, and a pegboard on which any course changes and gauged speed were marked. It was an inexact science, and during a long voyage the errors could multiply until the ship was hundreds of miles from her estimated position. Some were better at it than others, and to their illiterate shipmates reasonably skilled and educated pirate captains such as Blackbeard must have seemed to have almost magical powers.

In the deposition given by Henry Bostock on December 19, 1717, he claims that Blackbeard "took his cargo of cattle and hogs, his arms, books and instrument." The "instrument" was almost certainly Bostock's backstaff, or Davis quadrant. Invented by the arctic explorer Captain John Davis over a century before, the device was used to determine the altitude of the sun by observing its shadow, while simultaneously sighting the horizon. At noon (the sun's zenith), the navigator peered at the horizon through a slit in the wooden base. He then slid an adjustable crosspiece that reflected the sun's shadow up or down the arm until the shadow lined up directly with the slit. The angle this took place at was read off, which at least in theory gave the altitude of the sun from the horizon. Then, by consulting a book of printed mathematical tables, it was possible to use this information to work out the observer's latitude above or below the equator.

The backstaff was a simple enough wooden instrument, but it worked. Its only real drawback was that it wasn't much use at sighting the moon, the planets, or the stars. That trick would have to wait until the invention of double-reflection optics and the marine sextant in 1731. Blackbeard might well have considered Bostock's instrument to be superior to his own, hence he took it for his own use. The "books" taken by Blackbeard probably included Bostock's table of sun declinations, which he would have used to determine latitude, and possibly a series of rutters or pilot atlases, manuals that gave details of anchorages, harbors, tides, and prevalent weather conditions for a particular area. In addition, a book called the *English Pilot*, published in 1671, gathered together information on the coastline of North America from Hudson Bay down to the West Indies. It was still in print in 1718, and would remain in use until the volume was updated by Captain James Cook in the mid-eighteenth century.

The first printed atlas of sea charts was produced by the Dutch pilot Lucas Jansz Waghenaer in 1584, and by Blackbeard's day these volumes of charts (also known as "wagoners," after their creator) were widely available—for a price. Most navigators of the period relied on hand-drawn copies, and often added their own notes, covering such things as the best approaches to anchorages, soundings, the pattern of local tides, and prominent navigational landmarks. A seaman like Blackbeard wouldn't pass up the opportunity to take any charts or atlases he stumbled across, because they provided him with useful information. His looting of Bostock's navigational instruments and books was no doubt repeated by Blackbeard and his contemporaries whenever they looted a prize. Armed with this information, Blackbeard could greatly increase his knowledge of the area he operated in. At the same time, he would have quizzed local fishermen and coastal traders, gathering information that one day might give him the edge in a chase or in combat.

The business of cruising for prizes was something of a pirate art form. The benefit of cruising in consort with other vessels has already been mentioned—it extended the radius of the search, allowing pirates to comb a wider swath of ocean. The buccaneers and privateers of the previous century worked out a series of signals between these ships, such as a particular combination of sail evolutions combined with the firing of a gun. These prearranged signals were also adopted by pirates, and although we have no detail of what they were, it is pretty certain that they were similar to those used by most privateers of the time. That wasn't the only trick men like Blackbeard used from their privateering days. Other habits were equally useful, such as keeping just over the horizon from the coast as much as possible, so as to avoid being seen from the shore. The chances of detection were further reduced by having a minimum of sails set. If the pirates wanted to check known anchorages, as Blackbeard did in the Gulf of Honduras, he would send in a sloop or smaller vessel under cover of darkness.

The best vessel in these circumstances was a small prize such as a local fishing boat, as it would attract little attention.

When Blackbeard operated off the mouth of the Delaware River he would have used all these tricks to his advantage, while keeping his sloop ready for a fast pursuit if required. We have already demonstrated that he saw the importance of gathering intelligence such as navigational information. For the same reason, he would interrogate the captain and crew of any vessel he captured, asking whether other ships were due to sail from the same port, or were expected to arrive over the next few days. He would also ask about the presence of any warships. Any interrogation would be augmented by the reading of any dispatches, orders, and even private letters. It all helped to build up a picture of what was happening in a port. This was where Blackbeard's fearsome appearance came in handy. Even though he never developed a reputation for torture, he certainly looked as if he would stop at nothing to get what he wanted. We know from the accounts of the prisoners he captured off Charles Town Bar that most captives would tell him whatever he wanted to know.

At the height of his powers Blackbeard had a powerful forty-gun flagship and three sloops under his command, crewed by at least three hundred pirates. The trouble with a force like this was that his reputation would have preceded him. While Blackbeard lay off Charles Town the governor of the South Carolina colony sent word of the pirates to neighboring colonies, and to the nearest representatives of the Royal Navy, then at anchor in Virginia's James River. The news would also have spread to merchant captains and even local fishermen, who would have tried to delay their sailing until the pirate threat had passed. This meant that it was advisable to operate in an area for a limited period, probably no more than a week, then move on to fresh hunting grounds. Blackbeard's abandonment of his ships and crew at Topsail Inlet was a dramatic solution to the problem, but it meant that his progress would no longer be common knowledge. He was much more successful in the West Indies, where with just two ships he managed to capture a string of prizes and keep one step ahead of any naval pursuers.

During the Golden Age of Piracy there were several near clashes between pirates and warships, and a small number of bona fide engagements. Blackbeard narrowly avoided running into HMS *Scarborough* in the Leeward Islands, and even Captain Johnson credits the pirates with fighting an engagement against the British warship. An engagement of this kind held no appeal for pirates, as it meant a hard and often risky fight, with little or no chance of plunder at the end of it. Blackbeard was wise to make himself scarce, but other pirates were not so pragmatic, or so fortunate. The most spectacular engagement of this type was fought between the pirate Bartholomew Roberts's *Royal Fortune* and HMS *Swallow*, commanded by Captain Chaloner Ogle, off the West African coast. It is worth describing here, as it shows what could happen if a pirate crew let itself be cornered by a well-trained warship.

Captain Ogle had been hunting Bartholomew Roberts for weeks, and soon after dawn on February 5, 1722, he came upon the pirates as they lay at anchor near Cape Lopez near the slaving port of Whydah. Roberts and

Bartholomew Roberts, pictured off Whydah on the West African coast with his ships Ranger *and* Royal Fortune *entering the harbor. A group of slave ships are shown at anchor in the roads beyond, trapped by Roberts and his pirates. Although Blackbeard was less successful than Roberts, the Welsh-born pirate never managed to threaten the stability of colonial America as successfully as his English-born colleague.*

his men had captured a slave ship the previous day, and had spent the night drinking their way through her stocks of liquor. Consequently, the pirates were literally caught napping. As a sandbar lay between him and the pirate ships, Ogle veered out to sea slightly, a move that the pirates interpreted as an attempt to flee. Captain Skyrm in Roberts's consort, the thirty-two-gun *Ranger*, was the first to raise sail and pursue. Ogle realized that the pirates still hadn't recognized that the *Swallow* was a warship, so he reduced sail to improve the illusion. As the pursuers came within range they fired their bow chasers without much success. Evidently the gunners were as hung over as the rest of the pirate crew. In fact, it was claimed they thought they were chasing a Portuguese merchantman rather than a British warship, which suggests Ogle was flying the Portuguese flag as a *ruse de guerre*.

When the *Ranger* was too close to escape, Captain Ogle sprang his trap. Captain Johnson's account told the story from the perspective of the pirates: "It was with the utmost consternation they saw her [the *Swallow*] suddenly bring to, and hawl up her lower ports, now within pistol-shot." The pirates panicked and lowered their black flag, a signal of surrender. However, after a few moments of reflection they decided to fight, and raised their colors once again. What followed was a two-hour sea battle, and by the end of it the heavily outgunned *Ranger* was a bloody shambles, her mainmast brought down and her decks scattered with dead or dying men. Captain Johnson continued: "They [the pirates] grew sick, struck their colours, and called out for quarter; having 10 men killed out right, and 20 wounded, without the loss or hurt of one of the King's men. She had 32 guns, manned by 16 French men, 20 Negroes, and 77 English." These men had one last dramatic gesture to make: "The colours were thrown overboard, that they might not rise in judgment, nor be displayed in triumph over them." They then unsuccessfully tried to set fire to their ship before she could be secured by Ogle's boarders.

The fight against the *Ranger* was only half the battle. Five days later the *Swallow* returned to the coast at dawn, and found the *Royal Fortune* still at anchor, her crew impatiently waiting for the return of the *Ranger*. Once again Roberts and his men had been drinking, this time following the capture of the British slave ship *Neptune* of London, which rode at anchor close to the pirate flagship. The befuddled lookouts at first thought the approaching ship was the missing *Ranger*, but they soon realized their mistake. Roberts and his men scrambled to raise sail and get under way, tacking out into the mouth of the bay to meet the *Swallow* head-on. Desperate straits called for extreme measures. The pirate captain now knew he was facing a well-trained British warship, and that he stood no chance in a straight fight.

Roberts's plan was therefore "to pass close by the Swallow, with all their sails, and to receive her broadside, before they returned a shot; if disabled by this, or if they could not depend on sailing, then to run on shore at the Point (which is steep to) and everyone to shift for himself among the Negroes; or failing in these, to board and blow up together, for he saw that the greatest part of his men were drunk, passively courageous, unfit for service." Once past the *Swallow* he could make good his escape from the bay, hoping that the warship was too slow to pursue him. The pirate captain had put on his finest clothes, "a rich crimson damask waistcoat and breeches, a red feather in his hat, a gold chain around his neck, with a diamond cross hanging to it, a sword in his hand, and two pairs of pistols hanging at the end of a silk sling slung over his shoulders (according to the fashion of pirates)." As he got under way Roberts also ordered the black flag to be hoisted. Whatever the outcome of the coming battle, Roberts intended to fight with as much style as he could, hoping to inspire his drunken shipmates by his example.

An officer of the *Swallow* recalled that "the pirate sailing better than us, shot ahead about half a gunshot," the naval gunners blasting their opponents with a full broadside of double-shotted grapeshot as they passed. "We continued firing (without intermission) such guns as we could bring to bear." It seems that Bartholomew Roberts was killed in the first broadside. Captain Johnson wrote that

> He [Roberts] had now perhaps finished the fight very desperately, if death, who took a swift passage in a grape-shot, had not interposed, and struck him directly in the throat. He settled himself on the tackles of a gun, which one Stephenson, from the helm. Observing, ran to his assistance, and not perceiving him wounded, swore at him, and bid him stand up, and fight like a man; but when he found his mistake, and that his captain was certainly dead, he gushed into tears, and wished the next shot to be his lot. They presently threw him overboard, with his arms and ornaments on, according to the repeated request he made in his lifetime.

The one-sided fight soon reached its inevitable conclusion. Captain Johnson tells how the death of their captain took the fight out of the pirate crew: "many deserted their quarters, and all stupidly neglected any means of defence, or escape." As the officer recounted, the *Swallow* continued firing, "till by favour of the wind we came alongside again, and after exchanging a few more shot, about half past one, his main-mast came down, being shot away a little below the parrel. At two she struck, and called for quarters . . . the total of the men on board were 152, of which 52 were negroes." Amazingly, only two other pirates apart from Roberts were killed in the action, and once again the Royal Navy crew didn't suffer any casualties in the action. Some fifty-two of the prisoners would soon be swinging at the end of a rope outside Cape Coast Castle in what was to be the last and largest mass pirate hanging of the age.

Clearly it didn't pay to trade shots with the Royal Navy. While poorly trained and poorly motivated pirate crews could go through the motions sufficiently well to frighten merchant crews into submission, the crew of a warship were more than ready to call the pirates' bluff. Roberts realized this, and planned to take his blows and escape. By contrast, when Blackbeard faced an attack by two small sloops crewed by British sailors, he decided to remain to fight it out—which meant that he saw an advantage in staying. Piracy was as much a matter of showmanship as anything else, and men like Roberts and Blackbeard realized that flight was often more risky than battle. Even if the pirates made good their escape, the crew would inevitably question the courage and skill of their elected leader—which is exactly what happened to Charles Vane. It was much better to keep out of the Navy's way altogether, which meant gathering good intelligence, moving your area of operations, and quickly and skillfully identifying any approaching sail.

It usually wasn't too difficult. There were simply too few ships and too much ocean to patrol for the Royal Navy to have anything more than sporadic success against pirates before 1719, when they significantly increased the number of warships available to hunt down pirates. Tactics were also to blame. After Blackbeard blockaded Charles Town, Governor Robert Johnson of the South Carolina colony complained that the existing policy of allocating guard ships wasn't working. His attitude was colored by the fact that no such guard ship was allocated to his own colony, but he did make the valid suggestion that instead of patrolling certain harbors, these guard ships should become more proactive, hunting in areas where pirates were likely to operate. As the pirates tended to quit

North American waters completely during the winter, he suggested that the guard ships should follow them south, rather than lying idly at anchor in northern harbors. As he put it, "Where the game is, there the vermin will be."

Piracy wasn't just a business of avoiding warships and lying in wait for merchantmen. You also had to catch them. Of course, wind was all-important. Most sailing ships of the time couldn't sail within about 40° of the direction the wind was blowing from, and ships tacking into the wind naturally enough made slower progress than vessels sailing with the wind on their beam (hitting them at right angles). The best angle was when the wind came from the port or starboard quarter, as the ship could use her full press of sails to best advantage. While landlubbers might think that sailing with the wind directly astern was the fastest of all aspects, in most ships this meant that some of the sails were blocked by others further aft, which meant that the sails didn't draw to their full potential. This was all basic stuff, and second nature to men who made their living as seamen. An experienced pirate captain would constantly compute where his ship and his prey would be in relation to the wind, and would be ready to change course slightly to take advantage of any vagaries in wind strength or direction.

As with anything else, there were tricks of the trade. By sailing on a parallel course, the pirate captain could learn fairly quickly which was the faster of the two vessels. If the pirate ship began the chase to windward (upwind) of her prey, this obviously gave the pursuer a marked advantage. He could run down on his opponent, or could maintain his distance until he was sure the vessel he had selected was a hapless victim rather than a warship in disguise. He could also react to changes in course or wind direction faster than his opponent. If the windward ship was also faster, then it could afford to make a series of tacks toward the enemy, getting a little closer to his prey every time—a useful alternative to a headlong chase, particularly if he thought the other vessel's captain didn't suspect he was being pursued. Before the victim realized it, the pirate ship would be in range. If the ships began on similar courses, the pirate would almost surreptitiously try to work his way over to windward of his opponent. The windward position had one other slight advantage. In a stiff breeze both ships heeled over, and a ranging shot from the windward ship would find a larger target in his opponent, as more of his hull would be exposed.

If the prize was spotted to windward of the pirates, then the chase became a little more difficult, as the attackers had to claw their way up toward their prey against the wind. It also meant that if the victim became suspicious of the passing ship it could sail away relatively easily, which inevitably meant a longer chase. If a pirate expected her victims to appear from a certain direction, such as along a popular shipping route leading to a major port, then he would try to lie hull-down to windward, wallowing under light sails until the victim was in range. They would then make their approach. In the waters of the Carolinas the predominant wind direction was from the south, which meant that the pirates would lie well away from the coast, then move inshore on a northwesterly heading when the victim drew level with them. This course would eventually intercept that of the prey, while it was hoped that the prey would take the approaching ship as a merchantman heading for the same port.

In most cases the pirate ship was faster and more maneuverable than the ship she was stalking, which gave her the edge in both the approach and the chase. Even large pirate vessels like the *Queen Anne's Revenge* had their uses—she might have carried up to forty guns, but her French-built hull was sleeker than most, and given time she could overhaul most vessels she encountered. However, for the most part pirates relied on sloops as their chase vessels. There are numerous accounts of the pirates deciding to keep a sloop they captured, or else letting her go—a decision that had more to do with her perceived speed through the water than with any notions of piratical charity. Not all sloops were built the same, and the fast, sweet sailing craft were the ones prized by the pirates. In particular, by the start of the eighteenth century the shipbuilders of Bermuda had developed a reputation for building fast vessels, and naturally enough these became the most sought-after vessels in the Americas.

Faced with the approach of a pirate ship, the merchant captain had the option to flee, to stand and fight, or even to run his vessel ashore, hoping to come back and save the cargo and ship after the pirates left the scene. While Blackbeard was operating in the Gulf of Honduras, one particular vessel, the *Protestant Caesar*, stood its ground against the sloop *Adventure*, driving it away. However, a few days later when his captain saw the *Queen Anne's Revenge* approach him, he opted to abandon his ship and flee into the jungle—a less dramatic version of the running-your-vessel-ashore gambit. The tactic backfired, as Blackbeard simply picked the vessel clean, then set her on fire by way of payment for the merchantmen daring to offer resistance to the *Adventure*. The fight option didn't always end up with a sea battle. Sometimes merchant captains would try and brazen it out, hoping to look like a confident, well-armed vessel. The risk was that if the pirates called the merchant captain's bluff, then he could expect little mercy once the pirates saw through his charade.

The best course of action was for a merchant vessel to flee from any approaching sail, but this wasn't always practical or expedient. Owners would have little time for merchant captains who greatly prolonged their voyages by running from every strange sail, so clearly a combination of luck, judgment, and rapid identification was usually called for. As the two ships approached, the options slowly declined, until a point was reached when flight was impossible. Successful pirate captains sought to delay the flight of their victim for as long as possible, either by disguising their intentions or by disguising their ship. The use of false flags was fairly common, the hunter trying to lull the hunted into a false sense of security. Another pirate trick was to disguise the vessel by covering her gunports with a canvas screen painted to look like the rest of the hull. They could also add clutter to the deck such as animal pens or chicken coops, piles of deck cargo, or even female passengers—anything to buy a few more precious minutes. Similarly, many merchant ships painted fake gunports on their hull sides to make their vessels look better armed than they actually were.

Another useful ploy was to drag barrels astern of the pirate ship as she made her approach, which would create resistance and make the vessel seem less threatening than it really was. At the right moment the barrels would be cast adrift and the pirate ship would surge forward, catching its victim by surprise. As for false flags, everyone seemed to resort to this legitimate ruse, and pirate ships rarely hoisted the black flag or Jolly Roger until their victim was well within range. Instead they would fly the British Union flag, or a French or Spanish ensign—whatever would make them blend in with the local shipping. Once within range the pirate vessel would usually haul down any false colors, haul up her own, and demand that the quarry surrender by firing a gun across her bows. At closer range this would be accompanied by demands yelled through a speaking trumpet across the narrowing gap between the two ships. By then it was too late, and the victim was best advised to haul up her sails, haul down her colors, and surrender.

This was where Blackbeard's reputation came in. Merchantmen were often undermanned, and barely had sufficient crew to man their guns. Against a well-armed and well-manned pirate ship this made resistance an extremely risky business. In many cases the mere thought of standing your ground was enough to invite savage retaliation by the pirates once they finally captured their prey. There are several accounts of pirates killing or torturing their victims as an example to others not to resist in the future. It is a testimony to the fearsome name Blackbeard developed for himself that he never seemed to have to resort to such measures. His ferocious appearance and reputation were enough to encourage most merchant captains to surrender. Clearly he understood that intimidation was a major tool in the pirate arsenal.

A typical pirate attack was recounted in detail in the *Boston Gazette*. On July 13, 1720, the merchant ship *Samuel* of London was off the Newfoundland Banks, on the last leg of her transatlantic voyage between London and Boston. Captain Cary spotted two sails approaching from the southwest, a three-masted square-rigged ship and a fast sloop of around eighty tons. The sloop was flying the British flag, but as she drew closer she and her consort lowered their false colors and raised the piratical black flag. With only ten men in his crew and three guns on each broadside, the Englishman realized he was outmanned and outgunned. He later estimated that the larger attacker carried twenty-six guns and the sloop mounted a further ten pieces, and the combined pirate crew came to around two hundred men. He had little option but to lower his colors and heave to.

The pirates ordered that Cary lower his boat and come aboard the pirate flagship, which turned out to be the *Royal Fortune*, commanded by Bartholomew Roberts. With the merchant captain in custody, the pirates boarded the *Samuel*, plundering some of her cargo of merchandise and iron and throwing the rest over the side. They kept the forty barrels of gunpowder Cary had stowed in his hold, and added two of his guns to their haul, along with all his spare rigging, his stores, and even his ship's boat. According to the newspaper, the pirates swore and cursed throughout, acting "more like fiends than men." Next, all but one of the crew were forced to join the pirates at gunpoint, leaving Cary with just one other sailor and three passengers. While the pirates were debating whether to burn the *Samuel* or not they sighted another sail, and Cary was unceremoniously dumped back on board his ransacked vessel. As the pirates sailed off after a fresh victim, he managed to raise sail and limp off toward Boston.

This incident highlights a few other pirate tricks. First, the pirates almost always kept their prize to leeward, making it harder for it to escape. As the pirates closed within hailing distance, they would order their quarry to heave to. It was common for ships to exchange news and information in this manner, and even when hailed a victim might be slow to recognize the danger. By taking the merchant captain hostage the pirates reduced the risk of any insurrection on board while they were plundering their victim. If the pirate was still flying false colors it also maintained the illusion of legitimacy a little longer, as the demand for a hostage could be presented as an invitation, and one that was rarely refused by the master of the weaker vessel. If all else failed, the pirates would open their gunports and demand hostages at gunpoint.

Flying the black flag or skull and crossbones was designed as yet another means of intimidation. Like the blood-red flag used by privateers, it signified that resistance meant death. This made it a valuable psychological tool and helped ensure that most merchant captains would meekly surrender as soon as the black flag was unfurled. The term "Jolly Roger" came from the French *jolie rouge* (pretty red), a reference to the flag flown by privateersmen. By the early 1700s the term was associated with pirate flags, and by the end of the pirate crisis in the mid-1720s the term was firmly linked to the black piratical skull-and-crossbones flag. Even the use of images such as skeletons, skulls, and hourglasses was designed to reinforce this message of intimidation, danger, and imminent death. The black flag associated with Blackbeard was no exception; it carried the image of a grinning skeleton holding a spear in one hand and a glass in the other, the weapon poised over a blood-red heart dripping with blood.

This imagery had long been associated with death, and since the Middle Ages had been widely used on gravestones and other memento mori. It didn't take a lot of imagination to work out what the symbolism meant, particularly when some pirates used multiple images, like Blackbeard's skeleton and bleeding heart, or Christopher Moody's skull, crossbones, winged hourglass, and raised sword. Bartholomew Roberts went even further, showing a pirate standing on two skulls, labeled ABH and AMH — standing for "A Barbadian's Head" and "A Martiniquan's Head"—reflecting the pirate's feud with the authorities in the two islands. It can also be

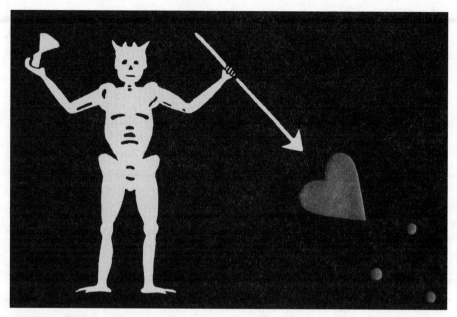

Blackbeard's own version of the Jolly Roger was supposed to depict a skeleton toasting the devil and piercing a heart with a spear.

argued that the imagery might also have reflected the fatalism of the pirates themselves, who realized that the odds were stacked against them.

Looking at the career of Blackbeard, we can see several examples where the prize contained very little of value. In such cases it was typical to demand a token donation of food or drink, or even just articles of clothing. It also seems almost a tradition that the pirate ship gave something back to its victim, probably in an attempt to maintain the illusion that the act wasn't piracy after all. No doubt the merchantmen smiled fixedly and hoped the pirates would just leave them in peace. On a few occasions the pirates allowed their victims to ransom their way out of trouble, negotiating with the predators in the hope that they would let them keep at least part of the cargo—usually goods the pirates couldn't eat, drink, wear, or fight with. This meant a delicate balancing act for the merchant captain, hoping that the pirates would see reason and avoid any wanton destruction—as happened to Captain Cary of the *Samuel*, who watched as the pirates tore his cargo of cloth to shreds, then threw it over the side.

It was extremely rare for a merchant captain to risk offering any resistance. When he did, the pirates were then forced to weigh up the odds. A sharply fought action might well result in the capture of a prize, but the risk was that the pirates would suffer casualties in the process. While some captains might opt to avoid pressing for an engagement, others were more than willing to continue the attack. That left the pirate captain with two more options—whether to attack the stubborn enemy vessel using his ordnance, which probably meant fewer pirate casualties, or to risk putting his ship alongside the enemy and boarding him. The pirates could usually guarantee that they outgunned their victim—even a ten-gun pirate sloop carried more firepower than the average three-masted merchantman of the time, and unlike Captain Cary of the *Samuel* they had more than enough men to crew the guns. In addition, the pirates almost certainly enjoyed an advantage in expertise, as many would have been former privateersmen, and most were used to handling ordnance. When it came to gunnery, the odds were heavily stacked in favor of the pirates.

The actual business of gunnery was a fairly straightforward mechanical process—easy to grasp but hard to master. Almost without exception, all larger pieces of ordnance were mounted on low carriages fitted with four wooden truck wheels. Lading meant pulling the gun inboard; filling the chamber with powder, wadding, and shot; then running the gun out again. The angle of traverse was limited by the gunport, which meant that ships really had to fire their guns in broadsides—to one side or another. There was little latitude for aiming, so in most cases all large guns except bow chasers were fired when their target appeared in view through the gunport itself. The only leeway was knowing exactly when to fire—waiting for the firing ship's roll to approach its height before clapping the slow match against the touchhole. Accurate fire meant that the gunner needed to have mastered the art to perfection—a skill that was even more in demand when it came to the accurate aiming and firing of bow chasers.

Archaeological evidence from the shipwreck believed to be the *Queen Anne's Revenge* shows that Blackbeard armed his flagship with a mixture of guns of various nationalities, presumably looted from *La Concorde* and other prizes along the way. So far eighteen cannons have been recovered, including four-pounder "minions" and six-pounder "sakers," both fairly typical shipborne guns of their day. Even larger guns might well still be down there—after all, Bartholomew Roberts's thirty-six-gun *Royal Fortune* reportedly carried twenty eight-pounder guns and four twelve pounders, as well as lighter pieces, making her the equivalent in firepower to her opponent HMS *Swallow*. A typical minion had an effective range of around a thousand yards, and a saker could fire her shot about sixteen hundred yards, just short of a mile. This extra range made guns of this type perfect for bow chasers, the guns used to fire warning shots at a vessel running away from its attackers.

Of course, effective range was a relatively elastic term. Firing a shot so it scared another ship was one thing, but firing a roundshot so it pierced the hull of an opponent or brought down her mast meant that ranges usually had to be a lot shorter—at least within five hundred yards. Any closer and the two sides could fire grapeshot at each other—the ammunition used by Captain Ogle in his first broadside against Bartholomew Roberts. Also known as "diced shot" or "lagrange," this mixture of musket balls, old nails, and scrap iron would have a devastating effect on the densely packed decks of a ship trying to board or prevent itself from being boarded. The same ammunition could be loaded into swivel guns—the shipborne machine guns of their day, which could be fired and reloaded far more rapidly than larger guns. In many ways this was an ideal form of ammunition for pirates—it damaged people, but didn't harm the enemy ship too much.

One final ammunition type that was relatively widely used was chainshot—roundshot linked together by a rod. This spun through the air and was designed to knock down masts and cut rigging, disabling a ship so she couldn't escape. A pirate captain had to gauge his enemy, and choose his ammunition accordingly. From contemporary accounts it seems that if pirates had to resort to broadside gunnery rather than simply firing warning shots, then the ammunition of choice was grapeshot, fired just seconds before the two vessels came alongside each other. The pirates would then board through the smoke, hoping that the close-range firepower would have knocked the resistance out of any defenders. Of course, the defenders might also have been saving up their grapeshot broadside for the same moment, a lethal game of maritime chicken—fire too soon and the effect was dissipated by too long a range, too late and the enemy fired first.

A similar tactic was to fire a volley of grenades just before the two vessels crashed together, a weapon that had much the same effect as grapeshot. In a battle between two pirate-hunting sloops and a pirate vessel off Jamaica in 1718, the pirates "threw vast numbers of powder flasks, grenado shells, and stinkpots into her which killed and wounded several and made others jump overboard." The term *grenado* (grenade) comes from the Spanish *granada*, meaning pomegranate. Once the ships were alongside each other, the pirates would use grappling hooks to make sure the two vessels stayed locked together, then would cross over to the enemy deck in the way so beloved of Hollywood. Grappling was a skill all its own, as the vessels could damage each other's rigging if they grappled the wrong way.

Once the pirates swarmed on board the enemy ship, they would still be relying on intimidation to help win their battles—yelling, roaring, and cursing like banshees in an attempt to cow the enemy. If that failed, then there was nothing for it but to launch into a free-for-all melee, using muskets, blunderbusses, pistols, swords, axes, cutlasses—whatever lay at hand. When it came to cold steel, the most popular weapon was the cutlass. It was made in great quantities for use at sea, and with time it came to be associated with sailors in general and pirates in particular. It was related to the older English or Scottish broadsword, or even to contemporary cavalry blades, but it was a far cruder weapon, poorly balanced, but with a lot of weight behind any cutting stroke. Other edged weapons used in boarding actions were six-foot boarding pikes, ship's axes, and hunting swords (hangers). Every seaman also carried a knife and knew what to do with it.

While Blackbeard fought at least one close-quarters boarding action off Ocracoke in November 1718, there is no evidence that he ever had to cross swords with anyone else during his career. This didn't mean that he was unwilling to test his mettle in combat, but rather that he was highly successful at what he did. Put simply, he managed to overpower his victims without having to resort to fighting. He was gifted in all the other skills a pirate captain needed, and therefore knew where to find his prey, how to approach them, and above all, how to intimidate them into submission. Benjamin Hornigold recognized this ability and promoted Blackbeard into a position where he could do his mentor some good. Blackbeard probably knew his craft pretty well through his days as a privateer, but under Hornigold he honed his skills to perfection. By the time Blackbeard was unleashed as a pirate captain in his own right, he knew exactly what was expected of him.

7

The Lord of the Outer Banks

Anyone standing on the waterfront of Beaufort in the North Carolina colony that morning in early June 1718 would have seen a cluster of four vessels heading toward them from the southeast. We know Blackbeard arrived off Charles Town Bar on May 22, and he remained there for at least five days. A report filed in London in 1719 reported of Blackbeard's flotilla that "about six Days after they had left the Bar of Charles-town, they arrived at Topsail-Inlet in North Carolina, having then under their Command the said Ship Queen Anne's Revenge, the Sloop commanded by Richards, this Depondent's Sloop, commanded by one Capt. Hands on of the said Pirate Crew, and a small empty Sloop which they had found near the Havana." The "Depondent" was Captain David Herriot, the commander of the Jamaican sloop *Adventure*, which Blackbeard captured in the Turneffe Islands off modern-day Belize. His vessel was now commanded by Israel Hands, while Captain Richards commanded Stede Bonnet's *Revenge*. The last and smallest of the three sloops was the Spanish prize Blackbeard captured off the Cuban port on his way north. That means Blackbeard would have appeared off Topsail Inlet on or just after June 2, 1718.

A chart dated 1777 shows Topsail Inlet (then called New Topsail Inlet) snaking its way northward through the sandbars, passing between the two sand-blown spits of land that separated the inland waterway of the Back Sound from the Atlantic Ocean. It marked the channel as being between 3 fathoms and 7 fathoms deep (18 to 42 feet) and about 300 yards wide. It passed close to the western spit, now part of Money Island, on which the Civil War–era Fort Macon stands guarding the entrance into Beaufort. Of course, in Blackbeard's day there was nothing there apart from sand dunes, sea grass, and land crabs. About a half-mile beyond the point the channel opened out into the Back Sound, allowing ships to enter the equally narrow coastal channel running east and west from Beaufort, or else anchor off the small settlement on the North Carolina mainland. Today the channel is called Beaufort Inlet, and the same harbor plays host to white-hulled yachts and jaunty pleasure boats, or is passed by more workmanlike vessels steaming up and down the Intracoastal Waterway. However, on that early June morning in 1718 only a handful of whalers and fishermen were on hand to watch Blackbeard sail into their lives.

Blackbeard had sailed off the same coast the year before, so we have to assume he had some knowledge of the area. That made his next action all the more shocking. As the pirate squadron entered the inlet, the *Queen Anne's Revenge* was in the lead, carrying more sail than would normally have been thought prudent. The helmsman must have been party to Blackbeard's scheme, as without any warning the pirate flagship veered to starboard and ran hard aground. The ship struck the submerged sandbar with enough force to spring several of her planks and shatter her mainmast.

They say a wooden-hulled sailing ship is virtually a living, sentient being. If so, that was the moment when the *Queen Anne's Revenge* suffered a mortal blow. In theory she could still be saved—if Blackbeard moved quickly enough. He would have to drag her off the sandbar, then beach her somewhere suitable at low tide, which would allow her crew to repair the damage to the hull. Once she was safely floating again, the men could work on any other damage to her masts and rigging. It would be a slow, laborious business, but it could be done.

At first Blackbeard appeared to rise to the occasion. He hailed Israel Hands in the sloop *Adventure*, and asked him to pass a tow rope and haul the pirate flagship off the sandbar. The submerged sandbar lay on the starboard side of the channel, so the *Adventure* would have passed close alongside the port side of the larger ship, and a cable would be paid out. We don't know exactly how Hands performed the operation, but we certainly know the result. The *Adventure* only managed to pull the *Queen Anne's Revenge* further onto the sandbar, damaging her keel and lower hull beyond repair. Even worse, the *Adventure* also managed to run herself ashore, her planks springing apart under the force of the impact. Both pirate ships were now stranded wrecks, and as the water poured into their immobile hulls they settled in the shallow water. Nothing could now save the two pirate ships, which left just the sloop *Revenge* and the smaller Spanish prize sloop still afloat in the middle of Topsail Inlet. To anyone else this would have been a disaster. For Blackbeard, it was all part of the plan. Without any doubt Israel Hands was a party to Blackbeard's scheme, as was the helmsman on the pirate flagship and up to forty of their shipmates. However, this was only the first stage of Blackbeard's masterstroke. He wasted no time laying the groundwork for the great betrayal that would follow.

Blackbeard began with the hapless Stede Bonnet. The major was still ensconced in the great cabin of the *Queen Anne's Revenge*, and it was probably there that Blackbeard shared his plan with his fellow captain—or at least gave him a heavily censored version of it. Blackbeard confessed that he intended to seek the royal pardon from Governor Eden of the North Carolina Colony, and suggested that Bonnet do the same. The original offer was open to pirates who "shall on or before the 5th of September, in the Year of our Lord 1718, surrender him or themselves, to one of our Principal Secretaries of State in Great Britain or Ireland, or to any Governor or Deputy Governor of any of our Plantations beyond the Seas." It then added a clause that read that while it offered immunity, this only applied to crimes committed before January 5, 1718. If Blackbeard, Bonnet, and their shipmates surrendered, they would surely hang for their actions in the Gulf of Honduras and off the Charles Town Bar. However, while he was off Charles Town Blackbeard must have learned that most authorities had the legal ability to waive this clause and to extend immunity up to the moment the pirate surrendered. We can be pretty sure Blackbeard considered Governor Eden a man he could do business with, but he still had little desire to offer himself up without discovering how flexible the governor might be.

He needed someone to act as a guinea pig, and the perfect candidate was seated in front of him. Blackbeard suggested that while he remained behind and salvaged what he could from the pirate flagship, Major Bonnet should race ahead to Bath Town in North Carolina, seek out the governor of the colony, and apply for the pardon. The pirate captains knew that their actions off Charles Town invited pursuit by the Royal Navy, and with the *Queen Anne's Revenge* a wreck, they had little chance of holding their own against a determined attack. Blackbeard must have stressed the risks involved in staying behind, but no doubt he convinced Bonnet that as the premier seaman of the two, Blackbeard had to remain in Topsail Inlet. As a sweetener Blackbeard offered Bonnet his old sloop back, although he would retain it a little longer to help with the salvage work. Both men must have heard the rumors that a new war was likely to break out between Britain and Spain, and so as an added sweetener Blackbeard suggested to Bonnet that he apply for a privateering "letter of incentive" or license, which would allow the Barbadian gentleman to continue his cruise with the full backing of the government. This would have appealed to Bonnet, as it offered him a way out. He must have recognized that his lack of maritime skill meant he made a poor pirate captain. Also, now that his men had tasted the egalitarian pirate life and witnessed his humiliation at the hands of Blackbeard, it would be difficult to make them accept his return to command. If they joined him in accepting the pardon, then Bonnet would once again enjoy the same legal control over his men as enjoyed by any merchant or privateering captain on the right side of the law.

Stede Bonnet gathered together the bulk of his old crew and embarked them in a small sailing boat—either a single-masted longboat from the *Queen Anne's Revenge* or else a slightly larger vessel supplied by the local Beaufort fishing and whaling community. In the latter case, no doubt Bonnet remained true to form and hired her rather than simply commandeering her. The remainder of his crew were ordered to set Bonnet's sloop the *Revenge* to rights, and to prepare her for a voyage to the West Indies on his return from Bath Town. When Bonnet and forty of his men sailed away to the north through the inland waterways leading toward Pamlico Sound, Blackbeard must have enjoyed the satisfaction of seeing his plan taking shape.

When Stede Bonnet and his men arrived in Bath Town they were pointed in the direction of the settlement where Governor Eden had his residence. In 1718 the colony had no official center, and the governor did business from one of his two plantation houses, a secondary one outside Bath Town and a larger residence to the north, outside the colony's oldest settlement, a place known simply as "the Towne on Queen Anne's Creek." Four years later the governor would immodestly change the name of this settlement to Edenton. By the end of the year the colony's first courthouse opened for business in the northern settlement, and Governor Eden officially named his Queen Anne's Creek residence as his official home. The two towns were just over fifty miles apart, so the journey there and back would have taken about three days for a group of pirates who still had their sea legs. From the timing it seems unlikely that the governor was in residence at his Bath Town plantation when Bonnet called on him.

Given that Bonnet's audience could have been granted immediately and that the governor was forthcoming, the whole trip would have taken the men a week. Added to that was the three-day sail each way from Beaufort to Bath Town, which meant that Blackbeard had the best part of two weeks to pick the wrecks clean and abandon his men. As Captain Johnson states that Bonnet returned just two days after Blackbeard set sail, then it becomes clear that Blackbeard's betrayal was both well planned and well timed. Major Bonnet was received cordially, and when he and his men surrendered to the authority of the governor they were immediately pardoned. Further pardons would have been extended to the crewmen Bonnet had left behind on board the *Revenge*—and who were soon to be marooned. It was also claimed that Bonnet managed to secure permission to take the *Revenge* to Danish-owned St. Thomas in the West Indies, where he hoped to obtain a privateering letter of marque from the Danish governor there. He might even manage to convince Governor Hamilton in Barbados or one of his deputies in the British-owned Leeward Islands that he was worthy of a privateering commission. He must have felt somewhat pleased with himself as he headed south again toward Beaufort.

This pleasure came to an abrupt end when he discovered his fellow pirate had absconded with all the loot. Worse, he soon discovered the sloop *Revenge* had been stripped of anything useful, and her crew marooned.

While Bonnet was away, Blackbeard was left with around 250 to 300 pirates under his command. Many of these cutthroats would have been incapacitated most of the time. There was nothing like a shipwreck to invite a lapse of discipline, and no doubt Blackbeard encouraged the majority of his men to drink their way through whatever spirits remained on board the pirate flagship.

The next stage was to transfer whatever plunder the pirates had onto the smaller of the two remaining sloops. After all, with the *Queen Anne's Revenge* and the *Adventure* wrecked and the *Revenge* ostensibly being handed over to Bonnet, it would have seemed a logical next step. By this time the pirates had established a small camp on the mainland at Beaufort, and Blackbeard himself probably established himself there alongside his men. Local legend has it that he made Hammock House his home during this period, an "ordinary" or small inn located within sight of the two stricken pirate ships. It was built around 1700, on a "hammock" of raised ground overlooking the harbor. The building also served as a recognizable landmark for mariners navigating their way through the channel of Topsail Inlet. The legends suggest that Blackbeard and his men actually built the house and that the pirate lived there for a while with a teenage French "wife." Unfortunately, Blackbeard never remained there long enough to put down roots, as in his plans it was important that he quit Beaufort before Stede Bonnet returned. This meant that the pirate would have remained in Beaufort for about two weeks at the most—hardly enough time to transfer stores from the two wrecks, let alone build a house and set up with a French mistress!

Blackbeard selected fewer than forty of his men to crew the small sloop, using her to transfer stores and men from ship to shore. Twenty or so of these pirates were his chosen men, the force he elected to keep with him while he abandoned the rest. With the plunder on board the small Spanish sloop and whatever stores could be crammed aboard her, Blackbeard was ready for the great betrayal. The remainder might well have been part of the crew Bonnet left aboard the *Revenge* to put her to rights. They were powerless to prevent Blackbeard as he stripped the *Revenge* of anything Bonnet would find useful, such as stores, guns, ammunition, and charts. Then, when he judged the time was right, he gave orders to head out to sea. The remaining 200 to 250 pirates left ashore in their temporary camp at Beaufort must have howled with rage as they watched their captain abandon them and sail into the sunset.

Some of the crew of the prize sloop or more likely their colleagues on the *Revenge* joined in the protest—prompting Blackbeard and the rest of their shipmates to turn on them. As Captain Johnson described it, "Teach goes in the tender sloop, with forty hands and leaves the Revenge there; then he takes seventeen others and maroons them upon a small sandy island about a league from the main, where there was neither bird, beast or herb for their subsistence, and where they must have perished if Major Bonnet had not two days after taken them off." It has been suggested that the marooned pirates were set ashore somewhere close to the present site of Fort Macon, on Money Island. Certainly this barren sand spit not only fitted Captain Johnson's description, but was less than a mile from the two shipwrecks. However, it seems surprising that their fellow pirates on the mainland didn't use local fishing boats to try and rescue them immediately, as the spit was less than two miles from the mainland, and well within sight of Beaufort. For this reason, Shackleford Bank on the other side of the inlet seems a more likely candidate. Not only was it equally barren, but it was just far enough from Beaufort to prevent an observer from seeing the marooned pirates with the naked eye. Bonnet set about rescuing the stranded pirates, who confirmed his worst suspicions. Blackbeard had double-crossed him.

Captain Johnson said of the marooned pirates, "They remained there two nights and one day, without subsistence, or the least prospect of any, expecting nothing else but a lingering death; when to their inexpressible comfort they saw redemption at hand; for Major Bonnet happened to get intelligence of their being there, by two of the pirates who had escaped Teach's cruelty, and had got to a poor little village at the upper end of the harbour, sent his boat to make discovery of the truth of the matter, which the poor wretches seeing, made a signal to them, and they were all brought on board Bonnet's sloop." The poor little village would have been Beaufort, so presumably the two pirates had eventually seen something on the sand spit, pressed a local rowing boat into service, and had set off to investigate.

Bonnet reclaimed his sloop, and would have crewed her with his own men, although no doubt the double-crossed pirates left stranded on the mainland would have eagerly tried to volunteer. Over the next few days Stede Bonnet and his crew would have hurriedly prepared the Revenge for sea as best they could, all the while dreaming of furious and bloody revenge against Blackbeard. This was a difficult moment for Bonnet. He never enjoyed the full support of his men, and so it would have been hard to balance the desire for revenge with his plans to become a legal privateer. To go chasing after Blackbeard was to invite the loss of what little control he enjoyed over his crew, as such a pursuit could easily be transformed into a lawless rampage, where his men would plunder any ship they encountered along the way. It also meant the risk of defeat at the hands of the unpardoned pirates. In the end Bonnet's hatred for Blackbeard overcame logic. Captain Johnson described the event that tipped the balance:

> Major Bonnet told all his company, that he would take a commission to go against the Spaniards, and to that end was going to St. Thomas, therefore if they would go with him, they should be welcome; whereupon they all

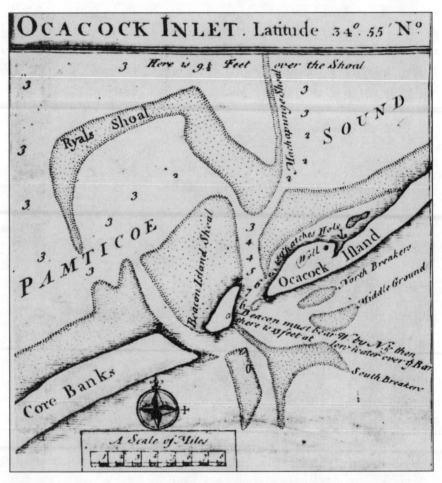

This early-eighteenth-century chart of Ocracoke Inlet shows the twisting narrow channels and sandbars that made navigation on the Pamlico Sound side of the Outer Banks so notoriously difficult. The location where Blackbeard anchored his sloop the Adventure is marked as "Thatches Hole."

consented, but as the sloop was preparing to sail, a bumboat, that brought apples and cider to sell to the sloop's men, informed them, that Captain Teach lay at Ocracoke Inlet, with only eighteen or twenty hands.

When this news broke there was no doubt what the crew of the *Revenge* should do. Ocracoke Island was some seventy miles to the northeast as the crow flies, or ninety miles by sea, a short day's haul around Cape Lookout and north along the line of the Outer Banks. We can assume that Bonnet had around eighty men at his disposal, so he would have outnumbered Blackbeard four to one. Even the most incompetent pirate captain would have felt confident given those odds. Bonnet gave the orders, and all thoughts of privateering were abandoned. Instead, the *Revenge* raced off in pursuit of Blackbeard. The news supplied by the bumboat would have been at least three days old when Bonnet heard it. It was already out of date. As Captain Johnson said of Bonnet's race to Ocracoke, "It happened too late, for he missed of him there, and after four days cruise, hearing no farther news of him, they steered their course towards Virginia." By the time the *Revenge* worked its way through the shallows of Ocracoke Inlet, Blackbeard had already sailed on to Bath Town. For some reason, although Blackbeard had no doubt mentioned that he planned to apply for a pardon, Bonnet must have assumed that his newfound enemy was bluffing and had continued on toward the north. Consequently, after waiting for fresh news that never came, Bonnet and his crew decided to continue the chase toward the Virginia Capes.

Stede Bonnet seemed a little unsure about what to do next. Common sense should have told him that his best course lay in legitimate privateering, or even quitting the maritime business altogether. It is all too easy to question his grip on reality, but being a little delusional wasn't necessarily a disadvantage for a gentleman turned pirate. He opted to return to piracy, or at least his crew did, and Bonnet would have had little option but to go along with them. Captain Johnson described Stede Bonnet's summer cruise off the Virginia coast: "In the month of July, these adventurers came off the Capes and meeting with a pink with a stock of provisions on board, which they happened to be in want of; they took out of her ten or twelve barrels of pork, and about four hundredweight of bread; but because they would not have this set down to the account of piracy, they gave them eight or ten casks of rice, and an old cable, in lieu thereof." Was this Bonnet's way of pretending he hadn't returned to piracy, but was merely a would-be privateer in need of supplies? If so, nobody was fooled by Bonnet's half-hearted attempt to pay his way, least of all his crew.

> Two days afterwards they chased a sloop of 60 tons, and took her two leagues off Cape Henry; they were so happy here to get a supply of liquor to their victuals, for they brought from her two hogsheads of rum and as many of molasses, which, it seems, they had need of, though they had not ready money to purchase them. What security they intended to give, I can't tell, but Bonnet sent eight men to take care of the prize sloop, who, perhaps, not caring to make use of those accustomed freedoms, took the first opportunity to go off with her, and Bonnet (who was pleased to have himself called Captain Thomas) saw them no more.

Deserted by part of his crew and having lost his prize, "Captain Thomas" was clearly having problems controlling his men. The rum couldn't have helped, nor did Bonnet's halfhearted attitude toward piracy. Captain Johnson continues the story:

> He took off Cape Henry, two ships from Virginia, bound to Glasgow, out of which they had very little besides a hundredweight of tobacco. The next day they took a small sloop bound from Virginia to Bermuda, which supplied them with twenty barrels of pork, some bacon, and they gave her in return, two barrels of rice, and a hogshead of molasses; out of this sloop two men entered voluntarily. The next they took was another Virginiaman, bound to Glasgow, out of which they had nothing of value, save only a few combs, pins and needles, and gave her instead thereof, a barrel of pork, and two barrels of bread.

Following that, the *Revenge* cruised the Delaware Bay, where they captured a small coastal schooner bound from North Carolina to Boston with a cargo of skins. The plunder was hardly worth the cost of giving up a royal pardon, and Bonnet must have realized this, hence the attempt to repay the last Glasgow-bound ship with provisions. It was all pretty feeble stuff, and hardly the successful cruise Bonnet needed to reestablish his authority with the crew. Certainly the provisions were necessary, as Blackbeard had pretty much stripped the *Revenge* of everything her crew needed.

Captain Johnson even suggests that despite this string of attacks Bonnet still thought it might be possible to continue on to St. Thomas to become a privateer. He wrote, "All this was but small game, and seemed as if they designed only to make provision for their sloop after they arrived at St. Thomas; for they hitherto had dealt favourably with all those that were so unhappy to fall into their hands." This was about to change. Evidently Bonnet's crew had a quiet word with their gentleman captain while the *Revenge* was cruising the waters of Delaware Bay, and whether by choice or coercion Stede Bonnet threw himself into the business of piracy with a vengeance. He captured two outward-bound snows off the mouth of the Delaware River and a 50-ton sloop bound from Philadelphia to Barbados called the *Francis*. All three vessels were thoroughly plundered and then sent on their way. On July 29 the *Revenge* captured another sloop bound for Barbados. This time the pirates kept the 50-ton vessel, and Bonnet manned her with a skeleton crew.

Two days later the pirates captured a third sloop, this time an inbound vessel sailing from Antigua to Philadelphia with the inappropriate name of the *Fortune*. She yielded a cargo of sugar and other goods valued at £500, but mostly she carried rum. Stede Bonnet and his men must have decided that they had overstayed their welcome off the Delaware, as to remain cruising there any longer was to invite the wrath of the Royal Navy. Consequently, as soon as the plunder from the Antiguan prize was secured and a prize crew sent over to man her, the trio of pirate sloops headed off to the south, their crews no doubt swilling rum like there was no tomorrow.

By this stage the sloop *Revenge* was badly in need of repair and careening, so Bonnet decided to put in to the Cape Fear River, where he planned to hide out and repair the pirate ship at his leisure. His two prizes remained at anchor in the river, while his flagship was beached for repair somewhere just inside the river mouth, probably at Prices Creek, where the small and picturesque town of Southport, North Carolina, now stands. Captain Johnson suggests the repairs were less than straightforward: "they stayed too long for their safety, for the pirate sloop which they now new named the *Royal James*, proved very leaky, so that they were obliged to remain here almost two months, to refit and repair the vessel." This account continued to describe how they captured a small shallop—a tiny single-masted coastal craft—and used her timbers to replace the rotten planks of the *Revenge*, now the *Royal James*.

This whole name change was another indication that Stede Bonnet had finally taken his new career seriously. The Jacobite name was designed to antagonize the British government of King George I, who was ever fearful of a Jacobite rising in Britain. One suspects the repair work had to wait until the pirates were sober enough to tackle the job, which would have added to the time they spent holed up in the mouth of the Cape Fear River. Reportedly Bonnet even had two of his drunken crewmen flogged for insulting their "superiors"—which no doubt meant Bonnet himself. Captain Mainwaring of the *Fortune* remained a prisoner of the pirates, and later reported that they treated him with civility. He also described the bacchanalian atmosphere in the pirate camp when he gave his statement to the authorities.

By this stage word of their activities had leaked out, and the news reached Charles Town at exactly the wrong moment. It was now early September, and the hard-pressed citizens of Charles Town were still smarting from another blockade of their port, this time by Charles Vane. He cruised off the Charles Town Bar for several days in mid-August, prompting Governor Johnson and the Council of South Carolina to take action. Despite the poor financial state of the colony it was felt that they needed to organize their own naval squadron, which would help defend the colony from any further pirate attacks. While the civic leaders were still arguing over the cost involved, Colonel William Rhett stepped forward to offer his services.

The British-born plantation owner first came to South Carolina in 1698 with his wife, Sarah, and he soon became one of the most prominent rice barons in the colony and a leading member of the South Carolina Assembly. He was also a man of action. In late August 1706 he led the small naval force that repulsed a halfhearted Franco-Spanish raid on Charles Town, and a dozen years later he was still the city's hero. He offered the use of two ships if the governor paid for fitting them out as antipiracy vessels. Governor Johnson wasted no time in accepting Rhett's proposal and commissioning him to become the colony's official pirate hunter. The governor hoped that Rhett would "very much irritate the pirates who infest the coast in great numbers." This description must have encompassed both Vane and Bonnet, and probably included Blackbeard as well.

Captain Johnson followed Colonel Rhett's preparations:

In a few days two sloops were equipped and manned: The Henry with 8 guns and seventy men, commanded by Captain John Masters, and the Sea

Nymph, with 8 guns and sixty men, commanded by Captain Fayrer Hall, both under the entire direction and command of the aforesaid Colonel Rhet, who, on the 14th September, went on board the Henry, and, with the other sloop, sailed from Charles town to Suillivants [Sullivan's] Island, to put themselves in order for the cruize.

By the time they were ready Vane had already quit the waters of the Carolinas and had joined Blackbeard at Ocracoke. However, Stede Bonnet was still in the Cape Fear River, and so it was that Colonel Rhett headed north, helped along by a following wind, his two sloops primed for action and his men eager for battle. He looked into every possible bolt-hole and anchorage on the way, just in case Vane was foolish enough to linger, but his principal objective was Bonnet. By the early afternoon of September 26 Oak Island lay ahead, and beyond it the narrow entrance to the river. He would have known that this wasn't the only channel—other, smaller channels pierced the sand spit that made up the eastern bank of the river mouth. As Captain Johnson put it, "in the evening, the colonel with his small squadron, entered the river, and saw, over a point of land, three sloops at an anchor, which were Major Bonnet and his prizes."

Even today the mouth of the river is difficult to navigate, as the sandbars and shoals shift with every winter storm. In 1718 it was much worse, as there was no clearly marked channel to follow. The local pilot hired by Rhett was clearly not up to the job of navigating the river, for as dusk began to fall one or both of the sloops grounded on a sandy shoal. Fortunately the tide was on the flood, and by nightfall the two South Carolina sloops were riding safely at anchor in the main channel. Rhett decided against a night engagement, and gave orders to his men to prepare themselves for an attack at dawn. Major Bonnet might have been a poor seaman, but at least he knew the basics of military tactics. He kept sentries posted, and when they reported that two strange sloops had anchored in the mouth of the river he decided to investigate. The pirates thought the vessels were merchantmen, and so they planned a nighttime assault, designed to catch the crews unawares. "The pirates soon discovered the sloops, but not knowing who they were, or upon what design they came into that river, they manned three canoes, and sent them down to take them, but they quickly found their mistake, and returned to the sloop, with the unwelcome news." The result was that the pirates as well as the South Carolinians prepared themselves for a battle at first light. From his conversation with his prisoner Captain Mainwaring of the *Fortune* it appeared that Bonnet's plan was to race past the two enemy sloops with guns blazing, then escape in the confusion—a bit like the tactic Charles Vane used in New Providence just two months before.

As the sun crept over the surface of the Atlantic the crews of the *Henry* and the *Sea Nymph* prepared to get under way. They had slept by their posts, their guns loaded and ready, but it was Bonnet who seized the initiative. The pirates had gotten the *Royal James* under way in the predawn darkness, and as the sun rose they were already heading into the main channel, straight for the two enemy sloops. Bonnet had around forty-five men under his command, and ten guns primed and double-shotted. Rhett saw the pirate sloop approaching, the Jolly Roger flapping in the early morning breeze, and he immediately gave the order to give battle. What followed should have been a spirited and hard-fought sea battle, but instead the drama soon turned into a black comedy. As the *Royal James* came within musket range of the two South Carolina sloops, she ran hard aground.

By this time the *Henry* and the *Sea Nymph* were under way, and closed in on their victim. Then, when the two sides were within easy pistol range, the advancing sloops shuddered and came to a sudden halt—trapped on the submerged sandbars of the river just like the pirates. It was enough to make any captain weep, especially as both sides now lay on opposite sides of the main channel, their guns unable to bear on the enemy. All three sloops would be unable to move until the flood tide lifted them clear. Then the first vessel to get under way would be able to slip across the bows of her wallowing opponent and rake her with a full broadside. However, as the three sloops lay there it soon became apparent that the pirates enjoyed a distinct advantage over their rivals. Coming downstream, the *Royal James* grounded on the starboard side of the channel, and heeled over to starboard. The other two sloops heeled to port, but they faced upstream.

This meant that while the hull of the *Royal James* acted as a bulwark protecting the men behind it, the sloping decks of the *Henry* and the *Sea Nymph* lay fully exposed to the enemy. As both sides began peppering their opponents with small-arms fire, it was the Carolinians who had the worst of the exchange. The two sides continued the gun battle for five hours, when the whispering trickle of the incoming tide promised an end to the torment for Rhett and his men. By that stage they had twelve men dead and eighteen more wounded, while inflicting only nine casualties on the pirates. However, revenge was sweet for the survivors. It was the *Henry* that righted first, and Captain Masters maneuvered his sloop across the bows of the pirate ship, where her four starboard guns could sweep her deck with grapeshot. The game was up. Bonnet ordered his crew to blow up the

A pirate crew holding a mock trial in a scene used to depict Johnson's "Life of Captain Anstis." While they tried to make light of such matters, most knew that they would eventually run afoul of the law.

sloop's magazine, but sensibly enough they ignored him, preferring to take their chances with the authorities rather than commit mass suicide. Bonnet was left with no option but to surrender, along with the rest of his crew. Before the sun had passed the yardarm Colonel Rhett had released the pirate's prisoners and returned their vessels to them, and was leading his flotilla back to Charles Town in triumph, with the captured *Royal James* following in its wake. Stede Bonnet's somewhat inglorious career had come to its sorry end, and all he and his men had to look forward to was death at the hands of a South Carolina hangman.

Meanwhile, Blackbeard was throwing a party. At roughly the same time that Stede Bonnet was fighting for his life, Blackbeard and his cronies were playing host to a group of visiting pirates led by Captain Charles Vane. The two crews met when Vane sailed past the Outer Banks. The previous three months had been good ones for Blackbeard, and while he had established himself on shore in Bath Town, he had also created his own pirate haven on Ocracoke Island. Vane had already quit the waters off Charles Town Bar by the end of August, although the authorities in South Carolina still thought he was lingering somewhere off their coast. It must have been mid- to late September when Vane put in to Ocracoke Inlet, and the celebratory "banyan" that followed lasted the best part of a week— which meant the festivities were still going on when Colonel Rhett sailed into the Cape Fear River. While nobody could class Charles Vane as a lucky pirate, Bonnet seemed to have a knack for meeting the wrong people at the wrong time.

Blackbeard certainly had plenty to celebrate. Around the middle of June he led his one remaining sloop through Ocracoke Inlet and crossed Pamlico Sound to Bath Town. The town itself was a modest affair of no more than two dozen houses, sited on Old Town Creek (now Bath Creek), a tributary of the Pamlico River. Another inlet known as Adams Creek (now Back Creek) joined the Old Town Creek just below the town, so the settlement lay on a stubby peninsula bounded by the two inlets. The town's waterfront faced west, onto Old Town Creek, and a single dirt road formed the main street, running parallel to the harbor itself.

The settlement was first founded in 1705, named after the English aristocrat John Granville, the Earl of Bath, who was one of Carolina's Lords Proprietor, and within three years it consisted of twelve houses and fifty people. Many of these first settlers were Huguenots—French Protestant émigrés who fled their native country to avoid persecution. Development was slow; by the time Blackbeard set foot on its main street it had doubled in size, but it was far from the booming regional center that the North Carolina authorities had hoped it would become. Still, a mill was built there in 1707, and a small shipyard was established later that year, to build the coastal vessels Bath Town needed to flourish as North Carolina's trading center. Tobacco, furs, and naval stores were all shipped through the port, although as the Outer Banks prevented the access of large merchant ships to the colony, most of these craft shipped the port's goods to other larger cities further up or down the coast. Despite this progress, the town was lucky to survive.

In 1711 it was devastated by a series of crises that all but wiped out the settlement. The first of these was an open rebellion between North Carolina's Quakers and the newly appointed governor of the time, Sir Thomas Hyde. The Quaker leader Thomas Cary refused to hand over his authority to the new governor, and his supporters gathered in Bath Town, causing the governor to fear that a rebellion was taking place. "Cary's Rebellion" was soon crushed in July 1711 when a Royal Navy warship arrived off Bath Town and a company of Royal Marines disembarked to round up the agitators. As a good Quaker, Cary prevented his supporters from opening fire on the marines, and consequently he was arrested and charged with treason. The charges were later dropped. By that time Bath Town had undergone two other disasters: a yellow fever epidemic that claimed the lives of several inhabitants and a severe drought that left the survivors faced with starvation.

If that wasn't enough, that September the local Tuscarora Indians rose up and attacked European settlements on the Pamlico and Neuse rivers, most notably Bath Town and New Bern. The Tuscarora chief was King Hancock, who persuaded other tribes to join forces with him in launching this two-pronged attack. The assault came on September 22 and lasted for three days, during which most of Bath County was overrun. Refugees flooded into the town, and makeshift defenses were hastily thrown up. In all some 130 settlers were killed and several more captured as slaves, the dead including John Lawson, the man who first founded the Bath Town settlement. The threat to the settlement was soon over, but the war rumbled on until 1715, further disrupting life within the North Carolina colony.

Still, some seven years after the disasters of 1711 Bath Town had shrugged off all traces of these setbacks, and was beginning to expand again. At least two "ordinaries" or inns supplied the needs of the sailors who passed through the port, while Governor Eden and several other North Carolina worthies had built homes in the area and a handful of merchants set up temporary stores on the edge of town to hold their goods. It was unlikely to become more than a sleepy local harbor, but for the time being it fulfilled the needs of North Carolina's primitive economy. This was exactly what Blackbeard wanted. It had just enough trade to permit the selling of stolen goods if he needed to, but not enough for the merchants to form an antipiracy lobby. The colony's administration was a ramshackle affair, with no firm center. As the colony's premier port, Bath Town was subject to the languid scrutiny of officials such as customs men and minor officials, but there were sufficiently few of them to bribe when necessary. Blackbeard had found his new pirate haven.

The first meeting between Blackbeard and Governor Eden must have taken place in the last two weeks of June 1718. The governor already knew about the incident at Topsail Inlet, as he had only recently dealt with Stede Bonnet, but still he must have been relieved when Blackbeard appeared with just two dozen pirate followers rather than three hundred. The meeting might well have taken place in Eden's plantation, on the western side of Old Town Creek, a day or so after the pirates arrived in town. Certainly after his meeting with Bonnet, he had every reason to quit his residence in Chowan County near the town on Queen Anne's Creek and head to his plantation outside Bath Town. After all, securing the pardon of Blackbeard would have been something of a coup for him. Incidentally, his deputy Tobias Knight bought the neighboring Robert Daniel plantation on June 15, roughly the same time as Blackbeard arrived. Given the rumors of financial dealings between Knight and the pirates, the timing may not have been entirely coincidental. Certainly Blackbeard had little trouble convincing the North Carolina governor and his advisors that he was earnest in his desire to give up pirating, and so like Bonnet before him, he and his men received the royal pardon.

A pirate no more, Blackbeard set about establishing himself in the local community. At first the pirates would have based themselves in one of the ordinaries, but it appears that Blackbeard may well have set himself up in a house on the outskirts of town soon after his arrival. Local tradition places his Bath Town home across the Back Creek on Plum Point. It was even claimed that he married, although no hard evidence has so far appeared to support this claim. Certainly Captain Johnson waxed lyrically about Blackbeard's activities in the settlement:

> He married a young creature of about sixteen years of age, the governor performing the ceremony. As it is the custom to marry here by a priest, so it is there by a magistrate, and this I have been informed, made Teach's fourteenth wife, whereof about a dozen might still be living. His behavior in this state was something extraordinary, for while his sloop lay in Ocracoke Inlet, and he ashore at a plantation where his wife lived, with whom after he had lain all night, was the custom to invite five or six of his brutal companions to come ashore, and he would force her to prostitute herself to them all, one after another, before his face.

This wild statement might well be just Johnson's way of creating sensational copy to fill in an otherwise uneventful period in Blackbeard's life. Certainly rumors of such goings-on would have spread through such a small community like wildfire, and the gossip would have reached official ears. Nothing of this kind was ever reported, either by the colony's officials or in the newspapers. However, a letter sent by Governor Hamilton of Bermuda in late November or early December 1717 included a snippet of gossip about Blackbeard that must have been going the rounds at the time. It stated that "This Teach it's said has a wife and children in London." At this time it was common for sailors in port to select a mistress for a time, and these might have given the appearance of de facto common-law marriages. However, there is absolutely nothing to support that anyone performed a marriage ceremony on his behalf, be it a preacher, a colonial official, or even a fellow ship's captain. We have to assume that the Bath Town young girl referred to by Captain Johnson was his mistress, not his wife, and that he wasn't as willing to share her favors as Captain Johnson alleged.

As for him building a house on Plum Point, the local legend suggests that the house where Blackbeard lived with his teenage bride sat on top of a slight knoll above Plum Point, a site that would give good views of the Bath Town harbor and the approaches to the town from the south up Old Town Creek. With a small rowing boat it also allowed easy access to the plantation homes of Charles Eden and Tobias Knight, on the far side of the creek. In the 1970s state archaeologists examined the site and found traces of ceramics dating from the right period. However, there was nothing to link the site with Blackbeard. That certainly didn't stop the treasure hunters, and over the years dozens of holes have been dug by those eager to find pirate buried treasure regardless of the fact that apart from Captain Kidd, pirates didn't actually bury their plunder. An old round brick structure in the area was known locally as "Teach's Kettle," and tradition had it that he used it to boil tar to repair his ships with. Its ruins have since been buried, but from its description it is more likely the structure formed part of the town's shipyard than a pirate household. Blackbeard had better things to do than boil tar.

Today the site is owned by a North Carolina company, and one day soon may be developed like the rest of the area. However, for the moment it remains the last unexplored archaeological link with Blackbeard's past, waiting for a team of trained archaeologists to uncover the vital clue that will definitively link the house with the pirate. As for the notion that he built the house himself, Blackbeard's sojourn in Bath Town lasted less than six months, and for much of that time he was away at sea. This suggests he bought or leased an existing property, as the time span was hardly enough to build a house, let alone maintain an active social life there. While he no doubt maintained civil relations with Eden and Knight, he would also have established contacts among local plantation owners, merchants, and officials. These men would prove useful during the next stage of Blackbeard's plan, which involved the use of Bath Town as a conduit for plunder.

During July and early August 1718 Blackbeard shuttled between his base in Bath Town and his sloop and crew off Ocracoke. The written records suggest he visited his wife in the settlement, which suggested his principal base was on board his sloop. By way of encouragement Governor Eden also granted Blackbeard permission to take his sloop to St. Thomas in order to seek a privateering commission from the Danes—the same offer he made to Stede Bonnet. Blackbeard could rightfully call the sloop his own by then, as part of the process of surrender and pardon set down in the royal edict of 1717 stated that the slate was wiped clean and the repentant pirates were no longer liable for the return of most of the property stolen before their surrender, providing their origins were officially declared. It was a bargaining chip designed so that officials could levy a fine on pirates as they saw fit, or use the ruling to force them into cooperation.

As the North Carolina colony had no Court of the Vice-Admiralty, the governor acted as the British Admiralty's local representative. In this capacity he called the court into session, and immediately declared that Blackbeard's sloop was a legitimate prize taken from the Spaniards. While the vessel was certainly Spanish and was captured by Blackbeard off Havana earlier that year, Spain and Britain were not then at war, which officially made the seizure an act of piracy. Governor Eden effectively gave the sloop to Blackbeard, and even issued him new ownership papers to prove it. The pirate duly renamed the Spanish sloop the *Adventure*. As Captain Johnson commented about the cover-up, "These proceedings show that governors are but men."

Another advantage of allowing Blackbeard the legal use of the Spanish sloop was that it encouraged the pirates to leave the colony. While the ordinaries of Bath Town would have welcomed the extra business created by former pirates with money to spend, others were less impressed. Even Governor Eden had to report to his council of advisors that the pirates had committed "some disorders" in the small community. He wasn't specific, but even drunken brawling, womanizing, and gambling would probably have been regarded as too racy for a predominantly straightlaced Quaker and Huguenot community. Bath Town was no Nassau or Port Royal. By awarding Blackbeard the sloop the governor also hoped the former pirate would engage in commerce, taking his crew with him as they plied the trade routes between North Carolina and the Caribbean. This was all somewhat optimistic, and relied on the assumption that Blackbeard intended to keep on the right side of the law.

Captain Johnson claims that Blackbeard returned to sea in June 1718, a date a few months out of sequence with the surviving historical records. After all, Captain Ellis Brand of HMS *Lyme*, at anchor in the James River, learned that Blackbeard had run his ships aground by July 12, and placed the incident in Topsail Inlet as taking place "on the 10th of June or thereabouts." Blackbeard then spent at least a month off either Beaufort, Ocracoke, or Bath Town, so the earliest he could have returned to sea was in mid-July. Most probably it was early August, and during the weeks in between Blackbeard's crew had amused themselves by harassing fishing vessels and passing coastal traders in the waters of the Outer Banks. Certainly by August 11 Governor William Keith of the Pennsylvania colony had issued a warrant for Blackbeard's arrest, although whether this was for crimes committed immediately before or just after the pirate accepted the royal pardon is unclear.

In his history of Blackbeard published in 1974, Robert E. Lee claimed that when Blackbeard returned to sea he first headed to Philadelphia, but quit the port when word reached him of Governor Keith's warrant. This makes little sense, and a more likely variant would have been if Blackbeard returned to his old hunting ground in Delaware Bay, and that was where he and his men harassed the local trading vessels rather than the Outer Banks. That meant that Blackbeard's men would have spent a little over a month putting the *Adventure* to rights, and as soon as the legal claim for her had been decided in Blackbeard's favor, the pirates put to sea again. Captain Johnson claimed that Blackbeard then sailed toward Bermuda, encountering two or three British merchant vessels along the way. They were plundered for their provisions, and then allowed to continue. If Johnson was right, this means that by the end of August at the latest Blackbeard had already stepped back over the line from legitimacy into piracy. His law-abiding phase had therefore lasted less than two months. However, Blackbeard knew that while he might incur the wrath of other colonial governors and the Royal Navy, he could still count on the support of Governor Eden provided he avoided any flagrant breach of the law. Blackbeard must have thought he could get away with it.

His next victims were two French merchantmen outbound from the Caribbean, one carrying a cargo of cocoa and sugar and the other empty, carrying nothing but ballast. Britain and France were at peace, and had been for the past five years. A blatant attack on them would be tantamount to an act of piracy, so Blackbeard had to use his wits. He transferred the crew of the laden ship onto the second empty vessel, and then allowed her to continue her voyage. Blackbeard then not only kept the French prize, but took her back to Ocracoke with him—she was too large to navigate into Bath Town. He then spent the best part of September stripping his prize of her cargo before transferring the goods to Bath Town. This was a calculated risk. He needed to sell the cargo, and Bath Town was the obvious market. However, to do so he had to spin the governor a yarn, and convince him the cargo and the ship were his by right.

Around September 24, 1718, Blackbeard sought an audience with Governor Eden, and claimed that he had "found the French ship at sea without a soul on board her." In legal terms this made the vessel "unmanned and abandoned on the high seas," and by Admiralty law this made Blackbeard the salvor in possession. Just as it would today, this gave him legal rights to the vessel and cargo. The only snag was, he had to prove his story. As the representative of the British Admiralty in the North Carolina colony, Governor Eden called another meeting of the Court of the Vice-Admiralty to determine ownership. Of course, Blackbeard and four of his pirates who testified in support were the only witnesses on hand to tell the story of what happened—all the French crew were still in Philadelphia where they had been landed. Nobody told them the news, and consequently Governor Eden had no option but to grant Blackbeard salvage rights over the French ship.

By law the Court of the Vice-Admiralty could claim a fraction of the cargo for themselves—usually a fifth—ostensibly to offset any administrative costs involved. Blackbeard promptly delivered sixty barrels of sugar and cocoa to Governor Eden's plantation house, and a further twenty barrels to the home of Tobias Knight. Although both men were well within their legal rights, they had both profited from Blackbeard's piratical activities—and were now the owners of stolen property. The rest of the cargo was sold in Bath Town, and the profits divided among the pirates. After all, the pirates had need of money. They had just thrown a weeklong party. At some time in mid- to late September, Blackbeard's lookouts on Ocracoke Island would have seen a sloop approaching from the south, then watched as she altered course toward Ocracoke Inlet. Unlike the usual small trading vessels bound for Bath Town, this sloop was well armed. She turned out to be a pirate ship—none other than the *Ranger*, commanded by Charles Vane. Blackbeard would have already prepared the *Adventure* for action, but stood his men down when the *Ranger* heaved to under Blackbeard's guns. The presence of two pirate bands in the same waters called for a celebration.

The nautical term for what followed is a "banyan," an impromptu beach picnic involving drinking and merrymaking. It originally derived from a Hindu term that referred to the open-air markets held by Indian merchants beneath the trees of the same name. By the late seventeenth century it had been adopted by the buccaneers to refer to any open-air gathering on the seashore. Pirates were never known for their moderation, and both Vane and Blackbeard would have made sure that the rum flowed like water, and everyone ate their fill. This party lasted about a week, which was presumably when the rum ran out. Vane and his crew made

Although drawn a century after the real party, this woodcut provides a convincing impression of the banyan held on Ocracoke Island in September 1718, when the crews of Blackbeard and Charles Vane were temporarily united.

their farewells, and the *Ranger* headed back out to sea, sailing north. Without the benefit of hindsight this gathering could have been seen as something more ominous than it was, amounting to a reestablishment of the New Providence exiles in the heart of the Outer Banks. Pirate crews who played together could raid together. However, it was not to be, and within two months Vane and his men would part company, and Blackbeard would have his own problems to face in Ocracoke.

Governor Eden might not have been openly consorting with Blackbeard, as his severest critics later claimed, but he must have been aware that Blackbeard had returned to his old ways. Not only did news of Blackbeard's activities off the mouth of the Delaware and Bermuda spread throughout the English-speaking colonies, but so, too, did news of the pirate gathering on Ocracoke. The threat posed by these pirates was considered serious enough for Governor Keith of the Pennsylvania colony to fit out two sloops, just as Governor Johnson of South Carolina had done. These vessels, commanded by Captain Raymond and Captain Taylor, were charged with patrolling the waters off the Delaware Capes, in the hope of intercepting either Vane or Blackbeard. The vessels returned to port without incident in early October, as a claim was submitted for the expenses incurred on October 17. However, the antipiracy measures taken by Keith and Johnson were nothing compared to the response of Virginia's Governor Spotswood to the pirate threat.

As early as July 10 he had issued a proclamation that required all former pirates who set foot on Virginia soil to register with the authorities, regardless of whether they had been pardoned or not. By this time the first of the pirates Blackbeard had stranded at Beaufort had begun to straggle into Charles Town, Williamsburg, and Philadelphia, and it would not have taken long for their earlier association with Blackbeard to become general knowledge. Although most applied for and were granted a pardon, Governor Spotswood still saw these men as a nascent threat to his colony— prime recruits for any pirate captain willing to raise a fresh crew on the Atlantic seaboard, and a socially and politically divisive group that might entice law-abiding seamen to follow their example. The proclamation also forbade these men from associating with one another in groups of three or more. However, Spotswood was prepared to go much further than simply passing edicts. One of Blackbeard's old shipmates who drifted into Williamsburg after being abandoned in Beaufort was William Howard, the former quartermaster of the *Queen Anne's Revenge*. His capture would give Spotswood the opportunity to hold a show trial—to make an example of Howard that would send a signal to all former pirates in the American colonies.

William Howard was identified and arrested. He had some £50 on him (the equivalent of around $10,000 today), and was accompanied by two black slaves. The money and the slaves were duly confiscated, and Howard was arrested as a vagrant seaman. As such he was liable to impressment, and he soon found himself chained belowdecks on board HMS *Lyme*, anchored in the James River. The authorities began building a case, but were unable to prevent Howard from contacting his own lawyer, John Holloway. His legal advisor was of the highest caliber, a well-respected lawyer who would later become both the speaker of Virginia's House of Burgesses and the mayor of Williamsburg. Holloway lodged a claim of wrongful imprisonment and brought charges against Captain Brand, the commander of HMS *Lyme*. He also demanded compensation for Howard of £500. Governor Spotswood was on shaky legal ground here, and

Holloway knew it. Technically the governor had no legal power to try men for piracy, a legal loophole that would soon be closed by fresh legislation sent from London. He certainly didn't have the right to arrest someone without trial and confiscate his goods. The governor decided to charge Howard with piracy nonetheless.

The governor called a meeting of his council on October 29, and together they thrashed out the legal groundwork for the coming trial. Under a law passed by William III, in times of crisis the governor could hold a pirate trial without using a jury—and the worthy council decided that Blackbeard and his cronies constituted a pirate crisis that threatened the colony. The charges against Howard cited several attacks made by Blackbeard in 1717, then claimed the attacks continued after January 5— thereby making Howard and Blackbeard legally ineligible for a pardon. The lawyers ignored the fact that the governor of North Carolina had extended the pardon, making Blackbeard a legal claimant beyond the Virginia colony's southern border. In particular, the charge focused on the sloop Blackbeard captured off Havana—the one he now legally owned and had renamed the *Adventure*: "The Said Wm Howard in Company with the aforesaid Edwd Tach and other their Confederates. . . . On or about the . . . month of April 1718 a sloop belonging to ye subjects of the King of Spain upon the high seas near the Isl^d of Cuba did piratically take and seize ye same."

The charge went on to cite other attacks, including the capture of the slaver off the Charles Town Bar. This was important because one of the two slaves accompanying Howard when he was captured was first captured by the pirates on board that slave ship. The slave therefore provided proof that Howard took part in the attack. Howard was moved to the public jail in Williamsburg, and a trial date was set. Captain Brand and his colleague Captain Gordon of HMS *Pearl* refused to participate in the trial if Holloway was present, and the governor needed to include these representatives of the British Admiralty in his show trial to ensure that the outcome would be ratified by the British government. As he reported to his superiors in London, Governor Spotswood wrote to Holloway. "To prevent any disturbance on the Bench, which I apprehended would ensue upon their publickly excepting against Mr. Holloway, I sent him a civil Message to desire him not to expose himself by appearing on that Tryal." The lawyer was furious, but had no option but to accede, and poor William Howard was left to fight for his life in court without the support of a lawyer.

As a result, the outcome was never in doubt. William Howard was tried and convicted as a pirate, and in the process Blackbeard's legal support from Governor Eden was undermined. Even more importantly, during those few weeks in September and October Governor Spotswood gathered a lot of information about Blackbeard and his crew, and rightly perceived that his pretense of accepting a royal pardon was nothing more than a sham. He now had a legal case against the pirate, and therefore had the right to take action against him, regardless of whether Blackbeard was on Virginia soil or not. As for William Howard, he was still languishing in the Williamsburg jail in December, when the rest of Blackbeard's crew joined him in prison. Unlike most of them, however, Howard would cheat the gallows. Before a date was set for his execution a copy of a proclamation arrived from London, dated December 24, that effectively ratified the extension of the pardon and covered all acts of piracy committed before July 23, 1718. That meant that every member of Blackbeard's crew who had been abandoned at Topsail Inlet were now cleared of all charges. The quartermaster walked out of Williamsburg a free man. We don't know much about what happened to him after that, although his name appeared as a character witness in a pirate trial held in New Providence in December 1721. Presumably the former pirate knew when to quit and become a respectable Bahamian beach bum.

As the colder seasonal weather closed in on Pamlico Sound, Blackbeard and his men settled down for the winter. The *Adventure* was still based out at Ocracoke, and both captain and crew split their time between their island haven and the ordinaries of Bath Town. Neither they nor the North Carolina governor were aware that across the colonial frontier in Virginia a different kind of storm was brewing. Any act of piracy committed in American waters as winter set in was blamed on Blackbeard and his crew, including the attacks made by a new small-time pirate, Richard Worley, around the Delaware River in September and October. Merchants clamored for help, while the governors of New York, Pennsylvania, and Virginia all promised to take action. However, the situation in Virginia should have caused Blackbeard the most concern. He would have learned of the arrest of his old quartermaster, but despite rumors that the pirates planned to sally forth and rescue their shipmate, Blackbeard had already washed his hands of Howard. He was reasonably confident that his contacts in the

North Carolina government would warn him of any impending attack. In the meantime, he and his men planned to spend the winter peaceably and ready themselves for a new sailing season in the spring. Unfortunately for Blackbeard, Governor Spotswood had other ideas. If they wouldn't stir themselves, then he would take the fight against piracy to them.

8

Trouble in the Colonies

Philip Ludwell the Younger knew how to throw a party. Just about everyone in Williamsburg was invited, apart from the governor. Of course, not all of them accepted the invitation to Williamsburg's Capitol that evening, as they had a more prestigious prior engagement. The House of Burgesses met in one of the ground-floor chambers of the civic building at the end of Duke of Gloucester Street, and lights blazed in this chamber as Ludwell and his supporters held court. The festivities were capped by the lighting of a bonfire on the grounds, an event that attracted the dross of the town as well as the partygoers. It must have been all Ludwell could do to resist throwing an effigy of Governor Spotswood into the flames. It was the evening of May 28, 1718, and across town in the Governor's Palace Alexander Spotswood was holding a party of his own. It was a glittering event he held every year to celebrate the birthday of King George I. Although work on his new mansion was still not finished, the birthday celebration gave him an opportunity to show its splendors to Virginia society, and to reinforce his authority in America's richest and oldest colony.

Although this soiree was attended by the elite of the Virginia colony, several disaffected members of the House of Burgesses, along with many of the town's radicals, preferred the company of Ludwell to that of the governor. They had certainly been invited—four weeks later Spotswood was still smarting when he wrote, "An invitation to my House after this Reconciliation was slighted by them, and an Entertainment with all the freedom and Civility I could give, has not prevailed, with one of the Eight to make me ye common compliment of a Visit." It seemed as if the government of the Virginia colony was hopelessly divided, with Governor Spotswood and his supporters on one side and eight of the twelve members of the House of Burgesses on the other. These dissidents took exception to Spotswood's overbearing manner and open contempt for the colony's lower house of elected representatives. The faction was led by Philip Ludwell the Younger, speaker of the House of Burgesses, and the Reverend James Blair, president of William and Mary College, and the events of May 28 showed that they rejected any attempt at reconciliation. They weren't the only ones to oppose their governor, as several members of the higher chamber, the Governor's Council, had petitioned London for Spotswood's removal from office.

The problem lay in the way Virginia's government had been set up. Unlike the colonies of France or Spain, the administration of the English (later the British) colonies evolved piecemeal, with little direction given by the mother country. Originally the colonial settlements in North America had been established by merchant adventurers or feudal entrepreneurs, and royal authority over the colonies came later, when these bodies relinquished control, allowing their provinces to become "royal colonies." By 1718 North and South Carolina were still run by the Lords Proprietors as a private venture, but Virginia along with most of the other colonies outside New England were run by the British government as royal colonies. In 1696 King William III created the Board of Trade to replace the Lords of Trade and Plantations, the body that administered the colonies. All colonial governors and officials reported directly to the Board, which dictated policy. Governor Spotswood was their man on the spot in Virginia.

As the main purpose of the Board was to harvest revenue from the colonies on behalf of the British government, their policies did not always reflect the needs of the colonies they administered. For instance, the

Navigation Acts forbade the import or export of goods to the North American colonies by vessels with non-British crews, while a series of trade restrictions benefited British manufacturers at the expense of their American counterparts. The Board also sought ways to increase its control over the colonies, even though this might hamper their economic development. In effect, it still operated America as a commercial venture, but this time it was the British government that called the shots. Each colony was a miniature version of Britain, with its own ruler, upper chamber, and parliament. The only exception was that Virginia's ruler had to answer to his superiors at the Board of Trade, and ultimately to King George I.

In proprietary colonies like North Carolina, the system was pretty much the same, only the Lords Proprietor replaced the Board of Trade as the shadowy and distant superiors in London. Of course, this meant that the governor and his senior officials were appointed directly by the Lords Proprietor, not by the Crown (represented by the Board of Trade). In New England the system worked a little differently, where in the private corporate colonies of Connecticut, Massachusetts, and Rhode Island the governor was elected by local company representatives. In effect, the government of each colony developed in a slightly different way from its neighbors, and the relationship between colonial administration and the mother country varied from colony to colony. So, too, did the balance between the power of the governor and that of the elected assembly, although both enjoyed privileges unique to British North America.

For example, after Britain's civil wars of the mid-seventeenth century and the upheavals caused by the reign of King James II and VII and the Glorious Revolution that followed, royal authority was severely limited, the king becoming a relatively powerless head of state. In America the colonial governor retained powers and prerogatives that the British monarch had lost. In particular, while the king never vetoed Parliament after the Union of the English and Scottish parliaments in 1707, colonial governors could still and frequently did veto decisions made by colonial assemblies. The same prerogative was reserved by the Crown, following the advice of the Board of Trade. Governors could also dissolve colonial assemblies in their colony, and postpone elections indefinitely. At the same time the colonial elected assemblies enjoyed more wide-ranging powers than the British Parliament, particularly when it came to electing officials and sidestepping higher levels of authority. It was a strange and delicate balance, and it all but invited conflict between the governor, the upper assembly, and the elected lower assembly in each colony.

What complicated matters even further was the higher assembly. Both royal governors (such as Alexander Spotswood) and proprietary governors (such as Charles Eden) got to select the members of their own advisory council—the higher assembly, a post held for life. The exception was in the corporate but remarkably democratic colony of Massachusetts, where advisors were elected by the lower house. This upper house, usually known as the Governor's Council, was also the highest court of appeal within the colony. As the governor also had the right to appoint or dismiss judges and other leading officials, and the Council was also made up of his appointees, in most cases the governor was effectively the lawmaker within the colony. He could also grant pardons if required, an option used by Charles Eden when dealing with Blackbeard and Stede Bonnet. In cases such as the trial of William Howard, it was almost impossible for a ruling to be made against a governor's wishes—which is why the lawyer John Holloway had little option but to withdraw his legal case in support of Blackbeard's old quartermaster.

A colonial governor also commanded any local militia and any naval forces the colony might have and, as his commission often put it, "execute everything which doth and of right ought to belong to the governor," a clause that could be stretched to the limit—as Spotswood did when he decided to take his war against the pirates into the territory of a neighboring colony. While these powers might be seen to encourage tyrannical rule, in effect they seemed to have been used benignly, as after all the governor was responsible to his masters in London, and any conflict with the colonists he ruled could reflect badly on him back home. Increasingly, real power was held by the elected assemblies, whether the House of Burgesses in Virginia or the assembly in most other colonies. The qualification to vote was linked to the ownership of land, which was based on the early-eighteenth-century assumption that only those with a stake in the colony could be relied upon to vote responsibly in its assembly. However, most small farmers were eligible, and, in effect, the only groups excluded from voting were women and slaves.

The situation in Virginia reflected colonial politics of the time. Governor Spotswood frequently tried to use prerogatives that were no longer available to King George I back in Britain, and his colonial assemblies

Blackbeard's nemesis Alexander Spotswood, the deputy governor of Virginia during the pirate crisis of 1718. Spotswood's campaign against Blackbeard became a matter of great controversy, and may ultimately have cost him his job.

knew that. They also realized that when it came to policymaking in Britain, Parliament held the whip hand over the monarch. They saw no reason the same relationship shouldn't apply in Williamsburg as well as in London. Even in 1718 the lower assembly in Virginia, the House of Burgesses, was advocating for the rights of the American people they represented rather than serving the will of the governor. This was what lay behind the rift between Spotswood and the Ludwell–Blair faction — the old British feud between king and Parliament fought out on a new battleground, and presaging the culmination of the same argument in the American Revolution just over half a century later. For the moment it was a case of irresistible force meeting an immovable object, and although neither side had the ability to win the argument, Spotswood realized that unless he managed to divert the attention of his assemblies from the struggle, then his political position would eventually be undermined by the bickering. That was why Blackbeard was a godsend to him.

Alexander Spotswood might have begun life as a soldier, but he was also a consummate politician. He was an army brat, born around 1676 in the English military garrison of Tangier, which was then an outpost of the empire. Tangier might have seemed a strange place for a three-thousand-man English military garrison, but the former Portuguese colony became part of the dowry of Catherine of Braganza when she married King Charles II of England and Scotland in 1662. Spotswood's Scottish father, Dr. Robert Spotswood, served there as an army surgeon, but he died when Alexander was just four. Rather than return home to England, his mother, Catherine Maxwell, stayed in Tangier and married the garrison's school-teacher, the Rev. George Mercer. It was an exciting and exotic place for a young boy—the Moors outside the walls remained a constant threat, and skirmishes were commonplace. Charles II eventually ordered the troops home in 1683, and Alexander completed a more conventional childhood in England.

This was a time of great upheaval in Britain. Charles II's younger brother succeeded him in 1663 to become James II of England and VII of Scotland, but his Catholicism earned him the distrust of his subjects. He managed to crush a rebellion in 1685, but James's power base collapsed like a house of cards during the Glorious Revolution of 1688, when the throne was seized by the Dutch stadtholder William of Orange. King William III plunged England and Scotland into a nine-year war with France and Spain, so the young Spotswood would have grown up with warfare being a constant theme in his life. His elder half-brother Roger Elliot (the product of Catherine's first marriage) helped secure Alexander an appointment as an ensign in the Earl of Bath's Regiment in 1693, and he distinguished himself in active service in Flanders. He received his commission as a captain of foot (infantry) in 1698, and a resumption of the war in 1702 presented him with the opportunity for promotion. In 1703 he became a lieutenant colonel, and was appointed to the staff of John Churchill, the Duke of Marlborough. Once again he distinguished himself at the Battle of Blenheim (1704) and through his staff work as the army's quartermaster general. Alexander Spotswood was clearly a man on the way up.

You didn't remain the quartermaster general of an allied army in wartime without learning the skills of a politician and a diplomat, and Spotswood proved adept at wooing British, Dutch, and Germans alike. He remained with Marlborough's victorious army until after the bloody Battle of Malplaquet (1709), when he was recalled to Britain. There he was given a new diplomatic assignment. Marlborough's trusted deputy during the campaigns in Flanders was George Hamilton, the 1st Earl of Orkney. The earl had recently been named as the titular governor of the colony of Virginia, and in 1710 he selected fellow Scotsman Alexander Spotswood as his lieutenant governor. In effect, Spotswood would run Virginia, while Orkney remained at home and earned half of all revenues the colony produced. Spotswood arrived in Williamsburg in late 1710, and soon began setting his stamp on the colony. He found that the job of balancing the needs of the colonists with those of the Earl of Orkney and the Board of Trade was difficult enough, but a radical element in the colony made his job all the harder. The crisis of 1718 was just one of many he faced during his twelve years in office, but somehow he managed to walk the political tightrope without falling—until the end.

Still, his tenure in office was marked by a string of clashes, the most serious being the imposition of a Tobacco Act in 1713, under which the governor's officials were required to inspect the quality of all Virginia tobacco designed for export or barter. Inevitably this led to a confrontation with the colony's wealthiest planters, and the governor's imperious handling of the situation did him few favors. From that moment on Spotswood was dogged by political opponents, and it was all he could do to avoid tripping up. In the years before 1716 he was still intent on pushing out the Virginian boundaries. In August 1716 Spotswood organized "an expedition over the Appalachian mountains" as a means of countering French expansion from New France (now Canada). Accompanied by scouts, servants, and a dozen gentlemen adventurers, he set off in search of a pass through the Alleghenies that would permit Virginia's westward expansion. Although Spotswood never found the pass, he was able to claim new lands for the British crown.

As one of the party, Lieutenant John Fontaine, noted in his diary,

I graved my name on a tree by the river side; and the Governor buried a bottle with a paper inclosed, on which he writ that he took possession of this place in the name and for King George the First of England. We had a good dinner, and after it we got the men together, and loaded all their arms, and we drank the King's health in Champagne, and fired a volley . . . the Princess's health in Burgundy, and fired a volley, and all the rest of the Royal Family in claret, and a volley. We drank the Governor's health and fired another volley . . . We called the highest mountain Mount George, and the one we crossed over Mount Spotswood.

As entertaining as this interlude was, it did little to divert Spotswood from the daily grind of Virginia politics. Still, it showed that he had his eye on posterity. The same impetus led to his foundation of a settlement at Germania in 1715, and within a few years the thousands of acres he owned in central Virginia were named after him, becoming Spotsylvania County.

By 1722 the higher and lower assemblies in Virginia had managed to convince the Board of Trade to remove Spotswood from office. With his days numbered, one of his last acts as governor was to deed further lands around Germania to himself, thereby creating a nice retirement nest egg. In the years that followed he made his money selling this central Virginia land to those wanting to settle, and within eight years he was one of the wealthiest men in the Americas. He returned to Britain in 1730, where he married Anne Butler Bayne. The fifty-four-year-old newlywed returned to Virginia with his bride, and served as the deputy postmaster-general of the American colonies before his death in Annapolis in 1740. However, in the fall of 1718 all this was in the future—only the wide rift between governor and assemblies pointed the way ahead. Like any good politician, he realized that a war or other external threat would help rally the people behind him. For Governor Spotswood, Blackbeard returned to sea at just the right moment. The pirate threat made him appear to be acting decisively in the interests of Virginia, and at the same time the seizure of plunder offered him the chance to make a tidy profit.

As early as May 1718, Governor Spotswood was busy laying the groundwork for an offensive against pirates in Virginia waters—and anywhere else he saw fit. Blackbeard was still off Charles Town Bar, but the Virginia governor was not targeting Blackbeard specifically. He was well aware that piracy was bad for trade and therefore hurt his own pocket. Pirate rampages also made him appear incapable of protecting the colony's merchants, which played directly into the hands of his opponents. Just as importantly, pirate hunting could be profitable. Under the terms of the king's pardon, those pirates who surrendered got to keep their plunder. However, the property of those caught red-handed was held by the authorities and divided according to predetermined Admiralty rules about ownership and salvage. If the authority involved was Virginia, then Spotswood stood to gain.

Appropriately enough, he began his antipiracy campaign by reinforcing his claim to ownership of any recaptured booty. On May 26 he declared: "If the owners make out their property, the produce must be paid to them according to His Majesty's Treatys, allowing a usual Salvage to those who rescued them from the Pyrats. If no Claimer appears and that the same comes to the King, no doubt his Majesty will think fit to reward the Officers of his Ships and other Concerned in so considerable a Service as the destroying of that crew of Pyrats." In Spotswood's view, the onus was on the wronged shipowners to make the case for ownership to the Virginian authorities, not for Spotswood to try to seek out the original owners. Given the poor communications in colonial America, and the fact that Blackbeard had plundered ships from Long Island to the Gulf of Honduras, it was clear that he was only paying lip service to doing the right thing.

The steps Spotswood should have taken were clearly laid down in his brief from the Earl of Orkney and the Board of Trade, issued just over three years earlier on April 15, 1715. This made clear the rules concerning the ownership of pirate plunder: "In case any goods, money or other Estate of pirates or Piratically taken, shall be brought in or found within said Colony of Virginia, or taken on board any Ship or Vessels, you are to cause the same to be seized, and secured, until our Pleasure Concerning the disposal of the same, but in Case such Goods, or any part of them, are perishable, the same shall be publicly sold and disposed of, and the produce thereof in like manner secured, until our Further order." This allowed Spotswood little leeway for making a profit. However, he had a loophole. His legitimacy as a pirate-hunting governor was based on a rocky legal foundation—a proclamation by the late King William III, who died in 1702. His successor and sister-in-law, Queen Anne, who reigned from 1702 to 1714, did not reissue the proclamation, and George I also did nothing about it during the first three years of his reign. When he finally got around to issuing one, the document only arrived in Virginia in December 1718. This meant that Spotswood could claim he had no direct guidance from London, and so had to take action first and seek legal approval for his actions later.

Other colonial governors were in the same position. In the colony of South Carolina Governor Johnson had already taken matters into his own hands by sending out Colonel Rhett's antipiracy patrol—the one that cornered Stede Bonnet in the Cape Fear River. In the New York colony and in the West Indies the governors were better served by the Royal Navy, and enjoyed the protection of warships serving within their boundaries. As for poor Governor Eden in North Carolina, he had neither the protection of the Royal Navy nor the resources to create his own antipiracy flotilla. Alexander Spotswood knew this, and sought to take advantage of his neighbor's weakness. If Eden lacked the power to deal with pirates within his own dominions, then Spotswood would do the job for him. This went far beyond the remit of the powers granted to him when he took the job—they specifically stated that he could only intervene in the affairs of other colonies "in case of Distress of any other of our plantations," and only then "upon the Application of the respective Governors thereof to you."

Governor Eden had made no such request. Spotswood was not only planning to meddle in the affairs of another colony, but he also planned to do so using military force—an event that Governor Eden and the Lords Proprietor would view as tantamount to invasion. From his letters it is evident that Spotswood had little time for both Governor Eden and North Carolina. He certainly viewed proprietary colonies (owned by individuals) as inferior to crown colonies (run on behalf of the monarch) like Virginia, and there is little doubt that he hoped his actions would highlight the inefficiencies of the Carolinian proprietary system. He probably harbored plans to incorporate the North Carolina colony into Virginia—an event that would significantly increase his own influence and almost certainly earn him even greater wealth.

Throughout history, leaders have used external threats and the prospect of military force as a means of diverting attention away from unpopular domestic policies. Spotswood was no exception, but by intervening in North Carolina's affairs he also raised the stakes. Win against the pirates and, while he could expect the censure of Eden and his superiors, he would have demonstrated Eden's inability to keep his own house in order. That in turn would improve the prospects of a Virginian takeover. Whichever way you looked at it, Spotswood had a lot to gain from taking the initiative against Blackbeard and his fellow pirates, and he had very little to lose—unless it all went wrong. Failure meant he would have played straight into the hands of his opponents, and the clamor for his removal would have been almost impossible for his superiors to ignore.

The most worrying thing for Spotswood was the whole legal question. It was all very good to take action against Blackbeard, but what happened when he caught the pirate? Presumably the arrest would be made on North Carolina soil or on the high seas, and then the pirate would be brought back to Williamsburg to stand trial. All it needed was another rabble-rousing lawyer like John Holloway for his whole antipiracy policy to be exposed as a legal house of cards. Without the express permission of King George I to hold pirate trials on his own authority, Spotswood was open to attack for overstepping his authority. His one advantage lay in his role as Virginia's Vice-Admiralty representative. Unlike normal legal procedures, there was no requirement for cases heard under Admiralty law to be put to trial by jury. As the Admiralty's representative, Spotswood could control the trial, and in effect stage-manage it as he had the case against William Howard. He also had legal precedent. By late 1718 Spotswood wasn't the only British colonial governor to have gone through the problems of trying pirates without specific authority to do so. In extremis he could always claim he was following the lead of his fellow colonial governor, Woodes Rogers.

The last time we heard of Governor Rogers was on the morning of July 27, after Charles Vane had forced his way past the British squadron outside Nassau Harbor and escaped out to sea. It could be argued that Vane's spectacular departure helped Rogers enormously, as not only did it rid New Providence of its radical element, but it meant that those who remained were all the more eager to toe the line. The task facing Rogers was monumental—he had to establish British authority where nothing but a semi-anarchic pirate fraternity had existed before. Then he had to make sure the former pirates remained on the right side of the law. He was under no illusions. However, he had useful allies in Henry Jennings and Benjamin Hornigold. Although Jennings retired from the scene soon after Rogers's arrival, Hornigold remained in New Providence, and accepted a commission from the governor as the colony's principal pirate hunter. He engaged in his new role with all the passion of a convert, fitting out a brig and setting off in pursuit of Charles Vane. Although the die-hard pirate escaped him, Hornigold had already stamped his authority on the Bahamas, regaining the authority over the pirate community he had lost the previous summer.

With Hornigold patrolling the waters of the Bahamas, Rogers set to work in Nassau. His first task was the formation of a council and the appointment of senior officials in the colony, many of whom were former pirates, as there were few other suitable candidates. With a war with Spain looming, his next task was to repair the defenses of the port, rebuilding the crumbling earthen walls of the small fort overlooking Nassau Harbor and equipping it so it could play its part in defending the harbor in the event of an assault. After all, New Providence was vulnerable to an attack from Havana, as the Spaniards could be lying off the harbor before Rogers could send word of their approach to the naval commander in Jamaica. It was clear that if he wanted to defend the island, he needed the help of men like Hornigold.

Most of the former pirates who accepted the offer of a pardon in the spring and summer of 1718 kept their word and became law-abiding seamen again. However, a few slipped back into their old ways, and without the example of men like Benjamin Hornigold and the former pirate Thomas Cocklyn, many more would have reverted to piracy. After all, New Providence had little to offer them—it was off the beaten track, there were few legitimate jobs to be had, and the pirates had been used to a time of plenty. As a former privateersman himself, Woodes Rogers was well aware of the temptations, so he developed a policy that was designed to discourage temptation. Hornigold and his antipiracy patrol was the cornerstone, providing paid employment for ex-pirates, discouraging others from slipping back into their former business, and hunting down those who crossed the line. Hornigold remained true to his word and remained an exemplary character for the remainder of his life. Rogers's policy of setting a thief to catch a thief came up trumps.

It is likely that Hornigold set off in pursuit of Charles Vane within days of the die-hard's spectacular departure from New Providence, but the pirate raced through the Northwest Providence Channel and was swallowed up in the emptiness of the Atlantic before Hornigold could catch him. We know that Hornigold had returned to New Providence by mid-September to reprovision his ship for a longer voyage, as he was mentioned as being in Nassau in mid-September in some of Rogers's correspondence. The governor then sent Hornigold out again, and although the pirate hunter never found Vane, in early November he did come across a sloop that had traded with the pirate. Hornigold had been waiting in ambush for the pirates off the Georgia coast, and from Nicholas Woodall of the sloop *Wolff* he learned that by that time Vane had passed through the Carolinas and headed north toward New England. Hornigold decided to return to New Providence with his prize. Many former pirates thought he might have used the opportunity to slip the leash, but Rogers retained his faith in Hornigold, a belief that was rewarded when the pirate hunter arrived off Nassau in late October accompanied by the *Wolff*, her captain charged with dealing in stolen goods and consorting with pirates.

The governor was delighted. On October 31 he wrote, "Captain Hornigold having proved honest, disobliged his old friends by seizing this vessel and it divides the people here and makes me stronger than I had expected." The sloop *Wolff* was duly impounded and Woodall thrown into the cells in Nassau fort. It soon turned out he was small fry—merely a trader caught up in piratical activities. Still, others faced the rope for less, and Woodall was lucky to lose nothing more than his vessel. However, by that time Rogers and Hornigold had more important matters to consider. During the late summer of 1718 Governor Rogers entrusted a Captain John Auger (also written Augur) with a cargo for a trading voyage on behalf of the Bahamian colony. These men were New Providence pirates who had accepted the royal pardon—the kind of men Rogers needed to trust if the colony was to thrive.

However, as soon as they cleared the island Captain Auger and his men resumed their piratical careers, and the sloop *Mary* of (New) Providence became a pirate ship once again. As Captain Johnson described it, "In their voyage they met with two sloops, and John [Auger] and his comrades not yet forgetting their former business, made use of their old freedom, and took out of them, in money and goods, to the value of 500 pounds." Worse still, Auger managed to convince many crewmen from the Bahamian sloops *Lancaster* and the *Batchelor's Adventure* to join him when he came upon them off Green Cay. He then "steered away for Hispaniola, not being satisfied whether the governor would admit them to carry on two trades at once, and so thought to have bidden farewell to the Bahama islands; as luck would have it, they met with a violent tornado, wherein they lost their mast, and were drove back to one of the uninhabited Bahama's." Auger and his men found themselves on Exuma, a small desolate island on the eastern side of the Tongue of the Ocean some 150 miles south of New Providence. While a remote and deserted island, it did provide a useful refuge for the pirates.

The defection of the other Bahamians made the recapture of Auger doubly important—not only had he and his men made off with a valuable cargo, but they had betrayed Rogers's trust. If Auger was allowed to escape, then others would undoubtedly follow his lead. Neither of the two sloops was released by the pirates before Auger headed down the Tongue of the Ocean, a wide deepwater expanse lying between the Bahamian islands of Andros and Exuma. We can assume that the pirates kept the other sloops with them. According to Captain Johnson, the pirates were cast ashore on the island by the tornado, as he claims "the men got ashore, and lived up and down in the wood, for a little time, until Governor Rogers happened to hear of their expedition, and where they had got to, sent out an armed sloop to the aforesaid island; the master of which, with good words and fair promises got them aboard, and brought them all to New Providence, being eleven persons."

The truth may have been even more dramatic. Johnson might well have confused the accounts of the sailors marooned by the pirates on Green Cay with references to the pirate base on Great Exuma. According to the court records Auger and his men came upon the two Bahamian sloops on October 6, 1718, at Green Cay, where they captured the *Batchelor's Adventure* and the *Lancaster*, and seized their cargo. The document claims that the pirates then marooned Captain James Kerr and others from the two sloops on the small, desolate island, then sailed off to the south. Somehow Kerr and his men managed to escape and raise the alarm, probably with the help of local fishermen. After all, the deep waters of the Tongue of the Ocean were as good for fishing then as they are today, and boats regularly set out from Nassau into the fishing grounds to the south. It would have been a relatively simple matter for Kerr and his men to light a signal fire and attract the attention of a passing boat. According to the report written by Rogers the pirates had at least one operational sloop at their disposal, and even though the *Mary* might have been dismasted or even cast ashore, they could still escape if they wanted to—or resume their piratical attacks using one or both of their prizes.

Hornigold put to sea again with three sloops, and by late November he had returned—with Auger's sloop following him into the harbor. Hornigold had learned where Auger and his men were hiding out through a combination of the reports from the original pirate victims and, possibly, the reports of local fishermen. It certainly appears that the pirate hunter knew where to look for Auger and had time to come up with a plan. He approached the island from the south, his sloops disguised as a small convoy of Spanish trading vessels. It was common for smaller Spanish craft to thread their way through the lower Bahamas archipelago in times of danger rather than risk the open-water passage from Hispaniola to Havana. To increase the chances of his deception working, Hornigold approached the pirate den as dusk was falling, making it less likely that any of the pirates would identify the approaching sloops as vessels from New Providence rather than Hispaniola.

The ruse worked. Auger and his fellow pirates sallied out to attack the Spanish convoy, expecting little or no resistance. Almost certainly they used only one of their two sloops in the attack, but they must have thought that even though they were outnumbered they still had sufficient force to intimidate the Spaniards. They realized their mistake too late, and must have watched with horror as Hornigold's sloops ran their guns out and the Spanish flag was replaced by Britain's Union Jack. At point-blank range the pirate-hunting flotilla let loose a broadside of grapeshot. Eight to twelve four- or six-pounder guns firing bags of scrap metal, old nails, or musket shot at a target less than a hundred yards away would have a devastating impact on the target—scything men down, slicing through rigging, and forcing the remaining enemy to cower behind the bulwarks of their ships. Hornigold's men then boarded through the smoke, and within minutes they had subdued the pirates. Auger survived the assault, although a dozen or so of his men lay on the pirate decks, while many others were wounded in the battle. Hornigold captured the ship, rounded up the pirates left behind on Green Cay, then returned to Nassau in triumph.

With Auger and his men in prison, Rogers now faced the thorny legal problem of jurisdiction. First of all, he had little authority, apart from the general rights granted to him when he accepted the post of governor. Officially he had just as little legal authority to try men for piracy as Governor Spotswood in Virginia, although both men used the carrot-and-stick authority vested in the pirate pardon to achieve their ends. On November 28 Rogers even admitted to his council that he didn't hold a direct commission to try Auger. He should really have sent the pirates to London to stand trial, but to do so would be to deny himself his one real chance of stamping his authority in the Bahamas. Any good lawyer could probably have made a convincing case for the defense—if he had been allowed to represent the condemned men. In Spotswood's case he had successfully driven off the only willing lawyer by hiding behind his powers as Virginia's Vice-Admiralty representative. Woodes Rogers relied on the same authority, but he had the advantage that in his primitive hand-to-mouth colony there was no legal hotshot willing to stand his ground against the governor.

The pirate act gave Rogers the opportunity to use Admiralty law, which meant he could try the pirates without a jury—and a jury trial would have been fraught with danger in New Providence. Finding twelve men without a pirate past on the island would have been well-nigh impossible. He could also limit the Vice-Admiralty commissioners who collectively sat in judgment to just seven men—which meant he could select them from among his loyal staff and officers of the garrison. However sympathetic the rest of New Providence's population might be to the captured pirates, Rogers could be assured the trial would proceed the way he wanted. The only danger was a general rising in favor of John Auger and his men, so Rogers doubled the guard in the fort and sent patrols out into the streets of Nassau. This would be a trying time for the new British regime, and for both Rogers and Hornigold.

As the leading representative of the Vice-Admiralty in the Bahamian colony, Governor Rogers presided over the trial, which was held in the Guard Room of Nassau Fort. He was assisted by the seven commissioners, whose number included William Halifax, who as the leading judicial figure on the island also doubled as the official judge of the Vice-Admiralty, and Captain Wingate Gale, commander of Rogers's guard ship the *Delicia*. Both were reliable Rogers appointees, as were the naval officers Captain Josias Burgess and Captain Peter Courant. The remaining commissioners were trusted locals—almost certainly former pirates who had been recommended to Rogers by Hornigold—and selected for their loyalty to the pirate hunter. Ten men stood in the dock, including John Auger; John Hipps, the boatswain of the sloop *Lancaster*; and William Cunningham, the gunner on board the *Batchelor's Delight*. All pleaded not guilty.

The trial was held on December 9 and 10, while soldiers with loaded muskets lined the walls of the fort. There was little to discuss, as the proof against John Auger and his men was damning. After all, he had been caught in the act. However, it was important that everything should be seen to be fair, and so Rogers and the commissioners went through their deliberations with some care. Each man was tried separately, but with Captain Kerr to accuse them they stood little chance of escaping justice. The result was that on December 10 Auger was sentenced "to be hanged by the neck 'till you shall be dead, dead, dead," along with eight of his fellow pirates. One man, the mariner John Hipps, was reprieved, as he was able to offer proof that he had been coerced into joining the pirates. The rest would be executed without delay, sure proof that the governor needed to make an example of the condemned men, while realizing that the longer they remained alive, the more chance there was that their former shipmates might try to rescue them.

The execution was set for 10 A.M. on December 12, just two days after the trial. The pirates asked for a temporary stay of execution to help their spiritual preparation for their deaths, but Rogers was unrelenting. He replied that he "thought himselfe indispensably obliged for the welfare of the Settlement to give them no longer time." The governor even expanded on this bald statement, claiming that with the prospect of war with Spain on the horizon, the colony was facing a crisis. There would be no stay of execution. The official account of the proceedings detailed what happened: "Wherefore about ten a clock the prisoners were released from their irons and committed to the charger and care of Thomas Robenson Esq., commissioned Provost Marshal for that day, who according to custom in such cases pinioned them and ordered the guard appointed to lead them to the top of the ramparts fronting the sea, which was well guarded by the Governor, soldiers and people to the number of about one hundred." The moment must have been a tense one. Would the crowd try to rescue their colleagues? Could the militiamen trained by Rogers be relied upon in a crisis? The next hour would determine the fate of Governor Rogers and the New Providence colony.

> At the prisoners request several prayers and psalms selected were read in which all present joined. When the service was ended, orders were given to the marshal, and he conducted the prisoners down a ladder provided on purpose to the foot of the wall, where was a gallows erected, and a black flag hoisted thereon and under it a stage, supported by three butts [barrels] on which they ascended by another ladder, where the hangman fastened the cords as dexterously as if he had been a servitour at Tyburn. They had ¾ of an hour allowed under the gallows which was spent by them in singing of psalms and some exhortations to their old consorts, and other sort of spectators who got as near to the foot of the gallows as the marshal's guard would suffer them.

This was the moment. An impassioned plea by any of the condemned men might well ignite the crowd, even though soldiers lined the fort walls with muskets primed and ready.

John Auger was the first to take the opportunity to speak to the assembled crowd. It was customary for the condemned man in these circumstances to make a short speech, and from the report it seems clear that each man was given five minutes to say his piece. Auger rose to the occasion. He was well known in New Providence, having served as a privateering master in Jamaica before he turned to piracy the first time. He apologized for his crimes, and for reneging on his word. He then asked for a glass of wine, and when it was brought to him he toasted the assembled throng "with wishes for the good success of the Bahama Islands and the Governor." The eight others followed him in rapid succession, and again most proved penitent. Their number included William Cunningham, who had served with Blackbeard as his master gunner when the pirate sailed in consort with Hornigold. Cunningham had returned to New Providence with Hornigold, and accepted the pardon. For that sin alone he could expect no mercy, and said as much, adding that he was conscious of his sins. Another, thirty-four-year-old William Lewis, defiantly asked for rum, claiming that he had never wanted to die sober, and wished to toast his fellows. His fellow pirate William Ling retorted that water would serve them better at a time like this. The governor assented to Lewis's wishes, and when the end came it is hoped the unfortunate pirate was oblivious to his fate.

For the most part the younger pirates were less penitent than Auger, and most displayed bravado in their last moments. Twenty-four-year-old William Dowling, described as a hardened pirate, lacked much remorse, while twenty-two-year-old Thomas Morris dressed well in red ribbons and defiantly shouted that he wished he had been a greater plague on the Bahamas than he had been. Similarly, eighteen-year-old George Bendall remained sullen throughout the proceedings, claiming that unlike the rest he had never been a pirate before, so he didn't deserve his fate. It was to little avail. The governor wasn't there to show clemency, only hardened resolve. However, it was politic to show some mercy when appropriate, just to prove he was no monster. One of the Barbadian mariners captured who joined the pirates at Green Cay was another teenager, George Rounsivel, and evidence from John Hipps and others suggested that he had become involved with the pirates through intimidation by his elders. He would serve Rogers's purpose perfectly.

The most impressive display came from Irish-born Dennis McCarty, a former ensign in the island's militia who dressed in his finest clothes for the occasion, "adorn'd at Neck, Wrist, Knees and Capp with long blew Ribbons." He harangued the crowd, saying, "he knew the time there were many brave fellows on the Island who would not suffer him to die like [a] dog." Cowed by the line of muskets, the crowd of former pirates refused to rise to his challenge. He then kicked off his shoes, as he had no desire to die with his boots on. McCarty had provided the New Providence pirates with their last hurrah, a rallying cry harking back to happier, more carefree days. Rogers must have been delighted that the crowd gathered to watch the execution proved as docile as the Irishman had been spirited. The official report concluded, "Then the Governor ordered the marshal to make

Woodes Rogers, the governor of the Bahamas, pictured during his buccaneering days a decade and a half before he took over control of New Providence in the name of King George. His experience as a buccaneer and privateering captain stood him in good stead in Nassau.

ready, and all the prisoners expecting the launch, the Governor thought fit to order George Rounsivel to be untied, and when brought off the stage, the butts having ropes about them were hauled away, upon which the stage fell and the eight swang off." Auger and his men had paid the ultimate price for their crimes.

The successful conclusion of the John Auger episode must have been a great relief to Woodes Rogers. However, as his secretary wrote in a statement at the time, the governor still had a lot to worry about: "he was obliged to employ all his People to assist in mounting the Great Guns, & in finishing the present works, with all possible dispatch, because of the expected War with Spain, & there being many more pyrates amongst these Islands." It added that New Providence was "left destitute from all Relief, from any man of War, or Station'd Ship." In other words, the governor still had to rely on Hornigold and loyal former pirates to protect the colony from attack, or to prevent any further slip toward piracy by the Bahamian brethren who made up the bulk of his colonists. In fact, Hornigold was probably the one cause for optimism that winter. On December 24, 1718, he wrote to the Board of Trade in London, "I am glad of this new proof that Captain Hornigold has given to the world to wipe off the infamous name he has hitherto been known by, though in the very acts of piracy he committed most people spoke well of his generosity."

The next trial of strength between Woodes Rogers and the Bahamian pirates came the following spring when Charles Vane's die-hard pirates returned to the Bahamas—without Vane, of course, who had been deposed, and was currently languishing on a deserted island in the Gulf of Honduras. When the pirates returned it was Vane's old quartermaster, "Calico" Jack Rackam, who was in charge. After a spree of attacks off Bermuda, Rackam and his shipmates took shelter in the Bahamas, thinking their old base was big enough to hide in. They soon discovered that Captain Hornigold had sent out patrols looking for him, and that since their rapid departure ten months before things had changed. The islands were now a relatively law-abiding part of the British Empire, and both Governor Rogers and his pirate hunter planned to keep it that way. With a fresh offer of a pardon on the table, Rackam, or at least the majority of his crew, opted to return to New Providence and surrender themselves to Rogers. It must have been a particularly sweet moment for the governor as he watched those who had defied him on his arrival return cap in hand, asking for mercy.

Since December 1718 Britain was at war with Spain, and the news would have reached Rogers around January 1719—who used the opportunity to reissue the offer of a pardon to draw in any last pirates. The policy certainly seemed to work. In late January 1719 Rogers wrote to Secretary Craggs at the Board of Trade, informing him that Captain Congon (or Coudon), who commanded two pirate sloops, had turned himself in under the terms of the new amnesty. This meant that Rogers wasted no time in taking advantage of the opportunities presented by the war, even though his colony lay on the front line, too close to the Spanish base at Havana for comfort. Britain now needed legitimate privateers, and these former privateersmen turned pirates had once been the best hunters of Spanish shipping around—and might be able to help defend the Bahamas in the process. Many of the former pirates in New Providence quit the island for Jamaica or Barbados, where privateer commissions were being issued. A few even managed to sign on as law-abiding privateersmen before the war came to an abrupt end in February 1720. However, a few lingered on, and could be pressed into service if Rogers needed them.

"Calico" Jack Rackam was still in the Bahamas when the war ended, and it was from there that he relaunched his piratical career in August 1720 when he stole the sloop *William* and slipped out to sea. While he might have been one of the last of the Bahamian pirates, he was little more than an irritant. He managed to plunder two Bahamian fishing boats before he headed south through the Windward Passage, where he officially became the problem of the governor of Jamaica rather than Woodes Rogers's responsibility. He was an exception to the rule, and while several pirates returned to piracy after accepting pardons, only Rackam deliberately flouted Rogers's authority by doing so in New Providence itself. Even more so than Auger, Rackam needed to be made an example of. It therefore made sense that as long as the pirate remained at large, Rogers would make every effort to pursue him. It is almost certain that Bahamian pirate hunters continued to hunt for Rackam until the pirate ran afoul of the Jamaican pirate hunter Captain Barnet in mid-November.

During the short War of the Quadruple Alliance between Britain and Spain, Governor Rogers busied himself improving the defenses of New Providence. According to Captain Johnson he concentrated on improving the defenses of the fort in Nassau "and garrisoned it with the people he found upon the island; the quondam pirates, to the number of 400, he formed into companies, appointed officers of those he most confided in, and then set about to settle a trade with the Spaniards in the Gulf of Mexico." Of course, when he first arrived that summer, Rogers brought with him a company of about fifty to sixty regular soldiers, and a small staff of experienced British military officers, engineers, and administrators. His pirate militia might not have been the best disciplined troops in the Americas, but at least they were experienced, and they were trained by some of the best instructors and drill sergeants around. However, it was fortunate that the Spanish never considered launching an attack on the island as they had done in previous wars, as the makeshift defenses might not have stood up against an all-out assault. Similarly, his militia of former pirates was never tested in battle.

However, Rogers had been thorough, not only in improving the defensive capabilities of New Providence but in attracting trade to the island. When the twenty-gun sixth-rate warship HMS *Flamborough* paid a visit to Nassau in the summer of 1720, the mate, Rowland Hildesley, was able to report that the fort on New Providence was in good order, with some sixty guns mounted overlooking the harbor and the landward approaches to the port. He added that the former East Indiaman *Delicia*, which had served as Rogers's flagship on his arrival in the Bahamas two years before, was in good condition and armed with thirty-six guns, which made her one of the most powerful warships in American waters. Finally, he claimed that New Providence was defended by a well-armed and motivated force of some six hundred to seven hundred militia. It seems that Governor Rogers had achieved something of a miracle during his first two years in office. Even more importantly, Nassau harbor was filled with over thirty trading vessels—sure proof that Rogers's policies were working.

Captain Johnson made the claim that one of Rogers's first acts as governor was to set up a trading link between the Bahamas and "the Spaniards in the Gulf of Mexico." This made little sense while Britain and Spain were at war—which meant from the time of John Auger's execution until early 1720. He also claimed that Rogers sent Hornigold on a trading voyage to Mexico. Once again, it seems highly unlikely that he would consider such a thing while the islands were still under threat from the Spanish. If any such trading route was established, then it began shortly before Rowland Hildesley visited the Bahamas in the summer of 1720, which left little time to build up trade to the level the naval observer suggests in his observations. It is therefore far more likely that after the Auger crisis passed, Governor Rogers then encouraged trade between New Providence and the other British colonies in the region, Jamaica, the Leeward Islands, and the Carolinas. After all, it made more sense—the principal exports of the Bahamas were dried fish and fruit, hardly produce of much financial value. This meant that trade involved small regular shipments to major ports or colonies—not long-range trading voyages halfway around the Caribbean basin. We have to assume Johnson got it wrong, although more work needs to be done on the development of Bahamian trade during this fledgling period in the archipelago's history.

This leads us to the next important question: What happened to Blackbeard's mentor, Captain Benjamin Hornigold? The last time we hear of him in official correspondence is around the time "Calico" Jack Rackam arrived in the Bahamas, some five months after the John Auger trial. Once again Captain Johnson offers us a solution. After speaking of the colony's alleged trade with Mexico, he claimed, "in one of which voyages, Captain Burgess aforementioned, died, and Captain Hornigold, another of the famous pirates, was cast away upon rocks, a great way from land, and perished, but five of his men got into a canoe and were saved." The suggestion is that Hornigold was overtaken by a hurricane somewhere between New Providence and Mexico and drowned when his ship struck a reef. However, the account fails to provide us with any more details. Above all, it doesn't provide us with any clue as to when the disaster happened. To answer the question, we need to do a little bit of detective work, and we need to make a few suppositions.

The hurricane season in the Caribbean lasts from the start of June until the beginning of November, with the worst storms usually coming in the latter half of the period. That means that Hornigold met his fate during the summer and fall of 1719, or just possibly during the same hurricane season of 1720. We know that in February 1720 Governor Rogers wrote to his superiors complaining of the lack of protection afforded to the colony, and no mention of his principal pirate hunter was made in the letter. This makes 1719 the most likely date for Hornigold's demise. Whether this shipwreck took place on a voyage to Mexico—possibly off the Florida Keys or the Yucatan Peninsula—or somewhere else entirely is uncertain. If we assume he was kept on hand to combat any threat from the Spanish, then he might well have lost his life somewhere in Bahamian waters. Certainly the reference to survivors of the shipwreck being able to make their way back to a friendly port suggests that the disaster took place reasonably close to home, or at least close to a major shipping route. Wherever the shipwreck happened, it seems that by the end of 1719 Woodes Rogers appears to have lost his most trusted lieutenant.

The next few years proved something of an anticlimax for Rogers. The end of the war with Spain didn't necessarily bring an end to the threat of invasion, as the two sides remained hostile, a little like Cold War protagonists. The Bahamas would remain the front-line colony for some time to come. The pirate threat might have diminished, but it didn't entirely go away. Eventually ill health forced Rogers to return to Britain in 1721, and he was duly replaced by George Phenney, a man who lacked Rogers's resolve and experience. His corrupt administration tottered on through the 1720s until the clamor for his dismissal forced the Board of Trade to react. Rogers duly petitioned King George for his reinstatement as governor, an application supported by none other than Alexander Spotswood of Virginia as well as the majority of the grandees running the Board of Trade. He was the obvious choice, and so in the summer of 1729 Woodes Rogers returned to Nassau, this time supported by powers he had lacked the first time around.

Today Woodes Rogers is known as the founding father of the Bahamas, or at least of Bahama's Anglicized administration. He was clearly an accomplished man: a successful privateer, a bestselling travel and adventure writer, and a colonial administrator who helped tame the piratical frontier of eighteenth-century America. During his final years he continued the uphill struggle to transform the fortunes of his adopted island home, supervising the introduction of new crops and encouraging trade. It is ironic that these crops were tobacco and sugar, which inevitably meant the introduction of slavery to the islands. His last few years might have seen a revival of Bahamian fortunes, but they also witnessed the involvement of the islands in the inhumane business of slavery. Today the descendants of these slaves make up the bulk of the Bahamian population.

However, he almost singlehandedly turned the islands from a pirate haven into a self-sufficient British colony, and ended the days when the Bahamians were regarded as the pariahs of the seas. He finally died in Nassau on July 15, 1732. Of all Woodes Rogers's legacies, it was his determined stand against piracy that was to have the most lasting effect on the

Americas. By denying pirates like Blackbeard a base of operations off the American coast, he did his fellow colonial governors an immeasurable service. It was now up to men like Alexander Spotswood, Robert Johnson, and to a lesser extent Charles Eden to end the pirate threat once and for all. The trouble was, not all colonial governors had the resources available to Spotswood, nor the determination of Johnson and Rogers. Blackbeard was well aware that the administration of North Carolina lacked the funding, the military force, and the resolve to tackle the pirate threat head-on. During the fall of 1718 the pirate did what he could to ensure that the administration would not only tolerate him but also discreetly support his activities.

Charles Eden was certainly no Woodes Rogers. However, there is no hard evidence that he was a corrupt one, either, despite the later claims of Governor Spotswood of Virginia. He was certainly in an unenviable position. For a start, even if he had wished to take a firm line with pirates such as Blackbeard, he had no troops to speak of. North Carolina boasted a militia, but it was organized on an ad-hoc basis, grouped around each settlement. It was also designed to fight off attacks by Native Americans, not take a stand against pirates, and men were unwilling to serve far from their homes. The colony was also in dire financial straits, having just emerged from a bitterly contested Indian war. Worse, a long-running border dispute with neighboring Virginia meant that Spotswood's administration had forbidden the import or transport of Carolinian tobacco from one colony to the other. This meant that what few North Carolina tobacco planters there were were forced to ship their goods south to Charles Town rather than Williamsburg, which was considerably closer.

Even more importantly, Governor Eden's dealings with Blackbeard were all aboveboard. In the year following the climax of our story, Governor Eden was heavily criticized for his involvement of Blackbeard, and was accused of offering the pirate his tacit support. It was also claimed that he was corrupt, and received consignments of stolen goods from the pirates in return for ignoring their activities. All these accusations can be traced back to one source—Alexander Spotswood. In order to justify his intervention in the affairs of another colony, Virginia's governor had to prove that his action was necessary. That meant proving that his neighbor Charles Eden was a man who couldn't be trusted. The bulk of these accusations came during the legal disputes of 1719, but at the time even the imperious Spotswood wasn't willing to challenge Eden to his face, or to level wild accusations without some sort of proof. One can only suppose he hoped hard evidence would be forthcoming, and after all, Spotswood's agents did find at least one incriminating document linking the Eden administration with Blackbeard. However, Spotswood was well aware that in openly challenging the running of the North Carolina colony or by intervening in its affairs he was laying himself open to counteraccusations of grossly overstepping his authority.

Everything centered on the Vice-Admiralty Court convened by governor Eden in Bath Town in late September 1718. Critics claim the argument proposed by Blackbeard and his men that they simply found a French merchant vessel drifting and abandoned on the high seas was completely unbelievable. However, this is based on reputation rather than facts, and all Governor Eden could rely on during the hearing was the evidence placed before him. Blackbeard and four of his crew had signed affidavits supporting the claim, and no representative of the French owners had appeared to question the salvors' claim. Such cases of abandonment on the high seas were unusual, but not unknown. In these circumstances Charles Eden had no recourse but to award salvage rights to the former pirates, and the French ship was duly declared a derelict vessel. Captain Johnson was clear that Eden had made the right decision based on the evidence, writing that the decision was made "as any other court must have done, and the cargo disposed of according to law."

In these circumstances the court usually awarded the ship and her contents to the salvors, less a portion that was retained by the Crown, or in this case by the North Carolina authorities. This portion of the cargo was what later caused most of the trouble. The French merchant vessel carried a mixed cargo, but the majority of it was sugar. Some sixty hogsheads (barrels) of sugar were duly delivered to Governor Eden's Bath Town plantation house, representing the legitimate share of the cargo claimed by the colony under salvage law. It was not a payoff by the pirates, nor did it suggest any complicity between governor and pirate. Slightly more controversially, another twenty hogsheads of sugar were delivered to the home of Tobias Knight, the secretary of the North Carolina colony and her chief justice. As such he led the Vice-Admiralty Council that heard the case, although as the "admiral of North Carolina," Governor Eden chaired the hearing.

Governor Spotswood later claimed that these twenty hogsheads were nothing more than a backhander, given by the pirates to Knight for his legal

*The execution of Stede Bonnet on the point of Charles Town in November
1718. Sailors crowd the mastheads of ships in harbor while a crowd watches
his final moments. The gentleman pirate is shown clutching a small bouquet
of flowers, a symbol for forgiveness.*

services. Both Eden and Knight countered with the much more believable
story that these barrels represented payment to the administration in lieu of
court fees. Knight also doubled as the colony's collector of customs, so it
was logical that he would be the man to collect such a payment. Still, in the

minds of their critics, all these barrels represented were evidence of complicity and corruption. Of course, it didn't help that soon afterward Blackbeard destroyed the evidence, burning the French ship to the waterline off Ocracoke Island. Although he claimed that the action was taken because the vessel was leaking badly and in danger of foundering in the inlet, it also conveniently disposed of a ship that could later be identified by its former owners, which would allow Eden's ruling to be challenged. Despite the rumors, it is extremely unlikely that Eden had anything to do with the ship's destruction.

If we are prepared to absolve Governor Eden of any direct complicity with Blackbeard, then that leaves his secretary, Tobias Knight. The case against him was built around a document that he allegedly wrote to Blackbeard, warning the pirate that Governor Spotswood planned to launch an attack against him. When this letter came into Spotswood's possession it became the central piece of evidence in a case that tried to prove that Knight was an accessory to piracy—with or without the knowledge of his superior Charles Eden. Further depositions followed where it was claimed that Knight was given several payoffs by Blackbeard, usually in the form of plunder. One went so far as to claim that in addition to the official hogsheads of sugar from the French ship, Knight received a consignment of cocoa (or chocolate). The pirates who delivered the consignment reached Knight's home shortly after midnight sometime in mid-September—a full two weeks before the Vice-Admiralty hearing.

The same deposition also claimed that on that occasion Blackbeard accompanied his men to Knight's plantation, and that Knight and Blackbeard remained talking together until just before dawn. If it could be proved, then it was clear evidence of collusion. However, if he was involved, Knight was smart enough to hide the evidence. What the case against him fell back on was the letter, written on November 17, 1718, when word of Spotswood's activities reached Bath Town. It is worth quoting it in full, as it is either a damning piece of evidence or a mere friendly note, depending on whether you believe the defense or the prosecution.

My friend,

If this finds you yet in harbour I would have you make the best of your way up as soon as possible your affairs will let you. I have something more to say to you than at present I can write; the bearer will tell you the end of our

Indian Warr, and Ganet can tell you in part what I have to say to you, so referr you in some measure to him.

I really think these three men are heartily sorry at their difference with you and will be very willing to ask your pardon; if I may advise, be ffriends again, its better than falling out among your selves.

I expect the Governor this night or tomorrow, who I believe would be likewise glad to see you before you goe, I have not time to add save my hearty respects to you, and am your real ffriend.

And Servant

T. Knight

This guarded letter was written as a warning—Knight had some important news to pass on to Blackbeard that he didn't want to put down on paper. It was sent from Bath Town to Ocracoke by two couriers, trusted associates of Knight. Was Tobias Knight trying to warn Blackbeard that he faced an attack? Governor Spotswood certainly thought so, and ended up putting Governor Eden's secretary on trial. However, as we shall see, Knight managed to avoid any official censure, largely by conducting a spirited defense, and then by dying from a lingering illness before any verdict could be reached. In other words, the case for corruption and complicity was never proven. In the end, the worst charges anyone could level against Charles Eden and Tobias Knight were that they had been foolhardy in their open dealings with a onetime pirate. They had been prepared to give Blackbeard the benefit of the doubt. Governor Spotswood had no intention of making the same mistake.

9

The Last Battle

Alexander Spotswood was not a man to be trifled with. Unlike his colleague Governor Eden of North Carolina, Virginia's governor wasn't prepared to put up with pirate attacks off the Chesapeake Capes. He certainly couldn't be accused of receiving any share of the plunder. A man of Spotswood's morals would never countenance striking a deal with a pirate, pardoned or not, and he certainly would never consider providing a pirate with a safe haven close to his colony's main township. His mind was made up; he would "expurgate the nest of vipers" at Bath Town, and end the threat posed by Blackbeard once and for all. All he needed now was a plan, and the men to help him carry it out.

In November 1718 two British warships were lying at anchor off Kecoughtan (now Hampton) in Virginia's James River, some thirty miles downstream from the colonial capital of Williamsburg. On Wednesday, November 13, Captain Ellis Brand, commanding HMS *Pearl*, and Captain George Gordon, commander of the *Lyme*, both received a summons from the Virginia governor, inviting them to meet him in his half-built mansion in Williamsburg. Although Spotswood and his family had moved into the new Governor's mansion the year before, work was still far from finished. The sound of hammering and sawing would have been heard in the background as the three men talked.

The three men had to confront a tricky matter of protocol, as Governor Spotswood had only the most tenuous authority over the navy in Virginia waters. Although he carried the imposing title of Admiral of Virginia, the honorary rank came with no fleet and no real power. In effect, it was a legal title giving him a certain amount of jurisdiction over what went on in Virginia's coastal waters or, more precisely, "below the tidal high water mark." The two naval officers and their men answered directly to the Admiralty in London, not the governor of Virginia, who had his own chain of command back to King George through the British Board of Trade. However, the two men also knew where their duty lay, and like most naval officers in American waters, when there was no proper admiral to answer to, they generally obeyed the orders of colonial governors. Even more importantly, both ships had been sent into Virginia waters that previous February specifically to protect the colony from attack by pirates.

The two officers listened to Spotswood outline his decision to attack Blackbeard, and they immediately offered their support. After all, since their ships arrived in the colony just over a year before, they had done nothing to take the war to the pirates. The *Lyme* reached Virginia from Britain in August 1717, and the *Pearl* arrived two months later. Since then, apart from the occasional voyage escorting ships from the mouth of the Chesapeake to New York and back, they had remained at anchor in the James River. While their presence in the James River would have been enough to protect the colony from attack, only a punitive expedition against the pirates would bring their mission to a satisfactory end. This was their chance to return home with the laurels of victory. If they had decided to refuse Spotswood's plea for help, the governor could have done nothing about it apart from penning a letter of complaint to the Admiralty. Unfortunately for Blackbeard, duty overcame protocol, and Brand and Gordon both appeared eager to do whatever they could.

As the senior of the two captains, Ellis Brand was put in charge of the operation. The intelligence supplied by Spotswood's informants placed Blackbeard and his crew at Bath Town, although he was also well aware of the pirate's base at Ocracoke Island. Even a cursory glance at the charts showed Brand and Gordon that their ships would be useless in the coming campaign against the pirates. HMS *Pearl* was a fifth-rate ship of the line of forty guns. Built in London's Rotherhithe ten years before, the two-decker displaced 531 tons and was just under 98 feet long, with a beam of 32 feet. A far more important statistic was that she drew 13½ feet of water from the waterline to the bottom of her keel, making her draft too great to pass over the coastal sandbars that linked the islands of the Outer Banks. During the age of fighting sail, navies divided their warships into six groups, or "rates," based on the number of guns they carried—from the largest first-rate ships of the line with one hundred or more guns to the smallest sixth-rate, twenty-eight-gun frigates. HMS *Lyme* was a good deal smaller than the *Pearl*, displacing 384 tons and reportedly a fast, well-built vessel, but she was also a ship that was past her prime. Originally classified as a fifth-rate with thirty-two guns, age had caught up with her after twenty-three years, and in 1717 she was reclassified as a sixth-rate man-of-war of twenty-four guns. Although slightly smaller and substantially lighter than the *Pearl*, she still drew 10½ feet of water. In taking the fight to Blackbeard in his lair, both ships might as well have been one-hundred-gun ships of the line for all the use they were.

The governor's solution was to charter two civilian vessels, then crew them with naval volunteers, a plan that won the approval of Brand and Gordon. So on November 15 Governor Spotswood summoned the owners of two Virginia trading sloops berthed at Jamestown, the *Ranger* and the *Jane*, and negotiated the hiring of their vessels. As there was no official means to do so, Spotswood paid out of his own pocket. Little is known about the two vessels, but they would have been typical of the merchant sloops that plied the waters of colonial America in the early eighteenth century.

The average sloop of this period was a small single-masted boat with its sails rigged fore and aft, like a modern racing yacht. Although there were several variations of the sailing rig, the basics of these craft remained the same: small vessels with fast, sleek lines, displacing around 100 tons and, more importantly, with a relatively shallow draft. These were the same type of vessels used by Blackbeard and his fellow pirates Stede Bonnet and Charles Vane (with the exception that most trading sloops were unarmed). These two were no exception, and although Brand had the option of transferring six-pounder guns into them from the warships, he decided to leave the sloops as they were. The extra weight could hinder the ability of the vessels to navigate the waters of the Outer Banks, and the delay in equipping the *Ranger* and the *Jane* went against Spotswood's demand for immediate action. Instead they were sent downriver to Kecoughtan under the charge of Captain Gordon, where they would be taken into naval service for the duration of the mission.

The three men soon developed a daring plan involving a two-pronged attack against the "nest of vipers." Captain Brand would command the main force of the expedition, which would march across country from the James River to Bath Town on the Pamlico River. It would cross the boundary line between the two colonies of Virginia and North Carolina near Windsor, at which point Spotswood's legal authority ceased to exist. Brand would be relying on speed and surprise to counter any move by the North Carolina authorities or the pirates to prevent him from carrying out his job.

He would then head south through Plymouth to attack Bath Town from the land. To avoid any trouble with Governor Eden, Brand's column would avoid the settlement of Albemarle where the North Carolina governor had his residence. The captain's force consisted of around two hundred men, half sailors and the rest a company of Virginia militia. Meanwhile, his first lieutenant (the executive officer in the modern U.S. Navy) on board the *Pearl*, Robert Maynard, would lead the second force. He was ordered to take command of Governor Spotswood's two sloops and then attack Bath Town from the sea. After all, the planners still expected to find Blackbeard in the small port.

Maynard's force would capture any pirates left behind on Blackbeard's base at Ocracoke Island before crossing the fifty miles of Pamlico Sound to the mouth of the Pamlico River. Once in place, Maynard could blockade the town from the sea while his commanding officer swept into the town from the landward side. Captain Gordon drew the short straw and remained behind on the James River, commanding the floating reserve of two warships with half-strength crews.

Just after dawn on Sunday, November 17, 1718, the two hired sloops reached Kecoughtan, and Gordon gave Maynard the pirate-hunting orders that were to make or break his career. The sloops were then prepared for their voyage. Maynard was given only fifty-seven men to crew them, thirty-three from the *Pearl* and twenty-four from the *Lyme*. The *Jane* was the larger of the two sloops, so Maynard used her as his flagship, crewed by his detachment from the *Pearl*. The men from the *Lyme* boarded the *Ranger*, which was placed under the command of one of Captain Gordon's junior officers, Mister Hyde. Equally importantly, Maynard was given two pilots (or local navigators) familiar with the waters of Pamlico Sound, and one was allocated to each sloop, bringing the total complement of both vessels up to a round sixty men. Both sloops would have been brought alongside the two warships to be loaded with supplies, weapons, and ammunition. Although none of the ship's guns were transferred to the two sloops, the crews would have been well provided with all the other paraphernalia of war at sea: pistols, muskets, cutlasses, daggers, boarding axes, grenades, and boarding pikes. The end result would have been two crews that looked little different from the pirates they were being sent to fight.

Maynard recorded the event in his report:

> Mod[erate] gales & fair Weather, this day I rec'd from Captain Gordon an Order to Command 60 men out of his Majsties Ships Pearl & Lyme, on board two small Sloops, in Order to destroy Some pyrates, who resided in N Carolina, This day Weigh'd & Sail'd hence with ye Sloops under my Command, having on board Proviso of all species with Arms, & Ammunition Suitable for ye occasion.

What Maynard didn't mention was that the civilian crews of the sloops seemed to have remained on board their vessels, no doubt to make sure the navy didn't cause too much damage. Three years after the event Captain Gordon recalled that the two masters of the sloops remained with their vessels, as did their crews, making "a twelfth part of the whole number of men that went with them." This means that the *Jane* carried at least two merchantmen as well as the sloop's own master, and the *Ranger* carried two. Although details of the charter no longer survive, these men must have been well paid to remain on board when the navy sailed off to fight the pirates.

As an added incentive to the crews of the two sloops, Governor Spotswood informed Captain Gordon that the Virginia Colony planned to pay a bounty for the pirates, dead or alive. Gordon duly told Maynard about this bonus, a variation on the established naval policy of paying out prize money for captured vessels. Spotswood ratified this a week later on November 24 when he issued a proclamation that offered "For Edward Teach, commonly called Captain Teach, or Black Beard, one hundred pounds." It continued, "For every other commander of a Pyrate Ship, Sloop, or Vessel, forty pounds; for every Lieutenant, Master or Quartermaster Boatswain, or Carpenter, twenty pounds; for every other inferior Officer, fifteen pounds, and for every private Man taken on Board such Ship. Sloop, or Vessel, ten pounds." If Brand's or Maynard's men caught the pirates and lived to tell the tale, they would be well rewarded for their efforts. No doubt Maynard wasted no time telling his crew the news.

Lieutenant Maynard had no intention of simply blundering into the "nest of vipers." After all, he was a thorough professional, the second-in-command of HMS *Pearl* and an experienced naval officer. Although we don't know much about Maynard's early career, we do know that he first gained his commission as a lieutenant on January 14, 1707, a full decade before he sailed off to do battle with Blackbeard. Two years later he was serving as third lieutenant on board HMS *Bedford*, a seventy-gun third-rate ship of the line. This warship then took part in several engagements against the French in both the English Channel and the Mediterranean, most notably a sea battle off Dunkirk in 1708. Few British naval officers went through seven years of naval warfare with France without putting themselves in harm's way.

From his report we know that Maynard slipped out of the Kecoughtan anchorage before nightfall on November 17 and probably gave the order to heave to for the night somewhere close to Cape Henry, probably in Lynnhaven Bay, where his men would finish the stowing of supplies and prepare their ships for the open sea. At dawn, as his two sloops passed Cape Henry, marking the southern limit of Chesapeake Bay, and entered the Atlantic Ocean, Maynard would have given the order to separate slightly. As his force headed south-southeast down the coast of what is now Virginia Beach, the two vessels would have formed a line abreast, some eight to ten miles apart (depending on the visibility), with the inner sloop stationed some five miles off the coast.

This was standard procedure during the age of fighting sail, before radar or aircraft extended the visibility of warships beyond the horizon. Lookouts in the mastheads of both sloops could see for ten or even twenty miles all around them, and also remained in sight of their consort vessel. This meant that during the hours of daylight, at least, Maynard would encounter any ship sailing within twenty miles of Virginia's Atlantic seaboard. We know he stopped passing vessels, making sure the pirates didn't escape him, and quizzing the masters of these coastal vessels for information. He learned that Blackbeard wasn't in Bath Town, but was on board his sloop the *Adventure*, anchored on the western side of Ocracoke Island. Maynard and Hyde continued on down the coast, a voyage that would take them the best part of four days, hampered by lumpy seas and a contrary wind.

Maynard timed his arrival off Ocracoke so that he arrived under cover of darkness just after dusk on Thursday, November 21. The tide was ebbing, and after consulting the pilot Maynard decided to wait until the following morning to launch his attack. Keen eyes could spot the mast of Blackbeard's sloop rising above the sand dunes on the southern tip of the island, so clearly at least some of the pirates were at their base rather than in Bath Town. With his ships riding at anchor off the seaward side of the island, Maynard ordered lookouts to keep a watch for any movement from the pirates, and to look out for the arrival of any ships approaching Ocracoke from the open sea. The last thing he needed at this stage was for a passing trading vessel to rouse the pirates, or worse still, to warn them. For his part, Blackbeard had become complacent after six months of inactivity. It would have been a sensible precaution to send a lookout party ashore to keep a weather eye out to sea. The very fact that no alarm was raised during the night meant that the pirates hadn't bothered to post a lookout. When Maynard launched his attack, it would come as a complete surprise.

On the other side of the island, Blackbeard was entertaining guests. After having operated in the same area since the spring, he knew most of the local vessels and their crews. One such trading sloop was also anchored off the island, and the pirates were playing host to at least two of her crew. The same two were still on board the following morning when the navy appeared. Johnson claims that the pirates entertained the sloop's master and three crewmen, in which case two were too drunk to return to their ship that night. The trading sloop had sailed from Bath Town, and it brought the pirate that infamous letter written by Tobias Knight, the Governor's secretary, five days earlier, on November 17. Clearly the letter offered no suggestion that an attack was being planned from the neighboring colony. The pirate sloop *Adventure* had only a skeleton crew on board. Blackbeard's first mate, Israel Hands, and about twenty-four of the crew were ashore in Bath Town, leaving Blackbeard with just twenty-five men to man his sloop. This was a far cry from the size of the company he had commanded off Charleston the previous spring, before he marooned half his crew and deliberately ran his flagship aground in Topsail Inlet. Others drifted away after that, as Blackbeard's dalliance with respectability offered them little in the way of plunder or profit.

Normally the pirates would have been ready for immediate action, with powder and shot stowed beside their guns, cutlasses close to hand, and pistols primed for use. Beyond that, the fact that Blackbeard failed to post a lookout and was feeling secure enough to carouse into the night suggests that he and his men were far from ready when dawn broke that morning. We know from British naval records that dawn on Friday, November 22, ushered in a gray, overcast day, with almost no wind, and calm seas. In the hour before dawn Maynard would have roused his men and allowed them to eat a cold breakfast, for fear that any fires might warn the pirates. He then gave the word to prepare for battle. His men probably had little to do, as they had been thinking of little else but the coming battle throughout the long winter night. With sunset around 5:30 P.M. and dawn at 6:30 A.M., there was plenty of time for the sailors to think about what lay ahead.

Even though Maynard had Master William Butler, the local pilot, on board, he took no chances, and ordered a boat to be lowered. It would lead the way for the two sloops, taking soundings as Maynard entered the inlet. Typically this would be an 18-foot, four-oared longboat. A contemporary chart shows that once past the sandbar between Ocracoke and Beacon Island, the twisting channel drew a respectable 6 fathoms, or 36 feet at low water. However, it became much shallower further on, and shoals extended well into the Sound. Worse, the pilots would have warned Maynard that the sandbars seemed to shift with every autumnal hurricane or winter storm. The pirate sloop lay tucked behind the southwestern tip of the island, a mile up a deep channel that led to the island's landing place. It must have been a slow, laborious business, but as the longboat rounded the tip of Ocracoke Island at around 7:30 A.M., men on the pirate sloop would have spotted her and raised the alarm. Looking beyond the point, they would have seen the masts of Maynard's two sloops creeping behind the rowers.

Blackbeard reacted by rousing his crew and preparing his ship for battle. According to Captain Johnson, one of the guns on the *Adventure* fired at the naval longboat, causing it to back away toward the safety of the two sloops. If this actually happened, then it would have taken a good five of ten minutes for Blackbeard's master gunner, Philip Morton, to prepare one of the sloop's eight guns, aim it, and fire. As the *Adventure*'s bows would have been facing south, pointing toward both the longboat and the incoming tide, it is more likely that he simply fired off a small swivel gun mounted in the sloop's forecastle. These light, swivel-mounted pieces, about the size of a modern machine gun, were antipersonnel weapons, capable of firing a small iron ball or a bag of scrap metal or pistol balls about sixty yards. However, while Maynard describes the *Adventure* as being armed with eight guns, the abstract of Maynard's report published in the *British Gazetteer* mentions nine guns. Swivel guns were never counted as main armament, so the possibility remains that Blackbeard mounted four guns on each broadside and his ninth gun as a bow chaser, where it would have been perfectly capable of firing on the longboat.

Whatever type of shot was fired, while the round had no chance of harming the men in the boat, it would certainly have gotten their attention. After all, the pirates had no idea who these strangers were, so the chances are that Morton fired the traditional shot across the bows. As Maynard recovered the longboat crew and took the boat in tow behind the *Jane,* the pirates would still have no idea who they were dealing with. Although courtesy demanded that a warship show her colors before opening fire, it was common to buy extra time by keeping any national flags furled until the last minute, or even to fly false colors. Therefore, neither Maynard nor Hyde would have hauled up the Union flag until they were within musket range, less than a hundred yards from the enemy.

Blackbeard's anchorage lay just over a mile and a half away from the southwestern tip of Ocracoke Island, and on the flood tide Maynard's sloops would have taken about twenty minutes to run down toward the *Adventure*. While this gave Blackbeard sufficient time to prepare his ship for action, it was not long enough to allow him to haul up his anchor. Even on a small sloop lying in thirty-six feet of water, the operation would have taken every available minute. Johnson records that Blackbeard opted for the more drastic Gordian solution of cutting his anchor cable. While this left the boat without any means of anchoring, it was probably not as dramatic as it seems. Being an experienced seaman, Blackbeard was probably ready for just such an eventuality and had a marker buoy and line ready, so he could recover his anchor cable later.

Freed from her tether to the seabed, the *Adventure* would have turned

An early-nineteenth-century depiction of Blackbeard's last fight. The cartoonlike quality of Blackbeard and the nineteenth-century uniform worn by Lieutenant Maynard are only the most glaring inaccuracies— another is the cannon. The fight took place on Maynard's sloop, but only Blackbeard's vessel carried any ordnance.

into the wind facing the island, and would have started drifting away from the oncoming sloops toward the northeast, parallel to the shore. The pirate crew would have taken a few minutes to hoist their two sails, and given the shallow draft of the *Adventure* and the benefits of the incoming tide, it would have been relatively simple for Blackbeard to evade his pursuers by escaping northward through the shoal waters into Pamlico Sound. The idea probably never crossed his mind. Everything Blackbeard did next showed that he was ready to fight to the death. He maneuvered his sloop so that her starboard guns faced the enemy, and waited for the strangers to come into point-blank range.

During this period a sloop in Royal Naval service was called a cutter, usually armed with three-pounder guns, each approximately 5 feet 6 inches long and weighing up to 7 hundredweight (784 pounds). However, Blackbeard's earlier ship, the *Queen Anne's Revenge*, also carried six-pounders, which would have been up to 8 feet long, with a weight of up to 22 hundredweight (2,464 pounds). While common sense would have restricted the armament of the *Adventure* to three-pounders or even four-pounders, Blackbeard might have been tempted to mount at least a couple of the heavier guns on his sloop, even though this would have placed a huge strain on the sloop's timbers when the pieces were fired. Probably Blackbeard cared very little for the wear and tear on his ship. After all, if he survived the battle he could easily find another sloop to replace the worn-out *Adventure*.

While gunnery was still very much a black art during the early eighteenth century, a handful of technical manuals provide us with the details of how these weapons operated. While these handbooks list the maximum range of a six-pounder at fifteen hundred yards and a four-pounder at a thousand yards, their effective range, when the shot had a good chance of hitting the target, was about half that. Common sense suggests that Blackbeard and his gunner, Philip Morton, would have waited until the advancing sloops came within at least five hundred yards before they would open fire, but for some reason Blackbeard held his fire until the British were even closer. In those days the habit was to keep guns loaded and ready for action when in hostile waters, with a charge down the barrel, the weapon loaded with its shot, and wadding rammed down to keep everything in place. This meant that to ready a gun for action all the crew had to do was unlash it from the ship's side, remove the wooden tompion that plugged the muzzle to keep out the damp, then prime the gun with loose powder poured into the touchhole. Underwater archaeology has shown us that many guns in merchant service were preloaded in this way, and at least one six-pounder recovered from the *Queen Anne's Revenge* was preloaded with shot.

In many cases the guns were double-shotted, with two roundshot placed in the barrel, or else they used grapeshot, an antipersonnel charge not unlike that used in swivel guns. The trouble was, double-shotting a gun reduced its effective range by at least a third, while grapeshot had an effective range of little more than two hundred fifty yards. Even then it was best to hold fire until the enemy were close enough to fire at with small arms. That way the grapeshot charge of scrap metal and musket balls would scythe

the enemy decks, cutting down the men who were preparing to board. It was a grisly business, but one that both Blackbeard and Morton understood thoroughly, and they were about to demonstrate their prowess in it.

Maynard was heading toward the pirates in line abreast, with Mister Hyde's *Ranger* on the port side of the *Jane*. After picking up the longboat crew it would have taken him about fifteen minutes to come within five hundred yards of the pirates, and effective range of their guns. It must have been a terrifying time for the sailors, crouching as low as they could and waiting for the enemy's broadside. The worst of it was that the British sloops were heading almost directly toward the *Adventure*, so if a roundshot struck one of the sloops in the bow it would travel the whole length of the vessel's deck, cutting down everything in its path. Fortunately, Maynard had planned ahead, and ordered at least half of his crew to stay belowdecks. The hatch covers were removed and extra ladders fitted, so that when the time came these men could rush on deck and join the fray. However, for the moment they enjoyed some protection from Blackbeard's guns.

Not everyone could stay under cover. The helmsman would have been fully exposed at the whipstaff, the forerunner of the ship's wheel, while undoubtedly Maynard had some of his crew standing by with sweeps, the oars that would help him maneuver if the light winds dropped away completely, or the current seemed to take him too close to the sandbars. Historian David Cordingly suggests that there was so little wind that the British sloops had to use their oars to make any progress, and Captain Johnson mentions that some of Maynard's men "laboured at the oars." However, Maynard himself makes no mention of the use of sweeps. Being an experienced officer he probably had the sweeps rigged, and used them to augment the sails to limit the time he remained in front of the pirate's guns.

Above all Maynard and Hyde, plus the two civilian pilots, would have remained exposed, although Captain Johnson suggests Maynard joined his men belowdecks before the pirates opened fire, so he could lead the bulk of his men in person. To encourage his men, Maynard ordered the Union flag to be unfurled on both ships. At last he was showing his true colors, and Blackbeard knew who he was dealing with. The London newspapers later reported that the pirates "accordingly hoisted their black Ensign with a Death's Head," but more than likely and far less romantically, Blackbeard probably saw no need to hoist a flag. After all, the crews of the oncoming sloops knew exactly who he was.

As the range closed to less than three hundred yards, Thomas Miller, the quartermaster, noticed that Blackbeard, who was at the helm of his sloop, was heading directly toward the landing beach of Ocracoke Island, a small inlet where the pirates often went ashore to draw water from a well. According to Johnson, Miller tried to warn Blackbeard of the danger, but the pirate captain knocked him aside and sent him sprawling. Far from risking his sloop unnecessarily, Blackbeard had a plan. Another sandbar lay parallel to the beach, and the pirate hoped to draw the attackers onto it, relying on his own local knowledge to avoid the danger to his own ship. When the two attackers came within a hundred yards, a mere minute's sailing away from the *Adventure*, Blackbeard and Maynard hailed each other.

According to Maynard, the dialogue was short and to the point: "At our first salutation he [Blackbeard] drank Damnation to me and my Men, whom he stil'd Cowardly Puppies, saying, He would neither give nor take Quarter." Naturally the version that later appeared in Captain Johnson's history and the newspapers was more expansive:

> Blackbeard hailed him in his rude manner: "Damn you for Villains, who are you? And from whence do you come?" The Lieutenant make him Answer: "You may see from our Colours we are no Pyrates." Blackbeard bid him send his boat on board, that he may see who he was, but Mr. Maynard reply'd thus: "I cannot spare my Boat, but I will come aboard you as soon as I can, with my Sloop." Upon this Black-beard took a Glass of Liquor, & drank to him with these words; "Damnation seize my Soul if I give you Quarters, or take any from you." In Answer to which, Mr. Maynard told him, "That he expected no Quarter from him, nor should he give him any."

It makes for a great story, but this whole dialogue probably never happened. It would take almost a minute for this exchange, by which time the British sloops would have been alongside the pirates. Also, as Maynard had already unfurled the British flag, his opponent knew perfectly well that the oncoming sloops were in the service of His Majesty, and meant business. Unfortunately, anything but the briefest of exchanges between the two commanders would have been impossible, given the circumstances, so Maynard's shorter version is probably accurate. Still, drinking damnation to the enemy and calling them cowardly puppies was colorful enough.

What happened next is still unclear. In a letter written after the battle,

Maynard wrote that after the verbal exchange, "Immediately we engaged, and Mr. Hyde was unfortunately kill'd, and five of his men wounded in the little Sloop, which, having no-body to command her, fell a-stern, and did not come up to assist me till the Action was almost over." Captain Johnson claims the two sides exchanged small arms fire, and that Blackbeard's sloop then ran aground. As the *Jane* and the *Ranger* drew more water than the *Adventure*, Maynard anchored within a "half-gunshot" of the pirates and lightened his ship, throwing overboard anything that was not going to be of use in the battle to come. He also claims that the *Adventure* ran aground, and Maynard's lightening of his ship was in order to come alongside the enemy in the shallow water, not to refloat his own vessel. Somehow this version fails to ring true, as no self-respecting naval officer would come to anchor within fifty yards of an enemy ship that was about to open fire. Another account claims that it was Maynard's sloops and not the *Adventure* that ran aground at the critical moment. As Maynard himself made no mention of all this, we have to assume that Captain Johnson got the sequence of events a little muddled.

Far more effective than any exchange of words with Maynard, Blackbeard then gave the order to open fire. Four of the *Adventure*'s guns would have been able to fire at that point, and from the impact the broadside had it seems clear that gunner Morton had preloaded most of his pieces with grapeshot. The account of the battle printed in the *Boston News Letter* described the events after the verbal exchange:

> Then Lieutenant Maynard told his Men that now they knew what they had trust to, and could not escape the Pirates hands if they had a mind, but must either fight or be killed. At that point Blackbeard opened fire. Teach begun and fired some small Guns, loaded with Swan shot [grapeshot], spick Nails, and pieces of old Iron, in upon Maynard, which killed six of his Men and wounded ten.

This four-gun broadside was devastating. Captain Johnson reported that on board the *Jane*, a full twenty men were killed or wounded by the discharge, plus a further nine on the *Ranger*, including Mister Hyde, who was killed. The next two ratings in the chain of command on board the *Ranger* were supposedly also killed or wounded, leaving the vessel with "no-body to command her," as Maynard put it. On February 6 the following year Captain Brand reported to the Admiralty that during the whole engagement "the Pearl sloop had killed and died of their wounds nine, my sloop had two killed, in both sloops there were upwards of twenty wounded."

Aside from confusing which sloop was crewed by men from his own ship, Brand painted a far less dramatic picture of the carnage caused by Blackbeard's broadside than Captain Johnson. Whether his men were killed or wounded made little difference to Maynard. In a single moment he had lost anywhere between a third and a half of his force. One more broadside would probably finish the attackers.

If the two British sloops went aground at all, then this was when it happened, with the *Jane* filled with wounded and dying men and her consort, the *Ranger*, drifting away out of action with nobody at her helm. The *Boston News Letter* claims that after Blackbeard fired his guns, "Lieutenant Maynard ordered all the rest of his Men to go down in the Hold: himself, Abraham Demelt of New York and a third at the Helm stayed above deck." Captain Johnson puts it another way: "The lieutenant, finding his own ship had way, and would soon be on board of Teach, he ordered all his men down, for fear of another broadside." The *British Gazetteer* quotes Maynard as claiming that "Continuing the fight, it being a perfect Calm, I shot away Teach's jib, and his Fore-Halliards, forcing him ashoar, I boarded his Sloop, and had 20 men kill'd and wounded."

Getting the story straight was even less of an issue in the early eighteenth century than it is today. First, neither the *Jane* nor the *Ranger* had any guns to fire back with, and second, if Maynard had waited until the ships were fifty yards apart before hiding half his crew, Blackbeard would never have been fooled into thinking the decks of the *Jane* had virtually been swept clear of men. Then again, concentrated small arms fire or even a swivel gun discharge from the *Jane* might just have cut through the *Adventure*'s jib sheet, causing her to veer toward the sandbar. Several versions of the story all state that at that moment the *Adventure* ran aground, caused either by the cutting of her jib sheet or by navigational error in the heat of battle. One account even suggests the accident was due to the recoil from firing her guns.

If both sides did indeed run aground, with the *Ranger* temporarily out of action it became a race of which sloop could be refloated first. The tide was still coming in, so floating off a sandbar would have been a reasonably straightforward process, involving little more than lightening the ship. An experienced naval officer like Maynard would probably have thought about keeping the bulk of his crew under cover long before he got into range of the *Adventure*, so he still retained the element of surprise even though most of the men on the *Jane*'s upper deck were dead or wounded. It only made the sloop appear more of a target.

However, if the *Jane* had run aground, Maynard would have to blow his cover, recalling his crew from belowdecks to help throw ballast and water casks over the side. If we accept that the pirate ship temporarily ran aground on a sandbar close to Ocracoke Island, possibly due to a lucky small arms shot from the *Jane*, then the panic to lighten ship would have taken place on Blackbeard's sloop rather than Maynard's. If the British commander was to stick to his plan, then the *Jane* would have dodged out of the arc of fire of the pirate ship, and kept up a harassing fire from muskets and pistols until the *Adventure* managed to break free of the sand. Appearing too rash was not part of the act.

With both the *Adventure* and the *Jane* back in action and the *Ranger* lying some way off, either aground or recovering from the pirate broadside, the dramatic battle entered its final phase. Maynard still had his trump card, the well-armed sailors hidden belowdecks in his sloop. His hope was that by appearing undermanned the *Jane* would look like an easy target for the pirates, and Blackbeard would bring the *Adventure* alongside. As soon as the pirates began swarming aboard his ship, Maynard planned to have his men swarm up from down below, taking the attackers by surprise. If he could sever the lines that linked the two ships, then he would be able to divide the enemy, and concentrate on defeating Blackbeard and his boarding party. The pirates fell for it.

Blackbeard steered the *Adventure* toward the *Jane* as his twenty-five men prepared to take the fight to the enemy. Maynard certainly needed the element of surprise on his side, because after deducting the casualties inflicted by the *Adventure*'s broadside, Maynard was clearly outnumbered. Just before the two sloops crashed into each other, Blackbeard gave the order to throw grenadoes onto the deck of the *Jane*. The grenado was the hand grenade of its day. In military and naval arsenals grenadoes were hollow cast-iron spheres, filled with gunpowder and plugged by a stopper with a hole bored through it. A fuse made from cord soaked in saltpeter was threaded through the hole, and the match was lit just before the grenado was thrown onto the enemy ship. Some grenadoes were even made from glass, and were designed to ignite on impact. Many of those were also packed with fragments of scrap metal.

Archaeological finds from ships of this period have shown that another, homemade version was also used. Glass and stoneware bottles were widely available, and could be used instead of hollow metal spheres. Although less elegant than their military counterparts, these empty rum bottles packed a similar punch. When the device exploded it would send shards of metal or glass in all directions, much in the same way as a modern hand grenade. If these devices exploded on the decks of a ship packed with men, the effects could be devastating. Fortunately for Maynard, most of his men were belowdecks, and it seems that none of the grenadoes were lobbed through the sloop's main hatch.

As the smoke lay thick over the enemy decks, Captain Johnson had Blackbeard exclaim, the enemy were "all knocked on the head, except three or four, and therefore let's jump on board and cut them to pieces." The account of the action given in the *Boston News Letter* had Blackbeard seize the foresheet of the *Jane* to help bring the two vessels together. Grappling hooks were thrown across to link the two ships together, and once these lines were made fast the two sloops were locked together in a fight to the death. Blackbeard led the charge onto the *Adventure*, boarding the British sloop over the bows. The three or four men he saw—Maynard, Abraham Demelt, the pilot William Butler, and possibly one other—must have looked forlorn standing in the stern of the *Jane*, with blood-spattered bodies littering their sloop's deck. However, as soon as Blackbeard and ten of his men swung themselves on board, Maynard gave the signal for his men to surge up out of the hold.

Smoke would have been lingering over the deck of the *Jane* as the pirates attacked, firing toward the group clustered in the enemy's stern. The outcome must have seemed a certainty to the pirates until the first seamen emerged from belowdecks, yelling and firing their pistols at the attackers. The surprise must have been total. In a letter quoted in the *British Gazetteer* Maynard claims that "He enter'd me with 10 Men; but 12 stout Men I left there, fought like Heroes, Sword in Hand." Captain Johnson placed the odds at "the lieutenant and twelve men, against Blackbeard and fourteen."

Once again Captain Johnson gives the most dramatic version of the battle, with Blackbeard and the naval officer singling each other out for a personal duel. Both crews knew that there was no way out of this fight, a battle for survival where surrender was not an option. Few can imagine the horror of a boarding action fought under such conditions, where the decks were already slippery with blood, and the senses of the men were dulled by the noise and smoke. It was too late for muskets or swivel guns, so the men fought with whatever they had or could reach, pistols, cutlasses, hatchets, half-pikes, knives, clubs, belaying pins, fists, or even teeth. It was a brutal, no-holds-barred fight to the death.

Blackbeard had armed himself with several pairs of pistols tucked into his sash and belt, and according to Captain Johnson, "Blackbeard and the lieutenant fired the first pistol at each other, by which the pirate received a wound." This did little to stop Blackbeard. Flintlock pistols were good for one shot only, and both men would have thrown theirs away, preferably toward the head of their opponent, before drawing their own close-quarter weapons. The pirate then drew a large cutlass, which he swung with incredible ferocity. He was known for his physical strength as much as for his terrifying appearance, and he used both to good effect, carving out a space on the crowded deck for his private fight with Maynard.

The *Boston News Letter* carried a dramatic account of the duel: "Maynard and Teach themselves begun the fight with their swords, Maynard making a thrust, the point of his sword went against Teach's cartridge box, and bended it to the hilt. Teach broke the guard of it, and wounded Maynard's fingers but did not disable him, whereupon he jumped back and threw away his sword and fired his pistol, which wounded Teach." The pirate had now been hit twice by pistol shot, but there seemed no stopping him. He took a step forward toward the now-fumbling Maynard, who was struggling to throw away his spent pistol and raise his cutlass.

Elsewhere the run of fighting seemed to be favoring the navy. Imagine a space just 20 feet long, the approximate distance from the main hatch to the bow, and 15 feet wide, littered with hatches, capstans, and bodies. While the fight between Blackbeard and Maynard was going on, the *Jane's* crew were slowly driving the *Adventure's* crew back, probably the result of firepower and training. In other words, Maynard's men had the advantage of quality, allied with a slight advantage in quantity. As the pirates were driven back toward the bow and their casualties mounted, Blackbeard was left isolated, allowing Maynard's men to move around behind him.

With Maynard bleeding and vulnerable, Blackbeard moved in to administer the coup de grâce. Then, as Captain Johnson described it, just as he raised his cutlass, "one of Maynard's men gave him a terrible wound in the neck and throat." The *Boston News Letter* was more specific. As Blackbeard moved toward Maynard, "Demelt struck in between then with his sword and cut Teach's face pretty much." Blood must have sprayed from the horrible wound, but Blackbeard remained standing, swinging his heavy cutlass in defiance like a wounded and cornered wild animal. It was clear that the heavily wounded pirate was running out of strength, or in Captain Johnson's words, "he stood his ground and fought with great fury, 'till he received five-and-twenty wounds, five of them by shot." Maynard and his men moved in for the kill.

Uncharacteristically, Captain Johnson described Blackbeard's final moments in largely unmelodramatic terms: "At length, as he was cocking another pistol, having fired several before, he fell down dead." The newspaper was more descriptive, claiming that "one of Maynard's men being a Highlander, engaged Teach with his broad sword, who gave Teach a cut in the neck, Teach saying well done lad; The Highlander replied, If it be not well done, I'll do it better. With that he gave him a second stroke, which cut off his head, laying it flat on his shoulder." The larger-than-life pirate Edward Teach had finally met his match.

As their leader fell to the deck, the fight went out of the surviving pirates. By that time eight of Blackbeard's fourteen shipmates had been cut down, lying dead or seriously wounded on the blood-soaked deck of the *Jane*. Captain Johnson claims that "all the rest, much wounded, jumped overboard and called out for quarter, which was granted, though it was only prolonging their lives for a few days." As Maynard and his men had a chance to draw breath, they saw that the fighting had spread onto the *Adventure*. The survivors of the *Ranger's* crew had managed to get their sloop under way, and brought their vessel alongside the unengaged starboard side of the pirate sloop. According to Captain Gordon, one of the men from his ship the *Lyme* became a victim of his own side, shot by a crewman on the *Jane* guilty of "taking him by mistake for one of the pirates."

Around ten pirates had remained behind on the *Adventure*, so according to Captain Johnson, "the sloop Ranger came up, and attacked the men that remained in Blackbeard's sloop, with equal bravery 'till they likewise cried out for quarters." However, there was one last bizarre twist. One of Blackbeard's crewmen was a former African slave known as Black Caesar.

According to Captain Johnson's account, just before the fighting began Blackbeard had "posted a resolute fellow, a Negro who he had brought up, with a lighted match in the powder room with commands to blow up when he should give him orders."

He remained belowdecks on the *Adventure* while Blackbeard and his men boarded the *Jane*, and he was still there when the *Ranger*'s men swarmed aboard the pirate sloop. Faced with certain death if he surrendered, Black Caesar tried to carry out his orders and start a fire in the *Adventure*'s powder store. The explosion would undoubtedly have blown the *Adventure* apart, along with the two sloops lying alongside her, together with all their crew. Fortunately the pirate was stopped from carrying out his task "by two prisoners that were then in the hold of the sloop." These were the two men from the trading sloop who had remained on board the previous night. Finding themselves in the midst of a sea battle, they stayed under cover in the *Adventure*'s hold, and were in the right place to stop Caesar and save their own lives.

The grueling, bloody fight was finally over. The surviving pirates who begged for quarter were dragged from the water and taken prisoner, although Captain Gordon might have hinted at a more grisly fate for any who tried to escape. In a letter to the Admiralty he stated that "in less than ten minutes tyme Tatch [Teach] and five or six men were killed; the rest of these rogues jumped in the water where they were demolished." Did this mean the British sailors fired at or stabbed the pirates in the water? This is fairly unlikely, as every pirate was worth money, dead or alive. Without a prisoner or a body, there was no proof to show the Virginia legislature, so no sailor would run the risk of pirate bodies sinking beneath the waters of Pamlico Sound. However, keeping the wounded prisoners alive would have been a low priority for the sailors, as dead bodies were as useful to them as live ones.

The decks of the *Adventure* and the *Jane* would have resembled a charnel house, slippery with blood and covered in bodies. As the blood lust died away, Maynard saw to the wounded, and allowed his own hand to be dressed. He then counted up the butcher's bill. In a letter written three weeks after the fight he claimed that eight of his men were killed and eighteen more wounded from the *Jane* alone, while, including Blackbeard, thirteen pirates were killed and another nine were taken prisoner (all of whom were wounded).

According to Captain Johnson, the pirate casualties included the quartermaster Thomas Miller, Master Gunner Philip Morton, Garret Gibbons the boatswain, and Owen Roberts, the ship's carpenter. He also named four other pirates among the dead: John Husk, Joseph Curtice, Joseph Brooks Sr., and Nathaniel Jackson. Captain Brand reported that ten rather than thirteen pirates were killed and the rest wounded, while nine of the crew of the *Jane* were killed or subsequently died of their wounds, together with two more from the *Ranger*. He added that "in both sloops there were upwards of twenty wounded." Governor Spotswood recorded that Black-beard and nine of his crew were killed, and that nine others were taken alive, "of which one is since dead of his wounds." If we accept Maynard's figure, the final toll was ten British sailors killed on the two sloops, while one more probably died of his wounds before Spotswood filed his report. There might have been another fatality among the score of British wounded, as by the following February Spotswood claimed that the navy lost "no less than 12 killed and 22 wounded."

Maynard remained off Ocracoke for at least two more days, patching up his three sloops and burying the dead. He also managed to send word to Captain Brand that Blackbeard was dead, probably by sending the trad-ing sloop anchored off the island to Albemarle with the news. The hunt for escaped pirates on the island continued, as Captain Gordon wrote some-time later of "one of them being discovered some days after in the reeds by the fowls hovering over him." He failed to mention whether the pirate was alive or dead, presumably because it made little difference.

Before he returned to the James River and a hero's welcome, Maynard had one last dramatic gesture to make. If the unnamed Highlander reported in the *Boston News Letter* hadn't actually managed to sever Black-beard's head in his second killing blow, the grisly job was completed in the aftermath of battle. The pirate's dismembered corpse was thrown over the side of the *Jane*, and we can discount the popular myth that the body swam around the sloop several times before sinking. Like the other pirate corpses, the body of the man who had once terrorized the whole Atlantic seaboard was now feeding the fishes of Pamlico Sound.

Blackbeard's head was kept as definitive proof that the pirate was dead, and as a final humiliation Maynard ordered it to be suspended from the *Jane*'s bowsprit, as a symbol of the lieutenant's victory, and as a warning to others. The three sloops then made their way to Bath Town, where Maynard was able to report to his commanding officer. Once his

Blackbeard's head hanging from the bowsprit of the sloop Jane *as it makes its way back to Williamsburg. It was a suitably gruesome end for a larger-than-life character.*

most seriously wounded men had recovered enough for the voyage home, Maynard left his prize the *Adventure* in the hands of the authorities in Bath Town, and the two battered but victorious sloops set course for the open sea and home. Blackbeard's grisly head still hung from the bowsprit of the *Jane*.

Back in Bath Town Captain Brand set about gathering evidence for the coming trial. First of all he rounded up six pirates who had missed the fight off Ocracoke, including Israel Hands. He placed them in irons, ready for transporting north to Virginia. When Maynard arrived he brought in plunder and stores he found on Ocracoke Island and on board the *Adventure*. Captain Johnson described the haul found in "pirate sloops and ashore in a tent where the sloops lay, 25 hogsheads of sugar, 11 tierces [barrels] and 145 bags of cocoa, a barrel of indigo, and a bale of cotton." It wasn't much of a haul, especially as the reference to sloops in the plural meant that the local vessel visiting Ocracoke from Bath Town was also included in the tally, and any stores she carried were seized with the rest.

Fortunately Captain Brand had managed to find more plunder scattered around Bath Town. First of all there were the goods stored in the barns and storehouses of Charles Eden and Tobias Knight. Although Brand was in charge of the operation, Captain Johnson credits their seizure to Maynard himself: "When the lieutenant came to Bath Town, he made bold to seize in the governor's storehouse the sixty hogsheads of sugar, and from honest Mr. Knight, twenty, which was their dividend of the plunder taken in the French ship; the latter did not long survive this shameful discovery, for being apprehensive that he might be called to account for these trifles, fell sick with the fright and died in a few days." Captain Johnson is somewhat racing ahead of the story here, as Tobias Knight was ailing long before the incident, and he survived long enough to conduct a robust defense against Governor Spotswood's allegations of complicity.

Interestingly enough, although Blackbeard maintained a house outside Bath Town, no plunder was reported as being found there, and there is no mention that the property was ever searched. It is unlikely that a seasoned officer like Brand would have passed over the chance to search any property associated with the parties, be it a rented house or the ordinaries of Bath Town. The conclusion has to be that whatever goods Blackbeard took from the French ships he plundered, the bulk of the cargo had long since been sold off and turned into other forms of assets—probably ready cash and rum for the crew. By the time Brand arrived the bulk of the evidence he sought had been drunk away. Despite protestations from Eden and Knight, the goods Brand seized from their properties were catalogued, then sent north to be sold at auction in Williamsburg. In the end some £2,238 was made from the sale of the sugar and Blackbeard's sloop, more than enough to compensate Spotswood, Brand, and Maynard for their time and trouble.

The seizure of property would lead to a long and bitter legal wrangle. After all, while Governor Eden might have lacked the military power to oppose Spotswood's "invasion," he still had his rights as a proprietorial governor and the political backing of his superiors in London, including the Lords Proprietor themselves. The end of one fight merely acted as the prelude to another, this time using writs and charges rather than pistol shot and cold steel. It was a fight that would see off Tobias Knight, and that almost led to the downfall of Governor Spotswood before it reached its squalid, sorry conclusion.

The battle lines were drawn when Brand seized what Eden and Knight insisted was the property of the colony of North Carolina. In a letter sent to Governor Eden by Alexander Spotswood dated December 21, 1718, the Virginia governor claimed to have "no news from Captain Brand since he went from here, nor do I know any thing of the success of the men of Warr sloops, further than the common report of their taking of Tache's sloop, and killing himself." This rather unbelievably suggests that Brand's decision to seize the property was made on his own initiative. In legal terms, it also left Brand wide open to attack.

The first thing Governor Eden did was to write to his friend and advisor Colonel Pollock. The colonel had acted as acting governor before Eden arrived in North Carolina four years earlier, and would stand in for Eden again after the governor's death in 1722. Eden must have been at Bath Town during its occupation, and deeply resented the occupation of his territory and, worse, the seizure of goods from his own house. As an attorney Pollock's response was measured, but he agreed that the Virginian governor had overstepped his bounds and had certainly exceeded the authority granted him in the statute signed by the king when he first took on the role of governor. This, then, would be Eden's line of attack—his over-zealous neighbor had gone too far and should be made answerable for his actions to the Crown.

Pollock went on to condemn the seizure of property belonging to the North Carolina colony and the plan to spirit these goods away across the border, where their sale would benefit Virginia, not North Carolina. After all, such an act was tantamount to armed robbery. From his letters we know that despite his claims in his letter to Charles Eden sent on December 21, Captain Brand had already reported to Governor Spotswood and told him of the seizure. The following day, on December 22, Spotswood wrote that "I also expect from North Carolina a considerable quantity of sugar and cocoa, wch. were in the possession of Tach and his crew." Clearly he realized a storm might be brewing between the two governors, and his earlier denial of knowledge of any seizure was simply a means of deflecting the blame. This letter proves Spotswood was lying.

Captain Brand would soon realize how badly he had been exposed. He remained in the vicinity of Bath Town until early December, then marched north with his prisoners and plunder. The 180-mile journey involved river crossings and bad roads, and encumbered by baggage wagons and captives the journey north would have taken much longer than the rapid march south of a few weeks before. Given an average of 12 to 15 miles a day, the trip would have taken Brand the better part of two weeks. He probably arrived back in Williamsburg by December 18 at the latest, as three days later the log of HMS *Pearl* reports his return on board as the frigate lay at anchor off Norfolk, Virginia. The *Pearl* and the *Lyme* had slipped down the river to this new mooring off the mouth of the Elizabeth River on November 25, probably so they could be a little closer to the action. After all, slipping out to sea from Hampton Roads was decidedly faster than working down the James River to the sea. If for some reason Blackbeard had managed to escape, then the two warships were ready to set off in pursuit.

Soon after dawn on Thursday, December 1, lookouts on board the two British warships spotted two sloops approaching from seaward. It was Maynard, returning in triumph, with Blackbeard's head still swinging from the bowsprit of the *Jane*. The log of HMS *Lyme* recorded the event in the usual nonchalant, understated manner adopted by the Royal Navy: "Light Wind, Fair Visibility, Wind WSW. This Morn. Sloops returned from ye expedition in N. Carolina." Over two hundred sailors raced into the rigging and lined the sides of the two warships, cheering the arrival of their victorious shipmates. The battered men of Maynard's command cheered back. They had plenty to cheer about. They had survived a hard-fought battle with the pirates, they had been promised a bonus—and they expected a share of the plunder. Lieutenant Maynard would have anchored his two sloops beside the larger warships, then reported to Captain George Gordon. He was ordered to transfer his wounded, then continue on upriver to deliver his prisoners into the governor's care. It appears that the pirate sloop remained behind in Bath Town for two more weeks before a prize crew sailed her north to the James River. However, the two naval vessels were free to return to Williamsburg without further delay. The following morning the *Ranger* and the *Jane* set off again, Blackbeard's head leading the way.

Maynard would have berthed at Jamestown, the original settlement of the colony and Williamsburg's port. Word of his approach would have reached the town shortly before his arrival, and townspeople would have left work to see the arrival of their hero, and to catch a glimpse of the cutthroats. A detachment of militia would also have met him, ready to escort the pirates the eight miles from the river to the public jail in Williamsburg. Given the wounds suffered by several of the prisoners, it is likely that carts would have been used—more to speed the business of transportation than to ease the suffering of the pirates. In those days prisoner welfare was not considered a high priority. On board the sloops and during their transportation to Williamsburg the prisoners were shackled with leg and wrist irons, and tethered together by lengths of chain.

At least a doctor was on hand to inspect them when they arrived at the jail, around the corner from the Capitol building. They would remain there for over three months, crammed together throughout the winter in a freezing, cramped chamber, with little in the way of light or comfort save dirty straw and rats for company. They remained fettered throughout their incarceration, even though the likelihood of escape was almost nonexistent. The coming pirate trial was important for Spotswood, as it would serve as a vindication of his actions. He had no intention of letting his performers slip away. Therefore the pirates were kept alive, but only just. Their wounds were tended, they were given a diet of salt beef and meal, and while Spotswood and his lawyers gathered evidence against them, they were left to contemplate their fate. It must have been with some relief that Lieutenant Maynard watched his prisoners disappear inland, allowing him to escape back to the clean open air of Hampton Roads.

The sloops were returned to their original owners, who were paid well for their lease, and for their involvement in the adventure. It was under their care that Maynard and his men returned downriver, with or without Blackbeard's skull swinging in front of them. Nobody knows what happened to the head afterward. Naturally enough, there were plenty of rumors. Some reports claim that Lieutenant Maynard handed his grisly relic over to the Virginia authorities along with his cargo of prisoners, and that for several years afterward Blackbeard's skull hung from a pole mounted on the western bank of Hampton Roads, probably on Newport News Point, where some 144 years later naval history would be made as the world's first battle between two ironclads took place just off the shore. If the rumor is true, then the skull would probably have remained in Maynard's keeping when he returned back downriver to Norfolk. The area of Newport News known as Wharton's Wharf has also been linked to the name "Blackbeard's Point," which somewhat reinforces the legend.

Sometime later the skull was removed, and again according to legend it landed up in the Raleigh Tavern in Williamsburg, where it was used as a novelty drinking vessel. Late-nineteenth-century antiquarian John F. Watson stated that the "skull was made into the bottom part of a very large punch bowl, called the infant. It was enlarged with silver, or silver plated; and I have seen those whose forefathers have spoken of their drinking punch from it, with a silver ladle appurtenant to that bowl." Virginian historian John Esten Cooke claimed that the cup was still preserved in the state collection at the start of the twentieth century, but by the 1920s it seems to have disappeared. Various sightings were reported over the years—in coastal North Carolina in the 1930s and in New England in the 1950s. Finally in the 1990s it—or at least an object that was declared to be Blackbeard's skull—reappeared in Massachusetts, when it was donated to the Peabody-Essex Museum in Salem. It now forms part of the museum's Edward Rowe Snow collection, named after the New England collector and pirate historian. Rowe himself claims to have owned the skull during the mid-twentieth century.

The author saw the skull in 1998, when it held pride of place at a pirate exhibition at the Mariner's Museum in Newport News, Virginia. It certainly didn't look like anything special, and the museum director admitted that there was no way the object could be authenticated after all these years. It was there as a talking point, an object to be admired, and despite requests the curators refused to let it be used as a punch bowl again. One was left with the uneasy realization that if the skull is indeed genuine, then it had come home—Blackbeard's Point was less than a mile away. Using a skull as a drinking vessel is not as gruesome or far-fetched as it sounds. Roman historians such as Livy, Plutarch, and Herodotus record Celtic and German tribes making drinking cups out of skulls in the time of Hannibal and Julius Caesar, while similar accounts have emerged from the steppes of Central Asia, where the Scythians, the Huns, and later the Mongols performed the same party trick. Blackbeard liked his rum, and it would be pleasing to think he would have approved of the use that had been found for his skull. In the midst of the exhibition's opening reception the author quietly raised his glass of rum and Coke and toasted the skull, and the memory of the long-dead pirate. Somehow it felt reassuring that a layer of reinforced plate glass lay between us.

10

The Blackbeard Legacy

Sixteen wounded pirates lay shivering in Williamsburg's rat-infested jail, with nothing to look forward to but a short trial and a long rope. While Governor Spotswood made sure the case for the prosecution was watertight, these men were barely allowed to see a doctor, let alone a defense attorney. It was understandable that some of them would do anything to avoid the inevitable. Consequently several proved willing to turn informant in a last-ditch effort to save their skins. Israel Hands was one of these turncoats. The man who had been Blackbeard's first mate was captured by Captain Brand in Bath Town rather than in the fight on board Blackbeard's sloop, and he might well have offered to turn informant before he even reached Williamsburg. Four other men, all African American pirate crewmen, also offered to tell the authorities what they knew in exchange for the chance to remain alive, albeit as slaves.

Discounting the unfortunate Samuel Odel, who was a noncombatant caught up in the fighting when Lieutenant Maynard attacked, fully a third of the remaining pirates were therefore willing to testify against their fellows. The four black informants—James Blake, Thomas Gates, Richard Stiles, and James White—were all considered dubious informants, as the law specifically forbade slaves from testifying in court. Of the five African American pirates, only Black Caesar refused to bargain with the authorities. As the man who tried to blow up Blackbeard's sloop at the end of the battle, he probably considered his life forfeit anyway. Apart from Israel Hands that left nine badly wounded pirates who, like Caesar, had nothing to say to Spotswood's lawyers, and who refused to plead for their lives. As winter turned into spring, these men were still there, lying amid the rotten straw and waiting to play their part in the final drama.

During the three months the pirates were imprisoned, Spotswood's officers interrogated the men, both the informants and their companions, while statements were gathered from the naval officers who took part in the attacks as well as from prominent North Carolinian and Virginian colonists. The guilt of the pirates themselves was hardly an issue—they had been caught red-handed on board Blackbeard's sloop, and had crossed swords with Lieutenant Maynard's men. The weak point in the Virginia authorities' case was the fact that they had intervened in the affairs of a neighboring colony. Therefore, Spotswood and the men he appointed as his Vice-Admiralty commissioners concentrated their efforts on gathering evidence that might implicate the North Carolina government. Spotswood wanted to prove that the association between the authorities and Blackbeard went all the way to the top. His ultimate goal was to uncover something that tied Governor Eden to Blackbeard.

The most damning piece of evidence was the letter from Tobias Knight to Blackbeard, found among the pirate's possessions on board the *Adventure*. The letter had been sent on November 17, just five days before the action, and while it didn't prove any direct involvement between the two men, it did suggest they were on good terms. Knight ended it by writing, "I have not time to add save my hearty respects to you, and am your real friend"—hardly a phrase used by an official who wanted to distance himself from the pirate. However, this, combined with the discovery of the twenty barrels of sugar found by Captain Brand in Knight's store, was enough to convince Spotswood that Tobias Knight was as guilty as sin. The trial would serve as a vehicle to bring the Virginia governor's accusations against Knight into the open, and would begin a round of accusations that rocked the foundations of colonial America.

The trial date was set for March 12, 1719, and held in the upper floor of Williamsburg's Capitol building. The day before, Spotswood addressed the thorny issue of the African American contingent among the prisoners. He held a meeting of his council, and the minutes recorded that "he desired the opinion of this Board whether there be anything in the Circumstances of these Negroes to exempt them from undergoing the same Tryal as other pirates." In other words, as former slaves they had even fewer rights than the other pirates, and could be killed for their crimes without having to bother with the expense of a trial. In their wisdom, the council advised Spotswood that they should be held accountable for their crimes just like the other pirates. It seems that the policy of turning informant didn't do four of these unfortunate men much good. With that decision made, the way was clear for one of the fastest trials in Virginia legal history.

On the morning of March 12, the prisoners shuffled into the courtroom and the trial began. Although the trial records haven't survived, the event left behind enough supporting evidence to reconstruct what happened. As this was a Vice-Admiralty trial, there was no jury, just the Vice-Admiralty's representative—in this case almost certainly Governor Spotswood himself, supported by seven or more commissioners. These were probably the same men who sat in judgment over William Howard the previous year—men Spotswood had hand-picked for their reliability, and for their loyalty to the governor. It was not unusual for the governor himself to preside over the court, although in many cases this was done by the chief justice of the colony, who also carried the title of Judge of the Court of Vice-Admiralty. It seems that this trial was too important for Spotswood to leave anything to chance.

The procedure was reasonably straightforward. First, the charges were read to the prisoners, a fairly detailed indictment that would have been fascinating to read if it had survived. To strengthen Spotswood's case, it presumably demonstrated that Blackbeard resumed his piratical activities after receiving his pardon from Governor Eden, and it almost certainly included evidence to support the claim that his capture of the French merchantmen was an act of piracy, not salvage. After all, this was the core of the prosecution's case. The North Carolinian authorities had already decided that Blackbeard had been acting within the law, a decision reflected in them awarding the former pirate salvage rights over the vessels. By proving this to be false, Spotswood was exposing Governor Eden to public censure. The fact that the decision also would condemn the surviving pirates to a grisly death was almost irrelevant.

It was almost inevitable that the Vice-Admiralty Court ruled in favor of the prosecution. The men were deemed to be pirates who had reneged on their pardon, and were therefore subject to the ultimate penalty. With only one exception the prisoners were condemned "to be hanged by the neck 'till you shall be dead, dead, dead." The condemned men included the five African Americans, regardless of whether they had turned informant or not, as well as the other turncoat, Israel Hands. It is almost certain that these men furnished Spotswood with both the evidence and the ammunition he needed to pursue his vendetta against Charles Eden and Tobias Knight. However, Spotswood was evidently in no mood for clemency.

The court did perform one humane act when it decided that one of the accused, Samuel Odel, was simply a man who was in the wrong place at the wrong time. The Bath Town trader managed to prove that his sloop had arrived at Ocracoke only the night before Lieutenant Maynard's attack, and that he had spent the evening carousing with the pirates on board the *Adventure*. He was still on board when the Royal Navy began its attack, and so he was caught up in the fighting. Forced to defend himself when the two sides clashed, he was badly wounded in the fight, then captured and incarcerated along with the rest. Given the fate of others such as the turtle fishermen found in a similar position on board "Calico" Jack Rackam's sloop, he should have considered himself lucky to escape with his life.

Another man who escaped the noose was Israel Hands. He managed to prove that the drinking session that ended with Blackbeard shooting him in the knee took place before the attack on the French merchantmen. Under the terms of the latest guidelines to reach Spotswood from Britain, he was therefore still covered by the terms of the pirate amnesty. The former pirate was duly released. As Captain Johnson explained it, "Hands, being taken, was tried and condemned but just as he was about to be executed a ship arrived at Virginia with a proclamation for prolonging the time of His Majesty's pardon to such of the pirates as should surrender by a limited time therein expressed. Notwithstanding the sentence, Hands pleaded the pardon and was allowed the benefit of it."

This seems highly unlikely. The proclamation Captain Johnson referred to was the extension to the offer of pardon issued on June 24, 1715. This would have been the same extension dated July 23, 1718, issued as a result of Britain's imminent entry into a war with Spain. At the time Britain was part of an anti-Spanish alliance and saw the Spanish occupation of Sicily in July 1718 as an informal declaration of war. Aware of Spain's vulnerability in the Americas and its own naval weakness, the British Admiralty encouraged the extension of the pardon as a means of increasing its pool of privateers willing to wage their own private war against the Spaniards. This means that rather than arriving at the eleventh hour, the document that saved Israel Hands's life was already in Virginia by the fall of 1718. It had already been used when Spotswood granted clemency to William Howard. A more likely version of events was that while Hands was condemned with the rest, this was a ploy to cover his work as an informant. This, in turn, suggests that his subsequent pardon was a reward for services rendered.

Although we don't know the exact date of the mass pirate execution, if we discount the eleventh-hour theory regarding Hands, then we can assume it took place within days of sentence being passed. After all, this was usually the case in these circumstances, whether the trial was held in Britain or the American colonies. The condemned men were escorted down the Jamestown road, the same route they traveled after Lieutenant Maynard handed them over to the Virginia authorities just over three months earlier. The procession would have included the condemned men, representatives of the Virginia church and legislature, an escort of Virginia militia, and a baying crowd of bloodthirsty onlookers.

One after the other Joseph Brooks Jr., John Carnes, Stephen Daniel, John Gills, Richard Greensail, John Martin, James Robbins, Joseph Philips, Edward Salter, and Black Caesar were forced to stand on a cart, their hands tied behind their backs. A rope was looped over a convenient tree, or a gibbet purpose-built for the occasion, and the noose tightened around the pirate's neck. The condemned man would be given the chance to make a short speech, and a preacher would say an even shorter prayer. The cart and horse were then led away, leaving the pirate kicking in midair, the crowd watching his last moments with rapt attention. The process was then repeated every half-mile or so, so emulating the fate of Spartacus and his fellow slaves in 71 BCE, the pirates lining the length of the road from Williamsburg to the James River. The bodies of James Blake, Thomas Gates, Richard Stiles, and James White hung with their fellows. It seems that Governor Spotswood and his advisors decided that the clemency offered to Israel Hands did not apply to his fellow African American informants.

With the death of Blackbeard's crew, Alexander Spotswood was able to concentrate on his two remaining problems, the first of which was the division of the spoils, the second being the equally agreeable business of discrediting Governor Eden. The trial having apparently vindicated his decision to seize the goods held by the North Carolinian governor and his secretary, Tobias Knight, Spotswood was now free to sell the plunder. In a letter dated May 26, less than two weeks after the trial, he informed his superiors at the Board of Trade that the sale of these goods plus the sloop *Adventure* raised a total of £2,238, the equivalent of around $500,000 today. From this total Spotswood deducted what he considered appropriate to cover the cost of the operation to attack Blackbeard, the transportation of the goods and the sloop from North Carolina, the storage of the goods and the vessel for the past three months, and the costs incurred in organizing the sale of the plunder.

There was also the cost of the legal process to consider: housing the prisoners, the expense of the trial, and any costs involved in organizing the mass execution. This was duly deducted from the next round of Virginia's taxes paid to the British Crown, a revenue levied on the sale of tobacco. Finally, Spotswood had to decide what to do about rewarding the men involved in his adventure. Four days before Lieutenant Maynard sailed for Ocracoke, the governor offered £100 for Blackbeard, £10 for each ordinary pirate, and a range of sums in between depending on the post held by the man they captured or killed. The total haul earned by Maynard and his men should have come to around £400, the equivalent of $110,000 today. The proclamation signed by Spotswood added that "the said Rewards shall be punctually & justly paid, in current Money of Virginia, according to the directions of the said Act." It turned out that when it came, the reward was neither punctual or just.

For a start, the way the navy usually dealt with prize money was that the participants received the bulk of the reward, while additional portions were reserved for senior officers such as admirals or senior captains, even though they took no part in the battle. However, even though Lieutenant Maynard captured Blackbeard's sloop and killed the pirate, it was Captain Brand who led the land forces to Bath Town and who seized the bulk of the goods. Maynard was overruled by his superior officers, and the navy's share of the prize money—the reward issued by Spotswood—was divided among the entire crew of HMS *Lyme* and HMS *Pearl*. This meant that men who took no part in the venture received the same share as the men who placed their lives on the line during the assault against Blackbeard. It was monstrously unjust, and Lieutenant Maynard said as much to anyone who would listen.

Even more disgracefully, Spotswood's clerks took almost four years to pay the reward money. By that time many of those involved had died or retired from the service, and so never received a penny. In August 1721 a petition was forwarded to the Admiralty, a document drawn up by Maynard, which drew attention to the injustice. Back in London Captain Gordon was asked for his comments, and he reported that Captain Brand had been given just over £334 to distribute, while Governor Spotswood had already awarded one twelfth of the total reward (another £30 or so) to the masters of the two hired sloops to distribute among their men. He added that he had already given his own share to Maynard to share out among the men who took part in the attack—an impromptu danger bonus to the men who deserved it. He then added the bombshell that as he heard it, Maynard had already awarded himself and his men plunder to the value of £90.

Much of the Admiralty's sympathy for Maynard's plight evaporated with this revelation. It appears that the lieutenant retained much of the personal haul of plunder he found on board the *Adventure*, which included gold dust, silver plate, and other trinkets. By rights he should have turned this over to the Virginia authorities, but instead he retained it and divided it up among his men. This plunder, equivalent to $25,000 today, was divided among the forty-seven or so survivors of the attack. It wasn't much of a bonus, but it meant that the men who deserved the reward received something right away, and didn't have to wait for years before they saw any money. Spotswood learned of this illegal haul soon after Maynard returned, and he considered that the lieutenant had acted immorally. At the time he had been organizing the collection of a personal reward to present to Maynard, for services rendered to the colony. That notion was quietly shelved. The naval hero had damaged his reputation by seeing to the welfare of his own men.

Normally a bold action like the one he fought would have served as a stepping-stone to promotion, but instead Maynard descended into obscurity. It is likely that on the return of HMS *Pearl* to Britain in 1721, Maynard quit the king's service. In his account historian Robert E. Lee claimed that a Virginian account claimed that Maynard was killed by two slaves in Prince George County, Virginia, a few years after the event. The county lies some twenty-five miles southeast of Richmond, on the southern bank of the James River. As Maynard was still a petitioner of the Admiralty in August 1721 and his ship had returned home, this seems unlikely. As for Captain Brand, the lawsuits which Governor Eden filed against him for stealing the colony's property came to nothing, and like Spotswood the senior naval officer involved in the Blackbeard adventure emerged unscathed, and ended his service career as a rear admiral.

After organizing the sale of the plunder and any division of the spoils, Governor Spotswood still had to deal with his counterpart in North Carolina. Shortly after the trial he wrote to Governor Eden, enclosing evidence that pointed at Tobias Knight being in league with Blackbeard. "It has appeared to this Court Mr. Tobias Knight, Secretary of North Carolina, hath given Just Cause to suspect his being privy to the Piracys committed by Edward Thatche and his Crew, and hath received and concealed the Effects by them piratically taken, whereby he is become an accessary." Of course, he didn't say anything about the goods taken from Eden's own house, and from Knight's store. He concluded by suggesting to Eden that "the said Tobias Knight be apprehended and proceeded against, pursuant to the directions of the Acts of Parliament for the effectual suppression of Piracy." From other snippets we can suppose that the evidence provided consisted of the statements made by Spotswood's pirate informants.

Governor Eden responded by calling together an emergency meeting of his Council of Advisors. He had already discussed the problem of Tobias Knight with his friend and legal advisor Colonel Thomas Pollock, who was of the conclusion that the Virginia governor had overstepped his bounds. On April 4, 1719, Eden's council met to hear what Knight had to say. The five advisors included Colonel Pollock. Spotswood's evidence included a statement by Israel Hands and his fellow informants that claimed that he and four other members of Blackbeard's crew made Tobias Knight a gift of several barrels of cocoa from the French ships, as well as "some Boxes, the Contents of which they did not know." Another local witness, William Bell, claimed the visit took place on the night of September 14—before Blackbeard informed Governor Eden that he captured the French ships through salvage rather than piracy. In other words, the goods given to Knight constituted a bribe.

The evidence also included a statement by Captain Brand, who claimed that an informant told him that pirate plunder was being held in Knight's store. After an initial denial that any such goods were in his possession, he "owned the whole matter, and the piratical Goods aforesaid were found in his Barn covered over with fodder." Tobias Knight was a dying man, but he managed to defend himself with some style. He insisted that "he is not in any wise howsoever guilty of the least of these Crimes which are so Slyly, malitiously and falsely suggested and insinuated against him by the said pretended Evidence." He added that this evidence "ought not to be taken in any Court of record or else where against the said Tobias Knight or any other white man." There was the crux of the defense. The only white accuser was Israel Hands. Under North Carolinian and Virginian law, testimony from African Americans was usually considered inadmissible in court. Even without countering the allegations in detail, Knight felt that he could throw out the evidence against him on a technicality.

He also suggested that as a prisoner "under the Terror of Death," Hands was intimidated by the Virginian authorities, and could therefore be expected to say whatever they wanted to hear. He added that the evidence supplied by William Bell was circumstantial—there was nothing to link the pirates' presence in the area that evening with a visit to Knight's house. Anyway, Bell's encounter was with local ruffians, not Blackbeard's men. He also claimed that "the said Brand never did at any time speak one word or mention to the said Knight in any manner whatsoever touching or concerning the sugar mentioned in the said Evidence before the said Knight first mentioned them to him." He claimed he never denied holding the sugar, but that the property was being stored there "at the request of the said Thatche, only till a more Convenient store could be procured by the Governor for the whole." With no government store available to take possession of the goods levied by the colony from Blackbeard after the Vice-Admiralty court deemed his French prizes legal salvage,

Knight was within his rights to store the goods himself, at the behest of the governor.

He added that Blackbeard and his men never visited him unless on business in his capacity as the colony's secretary and collector of customs, and that he never saw Blackbeard during his summer foray on the high seas until September 24, when he reported the salvage of the French ships to the authorities. Even more importantly, Tobias Knight had witnesses. Edmund Chamberlaine was resident in Knight's house during the previous summer, and was willing to testify that as far as he was aware Blackbeard and his men never visited the property, and that Knight's ill health precluded his venturing out to meet the pirates in person. He also reported that the only present Knight received from Blackbeard was a gun valued at £2 (or $275 today).

Another prop of Spotswood's case was the testimony of William Bell. Chamberlaine testified that he was present when Bell visited Knight, and reported being attacked and robbed while sailing in Pamlico Sound. His attackers were named as local men, not pirates. This meant that Bell had made contradictory statements in North Carolina and Virginia, making his word worth almost nothing. Faced with this evidence, Governor Eden and his Council of Advisors issued the following statement: "This Board, having taken the whole into their Serious Consideration . . . as in the remonstrances set forth; and that the other Evidence, so far as it relate to the said Tobias Knight, are false and malitious, and that he hath behaved himself, in that and all other affairs wherein he hath been intrusted, as becomes a good and faithfull officer; and thereupon, it is of the opinion of this Board that he is not guilty and ought to be aquited of the said crimes, and every of them laid to his charge, as aforesaid." Tobias Knight was innocent of all charges.

This wasn't good enough for Charles Eden. The allegations Alexander Spotswood made against Tobias Knight had come about during a trial where the North Carolina secretary had no opportunity to speak, and which he was never invited to attend. He was also furious that Captain Ellis Brand, a supposed officer and gentleman, had leveled trumped-up accusations against Knight that the naval officer continued to repeat. Then there was the whole matter of the property taken by Brand and subsequently sold in Virginia. Officially it belonged to the colony of North Carolina rather than Blackbeard, and therefore Brand had been guilty of theft. Although Tobias Knight died later that summer, his superior continued the legal battle with Brand, Spotswood, and their minions, not just to clear the name of the colony, but also to punish the men responsible for her humiliation.

The argument rumbled on for years, with both governors soliciting the support of their superiors in London, and calling on their lawyers and advisors to support their claims. As a naval officer Brand was answerable only to the Admiralty, while claims by the Lord Proprietors and Governor Eden for justice seemed to have had little effect on either the Admiralty or the Board of Trade. However, the death of Charles Eden on March 17, 1722, brought the campaign for recompense to a close. It says something for his antipathy to Alexander Spotswood that he named the Virginia governor's legal opponent John Holloway as a beneficiary, the man who offered to defend Blackbeard's quartermaster William Howard. Although Spotswood was unable to topple the government of North Carolina, his actions did play their part in a move toward the transfer of proprietary colonies to royal control. Unfortunately for him, he wasn't able to make capital out of this, and his plans to add North Carolina to his own colony came to naught.

Governor Spotswood continued to malign Governor Eden, claiming that he had benefited from the presence of pirates in North Carolina waters. Although there was no proof of this, even Captain Johnson was taken in, and in the first edition of his *General History*, published in 1724, he insinuated that Charles Eden's morals were less than they should be. Although in those days the business of suing for slander was less widespread than it is today, nevertheless Captain Johnson's publisher, Charles Rivington, must have been uneasy, as the Lords Proprietor fully supported Governor Eden throughout the aftermath of the Blackbeard incident, and they wielded more than enough political power to unnerve a small independent publisher. In his 1726 edition Captain Johnson printed a retraction, which is worth quoting as it added one final twist to the story.

After stating that any reflection on the character of Charles Eden was groundless, Captain Johnson felt obliged "to take the calumny thrown on his character by persons who have misjudged his conduct by the light things appeared at that time." He could only have been referring to Alexander Spotswood. Captain Johnson continued: "Upon a review of this part of Black-beard's story, it does not seem . . . that the said governor held any pirate or criminal correspondence with this Pirate." So much for

Spotswood's accusations. Johnson had probably conducted the first impartial investigation into the controversy, and was "informed since, by very good hands, that Mr. Eden always behaved . . . in a manner suitable to his post." He added, "There did not appear from any writings or letters found in Black-beard's sloop or from any other evidence whatsoever, that the said Governor [Eden] was concerned at all in any malpractice; but on the contrary . . . he was honored and beloved by his colony, for his uprightness, probity and prudent conduct in his administration."

Captain Johnson saved his criticism for the governor of Virginia. First he implied that Captains Brand and Gordon had joined forces with Spotswood to deflect criticism of their own inability to counter the pirate threat. He then dropped his bombshell: "I am at a loss to know what acts of Piracy he [Blackbeard] had committed after this surrender to the Proclaimation. The French ship was lawfully condemned . . . and if he had committed any depredations amongst the [North Carolinian] planters . . . they were not upon the high sea . . . and could not come within the jurisdiction of the Admiralty, nor under the laws of Piracy." In other words, Blackbeard was unjustly attacked and killed. In effect, Captain Johnson was saying that Lieutenant Maynard, Captain Brand, and Alexander Spotswood had acted above the law, overturning a Vice-Admiralty court decision made in good faith and then killing Blackbeard without any hard evidence that he had returned to piracy.

Finally Captain Johnson turned his attention to "the secret expedition from Virginia, undertaken by the Governor and two captains-of-war" into Governor Eden's province, which seized goods legally held by the North Carolina authorities. As he put it, the attack "was certainly a new thing for the Governor of one Province, whose commission was limited to that jurisdiction, to exercise authority in another government, and the Governor himself upon the spot." Clearly Captain Johnson agreed with North Carolina's Colonel Pollock that Alexander Spotswood had grossly overstepped his authority. Equally appalling in Captain Johnson's eyes was Spotswood's subsequent campaign of vilification against Tobias Knight and Charles Eden. He commented that Knight was never given the opportunity to answer the allegations in a full inquiry, as he died in 1719, and added that in his opinion "there might be no occasion for it." As for Spotswood's attacks on Eden, Captain Johnson wrote, "Thus was poor Mr. Eden insulted and abused on all sides, without having the power of doing himself justice, and asserting his lawful rights." It was clear who Captain Johnson saw as the villain.

As for Governor Spotswood himself, by 1722 years of political infighting had taken their toll. The Blackbeard adventure did little to silence Spotswood's many critics. While the governor was busy with his war against the pirates, Philip Ludwell the Younger sent one of his political allies to

The female personification of colonial America beseiged by pirates, the line of bodies hanging from the gallows proving that she emerged victorious from the bloody struggle. From an early-eighteenth-century engraving.

London. Colonel William Byrd the Younger, a prominent plantation owner from Westover on the James River, presented a series of formal complaints against Spotswood to the British government, and demanded his removal from office. It took four years of lobbying, but in 1722 Byrd finally managed to persuade chief minister (prime minister) Robert Walpole to replace Spotswood, and the experienced Scottish soldier and diplomat Hugh Drysdale was duly named as his successor. However, by that time Alexander Spotswood had made so much money from land deals that his governorship had become immaterial. He would remain the wealthiest man in Virginia until his death in 1740.

The death of Charles Eden and the firing of Alexander Spotswood brought to an end the series of upheavals caused by Blackbeard's presence in the North American colonies—and by Spotswood's one-man crusade against the pirate. While Blackbeard's death might not have marked the end of piracy in American waters, it did signify a shift in fortune. Before the arrival of Woodes Rogers in the Bahamas, piracy was considered a spreading cancer, wreaking havoc on the fragile economies of Britain's American colonies in North America and the Caribbean. The events that followed—the death of Blackbeard; the executions of Stede Bonnet, Jack Rackam, and Charles Vane; and the stepping-up of antipiracy patrols in American waters—all contributed to the cutting out of the cancer. Although isolated groups of pirates would continue to appear until the mid-1720s, the worst of the crisis was over.

As for Blackbeard, Captain Johnson's argument that he was killed unjustly has been almost completely ignored. However, it was a powerful argument. First, although Blackbeard's story that when he encountered the French merchant ships on the high seas they were abandoned is pretty unbelievable, no evidence emerged to contradict his story. If indeed he did attack the ships, then the fictional pirate adage that "Dead men tell no tales" was extremely appropriate. Certainly, when the evidence was presented to Charles Eden, there was nothing to contradict Blackbeard's version of events. Consequently the decision to award him salvage rights was unavoidable. While there might have been rumors that Blackbeard was amusing himself by attacking shipping off the North Carolina coast, there was no hard evidence to support the allegation. Similarly, although the Vice-Admiralty court in Williamsburg listened to evidence that suggested Blackbeard attacked local vessels in the Pamlico River, the evidence given in the Tobias Knight hearing in North Carolina contradicted this. Again, there was no hard evidence linking Blackbeard to any piratical act.

There is no doubt that Blackbeard was widely regarded as one of the most dangerous pirates in the Americas by the time he arrived at Topsail Inlet. In late May 1718 Lieutenant Governor Bennett in Bermuda wrote to his superiors in London concerning "those pirate vessels that went lately out from Providence there were several others att sea (vizt) one Tatch with whom is Major Bonnett of Barbados in a ship of 36 guns and 300 men, also in company with them a sloop of 12 guns and 115 men, and two other ships, in all which, it is computed there are 700 men or therabt." After the blockade on Charles Town the authorities were running scared, and greatly overestimated Blackbeard's strength and capabilities. With a force of seven hundred men he could terrorize any port on the North American coast. Bennett also included other pirate commands in his letter, "one Coudon . . . and 130 men, a French ship of 30 guns and 350 men, most of that Nation, a French sloop of 6 guns and 40 men, one Vaine in a sloop of 6 guns and 60 men." The list continued, but the point was clear. Blackbeard on his own was a serious threat. Blackbeard in association with other pirates was a threat reminiscent of a barbarian invasion.

If Blackbeard had managed to join forces with Captain Condon, Charles Vane, and others (presumably including La Bouche, given the French reference), then he would have had almost seven hundred pirates at his disposal—a figure the authorities doubled to almost fifteen hundred men—a small army in early-eighteenth-century America. It is little wonder that the colonial governors were rattled. With this number of men and fire-power Blackbeard could descend on New Providence and drive Woodes Rogers from the islands, he could threaten to repeat his blockade of Charles Town elsewhere along the North American coast, and he could even land his men and sack a major settlement—Williamsburg, Baltimore, even New York or Boston. This is what made Blackbeard so notorious—it wasn't his piratical attacks, it was his potential. The authorities must have been mightily relieved when they learned of the wrecking of the *Queen Anne's Revenge* and the dispersal of his crew.

Men like Woodes Rogers and Alexander Spotswood had little room for complacency. As long as Blackbeard remained at large, he remained a latent threat. It was probably Blackbeard's chance meeting with Charles Vane that sealed his fate. Even though the numbers of the two groups were pitifully small, it raised the specter of a pirate confederation. That was in September 1718, after Blackbeard had accepted a pardon, but before he approached Governor Eden with evidence that he had "salvaged" an abandoned French merchantman. Local fishermen and traders would have passed on rumors of Blackbeard's activities to the Virginia authorities, and so by early October Spotswood would have known that Blackbeard was at sea again, and that he had been consorting with another pirate group. This was evidence enough.

To a man of action like Spotswood, Blackbeard's legal status was a moot point—all the evidence suggested that not only was he returning to his piratical ways, but that he was actively recruiting others into his force. In Spotswood's eyes it was only a matter of time before Blackbeard would reemerge as a serious threat to the Virginia colony. That was when Spotswood made up his mind to deal with Blackbeard, regardless of law and jurisdiction. He realized that the shallow waters of Ocracoke Inlet prevented him from sending HMS *Pearl* and HMS *Lyme*. That meant that he had no option but to send a smaller force—and send it soon, before Blackbeard's band grew any bigger, or before he captured another flagship like the *Queen Anne's Revenge*. In other words, Blackbeard was a victim of his own reputation, attacked and killed more for what he represented than what he actually did.

It remains one of the great enigmas of the Blackbeard story—was he genuine in his desire to keep on the right side of the law, or was he harboring plans to rebuild his piratical empire? Was Spotswood justified in attacking Blackbeard to remove a threat to his colony, or were his actions a gross overstepping of authority? Did Spotswood send Captain Brand and Lieutenant Maynard to deal with Blackbeard as part of a legitimate campaign against piracy, or did he have ulterior motives? Was the campaign simply a means of distracting mounting criticism from Spotswood's domestic policies, or had Spotswood a greater goal in mind—the de facto annexation of North Carolina by the Virginia colony? We can read what we can into the evidence, but we cannot fully understand what Blackbeard and Spotswood's true intentions really were back in November 1718.

For all we know about Blackbeard, he remains a somewhat enigmatic figure. It seemed that at times his piratical career took on a life of its own, and the man himself was carried along with it. His disappearance from late 1717 until early 1718, for instance, seems to be the act of a man who wanted to lie low, to take stock of his fortunes. Similarly, the dramatic ship-wreck off Topsail Inlet could be interpreted logically as the reprehensible act of a man who coolly and calculatingly betrayed his companions. However, it could also be seen as an act of desperation, an attempt to divest himself of the apparatus of piracy. This was followed by a prolonged period when he at least gave the appearance of staying on the right side of the law. Whether this was genuine or simply a way of biding his time until the furor he created died down is now impossible to determine. If he was indeed planning to turn his back on piracy, then Governor Spotswood did him a terrible injustice.

As far as history is concerned, Blackbeard remained a pirate to the end, despite any reservations expressed by Captain Johnson or subsequent biographers. His piratical activities, his fearsome appearance, and above all the reputation he created all combined to overshadow the real man and his motives. Johnson's book became a bestseller because it was a sensational, titillating read, his world of pirates and tropical seas, brutality and vengeance far removed from the world of the reader. You just need to compare his dramatic description of Blackbeard himself with the far more reserved version given by the pirate's captive Henry Bostock to see how Captain Johnson could work up a good story. Those who followed in Johnson's footsteps simply followed his lead, and the man behind the blood-curdling façade was buried forever.

In the years that followed, Blackbeard became almost a caricature, the archetypal piratical captain of the Golden Age. Pirate fiction and then Hollywood played their part in this. For example, the Scottish novelist Robert Louis Stevenson relied heavily on Johnson's description of Blackbeard when he conjured up his pirate villain Long John Silver in *Treasure Island* (1883), although the pirate's physical appearance came from another Johnson passage describing a wooden-legged pirate in his "Life of Captain England." Surprisingly, Stevenson cast Israel Hands as the blackest pirate of them all. In *The Master of Ballantrae* (1889) Stevenson had his hero join Blackbeard's crew, but on finding the pirate captain little more than a drunken boor he led a revolt, overthrowing Blackbeard and seizing the ship for himself. This was the start of the slide from historical pirate figure into cartoonlike pirate buffoon.

The image of Blackbeard inspired by Captain Johnson and Robert Louis Stevenson was ignored by fiction writers such as Rafael Sabatini, whose swashbuckling novels inspired movies like *The Sea Hawk* and *Captain Blood*. These pirate heroes were clean-cut, dashing gentlemen, not hirsute, fearsome brutes, and it was not until the next round of pirate films, which satirized the Errol Flynn version of pirates, that Blackbeard would return to center stage. In the movie *Blackbeard the Pirate* (1952) the man himself was played by Robert Newton, who portrayed Blackbeard as a larger-than-life character full of bravado and menace, a figure drawn straight from the pages of Captain Johnson. It was Newton who introduced the whole "Yo ho heave ho," "Arrrr," and "Shiver me timbers" repertoire of pirate phrases so beloved of pirate impersonators today, but by his overacting exuberance Newton also encouraged the perception of Blackbeard as a somewhat preposterous figure.

One thing Robert Newton got right was the pirate's West Country accent. By making his character hail from Bristol or its hinterland, Newton showed that he had read Captain Johnson, and had based his character on Johnson's account. By this stage the fictional portrayal of Blackbeard had overshadowed any remaining scrap of fact, and subsequent versions of the pirate leaned heavily on Robert Newton's interpretation of the man. In the Walt Disney movie *Blackbeard's Ghost* (1968) Peter Ustinov went one step further, turning Blackbeard into a portly figure of fun, as far removed from the man who held Charles Town to ransom as you could possibly get. Director Steven Spielberg clearly drew on Captain Johnson for inspiration when portraying his black-bearded pirate captain One-Eyed Willie in *The Goonies* (1985), but again Spielberg's pirate is a sanitized character designed to stimulate the imagination of a young audience rather than incite fear.

More recently, the character of Barbossa played by Geoffrey Rush in *Pirates of the Caribbean: The Curse of the Black Pearl* (2003) appeared to be a reinterpretation of Robert Newton's Blackbeard, complete with West Country accent, fearsome beard, and repertoire of stock pirate phrases. Many contemporaries mention Blackbeard's charm and social ease. After all, he managed to impress Hornigold and Bonnet, keep his crew in check, and convince the North Carolina governor he was genuinely repentant. He was described as intelligent, and seems to have had a modicum of social grace. This is a completely different Blackbeard from the image developed by Hollywood. In fact, if any fictional pirate character of recent years reflected the real Blackbeard it was Jack Sparrow, played by Johnny Depp in the same 2003 blockbuster. While Depp may claim his character was inspired by Keith Richards or Groucho Marx, his appearance was drawn from Captain Johnson, and his persona was closer to the real Blackbeard than most fictional attempts to capture the real man behind the myth.

While Blackbeard himself may have become hidden behind a fictional curtain, a few more tangible reminders still survive to help maintain the historical legacy that has all but been submerged by myth. For a start, anyplace with even the remotest connection to the pirate boasts something with Blackbeard's name on it. For instance, we have already mentioned that the spot on the James River where his skull was displayed was known as Blackbeard's Point until relatively recently. Other locations in places where he operated such as the Outer Banks, Beaufort, Pamlico Sound, and the Bahamas all have genuine or mythical associations with the pirate, while others even lay claim to being haunted by Blackbeard's ghost. The notion that Blackbeard's headless body can still be seen swimming off Ocracoke Island or wandering the North Carolina coast carrying a lantern might seem fanciful, but stories of this kind, while remaining a good draw for tourists, also reflect local legend, a way of keeping the past alive through mythology.

Stores, entertainment centers, and watering holes from Bath to Ocracoke in North Carolina, Bristol in England to Nassau in the Bahamas, and even Bangor, Maine; Padre Island, Texas; and Bayville, outside Lakewood, New Jersey, all draw on Blackbeard's name as a means of attracting customers. Then there is the treasure. The only nonfictional pirate known to bury treasure was Captain Kidd, and then only to stash his Indian Ocean plunder before entering New York to meet the governor. However, from *Treasure Island* on, pirates and buried treasure have been inseparably linked, and it now forms part of the pirate image. The problem with Blackbeard lies in the passage in Captain Johnson's account that deals with the pirate captain's conversation the night before his death: "The night before he was killed, he sat up and drank 'till the morning, with some of his own men, and the master of a merchantman, and having had intelligence of the two sloops coming to attack him, one of his men asked him, in case anything should happen to him, whether his wife knew where he had buried his money? He answered that nobody but himself and the Devil knew where it was, and the longest liver should take all."

Since then many have looked for a hidden cache of plunder, but nothing was ever found. The supposed site of Blackbeard's house outside Bath Town was a favored location, and the area was extensively dug up by treasure hunters over the years, to no avail. Another prime location was "Teach's Oak," a tree on the banks of the Neuse River outside Oriental, North Carolina, where legend had it that Blackbeard buried his plunder and his spirit still protected the site. Similar searches were conducted near Blackbeard's encampment on Ocracoke Island, and even on Holiday's Island in North Carolina's Chowan River. Nothing was ever found, probably because Johnson's tale was included more for dramatic effect rather than historical accuracy. It is highly unlikely that Blackbeard ever buried a cache of money, as he had no reason to do so. Even if he had, the stash would have been a small one, bearing no resemblance to the buried treasure of pirate fiction. Without any evidence to the contrary, we have to write off the treasure story as just another Blackbeard myth.

One Blackbeard legacy that is altogether more tangible is the *Queen Anne's Revenge*. on June 19, 1718, Captain Brand of HMS *Lyme* reported that "on the 10th of June or thereabouts a large pyrate Ship of forty Guns with three Sloops in her company came upon the coast of North carolina ware they endeavour'd To goe in to a harbour, call'd Topsail Inlett, the Ship Stuck upon the barr att the entrance of the harbour and is lost; as is one of the sloops." This was the first official word that Blackbeard had lost the *Queen Anne's Revenge*. David Herriot, the master of the sloop *Adventure*, had been a prisoner of Blackbeard since his capture in the Gulf of Honduras, and so was a participant in the drama. He reported that "the Queen Anne's Revenge run a-ground off the Bar of Topsail-Inlet, and . . . This Depondent's Sloop . . . run a-ground likewise about Gun-Shot from the said Thatch." Somewhere off Beaufort, North Carolina, lay the wrecks of two pirate ships, just waiting to be discovered.

Some thirty years later the Spanish ship *El Salvador* was lost in the same area, supposedly with a cargo of Spanish treasure onboard. It was this shipwreck that drew the attention of the commercial salvage group Intersal, based in Boca Raton, Florida. Armed with a permit issued by North Carolina's Office of State Archaeology, they began a search of the Cape Lookout area. The work continued on and off beginning in 1986, but by June 1996 the group had found nothing of any real interest. It was then that a group of divers explored a site revealed by an electromagnetic survey close to Fort Macon on the approach channel to Beaufort, North

Carolina. Ray Giroux was the first down, and on surfacing he reported to chief diver Mike Daniels that he'd spotted three cannons. His dive partner, Eugene Brunelle, topped that by surfacing with a ship's bell! It was clear that the site was an old one.

Mike Daniels went down himself, and soon came across the three cannons, which to his experienced eye looked like six-pounders. Next he found a whole cluster of them, and on closer inspection he realized that they appeared to date from the eighteenth century. As Daniels put it, "Once I spotted that ball of cannons, I knew we were on to something." The aim of the dive was to recover artifacts that could help identify the shipwreck, and that's exactly what they achieved. Back onshore they discovered that the brass bell carried the date 1705 on it, while a blunderbuss barrel they recovered was identified as British, dating from the same time. When they first found the site, the salvors thought they had finally located the wreck of the *El Salvador*. Instead they found what seemed to be an earlier shipwreck, possibly of British origin. It appears that what they'd found that day was the *Queen Anne's Revenge*.

Phil Masters, the president of Intersal, combed the records in an attempt to figure out exactly what ship Daniels and his companions had found. It was then that he unearthed the story of Blackbeard's shipwreck— a vessel whose date tied in with the objects his divers had recovered. Over the next few months the divers returned to the site several times in the hope of finding some scrap of evidence that could positively link the shipwreck with Blackbeard and identify her as the *Queen Anne's Revenge*. Meanwhile, Mike Daniels founded the Maritime Research Institute, a not-for-profit organization charged with researching the shipwreck, its artifacts, and its history. By the fall of 1997 Daniels had teamed up with the North Carolina Underwater Archaeology Unit based at Fort Fisher near Wilmington, researchers from the University of North Carolina, and the staff of the North Carolina Maritime Museum in Beaufort, and together the four interested parties surveyed the site and recovered more artifacts to help figure out exactly what the ship was.

This teamwork was something fairly unique—the commercial divers of Intersal had realized that the historical importance of the shipwreck far outweighed any monetary value it might have, and threw themselves into a partnership with North Carolina's Department of Cultural Resources and the state-run maritime museum, a union designed to do whatever was best for the objects and the shipwreck. Clashes between the groups were inevitable, but somehow the coalition has survived and is still working together on a project that will continue on for at least another decade. The reason work is progressing so slowly is that the site itself is full of information. Every object the divers recover has to be conserved, a process that takes time and money. It has been estimated that for each month spent diving, enough artifacts are recovered to keep a full conservation team busy for the rest of the year. In some cases objects take years to stabilize and conserve to a standard where they could be displayed in a museum.

Part of the archaeological emphasis is on the shipwreck itself—mapping it, exploring it, and trying to understand it. But the work also includes a study of the environment itself—how the wreck site changes over the years, with sand covering and uncovering parts of the wreck with each new storm. During the hurricane-prone diving season of 2000 the recovery of artifacts deemed in danger due to being exposed in this way was made a top priority, a decision that resulted in the recovery of hundreds of precious artifacts. So far more than fifteen thousand objects have been recovered and put through the conservation process, ranging from pottery shards to pieces of gunnery equipment, from clay pipes to cannon. Many of these objects are now on display in the North Carolina Maritime Museum, whose staff viewed the discovery of the shipwreck as a unique opportunity—after all, maritime history was being made on their doorstep.

The business of identifying the shipwreck was always going to be difficult. Archaeologist Dave Moore from the North Carolina Maritime Museum conducted extensive research into the *Queen Anne's Revenge*, and recommended concentrating on her armament. The documentary evidence is somewhat contradictory. When she was captured, *La Concorde* carried either fourteen or sixteen guns. When Blackbeard transferred his French prisoners into one of his two sloops he almost certainly stripped the vessel of her own eight guns, adding these to the armament of his prize. This meant that in late 1717 the *Queen Anne's Revenge* carried around twenty-two or twenty-four guns in total. Over the next few months she was reported as carrying twenty-two, twenty-six, thirty-two, and thirty-six guns. By the time she appeared off Charles Town Bar, Governor Johnson of the South Carolina colony claims she was armed with forty guns, a figure that ties in with other reports. These additional sixteen or eighteen guns would probably have come from vessels looted by Blackbeard in the Gulf of Honduras.

Over the past eight years the salvors and archaeologists have recorded finding twenty-two of these guns, while surveys suggest that additional guns are scattered around the site, buried beneath the gray sand of the seabed. This ties in with the reports of twenty-six or thirty-two guns onboard, but it is more than likely that more pieces still lie buried out there, waiting to be discovered. The total of forty guns may have been an exaggeration, bandied about by the pirates off Charles Town in an effort to cow the port's inhabitants. The discrepancy of ten or so pieces could also be because the original total included small swivel guns, and the lack of these weapons among the finds suggests that Blackbeard took these portable weapons with him when he picked the wreck clean. Whatever the total number of guns carried by Blackbeard's flagship, it is clear that the ship that wrecked in Beaufort Inlet was exceptionally well armed. Only the *Queen Anne's Revenge* fits the description—she was the only ship carrying more than twenty-two guns known to have been wrecked in the area during the early eighteenth century. All the evidence points to the mystery wreck being the pirate ship.

In late 2000 the author visited old colleagues Dave Moore and project conservator Wayne Lusardi at the project's conservation laboratory in Morehead City, North Carolina. As a former ordnance authority from Britain's Royal Armouries, the author helped identify the recovered guns, suggesting they represented a mix of early-eighteenth-century French and British pieces. Two of the guns were French cast-iron six-pounders (sakers), and fourteen similar pieces still lie on the wreck site. Presumably these guns originally formed part of the armament of *La Concorde*. Another, smaller piece—a bronze three-pounder (minion)—was clearly British, as it carried a P mark showing she had been tested (or proofed) by the British authorities, and carried a British style of weight mark, divided into hundredweights (each of 112 pounds), quarters of hundredweights, and pounds. In her case the marks read "6-3-7," which meant she weighed 763 pounds, a typical size for a minion of the period. Incidentally, she was also virtually identical to similar guns recovered from the pirate ship *Whydah* and the slave ship *Henrietta Marie*. Again, that fitted the picture that the wreck was the *Queen Anne's Revenge*. Another four-pounder was raised in 2005.

Since then, other, smaller guns have been recovered, but work has moved away from the ordnance for the moment, as their conservation is a long and costly process. Of all the artifacts recovered so far, the most spectacular is the ship's bell. This cast-bronze bell was dated 1705 and carried a Catholic inscription—"IHS" (standing for *"Jesus Hominum Salvator"*) and the name "Maria." This suggests a Spanish origin, but the object is a little small for a ship's bell, at least for a vessel the size of the *Queen Anne's Revenge*. It has been suggested that the bell was taken from the sloop Blackbeard captured off Havana earlier that spring. That means the bell of Blackbeard's flagship is still down there.

A little more revealing was the selection of ship's timber that was raised for electrocarbon dating. The frames and hull planking were found to be built from oak, while a layer of pine sacrificial planking was attached to the outer hull to help protect the harder oak planking from the ravages of the *teredo* worm. Even more revealing, the dating placed the time of the ship's construction around 1710, which fits in exactly with the building of *La Concorde* in the French port of Nantes in the same year. The survey of the site has also meant that the size of the ballast pile and the nature of the hull planking still down there have been examined. Sailing ships carried stones as ballast to weight down their hull and so improve the vessel's center of gravity. When the ship sank, the wooden hull rotted away, leaving the ballast stones to form a pile on the seabed. Trapped beneath the pile were elements of hull structure.

This survey work helped to suggest that the mystery vessel was of a similar size and type to Blackbeard's flagship. It lay the right way, with its bows pointing northward toward Beaufort. The circumstantial evidence was starting to come together to form a pretty conclusive body of evidence. Everything was pointing toward her being the *Queen Anne's Revenge*. Another important benefit of studying her timbers is that they might help explain how the ship sank. In the 2005 season archaeologists found a part of the stern structure, which was damaged when the ship sank. It is almost too much to wish for, but it can only be hoped that in future seasons divers might find definitive proof that the vessel was run hard aground, adding another piece to the jigsaw puzzle of supportive evidence.

Of course, the artifacts weren't solely limited to the ship and her armament. They also included navigational and scientific instruments, the everyday items used by the crew, some of their personal effects, and even

medical equipment. A few of these have helped push that body of circumstantial evidence a little further along the road of identification. A seaman's
blunderbuss barrel made from brass was identified as being produced in
London sometime before 1702, while other gun fittings also appear to be
British. Two hollow cast-iron grenadoes (grenades) were found, of the type
used by Blackbeard during his final fight with Lieutenant Maynard in
November 1718. While these were commonly carried on board warships,
they were comparatively rare outside the service—except on board pirate
ships. While most steel objects have corroded away to nothing, a whetstone
suggests that the crew carried cutlasses and kept them ready for action.

As for the scientific and navigational instruments, we have already
mentioned how Blackbeard liked to plunder his prizes for navigational
equipment. So far the wreck site has revealed fittings from several complex
pieces of surveying equipment, a series of finds that remains something of
a mystery, and a collection of more recognizable navigational tools—
dividers, measuring rules, a brass sector (used in chart work), and a lead
sounding weight. Did Blackbeard capture the surveying tools on one of his
prizes, and if so, did he keep them with him while he tried to figure out
what they were used for? Although he probably never came across land surveying tools before, he would have probably figured out what they were
and how they were used—after all, he understood navigation, and the two
fields are not dissimilar.

Finally, two personal artifacts give us a direct link with Blackbeard.
Even though their presence on board might not be conclusive, the two
together have pushed that circumstantial evidence as far as it could
possibly go. The first was a syringe, the kind used to treat venereal disease
in the early eighteenth century. This intimidating-looking object was used
to inject mercury into the urethra, a surefire if painful and potentially
dangerous cure for venereal ailments. This is exactly the type of medical
instrument Blackbeard requested from the townspeople of Charles Town.
It is possible that it once formed part of the medical bag sent out to the
pirate flagship in an attempt to speed Blackbeard on his way.

Then there was the gold dust. So far just seventy flakes have been
recovered—no more than 2 grams, but these were all found in one spot,
suggesting they once formed part of a private stash. Analysis has shown that
the gold doesn't come from North America, which suggests it might well
have come from West Africa. According to reports, La Concorde carried

around 14 ounces of gold dust on board when Blackbeard captured her, the personal trading spoils of her French crew. Could this bag have once belonged to one of these Frenchmen, who hid it and then had no chance to retrieve his stash? Could it have belonged to one of Blackbeard's shipmates, forced to abandon the pirate flagship without his own plunder? While we might never know who the gold belonged to, we can certainly argue that it provides one final link between the shipwreck and Blackbeard.

No brass name plate will ever be discovered, and anything else that provides a positive identification of the wreck is extremely unlikely. Instead, what we have is an impressive collection of evidence that leads to the almost unavoidable conclusion that the shipwreck is almost certainly

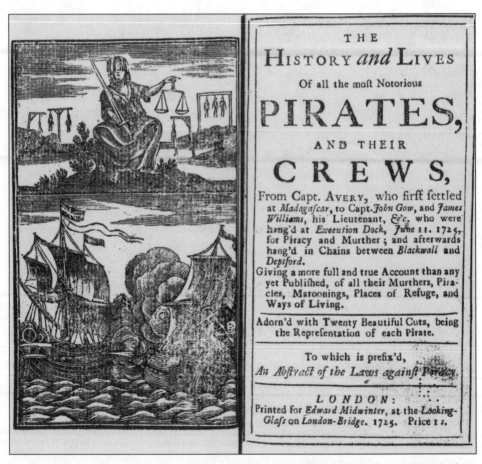

The frontispiece of the second edition of Captain Johnson's History, *published in 1725, with plates showing blind justice and a sea battle between a pirate ship and a vessel of the Royal Navy.*

that of Blackbeard's flagship. Of all the objects he could have left behind him, the *Queen Anne's Revenge* is the most revealing, and with time she will help broaden our understanding of Blackbeard and how he operated. There is some truth in the much-hackneyed phrase that archaeological shipwrecks are time capsules just waiting to be opened. In this case the time capsule is pretty unique—it represents a major part of American colonial history and dates from a specific dastardly moment in the early summer of 1718, when Blackbeard abandoned his crew and escaped into the sunset with the loot. It can only be hoped that everyone concerned continues their groundbreaking work, and helps us understand a little more about Blackbeard and his times.

However, Blackbeard is bigger than a collection of objects in a museum, or documents neatly tied up with ribbon in an archive. No other pirate managed to capture the public imagination like Blackbeard, or has retained this fascination over the centuries. He remains the archetypal pirate of the age, not just because of his subsequent portrayal by Holly-wood, but because to his contemporaries he was one of the most fearsome figures around. It was Captain Johnson who described Blackbeard as "a frightful meteor," a man who "frightened America more than any comet that has appeared there a long time." This was his secret—put simply, he scared people. Blackbeard was the bogeyman of early-eighteenth-century colonial America—a man who had colonial governors, merchants, shipowners, and fishermen running scared.

Almost single-handedly he engineered the pirate crisis that swept North America in the summer of 1718, and played no small part in the perception that the Americas were gripped in an even larger pirate scourge that was duly dubbed the Golden Age of Piracy. Warships were diverted from Britain, colonial governors scrambled to send out antipiracy patrols, and merchants demanded naval escorts. The establishment of a piratical blockade off Charles Town shook the burgeoning confidence of colonial America just as it was beginning to develop as an economic and maritime power. The panic Blackbeard created was out of all proportion to the num-ber of ships he seized or the goods he plundered. Blackbeard's notoriety— the reason he couldn't be allowed to live—was achieved at the expense of the confidence of an emerging nation. That is what made him such a fear-some figure, and why his image, if not his exploits, is still remembered today.

Notes

References

ADM   Admiralty and Navy Board Records (UK)
BNL   *Boston News Letter* (US)
CO   Colonial Office Records (UK)
HCA   High Court of the Admiralty Records (UK)
CSPC   Calendar of State Papers: Colonial, American and the West Indies Records (UK)
NMM   National Maritime Museum Records (UK)
PRO   Public Record Office Records (UK)

Preface

vii   *"I remember him"*   Robert Louis Stevenson: *Treasure Island* (London, 1883), reprinted by Penguin (London, 1994), 16.

vii   *"the bloodthirstiest buccaneer"*   Ibid, 29.

viii   *"In time of Action"*   Captain Johnson: *A General History of the Robberies & Murders of the most notorious Pirates* (London, 1724), reprinted by Lyons Press (New York, 1998), 60.

ix   *Indeed, the so-called Golden Age of Piracy*   Angus Konstam: *The History of Pirates* (New York, 1999), 94.

Chapter 1. The Pirate Apprentice

2   *Much of what we do know*   For a detailed account of the identity of Captain Johnson, see David Cordingly's commentary on Captain Johnson, vii.

2   *Daniel Defoe was a different type of man altogether*   See Daniel Defoe: *Robinson Crusoe* (London, 1719), reprinted by Penguin Popular Classics (London, 1998), and *The Life, Adventures, and Piracies of the Famous Captain Singleton* (London, 1720), reprinted by Wildside Press (Rockville, MD, 2003). Also, John R. Moore: *Defoe in the Pillory & other studies* (Chicago, 1939); *Daniel Defoe: Citizen of the Modern World* (Chicago, 1958); Philip N. Furbank & W. R. Owens: *Canonisation of Daniel Defoe* (New Haven, CT, 1988); *Defoe De-attributions: Critique of J. R. Moore's Checklist* (London, 1994).

3   *What we know about the book*   Johnson (reprinted 1998), vii.

3   *"Plutarch, and other grave historians"*   Ibid, 60.

4   *In his recent introduction to a reprint*   Philip Gosse: *The History of Piracy* (New York, 1925), a reprint of Captain Johnson with additional commentary, reprinted in turn by Rio Grande Press (Glorieta, NM, 1988); Johnson (reprinted 1998), xiii.

5   *"Edward Teach was a Bristol man"*   Johnson (reprinted 1998), 46.

5   *Captain Johnson was clear about naming Bristol*   For a more detailed account of Thomas J. Upshur's claim, see Robert E. Lee: *Blackbeard the Pirate: A Re-appraisal of his life and times* (Winston-Salem, NC, 1974), reprinted by John F. Blair (Winston-Salem, NC, 2002), 176.

6   *The Venetian immigrant John Cabot*   For a more detailed account of Bristol's early history, see Peter Aughton: *Bristol: A People's History* (Lancaster, Lancashire, UK, 2003); Bryan Little & John Sansom (eds.): *The Story of Bristol: From the Middle Ages to Today* (Tiverton, Essex, UK, 2003). Comments are also based on the research of Peter Martin and Rodney Broome.

8   *Privateering was little more than officially sanctioned piracy*   Konstam (*Pirates*, 1999), 10, but also see David J. Starkey, E. S. van Eyck, & J. A. de Moor (eds.): *Pirates and Privateers: New Perspectives on the War on Trade in the Eighteenth and Nineteenth Centuries* (Exeter, Devon, UK, 1997), 1–25.

13   *There is one possible clue*   Konstam (*Pirates*, 1999), 118.

14   *Later on both men served as privateersmen*   Konstam (*Pirates*, 1999), ibid, and Lee (1974), 6. See also Alexander Winston: *No Purchase, No Pay: Sir Henry Morgan, Captain William Kidd and Captain Woodes Rogers in the Great Age of Privateers and Pirates, 1665–1715* (London, 1970).

15   *Although no official records*   Interview with Peter Martin (2005).

16   *In his history of English merchant seamen during this period*   See Peter Earle: *Sailors: English Merchant Seamen 1650–1775* (London, 1988), 83 et al.

17   *Not every English or French merchantman*   For a précis of transatlantic trade during this period, see Angus Konstam: *America Speaks: The Birth of a Nation—Merchants* (Danbury, CT, 2005), 34. For a more detailed discussion, see Ralph Davis: *The Rise of the Atlantic Economies* (London, 1973), 264 et al.

18   *The pirate captain John Martel*   Johnson (reprinted 1998), 42.

18   *Even the accounts of Blackbeard's piratical attacks*   Johnson (reprinted 1998), 51.

19   *A prime example is the English slave ship* Henrietta Marie   See Michael H. Cottman: *The Wreck of the Henrietta Marie: An African-American's Spiritual Journey to Uncover a Sunken Slave Ship's Past* (New York, 1999); George Sullivan: *Slave Ship: The Story of the Henrietta Marie* (New York, 1994); and Madeleine Burnside & Rosemarie Rabotham: *Spirits of the Passage: Transatlantic Slave Trade in the Seventeenth Century* (New York, 1997).

22   *In the late 1690s Port Royal was a mere shadow of its former self*   Konstam (*Pirates*, 1999), 92. Also see David Cordingly (ed.): *Pirates: Terror on the High Seas* (Atlanta, GA, 1996), 49; and David Cordingly & John Falconer: *Pirates: Fact & Fiction* (London, 1992), 38–39.

26   *A typical purpose-built privateer of the time*   Diana & Michael Preston: *A Pirate of Exquisite Mind: The Life of William Dampier* (London, 2004), 418–22. See

also David Cordingly: *Under the Black Flag: The Romance and the Reality of Life among the Pirates* (London, 1995), 139.

27   *Captain Johnson claims that Blackbeard*   Captain Johnson (reprinted 1998), 46.

28   *Logwood was the boom crop of its day*   Cordingly (1995), 147–150; Preston & Preston (2004), 23–24, 56–60; Joel Baer: *Pirates of the British Isles* (Stroud, Gloucestershire, UK, 2005), 52–54.

30   *Historian David Cordingly claims*   Cordingly (1995), 150.

31   *As Captain Johnson put it*   Captain Johnson (reprinted 1998), 60.

Chapter 2.   A Pirate's Life

34   *Piracy was clearly not an occupation*   Cordingly (1995), 245.

35   *The actual business of hanging*   Konstam (*Pirates*, 1999), 138–141.

35   *We don't know when Blackbeard first arrived*   Captain Johnson (reprinted 1998), 47.

36   *By the time he arrived in the Bahamas*   Konstam (*Pirates*, 1999), 120–121; Cordingly (1995), 152–153; Lee (1974), 10–11.

38   *Colonists from Bermuda*   Paul Johnson: *A History of the American People* (New York, 1997), 175. Also see George B. Tindall & David E. Shi: *America: A Narrative History* (New York, 1989); Paul Albury: *A History of the Bahamas* (London, 1975); and Sandra Riley: *Homeward Bound: A History of the Bahama Islands to 1850* (Nassau, Bahamas, 2000).

39   *The pirate historian George Woodbury*   George Woodbury: *The Great Days of Piracy in the West Indies* (New York, 1951), 73, also quoted in Lee (1974), 10, together with the quoted Lee passage.

40   *We can be reasonably sure*   For a further exploration of this theme, see Marcus Rediker: *Between the Devil and the Deep Blue Sea: Merchant Seamen, Pirates and the Anglo-American Maritime World, 1700–1750* (Cambridge, 1987), 254 et passim; and Marcus Rediker: *Villains of All Nations: Atlantic Pirates in the Golden Age* (Boston, MA, 2004), 38–59.

41   *Several seamen who would later become successful pirate captains*   Captain Johnson (reprinted 1998), 80, 132, 161.

42   *Many privateersmen would have deserted*   Rediker (2005), 7 et passim.

42   *Hornigold even claimed*   Ibid, 36.

43   *The most celebrated and controversial example*   For a detailed and readable account of the career of Captain Kidd, see Richard Zacks: *The Pirate Hunter: The True Story of Captain Kidd* (New York, 2002). See also Robert C. Ritchie: *Captain Kidd and the War against the Pirates* (Cambridge, MA, 1986).

44   *"Those people have been so farr"*   CSPC 1718–1719: 257 (PRO).

45   *"On the 3rd of November [1724]"*   Johnson (reprinted 1998), 333–334.

45   *The historian Marcus Rediker estimated*   Rediker (1987), 227–228; Johnson (reprinted 1998), 274–288.

47   *We have already said that the majority of pirates*   Rediker (2004), 49–50.

47   *As for nationality*   Ibid, 50–56; Cordingly (1995), 15–17.

49   *The injustice of all this*   Cotton Mather: *The Tryals of Sixteen persons for Piracy*   (Boston, MA, 1726), 14–15; Cotton Mather: *The Vial Poured upon the Sea: A Remarkable Relation of Certain Pirates* (Boston, MA, 1726), 110–112.

50   *After spending some time as a prisoner*   William Snelgrave: *A New Account of some parts of Guinea and the Slave Trade* (London, 1734), 114.

50   *For instance, Captain Haskins*   HCA 24/133 (1722) Philips v Haskins; Earle (2003), 146 et passim (PRO).

52   *The pirate Walter Kennedy*   Arthur L. Hayward (ed.): *Lives of the Most Remarkable Criminals* (London, 1735), reprinted by Dodd, Mead & Co. (New York, 1927), 37.

55   *The rules they laid down*   Barnaby Slush: *The Navy Royal: Or a Sea-Cook Turn'd Projector* (London, 1709), viii.

55   *Captain Johnson quotes the document*   Johnson (reprinted 1998), 180–181.

57   *David Cordingly claims*   Cordingly (1995), 94, quoting HCA 1/99.3 (PRO).

57   *Even more unfortunate were the crew*   Barry Clifford: *The Pirate Prince: Discovering the Priceless Treasures of the Sunken Ship* Whydah (New York, 1993), 20 et passim; Barry Clifford: *The Black Ship: The Quest to Recover an English Pirate Ship and Its Lost Treasure* (London, 1999), 9–10.

58   *"A counsel of war was called"*   Johnson (reprinted 1998), 134.

58   *The pirates "made such Waste and Destruction"*   Snelgrave (1734), 223 242.

58   *"It was a melancholy request to the man"*   Johnson (reprinted 1998), 202.

Chapter 3.   The Scourge of the Caribbean

62   *Benjamin Hornigold was an Englishman*   For a brief summary of Hornigold's career, see Philip Gosse: *The Pirate's Who's Who* (reprinted by Rio Grande Press, Glorieta, NM, 1988), 162–163.

63   *Blackbeard was already a leading member*   Johnson (reprinted 1998), 46.

63   *One account suggests it was the sloop* Revenge   BNL, November 4–11, 1717. The article was filed in Philadelphia on October 24, 1717.

63   *What is clear is that by the spring of 1717*   Johnson (reprinted 1998), 46.

64   *The first mention of Blackbeard*   Letter from Captain Mathew Musson to the Council of Trade and Plantations, received July 5, 1717, CSPC 1716–1717 (v29): 635 (PRO).

65   *In the summer of 1718 the governor of Virginia*   Articles . . . against William Howard "for Pyracy and Robbery committed by him on the High Seas," quoted at length in Lee (1974), 101–104; Lloyd Hanes Williams: *Pirates of Colonial Virginia* (Richmond, VA, 1937), 79–82.

66   *In May 1716 the* Boston News Letter   BNL May 21–28, 1716.

66   *In 1716 Virginia's Governor Spotswood*   CO 5/1364 (PRO).

67   *Hornigold must have protested the decision*   Rediker (2005), 7.

67   *In fact, a later account*   The articles against William Howard quoted in Lee (1974), 101–104, suggest that Blackbeard and Hornigold's sloops were not operating in concert during this period.

69   *"Arrived Captain Codd from Liverpool"*   BNL, November 4–11, 1717. The article was filed in Philadelphia on October 24, 1717.

69   *The November copies of the paper*   These reports were spread over two issues, BNL (November 4–11, 1717) and BNL (November 18–25, 1717).

70   *"On board the Pirate Sloop"*   Quoted from the article for the *Boston News Letter* filed in Philadelphia on October 24, 1717: BNL (November 4–11, 1717).

70   *There is little doubt*   Johnson (reprinted 1998), 63.

72   *"That the said Wm Howard"*   Quoted in Lee (1974), 101–104.

73   *We know from British naval records*   Log of HMS *Lyme*, 1717–1718: ADM 51/4250 (PRO).

73   *As recently as 1715*   For details, see Angus Konstam: *The History of Shipwrecks* (New York, 1999), 112–113.

74   *Although Captain Johnson fails to give us any dates*   Johnson (reprinted 1998), 47.

74   *In fact, the pirate historian Robert E. Lee*   Lee (1974), 30.

75   *In "The Life of Major Bonnet"*   Johnson (reprinted 1998), 63–65.

77   *This is where the story becomes a little confusing*   Johnson (reprinted 1998), 64.

77   *Less than two weeks later*   BNL (November 4–11, 1717). The article actually says of Bonnet, "He was not well of his wounds that he received by attacking of a Spanish Man of War, which kill'd and wounded 30–40 men. After putting into Providence, the place of Rendevouze for the Pirates, they put the afore said Capt. Teach. On board for this Cruise . . ."

78   *"In September 1717 the badly damaged sloop"*   Baer (2005), 169.

79   *"to him [Blackbeard] Bonnet's crew joined in consortship"*   Johnson (reprinted 1998), 64.

79   *The rest of the force*   BNL (November 4–11, 1717). Further evidence of Blackbeard's activities during this period is recorded in BNL (December 30, 1717–January 6, 1718). The article was filed in Philadelphia on December 10 and purports to cover a report received a few days before, around November 26. However, the dating of this report is somewhat suspect and must be viewed with caution, as the events almost certainly took place a week or more earlier than suggested.

79   *The next time we hear of Blackbeard*   Aix-en-Provence, Centre des archives d'outremer [AN Col C8A 22 (1717)], fol. 447.

80   *Captain Johnson gave a surprisingly terse account*   Johnson (reprinted 1998), 47.

80   *"Last 28 November [French dating]"*   Aix-en-Provence, Centre des archives d'outremer [AN Col C8A 22 (1717)], fol. 447. The report was filed on December 10, 1717, and given the discrepancy between French (New Style) and British dating at this time, the document was therefore written after November 17 (Old Style), the date of Blackbeard's attack.

81   *We know a little about the French slave ship*   I am grateful to John de Bry, director of the Center of Historical Archaeology in Melborne Beach, Florida, for his work in reconstructing the career and the appearance of *La Concorde*, and to the article by Richard Lawrence and Mark Wilde-Ramsin: "In Search of Blackbeard: Historical and Archeological Research at Shipwreck Site 003BUI," published in *Southeastern Geology* (Vol. 40, No. 1, February 2001). Finally, the research of Dave Moore of the North Carolina Maritime Museum has done much to piece together the missing parts of the story.

84   *For a start, Captain Johnson describes a handful of prizes*   Johnson (reprinted 1998), 82, 199, 277.

85   *We can see that converting a merchantman into a pirate ship*   Angus Konstam: *The Pirate Ship, 1660–1730* (Oxford, Oxfordshire, UK, 2003), 12–15.

87 *"They carried with them sails"* Johnson (reprinted 1998), 186.

87 *Many pirates expressed their support for the exiled James* For a brief discussion of Jacobean sympathies among pirates, see Peter Earle: *The Pirate Wars* (London, 2003), 170; Baer (2005), 170, 173.

88 *It reported that in late November* BNL (March 3–10, 1718), from a report filed in New York on February 24, 1718. The report claimed the attack took place *"in November last."* See also Johnson (reprinted 1998), 47; Aix-en-Provence, Centre des archives d'outremer [AN Col C8A 23 (1717)], fol. 47–55.

88 *He claimed that the pirates* Deposition of Henry Bostock, copied into a letter from Governor Hamilton dated January 5, 1718: CSPC 1717–1718 (v30): 298/i (PRO).

88 *On November 30 Richard Joy* Deposition of Richard Joy, copied into a letter from Governor Hamilton dated January 5, 1718: CSPC 1717–1718 (v30): 298/i. The encounter between Benjamin Hobhouse and the pirates is recounted in the Deposition of Thomas Knight, copied into the same letter by Governor Hamilton: CSPC 1717–1718 (v30): 298/ii (both PRO).

89 *"A few days later, Teach fell in with the Scarborough"* Johnson (reprinted 1998), 47. Interestingly, Johnson does describe the encounter between HMS *Scarborough* and the pirate ship of Captain Martel on January 20, 1717, an event supported by other evidence. As this confrontation took place in the same area (near the Virgin Islands), it is possible that Captain Johnson simply confused the activities of the two pirates.

90 *Henry Bostock, the master of the sloop* Margaret CSPC 1717–1718 (v30): 298/ii (PRO).

Chapter 4. Mixing with the Wrong Crowd

93 *Blackbeard wasn't the first pirate* For a more detailed account of New Providence as a pirate haven, see Lee (1974), 9–13.

94 *On July 24, 1715, a Spanish treasure fleet* The account of the wrecking of the 1715 flota is drawn from Robert F. Burgess & Carl J. Clausen: *Florida's Golden Galleons: The Search for the 1715 Spanish Treasure Fleet* (Port Salerno, FL, 1982), first published as *Gold, Galleons and Archaeology*, 1976, 5–41. The description of Spanish treasure is drawn largely from the author's own curatorial notes taken while developing the Spanish treasure exhibit in the Mel Fisher Maritime Museum, Key West, Florida. Also see Timothy R. Walton: *The Spanish Treasure Fleets* (Sarasota, FL, 1994); Kathryn Budde-Jones: *Coins of the Lost Galleons* (Key West, FL, 1989); and J. H. Parry: *The Spanish Seaborne Empire* (London, 1966).

96 *In November 1715 Lord Archibald Hamilton* Quoted in Burgess & Clausen (1982), 67–68. Note that this is not the same Hamilton as his namesake the governor of the Leeward Islands, based in Barbados.

97 As *Captain Belchin of HMS* Diamond ADM 1/1471/24 (PRO).

97 *In a document dated April 22, 1716* CSPC 1717–1718 (v30): 712 (PRO).

98 *"The rovers being now pretty strong"* Johnson (reprinted 1998), 11.

98 *"Among these masterless men"* Earle (2003), 159.

99 *"In November last [1715], Benjamin Hornigold"* Quoted in Burgess & Clausen (1982), 69.

99 *We know very little about Hornigold's activities* Johnson (reprinted 1998), 46.

100   *"The English plunder"*   Quoted in Burgess & Clausen (1982), 71.

101   *A common way this happened was accidental*   For a superb précis of the relationship between the Bahamian pirates of this period, see Rediker (1987), 267–269. Also see Rediker (2004), 46–49.

103   *A document issued by the Admiralty Office*   Summarized in Cordingly (1995), 250.

104   *The report of Captain Musson*   CSPC 1716–1717 (v27): 635 (PRO).

104   *As for the total number of pirates*   See Rediker (2004), 29–30.

107   *On September 5, 1717*   The proclamation is cited in full in Johnson (reprinted 1998), 13–14.

108   *"They sent for those who were out a cruising"*   Johnson (reprinted 1998), 15.

110   *By the time the* Phoenix *pulled up her anchor*   ADM 1/2282/2. ADM 1/2282/13 contains Captain Pierce's list of the pirates who surrendered (both PRO).

110   *"while he was in the Harbour"*   Johnson (1726 edition), 16. The subsequent events of Vane's career are based on Johnson's 1724 version (reprinted 1998), and on the following depositions: Deposition of Nathaniel Catling CO 37/10 — 10(v), Deposition of Edward North, CO 37/10 — 10(ii) (both PRO).

111   *As a former privateer captain himself*   This account of Rogers's arrival in the Bahamas is drawn from his own report: Governor Rogers to the Council of Trade and Plantations CSPC 1717–1718 (v30): 737. This version is supported by Johnson (reprinted 1998), 15–16.

112   *Captain Pomeroy of the sloop* Shark *wrote*   ADM 1/2282/2, dated 3 September 1718.

112   *Captain Johnson puts the clash*   Johnson (reprinted 1998), 15–16; Cordingly (1995), 152.

113   *As Vane made good his escape*   The subsequent summary of the actions of Hornigold and Vane is largely drawn from Johnson (reprinted 1998), 16–17, 103–110.

117   *By November 1719*   Johnson (reprinted 1998), 110. For details of Vane's execution and the comments made by Captain Vernon, see ADM 1/2624/6 (18 April 1721), CSPC 1720–1721 (v23): 20 (PRO).

117   *He headed into "the Caribbee islands"*   Johnson (reprinted 1998), 1111 et seq.

119   *In May 1719 he was mentioned as a supplicant*   Johnson (reprinted 1998), 120–121.

119   *It was during this period*   Account based on Johnson (reprinted 1998), 117–133.

120   *Governor Rogers immediately issued a proclamation*   Reprinted in the *Boston Gazette*, October 10–17, 1720.

120   *By the start of September*   CO 137/14 (PRO); Johnson (reprinted 1998), 113–114.

121   *With two exceptions the pirates threw up their hands and surrendered*   Taken from the contemporary pamphlet *The Tryals of Captain John Rackam and the other Pirates* (Spanish Town, Jamaica, 1721), 18–19.

122   *On November 16, the Vice-Admiralty Court*   The account of the trial is based on the *Tryals* (Spanish Town, Jamaica, 1721), 31–33; various records in CSPC 1719–1720 (v28) and CO 137/14 (all PRO); also see Cordingly (1995), 145.

Chapter 5.   The Devil Off Charles Town

123   *What followed is something of a mystery*   Johnson (reprinted 1998), 47. For Bonnet's association with Blackbeard, see BNL, November 4–11, 1717.

124   *The Henry Bostock deposition*   CSPC 1717–1718 (v30): 298/i (PRO).

124   *In a letter he sent to London*   CSPC 1717–1718 (v30): 298, received on January 6, 1718 (PRO).

125   *For a few months*   ADM 1/2274/1 (NMM).

127   *"At Turniff [Turneffe Islands]"*   Johnson (reprinted 1998), 47.

129   *According to Captain Johnson they skirted the Cuban coast*   Ibid, 48.

130   *During the afternoon of May 22, 1718*   The account of Charleston is drawn from Walter J. Fraser: *Charleston! Charleston!: The History of a Southern City* (Columbia, SC, 1992); and Robert N. Rosen: *A Short History of Charleston* (Columbia, SC, 1997), while John Buchanan: *The Road to Guilford Courthouse* (New York, 1997), 17–24, provides a useful summary of the colony's rice plantations. Also see Johnson (1997), 65; Konstam (2005), 28–31.

136   *The men in the pilot boat*   This account is based on Johnson (reprinted 1998), 48–49, and a letter from Governor Johnson to the Council of Trade and Plantations, CSPC 1717–1718 (v30): 556, received June 18, 1718 (PRO).

138   *Another account refers to*   CSPC 1717–1718 (v30): 660 (PRO), containing several letters from Governor Johnson and the South Carolina legislature.

139   *"The unspeakable calamity"*   CSPC 1717–1718 (v30): 556 (PRO).

139   *In his report to London, Governor Johnson wrote*   Ibid.

141   *The merchant ship* Crowley   CSPC 1717–1718 (v30): 660 (PRO).

142   *What all the sources do agree on*   Ibid; also, Johnson (reprinted 1998), 49.

143   *As for the men onshore*   Ibid. This account is corroborated by CSPC 1717–1718 (v30): 660 (PRO).

150   *The place he selected for this dastardly deed*   Johnson (reprinted 1998), 49–50.

Chapter 6.   A Cutthroat Business

153   *Henry Bostock wasn't having the best of mornings*   This account is based on Deposition of Henry Bostock, copied into a letter from Governor Hamilton dated January 5, 1718: CSPC 1717–1718 (v30): 298/i (PRO), and the description of the *Queen Anne's Revenge* supplied by John de Bry and Dave Moore.

154   *Standing before him*   This description is based on Johnson (reprinted 1998), 60.

156   *"In the commonwealth of pirates"*   Ibid, 60.

157   *"Once upon a cruise"*   Ibid, 61.

159   *"When the pistols were ready"*   Ibid, 59.

159   *Another part of Captain Johnson's account*   Ibid, 61.

161   *Pirates didn't just randomly sail around*   The following account of pirate methods is drawn from Konstam (*Pirates*, 1999), 116–117; Angus Konstam: *Pirates: Terror on the High Seas* (Oxford, Oxfordshire, UK, 2001), 13–16; Konstam (2003), 34–38; and Benerson Little: *The Sea Rover's Practice: Pirate Tactics and Techniques, 1630–1730* (Dulles, VA, 2005).

165   *In the deposition given by Henry Bostock*   CSPC 1717–1718 (v30): 298/i (PRO).

165   *The "instrument" was almost certainly Bostock's backstaff*   The following works were consulted to produce this précis of navigation in Blackbeard's day: John Blake: *The Sea Chart: The Illustrated History of Nautical Maps and Navigational Charts* (London, 2004); Dava Sobel, & William J. H. Andrewes: *The Illustrated Longitude: The True Story of the Genius Who Solved the Greatest Scientific Problem of His Time* (London, 1998), and W. E. May: *A History of Marine Navigation* (Henley-on-Thames, UK, 1973.

168   *Captain Ogle had been hunting Bartholomew Roberts*   Johnson (reprinted 1998), 208–209; also, Baer (2005), 213–219; Earle (2003), 196–198; Cordingly (1995), 209–216; and Konstam (*Pirates*, 1999), 106–107.

173   *While Blackbeard was operating in the Gulf of Honduras*   Johnson (reprinted 1998), 48.

175   *A typical pirate attack*   *Boston Gazette*, August 15–22, 1720, also, Johnson (reprinted 1998), 186–187.

176   *Flying the black flag*   See Cordingly (1995), 117–118; Konstam (*Pirates*, 1999), 98–101; and Konstam (2001), 55–58.

178   *Archaeological evidence from the shipwreck*   Based on discussions between the author and Wayne Lusardi, conservator, and Dave Moore, archaeologist, in the Queen Anne's Revenge Shipwreck Project Center, Morehead City, North Carolina, December 2000, and subsequent discussions with Moore. The information on ranges comes from Howard L. Blackmore: *Armouries of the Tower of London: Catalogue: Volume 1: Ordnance* (London, 1977).

Chapter 7.   The Lord of the Outer Banks

181   *A report filed in London*   Letter by Governor Spotswood of Virginia to the Council of Trade and Plantations, dated December 22, 1718, CSPC 1717–1718 (v30): 800. Also, Deposition of David Herriot, CSPC 1718–1719 (v31): 348/i. For a detailed account of the incident, see David D. Moore: "A General History of Blackbeard the Pirate, the *Queen Anne's Revenge* and the *Adventure*," in *Tributaries*, Vol VII, 1997 (North Carolina Maritime History Council), 31–35.

182   *The helmsman must have been party*   Johnson (reprinted 1998), 49–50. A report of the incident was also included in a letter by Captain Ellis Brand of HMS *Lyme* in a letter to the Admiralty dated July 12, 1718, ADM 1/1472 (PRO).

183   *The original offer was open to pirates*   Quoted in Johnson (reprinted 1998), 13–14.

184   *Stede Bonnet gathered together*   Ibid, 65.

187   *"They remained there two nights"*   The account of Bonnet's rescue of his men and his subsequent career are taken from Johnson (reprinted 1998), 65–71.

194   *As the sun crept over the surface*   The account of the sea battle in the Cape Fear River is drawn from Johnson, augmented by the letters of Governor Johnson to the Council of Trade and Plantations, CSPC 1717–1718 (v30): 787.

196   *Meanwhile, Blackbeard was throwing a party*   Johnson (reprinted 1998), 106–107.

196   *The town itself was a modest affair*   The following description of Bath Town and its history prior to Blackbeard's arrival is drawn from Herbert L. Paschal: *A History of Colonial Bath* (Raleigh, NC, 1955), and Hugh F. Rankin: *Upheaval in Albemarle: The Story of Culpeper's Rebellion, 1675–1689* (Raleigh, NC, 1962).

198 *The first meeting between Blackbeard and Governor Eden* The dating is based on the assumption that by the time Bonnet headed north in search of Blackbeard, his quarry was no longer at sea, but had headed across Pamlico Sound to Bath Town. For details of Eden's residence and a general discussion of Blackbeard's sojourn in the town, see Lee (1974), 59–62.

199 *Certainly Captain Johnson waxed lyrically* Captain Johnson (reprinted 1998), 50–51.

200 *During July and early August 1718* Evidence for this is provided by the division of the pirate crew between Bath Town and Ocracoke in November 1718 (as cited in the report of Captain Brand), and the accounts of disorders in the town caused by Blackbeard's men, North Carolina Colonial Records II, 322, 347, cited in Lee (1974), 199.

201 *As the North Carolina colony* Captain Johnson (reprinted 1998), 50.

202 *In his history of Blackbeard* Lee (1974), 78–79.

202 *His next two victims* Johnson (reprinted 1998), 51; North Carolina Colonial Records II: 341, 348–40; letter from Governor Spotswood of Virginia to the Board of Trade and Plantations 1719–1720 (v.31): 357; and a letter from Governor Spotswood to the Board of Trade and Plantations reprinted in R. A. Brock (ed.): *Official Letters of Alexander Spotswood* (Richmond, VA, 1885), volume II: 324.

202 *Around September 24, 1718* Captain Johnson, op cit, 51; Lee (1974), 80.

203 *At some time in mid- to late September* Captain Johnson, op cit, 106.

205 *As early as July 10 he had issued a proclamation* Reprinted in H. R. McIlwaine (ed.): *Executive Journals, Council of Colonial Virginia* (Richmond, VA, 1928), volume III: 612.

206 *The governor called a meeting* McIlwaine (1928), volume III: 484; CSPC 1717–1718 (v30): 658, 669, 800.

206 *"The Said Wm Howard"* Quoted in Lee (1974), 101–104.

206 *As he reported to his superiors in London* Letter of Governor Spotswood to the Board of Trade and Plantations, reprinted in Brock (1885), volume 2: 351–354.

Chapter 8.   Trouble in the Colonies

209 *It was the evening of May 28, 1718* Brock (1885), volume 2: 284. For an account of the general political situation see Hugh Jones: *The Present State of Virginia* (Richmond, VA, 1912), 237–239.

210 *The problem lay in the way Virginia's government* Johnson (1997), 105–111; Tindall & Shi (1989), 73–81.

212 *A colonial governor also commanded any local militia* CO 5/190 116 et seq. (PRO).

213 *Alexander Spotswood might have begun life as a soldier* This account of Spotswood's life is drawn largely from Leonidas Dodson: *Alexander Spotswood: Governor of Colonial Virginia* (Philadelphia, PA, 1932); Walter Havighurst: *Alexander Spotswood: A Portrait of a Governor* (New York, 1967); and Thomas E. MacMasters: *To the Preferments of Our Ancestours: Early Life of Governor Alexander Spotswood, 1676–1740* (New York, 1985). Also see Virginius Dabney: *Virginia: The New Dominion* (Charlottesville, VA, 1983); and Brock (1885).

215 *As one of the party, Lieutenant John Fontaine, noted in his diary* Transcript

of Fontaine's diary is included in a work by one of his descendants: Anne Maury: *Memoirs of a Huguenot Family* (Richmond, VA, 1853), while a more recent edition is found in Edward Alexander (ed.): *The Journal of John Fontaine: An Irish Huguenot Son in Spain and Virginia, 1710 and 1719* (Williamsburg, VA, 1972).

217 *"If the owners make out their property"* Letter of Governor Spotswood to the Board of Trade and Plantations, dated May 26, 1718, in Brock (1885), volume 2: 324.

217 *"In case any goods, money or other Estate"* CO 5/190 116 et seq. (PRO).

218 *This went far beyond the remit of the powers* Ibid, 84.

219 *The last time we heard of Governor Rogers* For a more detailed summary of Rogers's life and governorship, see Johnson (reprinted 1998), 16–17; Jennifer Marx: *Pirates and Privateers of the Caribbean* (Malabar, FL, 1992), 239–251; Rediker (2004), 93; Cordingly (1995), 153–157; and Baer (2005), 184–185.

221 *The governor was delighted* CSPC [1717–1718 (v30)]: 737.

221 *"In their voyage they met with two sloops"* Johnson (reprinted 1998), 16.

222 *According to the court records* *The Trial of Ten Pirates at Nassau in the Bahamas*, CO 23/1/18 ff. 75–82 (PRO).

223 *First of all, he had little authority* See Baer (2005), 164–168, for a detailed discussion of the legal challenges facing Rogers and Spotswood.

224 *As the leading representative of the Vice-Admiralty* The description of the trial is based on CO 23/1/18 ff. 75–82 (PRO), but also see Cordingly (1995), 153–154.

225 *The execution was set for 10 A.M.* Ibid, ff. 81–82.

228 *The next trial of strength* Johnson (reprinted 1998), 112; *Boston Gazette*, October 10–17, 1720; also *The Tryals of Captain John Rackam, and other Pirates*, CO 137/14 (PRO).

229 *During the short War of the Quadruple Alliance* Johnson (reprinted 1998), 16.

230 *When the twenty-gun sixth-rate warship* HMS Flamborough ADM 1/2646/6.

231 *What happened to Blackbeard's mentor* Johnson (reprinted 1998), 16; CSPC 1720–1721 (v33): 390.

233 *Worse, a long-running border dispute* North Carolina Colonial Records, volume II, xiv–xviii.

234 *Captain Johnson was clear that Eden had made the right decision* Johnson (1726 edition, reprinted London, 1955), 64–66. As most versions of Johnson's work (including the version reprinted in 1998) are drawn from the original 1724 edition, this revision of Governor Eden's involvement with Blackbeard and his subsequent dispute with Governor Spotswood is rarely seen or quoted.

236 *"My friend"* Quoted in Lee (1974), 146.

Chapter 9. The Final Battle

239 *In November 1718 two British warships were lying at anchor* Log of HMS *Lyme*, 1717–1718: ADM 51/4250 (PRO); Log of HMS *Pearl*: ADM/L/32 (NMM); Brock (1885), volume 2: 317.

240 *As the senior of the two captains* CSPC 1717–1718 (v30): 800 (PRO); Report of Captain Brand to the Admiralty, February 6, 1719, ADM 1/1472 (PRO). The information on the two vessels is drawn from David Lyon: *The Sailing Navy List: All the Ships of the Royal Navy, Built, Purchased, and Captured, 1688–1860* (London, 2001).

242   *He would then head south through Plymouth*   The account of Captain Brand's part in the operation is drawn from his own report to the Admiralty, ADM 1/1472 (PRO), and the letter of Colonel Pollock to the Governor of North Carolina, dated December 8, 1718, North Carolina Colonial Record, volume II: 318–320.

242   *Just after dawn on Sunday, November 17*   Letter of Lieutenant Maynard to Lieutenant Symonds of HMS *Phoenix*, dated December 17, 1718, abstracted and reprinted in *The Weekly Journal or British Gazetteer*, April 25, 1719.

243   *Maynard recorded the event*   ADM/L/P32 (NMM). The orders given to Lieutenant Maynard by Captain Gordon are also referred to in ADM 1/1826 (PRO).

243   *Three years after the event Captain Gordon recalled*   ADM 1/1826 (PRO).

243   *As an added incentive to the crews*   Johnson (reprinted 1998), 53–54.

245   *On the other side of the island*   Johnson (reprinted 1998), 54.

246   *We know from British naval records*   Log of HMS *Lyme*, 1717–1718: ADM 51/4250 (PRO); Log of HMS *Pearl*, 1717–1718, ADM/L/P32 (NMM). The following account of the engagement is drawn from Johnson (reprinted 1998), 54–58; Maynard's letter, abstracted and reprinted in *The Weekly Journal or British Gazetteer*, April 25, 1719; BNL, February 16–23, 1719, based on letters of December 17, 1718; BNL February 23–March 2, 1719, based on a report dated February 20; and the report of Captain Brand, ADM 1/1472, and Captain Gordon, ADM 1/1826 (both PRO). Also see Cordingly (1995), 195–199; Lee (1974), 113–126; and Earle (2003), 193.

249   *During this period a sloop in Royal Naval service*   Lyon (2001), Blackmore (1977)—various entries in each.

251   *According to Maynard*   Maynard's letter abstracted and reprinted in *The Weekly Journal or British Gazetteer*, April 25, 1719.

252   *The account of the battle printed in the* Boston News Letter   BNL, February 16–23, 1719.

259   *Governor Spotswood recorded that Blackbeard*   Letter of Governor Spotswood, dated December 22, 1718, CSPC 1717–1718 (v30): 800 ff. 431 (PRO). The second letter by Spotswood, dated February 14, 1719, is found in North Carolina Colonial Record, volume II: 325.

259   *The hunt for escaped pirates*   Report of Captain Gordon, ADM 1/1826 (PRO).

259   *The pirate's dismembered corpse*   Johnson (reprinted 1998), 59.

260   *Back in Bath Town*   Report of Captain Brand, ADM 1/1472 (PRO).

261   *"When the lieutenant came to Bath Town"*   Johnson (reprinted 1998), 58.

262   *In a letter sent to Governor Eden*   Letter of Governor Spotswood to Governor Eden, December 21, 1718, now in the Library and Archives of the Virginia Historical Society, quoted in Lee (1974), 216.

262   *Pollock went on to condemn*   Letter of Colonel Pollock to Governor Eden, North Carolina Colonial Record, volume II: 318–320.

262   *He remained in the vicinity of Bath Town*   Captain Brand, ADM 1/1472 (PRO).

263   *Soon after dawn on Thursday, December 1*   Log of HMS *Lyme*, 1717–1718, ADM 51/4250 (PRO).

264   *Nobody knows what happened to the head*   For a colorful discussion of the mystery of Blackbeard's skull, see Lee (1974), 124–125; also see the curatorial notes of the Mariner's Museum, Newport News, Virginia, and the Peabody-Essex Museum of Salem, Massachusetts.

Chapter 10.   The Blackbeard Legacy

267   *Sixteen wounded pirates*   Johnson (reprinted 1998), 62. The following account of the trial is based on North Carolina Colonial Record, volume II: 328, 341–349, as the original transcript has been lost. See Lee (1974), 136–138, for a discussion of the surviving documentation.

268   *The most damning piece of evidence*   Quoted in Lee (1974), 146.

269   *The day before, Spotswood addressed the thorny issue*   Executive Journal of the Council of Colonial Virginia, volume III: 496.

270   *With only one exception*   The wording is drawn from that used in similar trials, including those presided over by Governor Rogers in the Bahamas.

270   *"Hands, being taken"*   Johnson (reprinted 1998), 60.

272   *In a letter dated May 26*   Letter of Governor Spotswood to the Board of Trade and Plantations, dated May 26, 1719; Brock (1885), volume 2: 324.

272   *The proclamation signed by Spotswood*   Johnson (reprinted 1998), 53–54.

273   *In August 1721 a petition was forwarded*   Privy Council Register 2/87 ff. 293 (PRO).

273   *Back in London Captain Gordon was asked for his comments*   Letter dated September 14, 1721, ADM 1/1826 (PRO).

274   *"It has appeared to this Court"*   North Carolina Colonial Record, volume II: 341–349.

274   *On April 4, 1719*   North Carolina Colonial Record, volume II: 329–330.

275   *Tobias Knight was a dying man*   Together with other documents relating to this inquiry, Knight's rebuttal together with Council notes, findings and even Spotswood's accusations are found in North Carolina Colonial Record, volume II: 341–349.

277   *After stating that any reflection*   Captain Johnson (1726 edition, reprinted London, 1955), 64–66.

279   *While the governor was busy*   A valuable discussion of the problems facing Spotswood can be found in Jones (1912), Dodson (1932), Havighurst (1967), and MacMasters (1985).

281   *In late May 1718*   Letter from Governor Bennett, May 31, 1718, CSPC 1718–1719 (v31): 551.

283   *In the years that followed*   For a more detailed discussion of Blackbeard's role in cinema and literature, see Cordingly (1995), 3–9, 172–177; Jan Rogozinski: *Pirates!: An A–Z Encyclopedia* (New York, 1995), 26–28.

285   *"The night before he was killed"*   Johnson (reprinted 1998), 61. For a discussion of sites associated with Blackbeard, see Lee (1974), 171–174; and Nancy Roberts: *Blackbeard and Other Pirates of the Atlantic Coast* (Winston-Salem, NC, 1993), 16–17.

286   *One Blackbeard legacy*   The following account of the discovery, excavation, and study of the wreck is drawn from several sources, including Konstam (*Shipwrecks*, 1999), 144–145, and discussions with Dave Moore, Wayne Lusardi, and others at the North Carolina Maritime Museum in Beaufort, North Carolina, and the Queen Anne's Revenge Shipwreck Project Conservation Center in Morehead City, North Carolina. It is also based on the displays, curatorial notes, and published information made available both by the North Carolina Maritime Museum and the North Carolina Department of Cultural Resources. Finally, it is based on taped or filmed interviews given to the media by those involved in the project.

Selected Bibliography

Albury, Paul. *The Story of the Bahamas*. London, 1975.

Alexander, Edward (ed.). *The Journal of John Fontaine: An Irish Huguenot Son in Spain and Virginia, 1710 and 1719*. Williamsburg, VA, 1972.

Anonymous. *The Tryals of Captain John Rackam and the Other Pirates*. Spanish Town, Jamaica, 1721.

Aughton, Peter. *Bristol: A People's History*. Lancaster, UK, 2003.

Baer, Joel. *Pirates of the British Isles*. Stroud, Gloucestershire, UK, 2005.

Blackmore, Howard L. *Armouries of the Tower of London: Catalogue: Volume 1: Ordnance*. London, 1977.

Blake, John. *The Sea Chart: The Illustrated History of Nautical Maps and Navigational Charts*. London, 2004.

Brock, R. A. (ed.). *Official Letters of Alexander Spotswood*. Richmond, VA, 1885.

Buchanan, John. *The Road to Guilford Courthouse*. New York, 1997.

Budde-Jones, Kathryn. *Coins of the Lost Galleons*. Key West, FL, 1989.

Burgess, Robert F., & Carl J. Clausen. *Florida's Golden Galleons: The Search for the 1715 Spanish Treasure Fleet*. Port Salerno, FL, 1982.

Burnside, Madeleine, and Rosemarie Rabotham. *Spirits of the Passage: The Transatlantic Slave Trade in the Seventeenth Century*. New York, 1997.

Clifford, Barry. *The Black Ship: The Quest to Recover an English Pirate Ship and Its Lost Treasure*. London, 1999.

———. *The Pirate Prince: Discovering the Priceless Treasures of the Sunken Ship Whydah*. New York, 1993.

Cordingly, David. (ed.). *Pirates: Terror on the High Seas from the Caribbean to the South China Sea*. Atlanta, GA, 1996.

———. *Under the Black Flag: The Romance and the Reality of Life among the Pirates*. London, 1995.

Cordingly, David, and John Falconer. *Pirates: Fact & Fiction*. London, 1992.

Cottman, Michael H. *The Wreck of the Henrietta Marie: An African-American's Spiritual Journey to Uncover a Sunken Slave Ship's Past*. New York, 1999.

Dabney, Virginius. *Virginia: The New Dominion*. Charlottesville, VA, 1983.

Davis, Ralph. *The Rise of the Atlantic Economies*. London, 1973.

Defoe, Daniel. *Life, Adventures, and Piracies of the Former Captain Singleton*. London, 1719, reprinted by Wildside Press, Rockville, MD, 2003.

——. *Robinson Crusoe*. London, 1720, reprinted by Penguin Popular Classics, 1998.

Dodson, Leonidas. *Alexander Spotswood: Governor of Colonial Virginia*. Philadelphia, PA, 1932.

Earle, Peter. *The Pirate Wars*. London, 2003.

——. *Sailors: English Merchant Seamen 1650–1775*. London, 1988.

Fraser, Walter J. *Charleston! Charleston!: The History of a Southern City*. Columbia, SC, 1992.

Furbank, Philip N., & W. R. Owens. *The Canonisation of Daniel Defoe*. New Haven, CT, 1988.

——. *Defoe De-attributions: A Critique of J. R. Moore's Checklist*. London, 1994.

Gosse, Philip. (ed.). *The History of Piracy*. New York, 1925, reprinted by Rio Grande Press, Glorieta, NM, 1988.

—— . *The Pirate's Who's Who: Giving Particulars of the Lives and Deaths of the Pirates and Buccaneers*. New York, 1925, reprinted by Rio Grande Press, Glorieta, NM, 1988.

Havighurst, Walter. *Alexander Spotswood: A Portrait of a Governor*. New York, 1967.

Hayward, Arthur L. (ed.). *Lives of the Most Remarkable Criminals*. London, 1735, reprinted by Dodd, Mead & Co., New York, 1927.

Johnson, Captain Charles. *A General History of the Robberies and Murders of the most notorious Pirates*. London, 1724, reprinted by Lyons Press, New York, 1998.

Johnson, Paul. *A History of the American People*. New York, 1997.

Jones, Hugh. *The Present State of Virginia*. Richmond, VA, 1912.

Konstam, Angus. *America Speaks: The Birth of a Nation—Merchants*. Danbury, CT, 2005.

——. *The History of Pirates*. New York, 1999.

——. *The History of Shipwrecks*. New York, 1999.

——. *The Pirate Ship, 1660–1730*. Oxford, Oxfordshire, UK, 2003.

——. *Pirates: Terror on the High Seas*. Oxford, Oxfordshire, UK, 2001.

Lawrence, Richard, and Mark Wilde-Ramsin. "In Search of Blackbeard: Historical and Archaeological Research at Shipwreck Site 003BUI." *Southeastern Geology*, Vol. 40, No. 1, February 2001.

Lee, Robert E. *Blackbeard the Pirate: A Reappraisal of His Life and Times*. Winston-Salem, NC, 1974, reprinted by John F. Blair, Winston-Salem, NC, 2002.

Little, Benerson. *The Sea Rover's Practice: Pirate Tactics and Techniques, 1630–1730*. Dulles, VA, 2005.

Little, Bryan, & John Sansom (eds.). *The Story of Bristol: From the Middle Ages to Today*. Tiverton, Essex, UK, 2003.

Lyon, David. *The Sailing Navy List: All the Ships of the Royal Navy, Built, Purchased and Captured, 1688–1860*. London, 2001.

McIlwaine, H. R. (ed.). *Executive Journals of the Council of Colonial Virginia*. Richmond, VA, 1928.

MacMasters, Thomas E. *To the Preferments of Our Ancestours: The Early Life of Governor Alexander Spotswood, 1676–1740*. New York, 1985.

Marx, Jennifer. *Pirates and Privateers of the Caribbean*. Malabar, FL, 1992.

Mather, Cotton. *The Tryals of Sixteen persons for Piracy*. Boston, MA, 1726.

———. *The Vial Poured upon the Sea: A Remarkable Relation of Certain Pirates*. Boston, MA, 1726.

Maury, Anne. *Memoirs of a Huguenot Family*. Richmond, VA, 1853.

May, W. E. *A History of Marine Navigation*. Henley-on-Thames, UK, 1973.

Moore, David D. "A General History of Blackbeard the Pirate, the *Queen Anne's Revenge*, and the *Adventure*," in *Tributaries*, Vol VII, 1997 (North Carolina Maritime History Council), 31–35.

Moore, John R. *Daniel Defoe: Citizen of the Modern World*. Chicago, 1958.

———. *Defoe in the Pillory and Other Studies*. London, 1939.

Parry, J. H. *The Spanish Seaborne Empire*. London, 1966.

Paschal, Herbert R. *A History of Colonial Bath*. Raleigh, NC, 1955.

Pawson, Michael, & David Buisseret. *Port Royal, Jamaica*. Oxford, Oxfordshire, UK, 1975.

Preston, Diana, and Michael Preston. *A Pirate of Exquisite Mind: The Life of William Dampier*. London, 2004.

Rankin, Hugh F. *Upheaval in Albemarle: The Story of Culpeper's Rebellion, 1675–1689*. Raleigh, NC, 1962.

Rediker, Marcus. *Between the Devil and the Deep Blue Sea: Merchant Seamen, Pirates and the Anglo-American Maritime World, 1700–1750*. Cambridge, UK, 1987.

———. *Villains of All Nations: Atlantic Pirates in the Golden Age*. Boston, MA, 2004.

Riley, Sandra. *Homeward Bound: A History of the Bahama Islands to 1850*. Nassau, Bahamas, 2000.

Ritchie, Robert C. *Captain Kidd and the War against the Pirates*. Cambridge, MA, 1986.

Roberts, Nancy. *Blackbeard and Other Pirates of the Atlantic Coast*. Winston-Salem, NC, 1993.

Rogozinski, Jan. *Pirates!: An A–Z Encyclopedia*. New York, 1995.

Rosen, Robert N. *A Short History of Charleston*. Columbia, SC, 1997.

Slush, Barnaby. *The Navy Royal: Or a Sea-Cook Turn'd Projector*. London, 1709.

Snelgrave, William. *A New Account of Some Parts of Guinea and the Slave Trade*. London, 1734.

Sobel, Dava, and William J. H. Andrewes. *The Illustrated Longitude: The True Story of a Lone Genius Who Solved the Greatest Scientific Problem of His Time*. London, 1998.

Starkey, David J., E. S. van Eyck, & J. A. de Moor (eds.). *Pirates and Privateers: New Perspectives on the War on Trade in the Eighteenth and Nineteenth Centuries*. Exeter, Devon, UK, 1997.

Stevenson, Robert Louis. *Treasure Island*. London, 1883.

Sullivan, George. *Slave Ship: The Story of the* Henrietta Marie. New York, 1994.

Tindall, George B., & David E. Shi. *America: A Narrative History*. New York, 1989.

Walton, Timothy R. *The Spanish Treasure Fleets*. Sarasota, FL, 1994.

Wilde-Ramsin, Mark. "In Search of Blackbeard: Historical and Archeological Research at Shipwreck Site 003BUI," in *Southeastern Geology*, Vol 40, No. 1, February 2001.

Williams, Lloyd Hanes. *Pirates of Colonial Virginia*. Richmond, VA, 1937.

Winston, Alexander. *No Purchase, No Pay: Sir Henry Morgan, Captain William Kidd, Captain Woodes Rogers in the Great Age of Privateers and Pirates, 1665–1715*. London, 1970.

Woodbury, George. *The Great Days of Piracy in the West Indies*. New York, 1951.

Index

Page numbers in *italics* refer to illustrations.